Structural Composites:
ADVANCED COMPOSITES IN AVIATION

STERKENBURG & WANG

Production Staff

Designer/Lead Illustrator Amy Siever
Designer/Illustrator Dustin Blyer
Senior Designer Roberta Byerly
Production Manager Holly Bonos

© Copyright 2013 by
Avotek Information Resources, LLC.
All Rights Reserved

International Standard Book Number 1-933189-35-5
ISBN 13: 978-1-933189-35-2
Order # T-STCOM-0101

For Sale by: Avotek
A Select Aerospace Industries, Inc. company

Mail to:
P.O. Box 219
Weyers Cave, Virginia 24486
USA

Ship to:
200 Packaging Drive
Weyers Cave, Virginia 24486
USA

Toll Free: 1-800-828-6835
Telephone: 1-540-234-9090
Fax: 1-540-234-9399

First Edition
First Printing
Printed in the USA

www.avotek.com

Cover photo (right): Courtesy of Wichita State University, National Institute for Aviation Research

Preface

This book is a comprehensive text for students who are beginning their careers in aviation maintenance and aerospace manufacturing. The text is focused on the manufacturing, maintenance, inspection and repair of composite aircraft. However, the text is also very useful for students who are interested in the automotive, ship building or construction industry. Experienced aircraft technicians and engineers could use this text to learn more about the manufacturing and repair processes for new composite aircraft designs that will enter the fleet. The use of composite materials for general aviation aircraft, business jets and transport aircraft is ever increasing, and the aircraft maintenance technician and engineer must have an in-depth knowledge of these new advanced materials, manufacturing processes and repair techniques to successfully maintain these complex aircraft.

Textbooks, by their very nature, must be general in their overall coverage of a subject area. As always, the aircraft manufacturer is the sole source of operation, maintenance, repair and overhaul information. Their manuals are approved by the FAA and must always be followed. You may not use any material presented in this or any other textbook as a manual for actual operation, maintenance or repair.

The writers, individuals and companies which have contributed to the production of this textbook have done so in the spirit of cooperation for the good of the industry. To the best of their abilities, they have tried to provide accuracy, honesty and pertinence in the presentation of the material. However, as with all human endeavors, errors and omissions can show up in the most unexpected places. If any exist, they are unintentional. Please bring them to our attention.

Email us at comments@avotek.com for comments or suggestions.

Avotek® Aircraft Maintenance Series
Introduction to Aircraft Maintenance
Aircraft Structural Maintenance
Aircraft System Maintenance
Aircraft Powerplant Maintenance

Avotek® Aircraft Avionics Series
Avionics: Fundamentals of Aircraft Electronics
Avionics: Beyond the AET
Avionics: Systems and Troubleshooting

Other Books by Avotek®
Aircraft Corrosion Control Guide
Aircraft Structural Technician
Aircraft Turbine Engines
Aircraft Wiring & Electrical Installation
AMT Reference Handbook
Avotek Aeronautical Dictionary
Fundamentals of Modern Aviation
Light Sport Aircraft Inspection Procedures

Acknowledgements

Advanced Composite Structures

Airbus Industries

Alcoa Global Fasteners, Inc.

Blue Ridge Community College, Aviation Maintenance Technology

Brian Stoltzfus — Priority Air Charter

China Fibers

Classic Aviation Services

Coast Composites, LLC

David Jones — Aviation Institute of Maintenance

EHA®

Energistics, LLC

General Composites, Ltd.

Greg Campbell, Sherman Showalter, Stacey Smith — Shenandoah Valley Regional Airport

Harry Moyer, Virgil Gottfried — Samaritan's Purse

Hawker Beechcraft

IABG Dresden

Jeremy Nafziger

Jet Solutions, LLC.

Karl Stoltzfus, Sr., Michael Stoltzfus, Aaron Lorson & staff — Dynamic Aviation Group, Inc.

Lori Johnson, Larry Bartlett — Duncan Aviation

MAG

Mark Stoltzfus — Preferred Airparts

NASA

Pat Colgan — Capital Aviation

Phoenix Composites

Scaled Composites

Select Aerospace Industries, Inc.

Select Airparts

Smart Tooling

Steve Hanson, Jeff Ellis, Tim Travis — Beechcraft

Thermal Wave Imaging, Inc.

Pratt & Whitney

Wavelength NDT/Marine Results

Webber Tools

Wichita State University, National Institute for Aviation Research

Zwick GmbH and Co. KG

Contents

Preface iii

Acknowledgements iv

1 Introduction to Composite Materials

1-1   Introduction to Composite Materials

2 Advanced Composite Materials

2-1   Dry Fibers (Reinforcements)
2-21 Prepregs

3 Composite Structures

3-1   Design Criteria
3-2   Composite Laminate Structures
3-9   Honeycomb Structures

4 Manufacturing Processes

4-1   Hand Lay-up
4-5   Automated Processes
4-15 Vacuum Bag Molding

5 Tool and Mold Making

5-1   Tooling Design
5-8   Tooling Construction Techniques

6 Assembly Operations

6-1   Machining Operations
6-3   Drilling Operations
6-8   Sanding and Trimming Operations
6-13 Mechanical Fastening and Adhesive Bonding

7 Heating and Curing

7-1   Heating and Curing Equipment
7-10 Heating and Curing Operations

8 Inspection and Testing

8-1   Inspection and Testing

9 Testing

9-1	Materials Testing Methods	9-13	Other Testing Methods
9-9	Testing of Adhesive Bonded Joints		

10 Types and Causes of Damage

10-2	Damage Types	10-6	Repair Qualification and Authority
10-4	Damage Assessment		

11 Repair

11-2	Introduction to Designing for Repairability	11-17	Types of Repair
		11-33	Repair Processes and Procedures

12 Health and Safety

12-2	Material Safety Data Sheet	12-5	Personal Protective Equipment
12-2	Toxicity and Hazards of Composite Materials	12-7	Emergency and First Aid Procedures

Appendix A A-1

Index I-1

Courtesy of Airbus

1

Introduction to Composite Materials

Composite parts such as fairings, spoilers and flight controls were first used on aircraft beginning in the 1960s. Their high strength, corrosion resistance and low weight compared to aluminum parts were recognized immediately. As a result, composite materials are becoming more important in the construction of aerospace structures.

New generation large aircraft, as pictured to the left, are now designed with all-composite fuselage and wing structures. Today's aircraft technician is required to have an in-depth knowledge of composite components and structures; knowledge of the proper procedures for repair of these components and the tools used in these repairs is also necessary.

New aircraft such as the Boeing 787 and Airbus 350 incorporate up to 50 percent (by weight) composite materials in their construction, including carbon fiber as the primary material for fuselage and wing structures, as illustrated in Figure 1-1-1 and Figure 1-1-2.

Titanium makes up a large percentage of the materials used in new aircraft construction because of its compatibility with carbon fiber. The use of aluminum is reduced, but leading edges, wing ribs, fuselage frames and other structural components are still made from it.

History of Composite Materials

The development of composite materials in the aerospace industry started during World War II. Th to produce materials with specific strength and stiffness values that were significantly higher than existing structural materials. In addition, existing materials such as aluminum alloys were subject to corrosion and fatigue.

Learning Objective

REVIEW
- the historical development of composite materials

DISCUSS
- advantages and disadvantages of composite materials

EXPLAIN
- the application of composites in the aerospace industry

APPLY
- define various types of composite materials

Left: New generation composite aircraft use a high percentage of composite materials.

1-2 | Introduction to Composite Materials

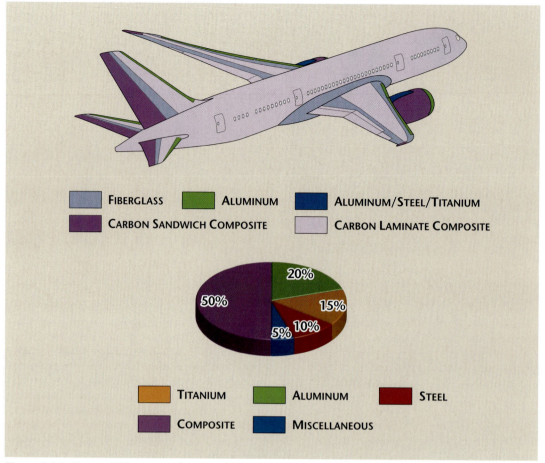

Figure 1-1-1. Boeing 787 structural materials distribution

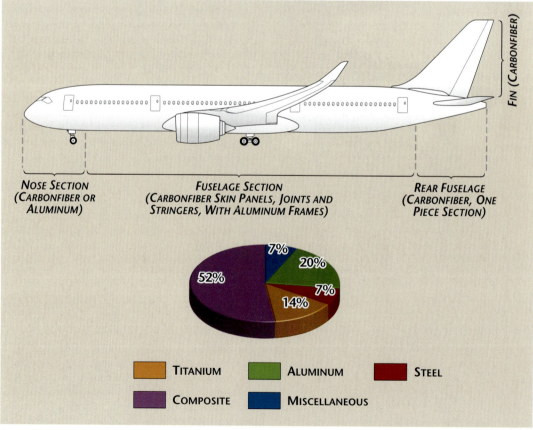

Figure 1-1-2. Airbus 350AWB structural materials distribution

Figure 1-1-3. The De Haviland Mosquito's primary structure was laminated wood.

The de Havilland Mosquito (Figure 1-1-3) was a British World War II attack bomber that was built from a natural composite material (wood) and used bonded joints extensively. Valuable lessons learned during the design and manufacture of this aircraft, especially the design of bonded joints and bonding techniques, are still used today in the building of modern carbon fiber aircraft.

After World War II, fiberglass materials were used successfully in filament-wound rocket motors and in other prototype structural aircraft applications. During the 1960s and '70s many military aircraft programs started to use high-performance carbon fiber material for secondary and primary structures. The Lear Fan was the first all-carbon fiber airframe, but it was never certificated. During this period, honeycomb fiberglass and carbon fiber flight control panels were increasingly used for commercial aircraft. The Airbus A300 was the first commercial jetliner that utilized a carbon fiber vertical tail section. New aircraft designs by most aircraft manufacturers started to use carbon fiber composite materials for the horizontal and vertical stabilizers of aircraft models such as the Airbus 320/330/340 and the Boeing 777.

The Beech Starship (Figure 1-1-4) in 1988 became the first all-composite civilian aircraft certificated by the FAA. On the military side, the B-2 bomber (Figure 1-1-5), introduced in 1989, has a carbon fiber fuselage and wing structure. Later military fixed wing aircraft programs such as the F-22 fighter (Figure 1-1-5) and F-35 fighter also use composite materials extensively.

Military helicopters like the V-22 tilt rotor (Figure 1-1-6) and the new CH-53K heavy lift helicopter have all-composite fuselage and wing/rotor construction. Composite materials

Figure 1-1-4. The Beech Starship
Courtesy of Scaled Composites

Figure 1-1-5. Military aircraft—a B-2 bomber (center) and F-22 fighters—with composite structures

Figure 1-1-6. The V-22 tilt rotor helicopter has a composite fuselage.

Definition of Composite Materials

A *composite* consists of two or more materials combined to achieve specific structural properties. Advanced composites used in aircraft construction contain strong, stiff, engineered fibers embedded in a high-performance matrix. The individual materials, such as resin and fibers, do not merge completely with one another in the composite, but rather act together to improve structural properties—like strength, stiffness and weight—over those of an individual material. Normally, the components of a composite can be physically identified and exhibit an interface between one another.

Advantages and Disadvantages of Composites

Advantages

are also widely used in unmanned aerial vehicles (UAV), where weight savings increase the time the vehicle can remain airborne.

Advanced composite materials are now considered for every new aircraft program, civilian and military. Composite materials are also used for commercial space applications, and several revolutionary aircraft designs by Scaled Composites have demonstrated the versatility of composite materials. Engineers at this company have incorporated composite materials in the structures of Proteus and Spaceship One, pictured in Figure 1-1-7, as well as Spaceship Two, White Knight, and Global Flyer. Composite materials allow the designer to develop lighter, more aerodynamic structures that cannot be manufactured from aluminum. The use of composite materials saves substantial weight and increases the payload of the spacecraft.

The advantages of composites include:

- A higher performance for a given weight leads to fuel savings.

- Composite materials have excellent strength-to-weight and stiffness-to-weight ratios. Strength divided by density is called *specific strength*, and stiffness (modulus) divided by density is referred to as *specific modulus*.

- Laminate patterns and ply buildup in a part can be tailored to give the required mechanical properties in various directions.

- It is easier to achieve smooth aerodynamic profiles for drag reduction. Complex double-curvature parts can be made with a smooth finish in one operation.

Figure 1-1-7. Two aircraft design by Scaled Composites, (A) Proteus, and (B) Spaceship One

(A) Courtesy of NASA, (B) Courtesy of Scaled Composites

Figure 1-1-8. Composite fuselage section with integrated stringers *Courtesy of Airbus*

- Part count is reduced.
- Production cost is reduced. Composites can be made by a wide range of processes.
- Composites offer excellent resistance to corrosion, chemical attack and outdoor weathering.

Disadvantages

Composites also have some disadvantages:

- Composites are more brittle than wrought metals and thus are more easily damaged.
- Repair can introduce new problems. Materials require refrigerated transport and storage and have limited shelf lives. Hot curing with special equipment is necessary in many cases. Both hot and cold curing take more time than other repairs.
- Repair at the original cure temperature requires tooling and pressure.
- Composites must be thoroughly cleaned of all contamination before repair.
- Composites must be dried before repair because all resin matrices and some fibers absorb moisture.
- Some chemicals, like paint stripper, are damaging to composites and some thermoplastics are not very resistant to some solvents. New types of paint and stripper are being developed to deal with this. Check the data sheets for each type.

Figure 1-1-9. Forward section of composite aircraft *Courtesy of Airbus*

Applications of Composite Structures in Current Aircraft

Composite materials are often selected because of their mechanical properties for the manufacture of aircraft parts and structures. Common carbon fiber components on today's production aircraft include fairings, flight control surfaces, landing gear doors, leading and trailing edge panels on the wing and stabilizer, and interior components. On large aircraft, carbon fiber is used in the vertical and horizontal stabilizer and in the primary structure. The structure of the commercial aircraft in Figure 1-1-8 uses large pieces of carbon fiber material, although the floor beams and frame sections are aluminum. Figure 1-1-9 shows the forward section of a commercial composite aircraft. The primary wing and fuselage structures on new generation large aircraft are carbon fiber.

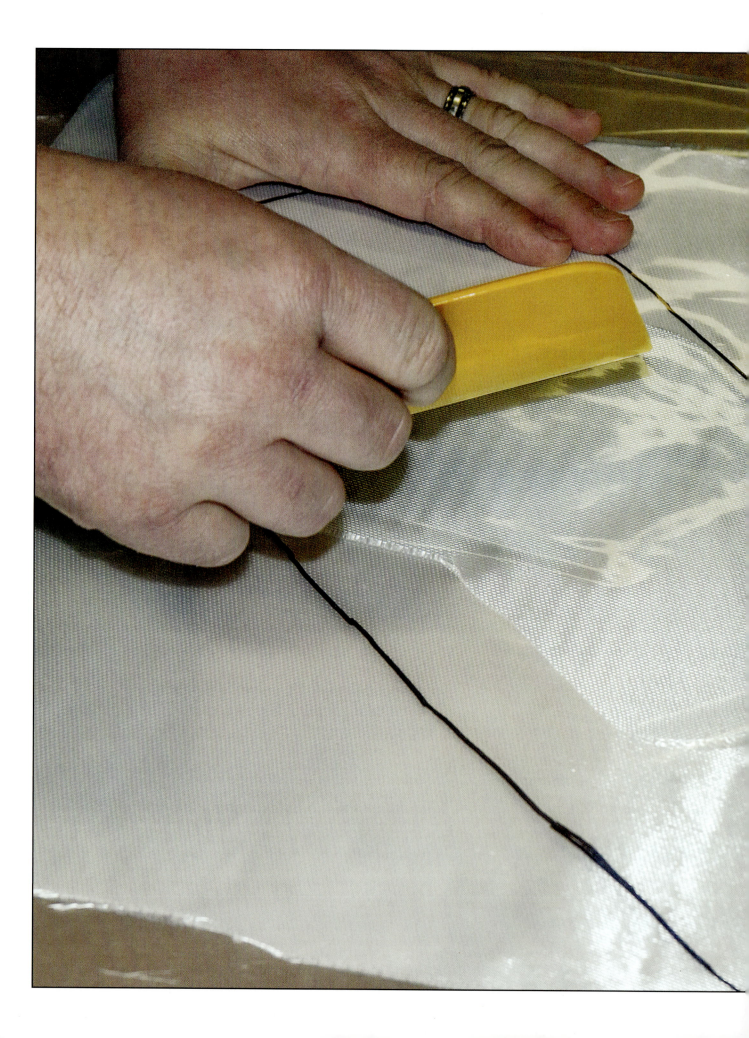

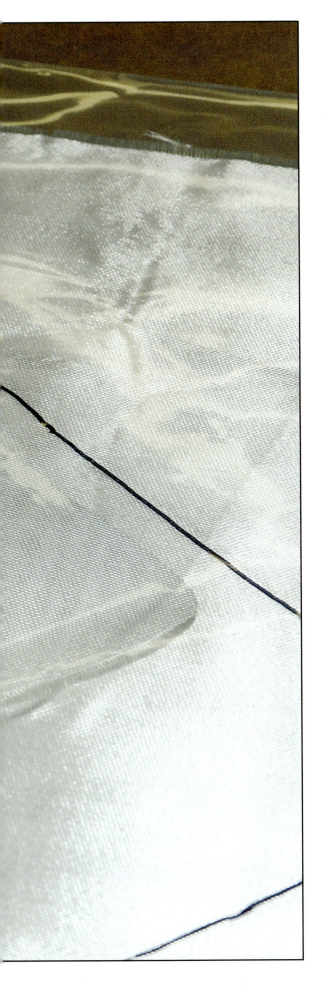

2

Advanced Composite Materials

Advanced composite materials for the aerospace industry consist of two main groups: dry fibers that must be impregnated with a resin and pre-impregnated (prepreg) materials.

Dry fibers are materials that will have to be impregnated with a resin to create the composite material. This will involve using resin transfer molding (RTM), vacuum assisted resin transfer molding (VARTM), resin film infusion (RFI) or wet lay-up processes.

Prepreg materials are those that are impregnated with a resin during the manufacturing process. These may include prepreg manual lay-up, automatic tape laying, filament winding or automatic fiber placement processes.

Learning Objective

DESCRIBE
- how dry fibers and prepreg materials are used in aerospace manufacturing
- curing processes used for dry and prepreg materials
- types of processing materials used for vacuum bagging
- resin systems and adhesives

Section 1

Dry Fibers (Reinforcements)

The most commonly used dry fibers for the aerospace industry are fiberglass, carbon fiber and Aramid (Kevlar®). Figure 2-1-1 shows, from top to bottom, fiberglass, Kevlar® and carbon-fiber fabric. All materials should be stored on a roll, off the ground, in a dry environment at room temperature. Figure 2-1-2 shows a storage rack with dry reinforcements.

Fiberglass

Glass is derived from one of our most abundant natural resources—sand. Glass melts are made by fusing (that is, melting together) silica

Left: A technician spreads epoxy laminating resin on fiberglass material.

Figure 2-1-1. Dry fiber reinforcements

Figure 2-1-2. Storage rack for dry fiber reinforcements

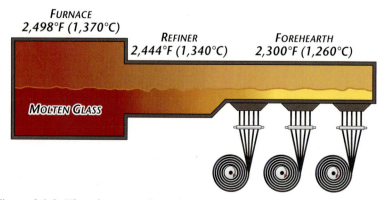

Figure 2-1-3. Fiberglass manufacturing

with minerals that contain the oxides needed to form a given composition. The molten mass is rapidly cooled to prevent crystallization and formed into glass fibers by a process also known as fiberization.

Nearly all continuous glass fibers are made by a direct draw process and formed by extruding molten glass through a platinum alloy bushing that may contain several thousand individual orifices, each 0.0312 to 0.125 in. (0.793 to 3.175 mm) in diameter. While they are still highly viscous, the resulting fibers are rapidly drawn to a fine diameter and then solidify. Typical fiber diameters range from 118 to 787 uin (3 to 20 um). Individual filaments are combined into multifilament strands, which are pulled by mechanical winders and wound onto tubes or forming packages. Figure 2-1-3 shows the manufacturing process for fiberglass.

Fiberglass is often used for secondary aircraft structures on aircraft such as fairings, radomes, wing tips, helicopter rotor blades and interior components. The strength properties of fiberglass are less than carbon fiber but the cost of fiberglass is substantially lower and therefore, fiberglass is an economical substitution if high strength and stiffness are not required.

Fiberglass materials are available as continuous rovings; yarn for fabrics or braiding; mattes; and chopped strand all with a variety of physical surface treatments and finishes. Most structural applications utilize fabric, roving, or rovings converted to unidirectional tapes. Perhaps the most versatile fiber type to produce glass product forms is *electrical glass*, or *E-glass*. E-glass is used as such for electrical applications and other applications. S-glass and S2-glass are structural fiberglass with higher strength than E-glass.

The various types of fiberglass offer lower cost than other composite materials and chemical or galvanic corrosion resistance. Fiberglass does not conduct electricity. Fiberglass is distinguished by its white color, as seen in Figure 2-1-4. It is available as a dry fiber fabric or as prepreg material (Figure 2-1-5).

Although the rapid evolution of carbon and aramid fibers, which have favorable mechanical properties when compared to fiberglass, have gained advantages in the composite market, glass composite products still prevail in many applications.

Cost per weight or volume, certain armament applications, chemical or galvanic corrosion resistance, electrical properties, and it's availability in many product forms are examples of the advantages of fiberglass.

Disadvantages include the coefficient of thermal expansion and modulus properties compared to carbon composites. When compared to aramid composites, glass falls short in tensile properties but has advantages in ultimate compression, shear properties and moisture pick-up.

Aramid (Kevlar®)

Aramid is an organic fiber that is 43 percent lighter than and twice as strong in tension as fiberglass. One of the outstanding properties of aramid is toughness; therefore, it is often used for ballistic and body armor. On the other hand, aramid fibers are generally weak in compression and are difficult to cut due to fuzzing.

Aramid composites were first adopted in applications where weight savings were critical, such as in aircraft components, helicopters, space vehicles and missiles. Armor applications followed from its superior ballistic and structural performance.

Kevlar® is a registered trademark for DuPont's aramid fibers. This type of fiber is manufactured by extruding a polymer solution through a spinneret. Major forms available from DuPont are continuous filament yarns, rovings, chopped fiber, pulp, spun-laced sheet, wet-laid papers, thermoplastic impregnated tows and thermo-formable composite sheets.

Bundles of aramid fibers are not sized by number of fibers but by the weight. Aramid is naturally yellow in color, as shown in Figure 2-1-6, and darkens when exposed to ultraviolet (UV) radiation. Aramids do not melt, but decompose at about 900°F (500°C). The main disadvantage is that the Aramid fibers are hygroscopic and can absorb 8 percent of their weight of water. For this reason, parts made from aramid fibers need to be protected from the environment.

Although the use of aramid fibers for aircraft parts has declined in recent years, two types are used. Kevlar®29 has the lowest modulus (stiffness) and highest toughness (strain to failure). These fibers are used in pneumatic tires, as well as in ballistics and other soft composite systems such as cut- and slash-resistance protective apparel, ropes, coated fabric and asbestos replacement. Kevlar®29 is also used for composites where maximum impact and damage tolerance are critical and stiffness is less important.

Kevlar®49, the other aramid fiber found in the aviation industry, is predominantly used in reinforced plastics. Secondary structures on some aircraft are made from Kevlar®, although due to the hygroscopic behavior of Kevlar® many of these secondary structures are replaced with fiberglass.

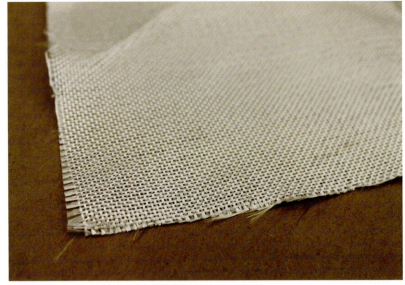

Figure 2-1-4. Dry fiberglass fabric

Figure 2-1-5. Prepreg fiberglass fabric

Figure 2-1-6. Aramid (Kevlar®) fabric

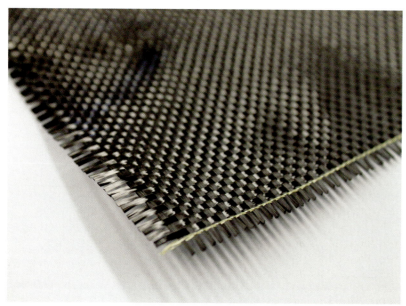

Figure 2-1-7. Carbon fiber fabric

Carbon Fiber

Carbon fibers, commonly called graphite, are made from organic materials. Although the terms are frequently used interchangeably, there are some differences between carbon and graphite fibers.

Both are based on the graphene (hexagonal) layer networks present in carbon. If the graphene layers or planes stack with three dimensional order, the material is defined as graphite. Usually extended time and temperature processing is required to form this order, making graphite fibers more expensive.

Because the bonding between planes is weak, disorder frequently occurs such that only two-dimensional ordering within the layers is present. This material is defined as carbon.

Graphite and carbon fibers can be identified by their dark gray or black color, as seen in Figure 2-1-7. They are moderately flexible. Graphite fibers have a high potential for causing galvanic corrosion when used with metallic fasteners and structures. Typically limitations on the use of carbon fibers in composite structures depend more on the resin matrix than the fiber. Carbon fiber is available as dry materials, as shown in Figure 2-1-7, and pre-preg materials.

Composites made from carbon fiber are five times stronger than grade 1020 steel for structural parts, yet are five times lighter. In comparison to 6061 aluminum, carbon fiber composites are seven times stronger and two times stiffer, yet one and a half times lighter.

Carbon fiber composites have fatigue properties superior to all known metals, and, when coupled with the proper resins, carbon fiber composites are one of the most corrosion resistant materials available. Carbon fiber is used for structural aircraft applications such as floor beams, stabilizers, flight controls and primary fuselage and wing structure.

Advantages are high strength, low fatigue and corrosion resistance. One disadvantage is lower conductivity than aluminum, and therefore, a lightning protection mesh or coating is necessary for aircraft parts that are prone to lightning strikes. Carbon also costs more than other materials.

Some key properties for carbon fiber, including cost, are listed in Table 2-1-1. Typical values for glass, aramid, and boron are shown for comparison. While some carbon fiber properties are fairly universal, different products from different manufacturers can have substantially different properties.

Carbon fibers are available in many of the same formats as glass fiber. These formats include continuous filament-spooled fiber, milled fiber, chopped fiber, woven fabrics, felts, veils, and chopped-fiber mattes. Most fiber today is spooled, and then processed into other formats in secondary operations.

The size of the carbon fiber tow bundle can range from 1,000 filaments (1k) to more than 200k. Generally, aerospace carbon fibers are available in bundles of 3k, 6k, 12k and 24k

	TENSILE MODULUS (MSI)	TENSILE STRENGTH (KSI)	DENSITY (G/CM^3)	FIBER DIAMETER (MICRON)	COST ($/LB)
Carbon (PAN)	30 - 50	350 - 1,000	1.75 - 1.90	4 - 8	20 - 100
Carbon (Pitch)	25 - 110	200 - 450	1.90 - 2.15	8 - 11	40 - 200
Carbon (Rayon)	6	150	1.60	8 - 9	5 - 25
Glass	10 - 12.5	440 - 670	2.48 - 2.62	30	5 - 40
Aramid	20	410	1.44	—	25 - 75
Boron	58	730 - 1,000	2.30 - 2.60	100 - 200	100 - 250

Table 2-1-1. Typical values for carbon, glass, aramid and boron

filaments, while most commercial-grade fibers are available in 48k or larger filament counts. Composite fabrication equipment, such as filament winders and weaving machines, must be adapted to handle the larger cross section of commercial grade fiber.

Carbon fiber manufacture using polyacrylonitrile (PAN). The manufacture of PAN-based carbon fiber can be broken down into white-fiber and black-fiber stages. Most manufacturers consider the details of these processes proprietary.

Production of the PAN precursor, or white fiber, is a technology in itself. Fairly conventional fiber processes are performed: polymerization, spinning, drawing and washing. Additional drawing stages may be added in the process. Characteristics of the white fiber influence the processing and results for black fiber processing.

The black fiber process consists of several steps: oxidation (or thermosetting), pyrolysis (or carbonizing), surface treatment and sizing. In the oxidation process the PAN fiber is converted from a thermoplastic to a thermoset. For this oxidation process the fiber diameter is limited by waste gas diffusion. In the pyrolysis process, which is performed under an inert atmosphere, most of the non-carbon material is expelled, forming ribbons of carbon aligned with the fiber axis.

In the surface treatment step the fiber may be etched in either gas or liquid phase by oxidizing agents such as chlorine, bromine, nitric acid or chlorates. This improves the wettability for the resin and encourages formation of a strong, durable bond. Additional improvement through removal of surface flaws may also be realized. This process can be electrolytic. The carbon fibers are often sized with a solution of unmodified epoxy resin or other products. The sizing prevents fiber abrasion, improves handling and can provide an epoxy-matrix-compatible surface. Figure 2-1-8 presents an overview of the PAN and PITCH process.

Resins and molten metals do not easily wet carbon fibers due to the relatively inert, non-polar fiber surface. Glass fibers depend upon coupling agents to chemically bond with resins; carbon fibers never achieve strong bonds. Instead, carbon fiber depends upon a combination of mechanical and weak chemical bonding with the matrix material.

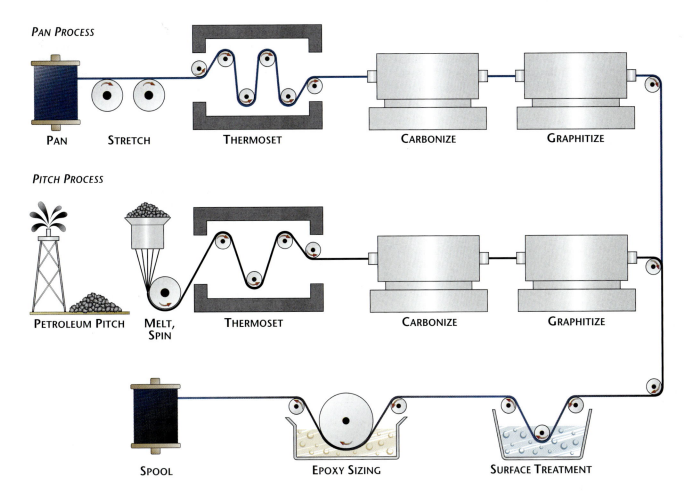

Figure 2-1-8. Comparison of PAN and PITCH processes

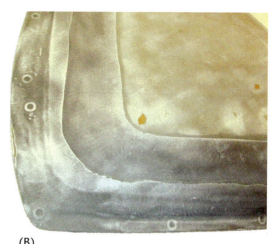

(A)   (B)

Figure 2-1-9. (A) Copper mesh lightning protection, (B) Aluminum mesh lightning protection

Surface treatments used by carbon fiber manufacturers populate the fiber surface with active chemical groups such as hydroxyls, carboxyls and carbonyls. These form bridges between the fiber and resin, and depend upon the number of bonds rather than the strength of the bonds to achieve a strong interface.

Lightning Protection

An aluminum airplane is quite conductive and is able to dissipate the high currents resulting from a lightning strike. Carbon fibers are 1,000 times more resistive than aluminum to current flow, and epoxy resin is one million times more resistive (i.e., perpendicular to the skin). High-energy lightning strikes can cause substantial damage to composite aircraft structures.

There are zones on the airplane with high probability of lightning strike occurrence. Protection of composite aircraft structure by conductive materials is required on these *lightning strike zones* and beyond them to enable conductivity of induced currents away from attachment zones. Attachment zones are areas where structures are connected together using steel or titanium fasteners. The lighting strike is attracted to these fasteners and if the energy cannot be released it will cause serious damage.

An all-composite wing may have to be completely covered by a conductive layer, even if the attachment zone is located near the wing tip. At fasteners and connections, electrical resistance to current flow generated by lightning produces heat that causes burning and delaminations. Minor lightning strikes also can cause significant damage, particularly to the tips and trailing edges if a conductive material is not used.

Many different types of conductive materials are used, ranging from nickel-coated graphite cloth to metal meshes (Figure 2-1-9) to aluminized fiberglass to conductive paints. The materials are available with wet layup and prepreg materials.

If a composite aircraft gets damaged, in addition to a normal structural repair, repair technicians must also recreate the electrical conductivity designed into such a part. These types of repairs generally require a conductivity test with an ohmmeter to verify minimum electrical resistance across the structure. It is extremely important in repairing these types of structures to use only the approved materials from authorized vendors, including potting compounds, sealants, adhesives, and so forth.

Figure 2-1-10. Tows can be used to construct tape or fabric products

Fabrics and Preforms

Product forms generally begin with spooled unidirectional raw fibers packaged as continuous strands. An individual fiber is called a *filament*. The word strand is also used to identify an individual glass fiber. Bundles of filaments are identified as tows, yarns or rovings. Fiberglass yarns are twisted, while Kevlar® yarns are not. Tows and rovings do not have any twist. Most fibers are available as dry fiber that needs to be impregnated with a resin before use or prepreg materials where the resin is already applied to the fiber. Figure 2-1-10 shows fiber products.

Roving

A *roving* is a single grouping of filament or fiber ends, such as 20-end or 60-end glass rovings. All filaments are in the same direction and are not twisted. Carbon rovings are usually identified as 3k, 6k, or 12k, where K equals 1,000 filaments. Most applications for roving products utilize mandrels for filament winding and then resin cure to final configuration.

Unidirectional (Tape)

Unidirectional prepreg tapes have been the standard within the aerospace industry for many years. The fiber is typically impregnated with thermosetting resins. The most common method of manufacture is to draw collimated raw (dry) strands into the impregnation machine where hot, melted resins are combined with the strands using heat and pressure.

Tape products have a high strength in the fiber direction and virtually no strength across the fibers. The fibers are held in place by the resin.

Figure 2-1-11. Carbon fiber tape (unidirectional)

Figure 2-1-11 shows a unidirectional carbon fiber prepreg material.

Bidirectional (Fabric)

Most fabric constructions offer more flexibility for lay-up of complex shapes than straight unidirectional tapes. Fabrics offer the option for resin impregnation either by solution or the hot melt process.

Generally, fabrics used for structural applications use fibers or strands of the same weight or yield in both the warp (longitudinal) and fill (transverse) directions. For aerospace structures, tightly woven fabrics are usually the choice to save weight, minimizing resin void size, and maintaining fiber orientation during the fabrication process. Figure 2-1-12 shows typical weaving equipment for weaving composite materials.

Woven structural fabrics are usually constructed with reinforcement tows, strands or

Figure 2-1-12. Weaving equipment for dry fabric materials

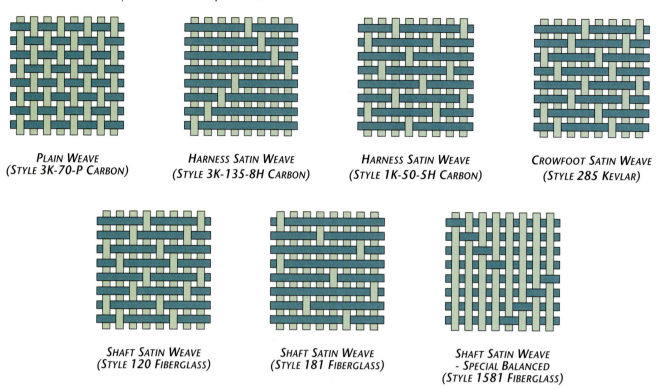

Figure 2-1-13. Typical fabric weave patterns

yarns interlocking upon themselves with over/under placement during the weaving process. The more common fabrics are plain, basket, or satin weaves. The plain weave is the most highly interlaced, and it offers the tightest of the basic fabric designs and is the most resistant to in-plane shear movement. The plain weave construction results from each fiber alternating over and then under each intersecting strand (tow, bundle, or yarn).

Basket weave, a variation of plain weave, has warp and fill yarns that are paired: two up and two down. With the common satin weaves, such as five harness or eight harness, the fiber bundles traverse both in warp and fill directions changing over/under position less frequently.

Satin weaves have less crimp and are easier to distort than a plain weave. Satin weaves can be produced as standard four-, five-, or eight-harness forms. As the number of harnesses increases, so do the float lengths and the degree of looseness and sleaziness, making the fabric more difficult to control during handling operations.

With plain weave fabrics and most five- or eight-harness woven fabrics the fiber strand count is equal in both warp and fill directions. For example, 3k plain weave often has an additional designation such as 12 x 12, meaning there are twelve tows per inch in each direction. This count designation can be varied to increase or decrease fabric weight or to accommodate different fibers of varying weight. Figure 2-1-13 shows some basic types of fabric weave styles.

Nonwoven (Knitted or Stitched)

Multi-axial fabrics are used more frequently for the manufacture of composite components. These fabrics consist of one or more layers of continuous fibers held in place by a secondary, nonstructural stitching thread.

The main fibers can be any of the structural fibers available in any combination. The stitching thread is usually polyester due to its combination of comparative low cost and fiber properties for binding the fabric together. The stitching process allows a variety of fiber orientations, beyond the simple 0/90° of woven fabrics, to be combined into one fabric. Multi-axial fabrics have the following characteristics:

Advantages. The two key improvements with stitched multiaxial fabrics over woven types are better mechanical properties, and improved component build speed. Better mechanical properties result from the fact that the fibers are always straight and uncrimped, and that more orientations of fiber are available due to the increased number of layers of fabric. Component build speed is improved because the fabrics can be made thicker and with multiple fiber orientations so fewer layers need to be included in the laminate sequence.

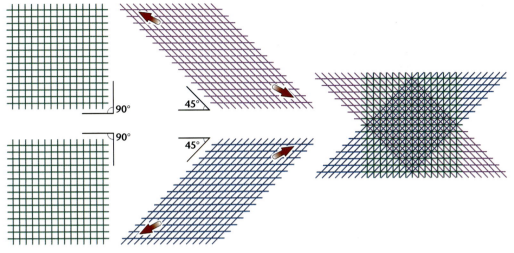

Figure 2-1-14. Weave and stitch process

Disadvantages. Polyester stitching fiber does not bond well to some resin systems, so the stitching can be a starting point for wicking or other failures. The fabric production process can also be slow and the cost of the machinery high. This, together with the fact that more expensive, small, fiber bundles are required to get good surface coverage for the low-weight fabrics, means the cost of good quality stitched fabrics can be relatively high compared to woven fabrics.

Heavyweight fabrics, while enabling large quantities of fiber to be incorporated rapidly into the component, can also be difficult to impregnate with resin without some automated process. Finally, the stitching process, unless carefully controlled, can bunch the fibers together, particularly in the 0° direction, creating resin-rich areas in the laminate.

Stitched fabric construction. The most common forms of this type of fabric are weave and stitch and simultaneous stitch. With the *weave and stitch method* (Figure 2-1-14), the +45° and -45° layers can be made by weaving weft unidirectional and then skewing the fabric to 45°. A warp unidirectional or a weft unidirectional can also be used unskewed to make a 0- and 90° layer. If both 0- and 90° layers are present in a multilayer stitched fabric, this can be provided by a conventional 0/90° woven fabric. Because heavy rovings can be used to make each layer, the weaving process is relatively fast, as is the subsequent stitching together of the layers via a simple stitching frame.

Simultaneous stitch manufacture is based on the knitting process. Fibers are drawn simultaneously along each axis/layer until the required layers have been assembled and stitched together, as shown in Figure 2-1-15. Unlike the weave and stitch method, each layer is unidirectional rather than woven.

Braiding

Braided structures are unique in their high level of conformability, torsional stability and damage resistance. *Braiding* is a system of three or more yarns intertwined in such a way that no two yarns are twisted around one. Braided material differs from woven and knitted fabrics in the method of yarn introduction into the fabric and in the manner by which the yarns are interlaced.

Dry or prepreg yarns, tapes or tows can be braided over a rotating and removable form or mandrel in a controlled manner to assume various shapes, fiber orientations and fiber volume fractions. Although braiding cannot achieve as high a fiber volume fraction as filament winding, braids can assume more complex shapes (sharper curvatures) than filament-wound preforms. The interlaced nature of braids also provides a higher level of structural integrity, which is essential for ease of handling, joining and damage resistance.

The braiding process allows for the introduction of axial yarns between the woven bias

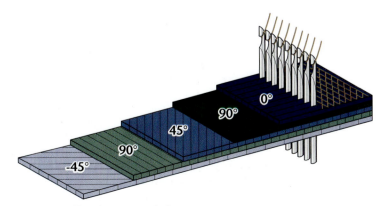

Figure 2-1-15. Simultaneous stitch process

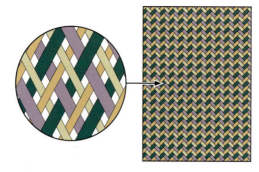

Figure 2-1-16. Braid can include axial yarn.

yarns. These axial yarns are not crimped by the weaving process. See Figure 2-1-16.

Braid is most commonly manufactured and used as a freestanding, tubular fabric with a constant braid angle for a given diameter. In this form, it is supplied on reels or festooned in cartons. In composite manufacturing tubular braids, as shown in Figure 2-1-17, are typically expanded open diametrically, applied to a molding tool or core, snugged down, impregnated with resin and then consolidated. For protrusion, tubular braids are continuously fed over a die mandrel to produce hollow cross sections.

Braided fiber architecture resembles a hybrid of filament winding and weaving. Like filament winding, tubular braid features seamless fiber continuity from end to end of a part. Like woven materials, braided fibers are mechanically interlocked with one another.

The combination, however, is quite extraordinary. When functioning as a composite reinforcement, all the fibers within a braided structure are continuous and mechanically locked, providing a natural mechanism that evenly distributes load throughout the structure.

With regard to strength and stiffness, properly molded biaxial braided composites exhibit properties that are essentially identical to unidirectional tape laminates of the same orientation and fiber volume. Because of the load distributing feature inherent in braided reinforcement, there is no design strength reduction due to fiber crimp.

This phenomenon is limited to tri-axial constructions that have significant fiber volume in the axial direction. The laid-in axial yarns force added crimp in the bias yarns, causing the biases to lose in-plane properties. The axial fibers also tend to inhibit the distribution of loads within the laminate, yielding lower breaking strength. However, tri-axial constructions are very cost effective in a myriad of applications because the automated formation of complex net-shape preforms frequently affords more savings than the additional cost associated with the fiber needed to meet design loads.

Braid's efficient distribution of loads also makes braided structures very impact resistant. Since all the fibers in the structure are involved in a loading event, braid absorbs a great deal of energy as it fails. This is why braid is used for energy absorbing crash structures, ballistic applications and fan blade containment in aircraft engine applications.

Braid greatly improves interlaminar shear properties when nested with other braids. While interlaminar adhesion is no different from other reinforcement products, the layers move together. As a result, it is very rare for cracks to form and propagate between layers of braided reinforcement. Since braids are woven on the bias, they provide very efficient reinforcement for parts subjected to torsional loads. Braid is an ideal reinforcement for drive shafts and other torque transfer components such as flanged hubs.

Matrix Materials (Resin) and Adhesives

Resin is a generic term used to designate the polymer, polymer precursor material, or mixture thereof with various additives or chemically reactive components. The resin, its chemical composition and physical properties fundamentally affect the processing, fabrication and ultimate properties of composite materials. Variations in the composition, physical state or morphology of a resin and the presence of impurities or contaminants in a resin

Figure 2-1-17. Braiding equipment for tubular materials

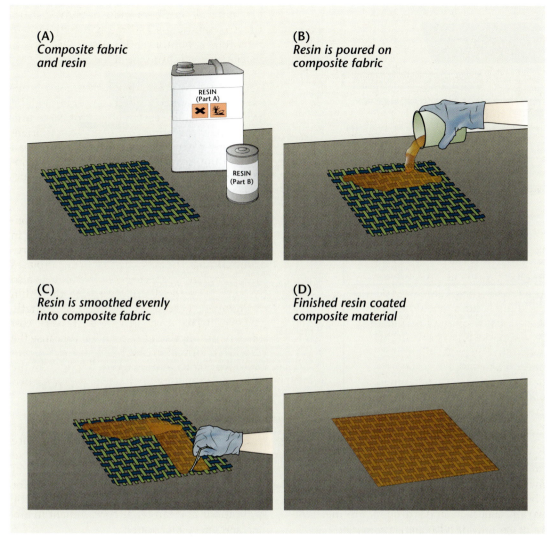

Figure 2-1-18. Resin bonds the individual fibers to each other creating a rigid, lightweight structure.

may affect handleability and processability, lamina/laminate properties, composite material performance and long-term durability.

The resin is often referred to as the matrix of a composite. The role of the matrix is to support the fibers and bond them together in the composite material. It transfers any applied loads to the fibers, keeps the fibers in their position and chosen orientation (Figure 2-1-18). The matrix also gives the composite environmental resistance and determines the maximum service temperature of a prepreg. The maximum service temperature is one of the key criteria for choosing the best matrix.

Figure 2-1-19. Two-part wet lay-up resin system

Thermoset and Thermoplastic Resins

Both thermoset and thermoplastic matrix material systems are used in the manufacturing of advanced composite parts. Thermoset materials are systems that take a permanent set or shape when cured. Cure temperatures range from room temperature to 350°F (180°C) for polyesters, vinyl esters, epoxies and cyanate esters, and are around 450°F (230°C) for Bismaleimide (BMI) materials, and close to 700°F (370°C) for polyimides. Cure pressures are usually less than 100 pounds per square inch (psi). Figure 2-1-19 shows a two-part room temperature cure-epoxy resin system.

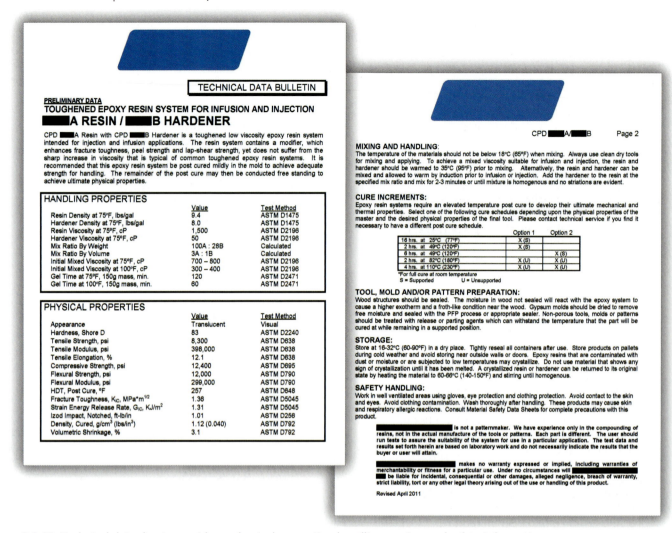

Figure 2-1-20. Technical data sheets provide mechanical properties, handling, curing and safety information.

Thermoplastic materials are noncuring systems that can be reshaped or reformed after the part has been processed or consolidated. Reshaping is accomplished by reheating the part until the material softens and then applying pressure to produce a newly molded shape. Thermoplastics are consolidated at temperatures up to 800°F (425°C) and pressures up to 200 p.s.i.

Thermoplastics have attractive mechanical properties for many supersonic aircraft requirements and for most commercial aircraft requirements. They offer dimensional stability and attractive dielectric characteristics. Good flame-retardant and wear-resistant characteristics also are common.

Most of the thermoplastic polymers have found commodity applications that typically have modest service temperature requirements. Less than a dozen polymers have been considered for engineering applications at higher temperatures, such as are required for many aerospace structural composites. The restricting factor has been the relationship of processing to elevated-temperature properties.

Many polymers may have a glass transition temperature (Tg) or melting temperature (Tm) that seems high. However, the stiffness and mechanical performance of thermoplastics progressively diminish as these points are approached. To have good properties at temperatures of 270°F (132°C) or higher, the Tg or Tm must be well above the intended use temperature.

Types of Thermoset Resins

Resins used in commercial composite applications can be loosely categorized as those suitable for structural or high-temperature applications, and those best suited to nonstructural or low-temperature applications. A primary indicator of service or use temperature of a polymeric composite is the glass transition temperature (Tg).

The Tg is the temperature below which a polymer exists in the glassy state where only vibrational motion is present. Above this temperature, individual molecular segments are able to move relative to each other in what is termed the "rubbery state."

The modulus of a material above its Tg is typically several orders of magnitude lower than its value below the Tg, so this becomes an important consideration when selecting an resin. The Tg is also strongly affected by the presence of absorbed moisture or solvents. Thus, exposure to moisture or solvents must also be taken into account when selecting or designing resins for particular applications.

Figure 2-1-20 shows the technical data sheet of an epoxy resin system. This data sheet contains material related to mechanical properties, handling, curing and safety. Always research the technical data sheet when selecting a new resin system. Note that this data sheet does not provide the Tg, rather a heat deflection temperature (HDT) is given.

Tg is measured in two primary ways: differential scanning calorimetry (DSC), which is the "official" method and thermo-mechanical analysis (TMA). Heat deflection temperature is defined as the temperature at which a standard test bar deflects a specified distance under a load. It is used to determine short-term heat resistance. It distinguishes between materials that are able to sustain light loads at high temperatures and those that lose their rigidity over a narrow temperature range.

Although HDT does not directly state the Tg, this test gives a good indication of the dry Tg of a resin. The HDT is typically a little higher than the Tg measured via the DSC method.

When selecting a thermoset resin, consideration is usually given to tensile strength, modulus and strain, compression strength and modulus, notch sensitivity, impact resistance, heat deflection temperature or Tg, flammability, durability in service, material availability, ease of processing, and price.

Figure 2-1-21 shows the relationship between service temperature and mechanical performance. The figure shows clearly that as service temperature increases, mechanical performance decreases. This should be carefully considered when selecting a resin system.

Polyester resins. Polyester resins are relatively inexpensive and fast processing resins used generally for low-cost applications. Low smoke polyester resins are used for interior parts of an aircraft. Fiber-reinforced polyesters can be processed by many methods, commonly including matched metal molding, wet layup, press (vacuum bag) molding, injection molding, filament winding, pultrusion, and autoclaving. In general, for a fiber-reinforced resin system, the advantage of polyester is its low cost and the capability to process it quickly.

Polyesters can be formulated to cure more rapidly than phenolics during the thermoset molding process. While phenolic processing is dependent on a time/temperature relationship, polyester processing is primarily dependent on temperature.

Depending on the formulation, polyesters can be processed from room temperature to 350°F (180°C). If the proper temperature is applied, a quick cure will occur. Without sufficient heat, the resin/catalyst system will remain plasticized. Compared to epoxies, polyesters process more easily and are much tougher, whereas phenolics are more difficult to process and more brittle, but have higher service temperatures.

Vinyl ester resin. The appearance, handling properties and curing characteristics of vinyl ester resins are the same as conventional polyester resins. However, the corrosion resistance and mechanical properties of vinyl ester composites are much improved over standard polyester resin composites.

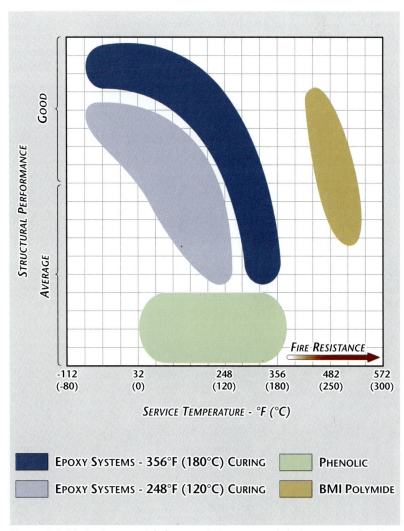

Figure 2-1-21. Resin material characteristics vary and designers use the best fit for the application.

Phenolic resin. Phenol-formaldehyde resins were first produced for commercial use in the early 1900s. *Phenolics* are thermosetting resins produced by the reaction of phenol or substituted phenol with an aldehyde, usually formaldehyde, in the presence of a catalyst.

Urea-formaldehyde and melamine-formaldehyde appeared in the 1920s and '30s as a less-expensive alternative for lower-temperature use. Phenolic resin composites offer superior fire resistance, excellent high-temperature performance, long-term durability, and resistance to hydrocarbon and chlorinated solvents. Phenolic resins are used for interior components because of their low smoke and flammability characteristics.

In the 1980s, the Federal Aviation Administration tightened specifications for smoke and heat release tests in order to increase the evacuation time for passengers in airplane fires to exit safely. Glass and carbon fiber composites made with phenolic resins met these severe fire specifications.

Today, phenolic composites are the material of choice for the walls, ceilings, and floors of aircraft interiors. Phenolic resin can be processed by the following fabrication processes:

Figure 2-1-22. Polyimide resins are commonly used in aircraft powerplant applications because of their heat-resistant properties.

solution/hot-melt process, pultrusion, vacuum infusion, filament winding, sheet molding and hand lay-up

Epoxy. *Epoxies* are polymerizable thermosetting resins and are available in a variety of viscosities from liquid to solid. Epoxies are used widely in resins for prepreg materials and structural adhesives. Most advanced composite parts in the aerospace industry use epoxy resins.

Epoxies have earned wide acceptance because of their excellent mechanical properties, extended service temperature range, and ease of part manufacture. The advantages of epoxies are high strength and modulus, low levels of volatiles, excellent adhesion, low shrinkage, good chemical resistance, and ease of processing. Their major disadvantages are brittleness and the reduction of properties in the presence of moisture.

The processing or curing of epoxies is slower than that of polyester resins. Processing techniques include autoclave molding, filament winding, press molding, vacuum bag molding, resin transfer molding and pultrusion. Curing temperatures vary from room temperature to approximately 350°F (180° C). The most common cure temperatures range between 250° and 350°F (120° and 180° C). Epoxy resins are also chemically compatible with most substrates and tend to wet surfaces easily, making them especially suited to composite applications.

Epoxy resins are routinely used as adhesives, coatings, encapsulates, casting materials, potting compounds and binders. Some of their most interesting applications are found in the aerospace industry where resins and fibers are combined to produce complex composite structures. Epoxy technologies satisfy a variety of nonmetallic composite designs in commercial and military aerospace applications, including flooring panels, ducting, vertical and horizontal stabilizers, wings, and even the fuselage.

The glass transition temperature of a cured epoxy resin is dependent upon the molecular structure that develops in the matrix during cure, which is driven by characteristics such as crosslink density, stiffness of the polymer backbone and intermolecular interactions. It is generally agreed, however, that cured resin formulations suitable for elevated temperature applications are largely determined by crosslink density.

The T_g is therefore closely related to cure temperature and changes as the cure temperature changes, so a resin system cured at a low temperature has a lower T_g than the same system cured at a higher temperature. Every system, however, has an ultimate T_g determined by its formulation that cannot be enhanced by an increase in cure temperature. In most cured epoxy resins Tg lags cure temperature by 20 to 35°F (10 to 20°C). It is important to remember that the molecular structure and other characteristics of the cured product are equally dependent on the base resin, the curing agent, and modifiers employed in the formulation.

Polyimides. Polyimide resins excel in high-temperature environments where their thermal resistance, oxidative stability, low coefficient of thermal expansion and solvent resistance benefit the design. Figure 2-1-22 shows a composite turbine engine fan housing. Their primary uses are in circuit boards and hot engine and aerospace structures.

A polyimide may be either a thermoset resin or a thermoplastic. Polyimides require high cure temperatures, usually in excess of 550°F (290°C). Consequently, normal epoxy composite consumable materials are not usable, and steel tooling becomes a necessity. Polyimide bagging and release films, such as Kapton® and Upilex®, replace the lower cost nylon bagging and polytetrafluoroethylene (PTFE) release films common to epoxy composite processing. Fiberglass fabrics must be used for bleeder and breather materials instead of polyester mat materials.

Bismaleimides. Bismaleimide resins (BMI) have compounds that contain maleimide groups that combine to form a cross-linked network during cure. BMI resins combine a number of unique features, including excellent physical property retention at elevated temperatures and in wet environments; almost constant electrical properties over a wide range of temperatures and non-flammability.

BMIs have epoxy-like processing characteristics yet have a higher temperature use limit. BMIs require higher cure temperatures than those used for epoxies, typically 375 to 450°F (190°F to 230°C). BMIs are used for aero engines and high temperature components. They are suitable for standard autoclave processing, injection molding, resin transfer molding and sheet molding compound (SMC), among others.

The advantages of BMI resins are best discussed in the relation to epoxy resins. Their primary advantage over epoxy resins is their high Tg, in the 500 to 600°F range (260 to 320°C). Glass transition temperatures for high-temperature epoxies are generally less than 500°F (260°C).

The second advantage of BMI resins is high elongation with the corresponding high service temperature capabilities. While the high-temperature epoxies have approximately one percent elongation when cured with diamino-

Figure 2-1-23. Composites containing benzoxazine resins are used in aircraft interiors because of their flame-retardant properties such as low burn time, low smoke density, low heat release and low toxicity of burned by-products.

diphenylsulfone (DDS), BMI's can have 2 to 3 percent elongation. Thus, bismaleimide resins deliver higher temperature capability and higher toughness providing excellent performance at ambient and elevated temperatures.

Benzoxazine. Benzoxazine resin systems are an emerging type of resin systems for aerospace applications. Benzoxazine resins offer high temperature performance, low moisture uptake, good flame, smoke and toxicity; and the potential for ambient storage.

These resins are processed just like epoxy resins but have higher operating temperatures, and Benzoazine prepregs can be stored at room temperature so there is no need for freezers. Benzoazine resin systems are available for prepreg, film adhesive and RTM/VARTM. They are frequently used in internal applications, as seen in Figure 2-1-23.

Adhesives

Epoxy-based adhesives are the most commonly used materials for bonding or repair of composite structures. Epoxy adhesives impart high-strength bonds and long-term durability over a wide range of temperatures and environments. The ease of formulation modification makes it fairly easy for the user to employ various materials to control specific performance properties, such as density, toughness, flow, mix ratio, pot life/shelf life, shop handling characteristics, cure time/temperature and service temperature.

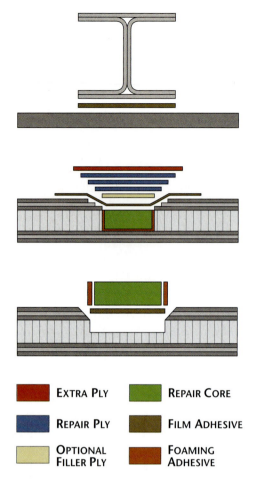

Figure 2-1-24. Film adhesives are used to join structural components.

Advantages of epoxy adhesives are excellent adhesion, high strength and modulus, low or no volatiles during cure, low shrinkage, and good chemical resistance. Its disadvantages include cost, brittleness unless modified, moisture absorption that adversely affects properties, and rather long cure times. A wide range of one- and two-part systems are available. Some systems cure at room temperature, while others require elevated temperatures.

Selecting the correct adhesive, surface preparation and bond line thickness control are critical for bonding processes. Controlling the thickness of the adhesive bond line is a critical factor in bond strength. This control can be obtained by matching the quantity of available adhesive to the size of the gap between the mating surfaces under actual bonding heat and pressure conditions.

For liquid and paste adhesives, it is a common practice to embed nylon or polyester fibers in the adhesive to prevent adhesive-starved bond lines. Higher applied loads during bonding tend to reduce bond line thickness. A slight overfill is usually desired to ensure that the gap is totally filled. Conversely, if the adhesive is squeezed out of a local area due to a high spot in one of the adherends, a dis-bond can result.

Film adhesives. Structural adhesives for aerospace applications are generally supplied as thin films supported on a release paper and stored under refrigerated conditions (0°F, or -18°C). Film adhesives are available using high-temperature aromatic amine or catalytic curing agents with a wide range of flexibilizing and toughening agents. Rubber-toughened epoxy film adhesives are widely used in the aircraft industry.

The upper temperature limit of 250-350°F (121 to 177°C) is usually dictated by the degree of toughening required and by the overall choice of resins and curing agents. In general, toughening of a resin results in a lower usable service temperature. Film materials are frequently supported by fibers that serve to improve handling of the films prior to cure, control adhesive flow during bonding and assist in bond line thickness control.

Fibers can be incorporated as short-fiber mattes with random orientation or as woven cloth. Commonly encountered fibers are polyesters, polyamides (nylon) and glass. Adhesives containing woven cloth may have slightly degraded environmental properties because of wicking of water by the fiber. Random matte scrim cloth is not as efficient for controlling film thickness as woven cloth, because the unrestricted fibers move during bonding, although spun-bonded nonwoven scrims do not move and are therefore widely used.

Adhesive films have a separator film or backing paper that is applied to keep the material from sticking to itself. Film adhesives are tacky at room temperature and above (provided the shelf life is good) and are available with one side tacky (OST) or both sides tacky (BST).

Film adhesives are manually cut to size, usually with knives, and placed in the bond lines. When applying film adhesives, it is important to prevent or eliminate entrapped air pockets between the adherend and the adhesive film by pricking bubbles or "porcupine" rolling over the adhesive prior to application. Figure 2-1-24 shows the different applications for film adhesives in aerospace manufacturing, and Figure 2-1-25 shows typical film adhesive products.

Liquid adhesives. These materials consist of low-viscosity resins used for injecting delaminations and disbonds and for laminating dry-woven cloth. These adhesives, consist of two components and come in separate containers. Part A contains the base resin and part B the curing agent. Just prior to use, the two parts are weighed to obtain the proper mix ratio and then mixed. Correct weighing and thorough mixing is required to ensure strength is not compromised.

Liquid adhesives are extremely exothermic after mixing and require special care when mixing quantities in excess of 3.5 oz. (100g). For most of these resin systems, the curing reaction begins immediately after mixing and provides only limited working time.

This working time is called *pot life*. Pot life is defined as the period between the time of mixing the resin and curing agent and the time at which the viscosity has increased to the point when the adhesive can no longer be successfully applied. To avoid potential exothermic conditions after application, excess mixed material should be removed from the container and spread out in a thin film. This prevents the risk of mass-related heat buildup and the possibility of a fire or the release of toxic fumes.

Some of these resin systems can be cured at room temperature. However, the cure time can be significantly shortened by application of heat. Liquid adhesives can be filled with chopped fibers or hollow microspheres to make low density filler compounds or pastes. Liquid adhesives sometimes require refrigerated storage to maximize their shelf life.

Application of liquid adhesives can be accomplished using brushes, rollers, manual sprays or robotically controlled sprays. A robot can apply tightly controlled quantities of adhesive to specific areas. Solvated two-part systems are sprayed using equipment with two pumps; preset quantities of each component are pumped through the spray head where they are blended into a single stream. Of course, many plants use several different application systems simultaneously for their various job shop requirements.

Filler materials/paste adhesives. Paste adhesives are liquid adhesives modified by the manufacturer with the addition of fillers or a chemically reactive modifier. Paste adhesives are used in the repair of composite parts as filler materials, for bonding repair core sections in place and for bonding repair patches. Like liquid adhesive systems, paste adhesives are two component systems requiring careful weighing and thorough mixing to ensure strength is not compromised.

Compared to film adhesives, paste adhesives have the advantage of lower temperature cure cycles and are easier to store and ship. However, they have the disadvantage of lower strength, poor bond line thickness control, and higher overall repair weight when compared to film adhesives.

Paste adhesives require refrigerated storage to maximize their shelf-life. In addition to composite bonding and repair applications, two-

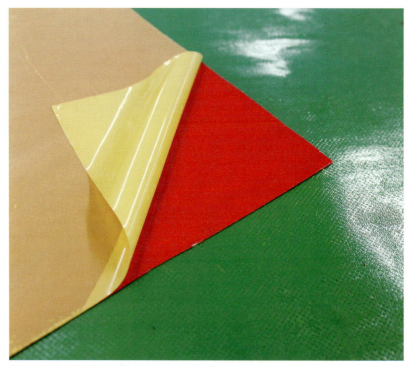

Figure 2-1-25. Film adhesive

part epoxy paste adhesives are also used for liquid shim applications during mechanical assembly operations. The ability to tailor flow, cure time and compressive strength make these materials ideal for use in areas of poor fit-up.

Application of paste adhesives can be accomplished by brush, by spreading with a grooved tool or by extrusion from cartridges or sealed containers using compressed air. For the latter, the combination of the orifice diameter and the applied pressure controls the size of the bead applied to the work. Figure 2-1-26 shows a two-part paste adhesive used for composite structural repair.

Figure 2-1-26. Two-part epoxy paste adhesive

Foaming adhesives. Foaming adhesives consist of a thin unsupported epoxy film containing a blowing agent. During the rise to cure temperature, an inert gas is liberated causing an expansion or foaming action in the film. The expansion must be performed under positive pressure to prevent over expansion and reduced strength.

Following expansion, the adhesive is cured into a strong highly structured foam. It is used as a lightweight splice material for splicing honeycomb core repair sections. Like film adhesives, foaming adhesives have the disadvantage of requiring a high temperature cure cycle and must be shipped and stored at or below 0°F (-18°C). They are sensitive to moisture, temperature and contamination in the uncured state and must be handled and stored properly to prevent degradation. Figure 2-1-27 shows how foaming adhesives are used for the splicing and repair of honeycomb structures.

Storage and Handling of Resins and Adhesives

Film adhesives are sensitive to temperature, moisture and contamination in the uncured state and must be handled and stored properly to prevent degradation. They require shipping and storage at or below 0°F (-18°C) in a sealed, water- and vapor-proof bag, unless otherwise specified in the manufacturer's technical data sheet. Storage life and maximum time out of the freezer, prior to use, are specified by manufacturers. A record of out-time shall be maintained for all film adhesives (Table 2-1-2).

The shelf life of material can be improved by cutting large batches into smaller sections (kitting) the first time it is thawed. This method permits the bulk of the material to be kept frozen while some pieces are thawed for use, thereby, reducing waste caused by exceeding out-time requirements.

When kitting, lay the material flat or wrap it around a tube that is at least 3 in. in diameter and 2 in. longer than the material. Do not fold the material as this will distort it. Before opening refrigerated packages containing film adhesives, the packages must be allowed to warm up, typically four to six hours or until moisture is no longer condensing on the package.

Backing or separator film must not be removed from the repair material until it is ready for use. If film adhesives were received without dry ice in the shipping container, determine how long it was out of the freezer, then add that time to the out-time log.

Wear latex or nitrile gloves when handling film adhesives. If powdered gloves are all that are available, ensure that the exterior of the gloves is cleaned before handling repair materials and wash your hands thoroughly immediately after removing the gloves to prevent contaminating the repair area and materials.

Prepreg and film adhesive should be supported on cardboard rolls, or in some other manner. They should be sealed in moisture-proof bags, with desiccant packages if possible. Once packaged, they should be stored in conditions as recommended by the manufacturer, usually at or below 0°F (-18°C) for a shelf life of six months or longer. Since the cure of thermoset materials continues to progress at room temperature, and even at these lower storage temperatures, a record must be kept of the time exposed at room and storage temperatures.

This record will be used to establish the useful life of the material and to determine when retesting is required. The time that material can be at room temperature and still usable, known as the out-time, can range from minutes to 30 days or longer. For some materials the processing characteristics can change dramatically depending on how much storage and out-time they have experienced.

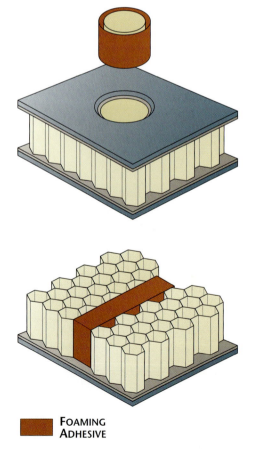

Figure 2-1-27. Foaming adhesives simplify repair and splicing tasks.

Perishable Material:				Initial Shelf Life:			Initial Expiration Date:		
Store at or Below:									
Material (Generic or Trade Name):				Manufacturer:			Batch/Lot:		
Roll/Can/Kit/etc.:		DOS/DOM:			Specification:		Type:	Class:	Grade:
Purchase Order Number:		Chemical Number:			LOC:		Part Number:		
ROOM TEMPERATURE STORAGE									
Maximum Allowable Out-Time									
Out		In		Out-Time (Hours)		User Signature		Inspector Signature	
Date	Time	Date	Time	Subtotal	Total				
CONTROLLED STORAGE RESET									
Test	Date			Lab Report		Signature		New Exp Date	
1st									
2nd									
3rd									
4th									
5th									
MATERIAL USE									
Initial Length/Quality									
Material Used	Material Remaining	Date	Material Use		Material Used	Material Remaining	Date	Material Use	

Table 2-1-2. Perishable material history sheet/out-time log

Since these materials require a carefully controlled environment, maintaining that environment while shipping the product can be challenging. Usually the material, still in its moisture-proof sealed bag, is placed in a shipping container approved for use with dry ice. Enough dry ice is placed in the container to allow some to be remaining upon the scheduled arrival, plus about 24 hours. Chemically based temperature sensitive materials, or electronic temperature recording devices (Figure 2-1-28) can be placed in the container to assure material integrity upon delivery.

Laminating resins and paste adhesives must be stored in clean containers and in accordance with the manufacturer's instructions. The containers must be kept closed to prevent moisture absorption that will degrade the resin properties. Many of the two-part systems can

Figure 2-1-28. Electronic temperature recording devices track storage temperatures.

Figure 2-1-29. A cold storage facility is required for some materials.

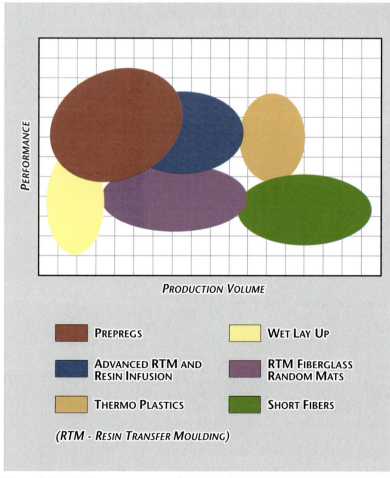

Figure 2-2-1. Performance vs. production volume comparison

be stored under normal ambient temperature conditions. Shelf-life limitations imposed by the manufacturer must be observed.

Before opening refrigerated materials, the containers must be allowed to warm up, typically for a few hours or until moisture is no longer condensing on the package. Wear latex or nitrile gloves when handling resins and adhesives. If powdered gloves are all that are available, ensure that the exterior of the gloves is cleaned before handling repair materials and wash your hands thoroughly immediately after removing the gloves to prevent contaminating the area and materials. When handling these materials, wear low-lint garments to prevent contamination of the repair area and materials.

Cold storage rooms. Non-frost-free cold storage equipment that can maintain material at 0°F (-18°C) or lower is required to maintain shelf life on the vast majority of pre-impregnated materials and adhesives. Frost-free freezers remove frost by temporarily heating up above 32°F (0°C), which can reduce the shelf life of the materials.

Because of moderate usage rates on pre-impregnated materials, and the number of different shelf-life-limited materials necessary for aircraft support, as well as long procurement lead-times, manufacturers and maintenance and repair facilities will require walk-in freezers that have sufficient capacity to meet local, and potentially field, needs for 6 to 12 months. Procurement and manufacturer lead times for most specification materials can mean waits of eight weeks to four months before delivery.

In case of power or freezer failure, an alarm system tied to a 24-hour notification site may avoid an expensive loss of shelf life and material. Figure 2-1-29 shows a cold storage facility.

Section 2
Prepregs

The position of prepreg technology in terms of performance and production volumes is compared in Figure 2-2-1 with other fabrication processes. Prepreg manufacturing processes have a low volume but the products provide the best performance and therefore are used frequently in the aerospace industry.

Prepreg material, as illustrated in Figure 2-2-2, consists of a combination of a matrix and fiber reinforcement. It is available in unidirectional

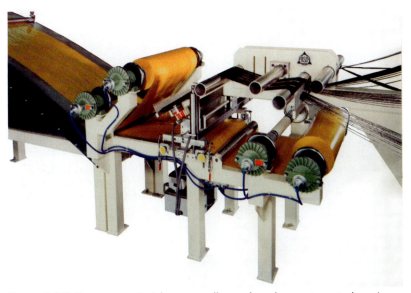

Figure 2-2-3. Prepreg materials are usually produced on automated equipment.
Courtesy of EHA

form (one direction of reinforcement) and fabric form (several directions of reinforcement). All the major families of matrix resins can be used to impregnate various fiber forms. The resin is then no longer in a low-viscosity stage, but has been advanced to a B-stage level of cure for better handling characteristics. The following products are available in prepreg form: unidirectional tape, woven fabric, continuous strand rovings and chopped matte.

Prepreg materials must be stored in a freezer at a temperature below 0°F (-18°C) to retard the curing process. Prepreg materials are cured with an elevated temperature. Many prepreg materials used in aerospace are impregnated with an epoxy resin and cured at either 250° or 350°F (120° or 175°C). Prepreg materials are cured with an autoclave, oven or heat blanket. During the prepreg manufacturing process backing paper is applied to either one or both sides of the prepreg. The backing paper is coated with a release agent to ensure the level of adhesion to the prepreg is consistent. It also must be very consistent in thickness and not have a propensity to rip when scored with a knife.

Prepreg Manufacturing Techniques

Two techniques are used to make prepreg materials: film transfer and solution transfer. Film transfer is used often for the aerospace industry. An advantage of the film transfer technique is high quality and no release of volatiles during processing. Prepreg equipment are large pieces of machinery that operate at close tolerances. Figure 2-2-3 shows a complete prepreg line.

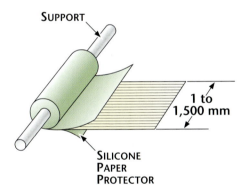

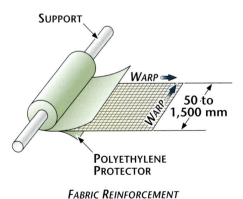

Figure 2-2-2. Unidirectional and fabric prepreg materials

Film Transfer

The film transfer, or hot melt process, consists of two steps, as shown in Figure 2-2-4. During the first step the resin is placed on release paper and the resulting film will be used to make the prepreg. During the second step the fiber reinforcement is added to the resin film and a release film is placed on top. After this the material is heated and pressed together (consolidated). The top release film is removed again and the prepreg is placed on a roll, ready for shipping. Film transfer is the most common method to prepreg aerospace-quality tape and fabric products.

Solution Technique

The solution technique (Figure 2-2-5) can be used in a vertical or horizontal set up. The fiber is run through a resin bath and impregnated, then passed through rollers to remove excess resin and consolidate the material. The material is dried in an oven and release film is placed on the prepreg material. During this process solvents are used to lower the viscosity of the resin so that it can impregnate the fiber. These solvents will have to be removed from the material.

Curing Stages of Resins

Thermosetting resins cure through a chemical reaction. There are three curing stages, known as A, B and C.

A stage. The components of the resin (base material and hardener) have been mixed but the chemical reaction has not started. The resin is in the A stage during a wet lay-up procedure.

B stage. The components of the resin have been mixed and the chemical reaction has started. The material has thickened and is tacky. To prevent further curing the resin is placed in a freezer at 0°F (-18°C). In the frozen state the resin will stay in the B stage. The curing will start when the material is removed from the freezer and heated again.

C stage. The resin is fully cured. Some resins cure at room temperature and others need an elevated temperature to fully cure.

Types of Prepregs

Prepreg is available in many different types. The most common are: prepreg roving for filament winding and automated fiber placement

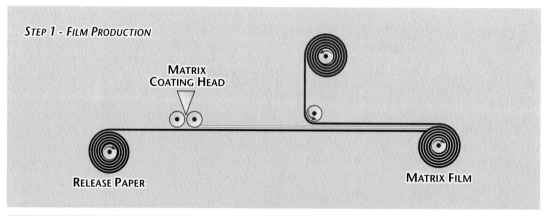

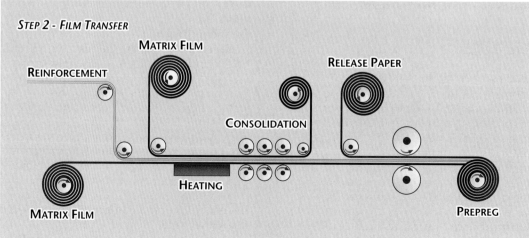

Figure 2-2-4. Film transfer (hot melt) prepreg manufacturing

processes; prepreg unidirectional tape for automated tape laying and hand lay-up processes; and prepreg fabric for hand lay-up processes. Figure 2-2-6 shows a prepreg fabric product.

Prepreg Roving

This impregnated product form generally applies to a single grouping of filament or fiber ends, such as 20-end or 60-end glass rovings. Carbon rovings are usually identified as 3k, 6k, or 12k but other counts are available. It is possible, preferably during the resin impregnation step, to combine two or more counts or filaments or ends, to increase the rovings weight or, width per linear length. For mechanical testing purposes individual rovings are usually wound, side by side, to form single-ply tapes and processed as such. The roving product form, with its packaging on individual spools, offers the means for automated fiber placement during the manufacture of parts.

Rovings can be placed in a unidirectional pattern, like tapes, or to generate a crossover interlocking effect. Most applications for roving products utilize mandrels for filament winding and then resin cure to final configuration. In addition, this product form is used for efficient build-up of oriented filaments to create preforms.

The preforms are combined with other layups or processed individually in closed tools rather than the conventional mandrel cure process. Most rovings are supplied untwisted, in nearly flat continuous bands. Band widths can be controlled to a degree during the impregnation step.

Compared to tapes or fabrics, roving areal weights (dry weight/area) for individual plies or wraps are more dependent on the winding process than the impregnation step. However, resin control of the pre-impregnated rovings shares a like degree of accuracy.

Prepreg Tape

All product forms generally begin with spooled unidirectional raw fibers packaged as continuous strands. Normally, untwisted tows or ends are specified for unidirectional product forms to obtain ultimate fiber properties. This particular product form depends on the proper fiber wet-out and the tenacity of the uncured resin to maintain proper fiber placement until the tape reaches the curing procedure.

Conventional unidirectional tapes. This particular form has been the standard within the user industry for many years and is com-

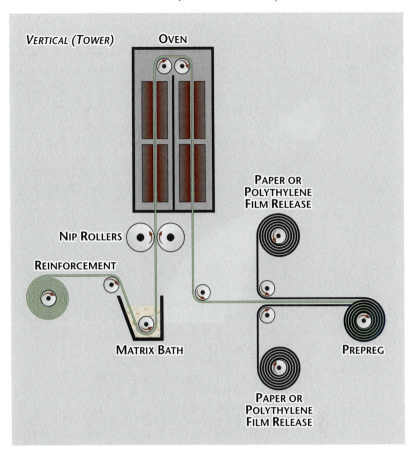

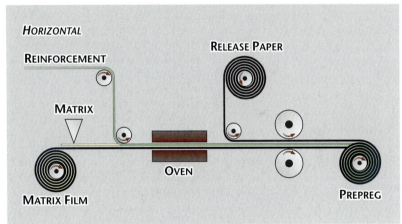

Figure 2-2-5. Solution transfer prepreg manufacturing

mon with thermosetting resins. The most common method of manufacture is to draw collimated raw (dry) strands into the impregnation machine where hot melted resins are combined with the strands using heat and pressure. The combination of fibers and resin usually travels through the machine between coated carrier papers or films for ease of release. The tapes are trimmed to specified widths. One side of the carrier is removed prior to the roll-up position to facilitate continuous visual inspection.

The remaining carrier is left in place with the tape to serve as a separator on the roll and as a processing aid for fabrication purposes. The tape manufacturing process is continu-

Figure 2-2-6. Prepreg carbon-fiber fabric

ous within the linear limits of the raw strands reeled to the machine or specified lot size or availability of resin.

Most impregnation machines are designed to permit in-line changeover to new rolls (take-ups) without interruption. Raw strand collimation is adjusted to control specified areal weight. Resin filming for tape machine operations is often done as a separate controlled operation. Some machines accommodate in-line filming that permit resin content adjustments during the impregnation process. Tapes as wide as 60 in. (1.5 m) are commercially available.

Two-step unidirectional tapes. Although they are not common in the prepreg industry, there are unidirectional tapes manufactured from pre-impregnated rovings. The collimation of these rovings to make tapes allows the use of solution-impregnated resins, rather than hot melt systems. Although the product form may be similar to conventional tapes, thin uniform flat tapes may be difficult to produce.

Supported unidirectional tapes. To enhance specific mechanical properties or part manufacturing handling operations, it is sometimes advantageous to add product form during the manufacture of unidirectional tapes. Generally, these added fibrous forms are lightweight to be accommodated during the normal tape manufacture operation. The added form may be combined in the machine dry or pre-impregnated prior to the tape production. More common added forms are lightweight mats or scrim fabrics of the same or unlike fiber type. The added product form will affect material properties compared to tapes without the supporting material.

Coated unidirectional tapes. Some tape suppliers offer added tape surface coating. These resinous coatings of films are usually of different rheology or viscosities from the fiber impregnation resin to remain as distinct boundaries between plies of the cured tapes. As with supported unidirectional tapes, the added layer may be combined during the tape manufacturing operation.

Pre-plied unidirectional tapes. These tapes originate as any of the above-described tape forms in single-ply form. Then through a process of stacking, two or more layers of tapes are oriented at predetermined angles to form a progressively generated tape or broad-goods form. The original individual tapes are located side to side in each angled layer to form a continuous linear form. The original single-ply tapes are usually precut in segments at angles to correspond to the new product form's edges. The progressive stacking sequence takes place on a continuous carrier (paper or film) atop a flat surface much like the fabrication process.

The carrier, with the pre-plied form in place, is utilized to take up the pre-plied tapes onto a shipping/handling core. The predetermined length of the individual precut segments will generally regulate the width of the pre-plied tapes. However, a final trim of both edges to control specified widths can be incorporated during the take-up step.

For economic purposes the pre-plying operation usually is done in widths of approximately 24 in. (0.6 m) or greater. Should narrow widths be required, they can be accommodated with a secondary slitting operation. To some extent the retention of this product form's continuity is, like single-ply tapes, dependent on the tack or tenacity of the uncured resin.

Prepreg Variables

Resin mixing and pre-impregnating operations can also influence the processability of the final prepreg. During normal mixing operations, air can be easily mixed into the resin. This entrained air can later serve as nucleation sites for voids and porosity. However, many mixing vessels are equipped with seals that allow vacuum degassing during the mixing operation, a practice that has been found to be effective in removing entrained air and may be beneficial in producing superior quality laminates.

Prepreg physical properties can also influence final laminate quality. Prepreg tack is a measure of the stickiness or self-adhesive nature of the prepreg plies. Many times, prepregs with a high tack level have resulted in laminates with severe voids and porosity. This could be due to the potential difficulty of removing entrapped air pockets during collation of the tacky prepreg. Again, moisture can be a factor. Prepregs with a high moisture content have been found to be inherently tackier than low moisture content material.

Prepreg physical quality can greatly influence final laminate quality. Ironically, prepreg that appears "good" (i.e., smooth and well impregnated) may not necessarily produce the best laminates. Several material suppliers have determined that only partially impregnating the fibers during pre-impregnating results in a prepreg that consistently yields high-quality parts, whereas a "good" prepreg can result in laminates with voids and porosity. Partially impregnated prepregs have the same resin content and fiber areal weight as the fully impregnated material.

Laminate configuration can influence final quality. Thin laminates are more prone to bleeding than thick laminates. In other words, it is quite easy to remove too much resin from a thin laminate and this can result in voids and porosity. On the other hand, thick laminates tend to be too thick if they are bled from only one surface.

Porosity in thick laminates has been observed in the surface plies, next to the bleeder pack, which can undergo severe over bleeding, while the center and tool plies of the laminate undergo little to no bleeding. It is easier to trap air during ply collation of thick laminates that cannot escape during "debulking" or processing. Furthermore, it is much more difficult to evacuate volatiles from the center of large thick laminates, where air and volatiles cannot escape horizontally to the edges.

Unidirectional laminates can be difficult to process. Unidirectional plies tend to nest and seal off at the edges, limiting the effectiveness of debulking. This leaves trapped air pockets in the laminate. In addition, it has been observed that volatiles will attempt to travel down the fiber lengths to evacuate out the edges. This has led to the term "linear porosity" for microscopic tubes of porosity that run parallel to the fiber orientation.

In cross-plied laminates, several plies oriented in the same direction have the same effect. Internal ply drop-off areas also tend to be porosity prone. Many times voids are present at ply terminations. This is especially true in low-flow systems where the resin does not flow and properly fill the gaps at ply terminations.

Once a laminate is collated, it must be bagged for autoclave curing. The bagging operation involves several variables that can affect part

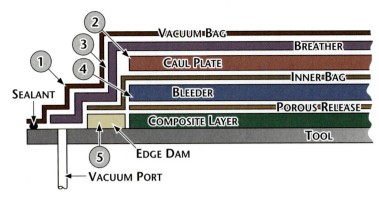

1. Vacuum bag ruptures at sharp corner or bridge causing pressure loss
2. Caul plate severs inner bag allowing resin to escape into breather pack
3. Caul plate bridges over top of dam causing low pressure area
4. Too much bleeder material overbleeds laminate
5. Improperly sealed dams allow resin to escape into breather pack

Figure 2-2-7. Potential bagging problems

quality, a number of which are illustrated in Figure 2-2-7. If too much bleeder is used, overbleeding can result in a large drop in the hydrostatic resin pressure, a condition conducive to porosity and void formation. If the resin has a low viscosity (i.e., high flow), the danger of over bleeding is even greater.

Even if the correct amount of bleeder is used, an improperly sealed inner bagging system can allow resin to escape into the breather system. For example, if the caul plate severs the inner bag or the dams are not properly sealed, the resin will escape and the hydrostatic resin pressure could fall below the volatile vapor pressure leading to voids and porosity.

Another variable that will occasionally cause a problem is if the caul plate is misallocated or slips and bridges over the top of a dam. This results in a localized low-pressure area along the edge of the laminate that will experience voids or possibly even large delamination. Finally, if the outer vacuum bag (usually nylon film) bridges and ruptures during the autoclave cycle, a partial or total loss of the compaction force can result. If the resin has not already reached the point of gelation in the cure cycle, massive amounts of voids and porosity can form.

Curing of Prepregs

Resin consolidation and cure processes are required to ensure that the individual sections or layers of a composite part are properly bonded, and that the matrix is intact and

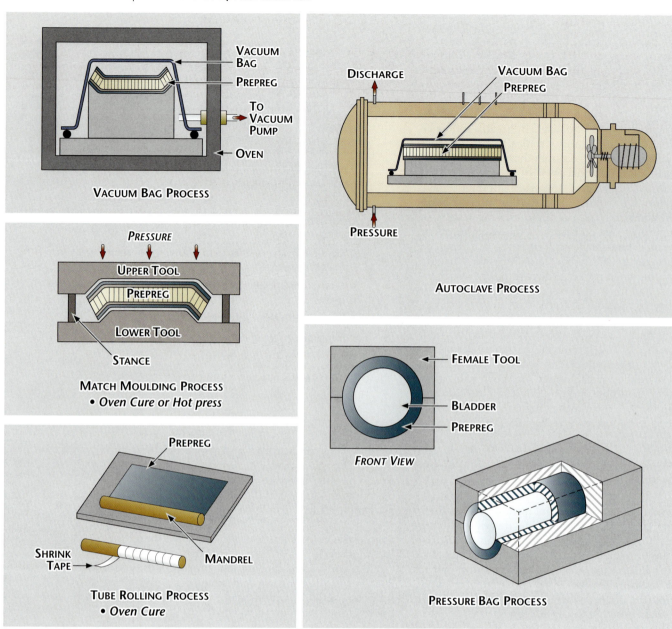

Figure 2-2-8. Structures made from prepreg materials can be cured using various processes.

capable of maintaining the placement of the fibrous reinforcement that will carry the loads applied to the part. These processes are among the most sensitive in the materials processing pipeline.

As a thermosetting composite part is formed during cure, the material is undergoing extensive chemical and morphological change. As a result, many actions occur simultaneously. Some of these actions can be controlled directly, others indirectly, and some of them interact. Such actions as evolution of voids or shifting of reinforcing fibers during matrix flow may result in large changes in properties of the cured composite.

In the case of a thermoplastic matrix composite, the matrix is not intended to undergo chemical change during consolidation. Changes such as chain scissions resulting in production of volatiles may occur inadvertently. In addition, resin flow is required for consolidation. Semi-crystalline thermoplastics may undergo morphological changes in the degree of crystallinity upon melting, flow and recrystallization, particularly in the fiber/matrix interphase.

These changes can cause significant alterations in the mechanical and physical properties of the consolidated composite. In amorphous thermoplastics, segregation of varying molecular weight materials in the interphase may also result in changes in composite properties. The various processes that can be used to cure prepregs are shown in Figure 2-2-8.

Vacuum Bag Molding

In vacuum bag molding, the layup is cured under pressure generated by drawing a vacuum in the space between the layup and a flexible sheet placed over it and sealed at the edges. The reinforcement is generally placed in the mold by hand lay-up using prepreg or wet resin. High-flow resins are preferred for vacuum bag molding. The following steps are used in vacuum bag molding:

1. Place composite material for part into mold.
2. Install bleeder and breather material.
3. Place vacuum bag over part.
4. Seal bag and check for leaks.
5. Place tool and part in oven and cure as required at elevated temperature.
6. Remove part from mold.

Parts fabricated using vacuum bag oven cure have lower fiber volumes and higher void contents than parts made in an autoclave. Vacuum bag molding is a low-cost method of fabrication and uses low-cost tooling for short production runs. Figure 2-2-9 shows a simple part being consolidated using a vacuum bag process.

Oven Cure

Composite material can be cured in ovens using various pressure application methods. Vacuum bagging, described above, can be used to remove volatiles and trapped air by using atmospheric pressure for consolidation. Another method of pressure application for oven cures is the use of shrink-wrapping or shrink tape. This method is commonly used with parts that have been filament wound because some of the same rules for application apply. The tape is wrapped around the completed layup, usually with only a layer of release material between the tape and the layup. Heat is applied to the tape, usually using a heat gun, to make the tape shrink. The shrinking tape, can apply a tremendous amount of pressure to the layup. After shrinking, the part is placed in the oven for cure.

High-quality parts can be made inexpensively using shrink tape, with a couple of limitations. First, the part must be of a configuration where the tape can apply pressure at all points. Second, flow of the resin during cure must be limited because the tape will not continue to shrink in the oven. If the resin flows excessively, the pressure applied by the shrink tape will be reduced substantially.

Autoclave Curing Processing

Autoclave curing uses relatively high heat and high pressure. An *autoclave* (Figure 2-2-10) is a heated pressure vessel typically capable of 300 p.s.i. (2 MPa) internal pressure and temperatures up to 700°F (370°C). Thermoset composite materials are generally processed at less than 100 p.s.i. and at temperatures ranging from 250 to 400°F (120 to 200°C). Thermoplastic composites may require higher temperatures and pressures. Due to the high temperatures during processing, the atmosphere within the vessel is generally purged of oxygen using an inert gas, such as nitrogen, thereby preventing thermal combustion or charring of the materials being cured.

Materials that are to be cured in an autoclave are located onto tooling that provides the eventual shape of the cured material. The tooling, frequently referred to as the mold, may comprise an assembly of mandrels or tool details to accommodate complex geometry. The mold may also include features such as locating devices, tooling tabs or net-molding details to enhance the subsequent processing of the final product or material.

Typically, an impervious layer of bagging film or a reusable elastic bladder is located over the material being cured and sealed against the mold. Vacuum is applied between the bagging material and the material being cured such that the plies of material are compressed through the thickness against the mold.

In some instances, an autoclave or oven is used to apply heat and pressure to only a portion of the material being cured as an interim de-bulk step to enhance the quality of the finished product through improved consolidation. As

Figure 2-2-9. Vacuum bag molding

the temperature in the autoclave is raised, the viscosity of the curing material is generally lowered to a fluid state and the gasses within and between the layers escape as the material consolidates. A porous bleeder layer or a breather in the form of sheet, strips or strands may be utilized under the bagging material to help enable the evacuation of gasses.

Surface films or in mold coatings may also be included against the tool surface to improve the surface finish of the cured material. Rigid caul plates or intensifiers may also be incorporated under the bagging material to locally control the thickness and quality of the finished product. In some cases, pre-cured or stage-cured components may be co-cured or co-bonded with the material being cured in the autoclave.

The primary sources of variability in the autoclave curing process are:

- Poor surface finish on the tooling or mold surface will transfer to finished product.
- More tools closer together in the autoclave will act as a heat sink and affect degree of cure.
- The more complex the part geometry, the more difficult to achieve uniform consolidation and avoid wrinkling.
- Non-symmetrical geometry and/or lay-up causes part warping or spring back.
- Non-symmetrical material location and alignment tolerances cause part warping.
- Vacuum bagging material movement or restriction from complete contact against curing material (i.e., bridging) causes nonuniformity in material compaction and resin flow affecting the quality of the finished product.
- Insufficient debulking causes thickness and surface finish variability as well as wrinkles in the finished part.
- Raw materials can vary batch to batch and their shelf life is typically time and temperature dependent.

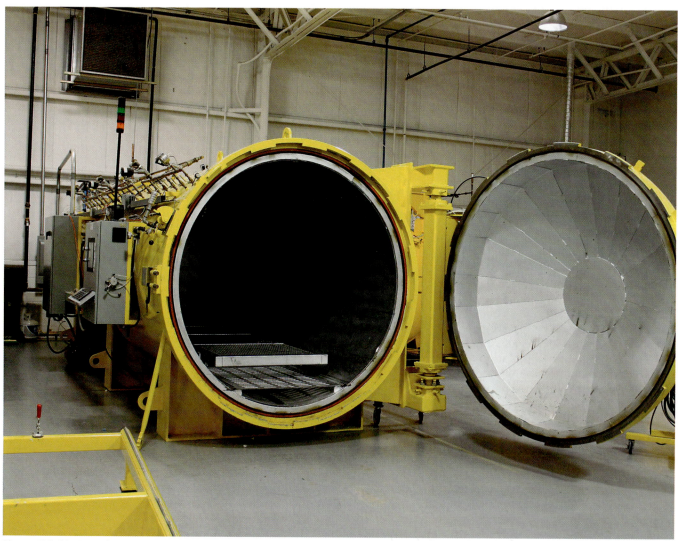

Figure 2-2-10. Autoclaves come in many sizes to handle various parts and assemblies.

- Moisture in material affects laminate quality, causing porosity as it turns to steam during cure.
- The number and location of vacuum ports and vacuum integrity during cure cycles affects the level of compaction.
- Autoclave temperature, pressure and time variations in the cure cycle affect the resin flow prior to cure, the level of cure and the finished product thickness.
- Part thickness variations may affect consolidation and curing uniformity.

Press Molding

Press curing uses heated platens to apply both pressure and heat to the part. Presses, in general, operate at 20 to 1,000 p.s.i. (140 to 7,000 kPa) and up to 600°F (320°C). Press curing is very economical for flat parts and high production rates, and it produces high-quality parts with low void content. Tooling requires matched die molds for contoured parts. The following steps are used in press molding:

1. Composite material is placed in the mold cavity.
2. Cure monitoring devices are installed.
3. Parts are placed into press and cured. Pressure, temperature and time are monitored during the cure cycle to ensure curing parameters are met.

Integrally Heated Tooling

With integrally heated tooling the heat required for cure is provided through the tool itself, rather than through external heating in an oven or autoclave. This can be used to make high-quality parts without using an autoclave if matched mold tools are used. The heat is usually provided by imbedding electrical resistance elements or hot oil circulation channels (Figure 2-2-11) within the tool. This can result in hot and cold spots within the tool. Heat surveys are necessary to ensure that all parts of the tool perform with a heat profile that allows the part to be cured completely and with high quality.

Storage and Handling of Prepregs

Reinforcements, pre-impregnated with an epoxy resin system or other type of thermoset matrix material, will generally require freezer storage. Storage life and maximum time out of the freezer prior to use are specified by material manufacturers. Store these materials in

Figure 2-2-11. Integrally heated tool *Courtesy of Webber Tools*

sealed, moisture-proof bags in accordance with the applicable technical data. A record of out-time shall be maintained for all prepreg materials.

The shelf life of material can be improved by cutting large batches into smaller sections (kitting) the first time it is thawed. This method will permit the bulk of the material to be kept frozen while pieces are thawed for use, thereby reducing waste caused by exceeding out-time requirements. All refrigerated and frozen item packages/containers must be sealed before storing and warmed to room temperature before opening.

Failure to warm to room temperature will result in moisture absorption which will degrade the resin. Backing or separator film must not be removed from the repair material until it is ready for use.

If film adhesives, foaming adhesives or prepregs were received without dry ice in the shipping container, determine how long it was out of the freezer, then add that time to the out-time log. Wear latex or nitrile gloves when handling film adhesives. If powdered gloves are all that are available, ensure that the exterior of the gloves is cleaned before handling repair materials and wash your hands thoroughly immediately after removing the gloves to prevent contaminating the repair area and materials.

Processing Materials

Several types of processing materials are required to make a part or a repair to a composite aircraft. These materials are removed after the repair or manufacturing process is complete. Table 2-2-1 provides information related to different materials and temperatures of processing materials. These materials are often placed on racks in dry places, as shown in Figure 2-2-12.

Peel Plies

Peel plies provide a surface that is ready for bonding; however, further surface preparation, such as scuff sanding, may be required. The material is peeled from the repair after the repair is cured. Peel plies are manufactured from polyester, nylon, fluorinated ethylene propylene (FEP), or coated fiberglass. They can be difficult to remove if overheated. Some coated peel plies can leave an undesirable contamination on the surface.

The preferred peel ply material is polyester that has been heat-set to eliminate shrinkage and scoured to eliminate contaminates. The theory is that the tearing or peeling process fractures the resin matrix coating and exposes a clean, virgin, roughened surface for the bonding process. The surface roughness attained can, to some extent, be determined by the weave characteristics of the peel ply.

Some manufacturers claim that this is sufficient, while others maintain that an additional hand sanding or light grit blasting is required to adequately prepare the surface. The abrasion increases the surface area of the surfaces to be bonded and may remove residual contamination and fractured resin left behind from the peel ply. The abrading operation should be conducted with care, however, to avoid exposing or rupturing the reinforcing fibers near the surface.

Release Films

Release fabrics and films are also referred to as separator film, parting film or release fabric. They are sometimes referred to by the material they are made from, such as polyvinyl fluoride (PVF), FEP or polytetrafluoroethylene (PTFE, that is Teflon®) coated fiberglass. Both the films and the fabrics are available in porous and nonporous forms.

Perforated release film. Perforated parting film is used to allow air and volatiles out of the part or repair, and it prevents the bleeder ply from sticking to the part or repair. Perforated release films and fabrics have small holes that allow excess resin to bleed out. The size and distance between perforations, in combination with the bleeder cloth used, directly affects the resin contact of the cured component; therefore, you must use the type specified for your particular repair.

Solid release film. Solid release films are used so that the prepreg or wet lay-up plies will not stick to the working surface or caul plate. Solid release film is also used to prevent the resins from bleeding through and damaging the heat blanket or caul plate if they are used.

Breather. Breather material allows air inside the vacuum bag to be removed and thus enables atmospheric pressure to be applied to the area. It is made of a loosely woven or nonwoven material. It does not come in direct contact with the part or repair area. Fiberglass cloth or commercially available breather materials may be used.

The commercially available breather cloths have been designed to provide better airflow

APPLICATION	MATERIAL	MAXIMUM TEMPERATURE[2]
Vacuum Bag	Polyethylene	<120 to 150°F
	Nylon	<400°F
	Polymide	<800°F
Sealant Type[1]	Low Temperature	<180 to 250°F
	General Purpose	<400°F
	High Temperature	<800°F
Breather/Bleeder	Polyester	<400°F
	Nylon	<450°F
	Fiberglass	<900°F
Release film	Polyvinyl Chloride	<180°F
	Polyvinyl Alcohol	<250°F
	Nylon	<400°F
	Flourinated Polymer Films	<450°F
	Polymide	<700°F
Peel ply	Polyester	<400°F
	Nylon	<400°F
	Coated Fiberglass	<550°F
	Aramid	<800°F
	Fiberglass	<900°F
Flash Tape	Polyester	<400°F
	Nylon	<400°F
	Coated Fiberglass	<550°F
	Polymide	<800°F

[1] Maximum temperature values reflect industry averages for each material type and are listed for reference purposes only. Use only vendor supplied material data when selecting materials for a given cure temperature.

[2] Sealant tapes are made from a wide variety of materials and blends of materials. For simplicity, they are listed by temperature application rather than specific chemical makeup.

Table 2-2-1. Materials temperature capabilities

Figure 2-2-12. Storage rack for processing materials

than fiberglass cloths. Breathers have been tailored to meet composite part manufacturers' needs and are available in different weights (thicknesses) and different levels of conformability. Breather cloth is available in 5 and 10 ounce weights. For vacuum bagging a 5 oz. breather is sufficient. For autoclave cure at pressures above 45 p.s.i. at least a 10 oz. polyester breather is required.

Bleeder. Bleeder cloths can be made from cotton, polyester or fiberglass. They absorb the surplus resin from the part or repair. When a specific number and type of bleeder cloth is called for in a manufacturing or repair instruction, it must be used to ensure the resin-to-fiber ratio meet the repair requirements.

Flash tape. Flash tapes are used to hold thermocouples and other materials in place inside the vacuum bag. Flash tapes are usually made from 2- to 5-mil polyester film and have a silicone or rubber adhesive on one side. The rubber adhesive is preferred if there will be subsequent bonding operations. They are available in a variety of widths and typically have a one-year shelf life.

Because the flash tape is not part of the completed manufacturing or repair process, the shelf life is not critical and the tape can be used as long as it has sufficient tack. For most repairs, flash tape 1-in. wide and 0.002-in. thick with silicone adhesive is usually sufficient.

Sealant tape. Sealant tape is often referred to as tacky tape. It is used to seal the vacuum bag to the part or tool surface. Sealant tape is usually $1/8$ inch thick and $1/2$ inch wide made of a synthetic rubber material that comes in a roll. It is available with different amounts of tack. Most have a shelf life of nine months to one year, after which they lose their tackiness. For field repairs, a sealant tape with good or excellent tack is recommended.

3

Composite Structures

Section 1

Design Criteria

Engineers establish the design criteria during the initial phase of an aircraft program, but these criteria often change during the development and production process.

Design engineering is often the art of compromise. The design/engineering team needs to know clearly the expectations of the end user, the expected life of the aircraft, and the expected environment that the aircraft will operate in. One of the advantages of composite materials is that the properties of the material can be adjusted to achieve specific design requirements.

Composites achieve their design flexibility from

- the large possible selection in material types, arrangements and forms
- the wide variety of processing methods available
- the many variations available when choosing a structural configuration

The following list of variables that can be considered during the design process illustrates this point: cost, strength, stiffness, weight, size, repeatability and precision of parts, environmental constraints in processing, use and disposal, aesthetics, manufacturability and production rates, assembly restrictions, life cycle durability and damage tolerance, maintainability and repairability, and non-mechanical properties such as flammability and conductivity.

> **Learning Objective**
>
> **REVIEW**
> - fiber orientation
> - laminate balance
> - laminate symmetry
>
> **EXPLAIN**
> - honeycomb sandwich structure theory, properties and application
> - composite laminate structure theory, properties and application

Left: Airbus A350 makes extensive use of composites in its primary structure.

Courtesy of Airbus

Section 2

Composite Laminate Structures

There are several terms associated with laminate structures:

Homogeneous. A homogeneous material has a uniform composition throughout and has no internal physical boundaries. The properties of a homogeneous material are constant at every point.

Heterogeneous. A heterogeneous material consists of dissimilar constituents that can be identified and regions of unlike properties separated by internal boundaries.

Anisotropic. An anisotropic material has mechanical and/or physical properties that vary with direction relative to natural reference axes inherent in the material.

Isotropic. An isotropic material has uniform properties in all directions. The measured properties of an isotropic material are independent of the axis of testing. Metals such as aluminum and titanium are isotropic materials.

Quasi-isotropic. A quasi-isotropic material has approximately the same properties as an isotropic material. An example is a composite laminate with the fibers orientated in the 0°, 90°, +45° and -45° directions to simulate isotropic properties, as shown in Figure 3-2-1. Many aerospace composite structures are made of quasi-isotropic materials.

Major Components of a Laminate

Broadly speaking, a composite laminate is composed of fibers and a matrix.

Fibers. The fibers in a composite are the primary load carrying element of the composite material. The composite material will be strong and stiff in the direction of the fibers. As a result unidirectional composites (Figure 3-2-2) have predominant mechanical properties in one direction and are said to be anisotropic. Components made from fiber-reinforced composites can be designed so that the fiber orientation produces optimum mechanical properties, but they can only approach the true isotropic nature of metals.

Matrix. The matrix supports the fibers and bonds them together in the composite material. The matrix transfers applied loads to the fibers and keeps the fibers in their position and chosen orientation. The matrix also gives the composite environmental resistance and determines the maximum service temperature of a composite structure.

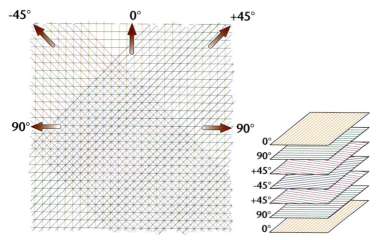

Figure 3-2-1. Quasi-isotropic material lay-up

Properties

One of the advantages of using a modern composite material is that the fibers can be oriented to respond to the load requirements of the airframe. Structural properties such as stiffness, dimensional stability and strength of a composite laminate depend on the stacking sequence of the plies. The stacking sequence describes the distribution of ply orientations through the laminate thickness. As the number of plies with chosen orientations increase, more stacking sequences are possible. For example, a symmetric eight-ply laminate with four different ply orientations has 24 different stacking sequences.

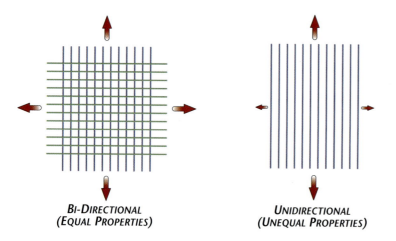

Figure 3-2-2. Bidirectional and unidirectional material properties

Fiber Orientation

The strength and stiffness of a composite laminate is depended on the orientation sequence of the plies. The practical range of strength and stiffness of carbon fiber extends from values as low as those provided by fiberglass to as high as those provided by titanium. This range of values is determined by the orientation of the plies to the applied load.

Proper selection of ply orientation in advanced composite materials is necessary to provide a structurally efficient design. The part might require 0° plies to react to axial loads, ± 45° plies to react to shear loads and 90° plies to react to side loads. Because the strength design requirements are a function of the applied load direction, ply orientation and ply sequence have to be correct.

Unidirectional fibers run in one direction and the strength and stiffness is in the fiber direction only. Prepreg tape is an example of a unidirectional ply orientation.

Bidirectional fibers run in two directions, typically 90° apart. A plain weave fabric is an example of a bidirectional ply orientation. These ply orientations have strength in both directions but not necessarily the same strength.

The plies of a quasi-isotropic lay-up are stacked in a 0°, -45°, 45° and 90° sequence or in a 0°, -60° and +60° sequence. These types of ply orientation simulate the properties of an isotropic material.

The strength properties of an isotropic material like aluminum or titanium are similar in all directions.

Reference plane. The reference plane, for the purposes of the laminate orientation code, is either the bottom or top ply of the laminate. When the laminate is symmetrical about the mid-plane, using either the top or bottom ply as the reference plane will yield the same results.

Reference direction. Selection of the reference direction or 0° direction is arbitrary. Standard convention is to select the 0° in the same direction as the main load, the fiber in the top ply, or the dominate fiber direction in the laminate.

Angles. The angle of each ply or lamina represents its orientation in degrees between the fibers in that ply (lamina fiber direction) and the reference direction of the laminate.

Positive angles. Positive angles can be measured either clockwise or counterclockwise. The ASTM International and MIL-HDBK-17 standard is to measure positive angles clockwise when looking at the layup surface. Figure 3-2-3 shows a warp clock that indicates the ply direction. Warp is the longitudinal fibers of a fabric. The warp is the high-strength direction, due to the straightness of the fibers. A warp clock is used to describe direction of fibers on a diagram, spec sheet, or manufacturer's sheets. If the warp clock is not available on the fabric, the orientation will be defaulted to zero as the

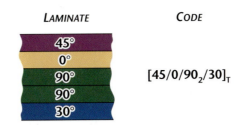

Figure 3-2-4. Laminate code

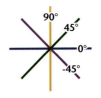

Figure 3-2-3. Warp clock for measuring positive angles

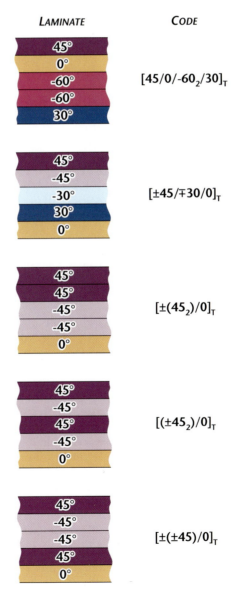

Figure 3-2-5. Example for positive and negative angles

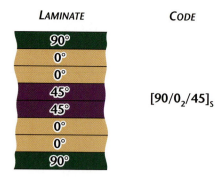

Figure 3-2-6. Code for an even symmetric laminate

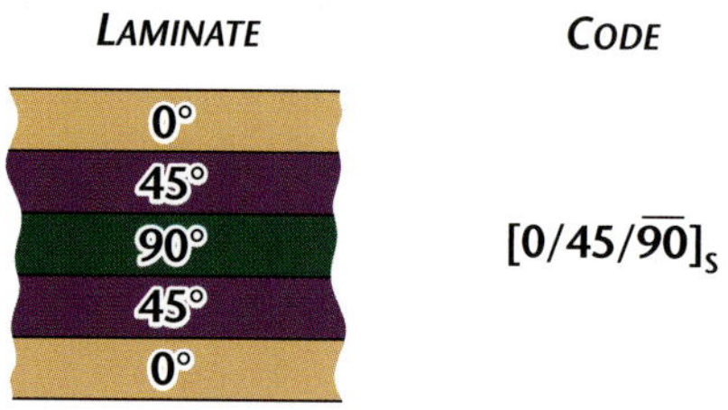

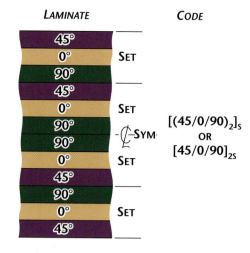

Figure 3-2-9. Code for sets of symmetric laminates

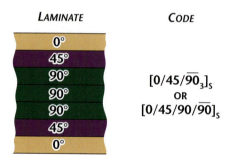

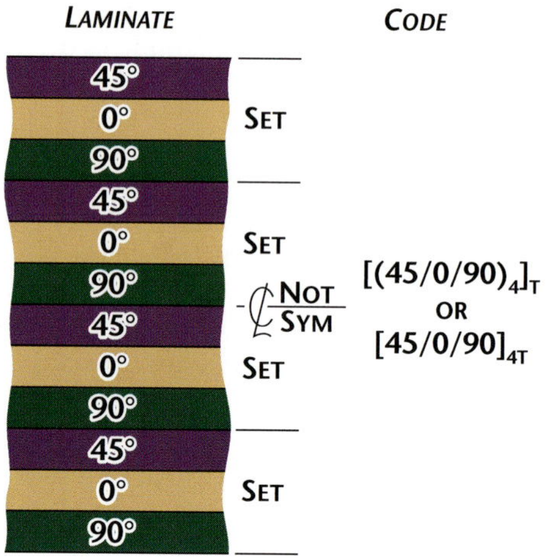

Figure 3-2-7. Code for an odd symmetric laminate

Figure 3-2-8. Code for an odd symmetric laminate with multiple same angled laminae

Figure 3-2-10. Code for sets of non-symmetric laminates

fabric comes off the roll. Therefore, 90° to zero will be across the width of the fabric. 90° to zero is also called the fill direction.

Standard laminate code. The Standard Laminate Code was originally formulated specifically for unidirectional laminates; a modification covered woven fabric and braided laminates. The standard code is used to uniquely describe a laminate and includes the following features:

- Each lamina is denoted by a number representing its orientation in degrees between its filament direction and the reference direction. Normally the angles are limited to between 90° and -90°.

- Individual adjacent laminate are separated in the code by a forward slash (/) if their angles are different. The laminates are listed in sequence from one laminate face to the other, starting with the first lamina laid up, with brackets indicating the beginning and the end of the code.

Adjacent laminate of the same angle are denoted by a numerical subscript. A subscript T to the bracket indicates the total laminate is shown. If no subscript is present on the brackets, the T is assumed to be there. See Figure 3-2-4.

- When adjacent laminates are of the same angle but opposite in sign, the plus (+) and minus (-) signs are employed. Each plus or minus sign represents one lamina and supersedes the use of the numerical subscript, which is used only when the directions are identical. Signs can be condensed to a plus-minus sign (±) with the sign on top representing the first lamina in the layup order. See Figure 3-2-5.

TYPE	EXAMPLE	COMMENTS
Symmetrical, Balanced	(45, -45, 0, 0, -45, 45)	Flat, Constant midplane stress
Asymmetrical, Balanced	(90, 45, 0, 90, -45, 0)	Induces curvature
Symmetrical, Unbalanced	(-45, 0, 0, -45)	Induces twist
Asymmetrical, Unbalanced	(90, -45, 0, 90, -45, 0)	Induces twist and curvature

Table 3-2-1. Symmetrical and balanced laminates

- Symmetric laminates with an even number of laminate still list the laminate in sequence, starting at one face, but stopping at the plane of symmetry instead of continuing to the other face. A bracket subscript S indicates only one-half of the laminate. See Figure 3-2-6.

Symmetric laminates with an odd number of laminate are coded the same as even symmetric laminates, except that the center lamina, listed last, is over-lined to indicate that half of it lies on either side of the plane of symmetry. See Figure 3-2-7.

Where an odd symmetric laminate has additional laminate of the same angle adjacent to the center lamina, a subscript is used with the over-line to indicate the number of half-laminate on either side of the center plane. See Figure 3-2-8.

- Repeating sequences of laminate are called sets and are enclosed in parentheses. A set is coded in accordance with the same rules that apply to a single lamina. See Figure 3-2-9 and Figure 3-2-10.

Symmetry

The geometric midplane is the reference surface for determining whether a laminate is symmetrical. In general, to reduce out-of-plane strains, coupled bending and stretching of the laminate and complexity of analysis, symmetric laminates should be used. However, some composite structures (e.g., filament wound pressure vessels) can achieve geometric symmetry so that symmetry through a single laminate wall is not necessary if it constrains manufacture.

To construct a midplane symmetric laminate, for each layer above the midplane there must exist an identical layer (same thickness, material properties and angular orientation) below the midplane. Table 3-2-1 shows the results of symmetrical and unsymmetrical laminates.

Balance

All laminates should be balanced to achieve in-plane orthotropic behavior. To achieve balance, for every layer centered at some positive angle there must exist an identical layer oriented at a negative angle with the same thickness and material properties. If the laminate contains only 0° and/or 90° layers it satisfies the requirements for balance. Laminates may be midplane symmetric but not balanced and vice versa.

Figure 3-2-11. Laminate composite structure

Composite Structures

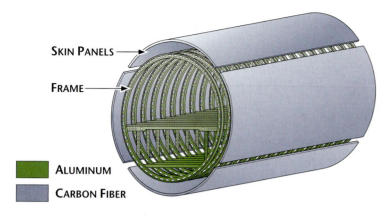

Figure 3-2-12. Four-panel fuselage design of Airbus A350

Laminate Aircraft Construction (Semi-Monocoque Construction)

Many secondary aircraft structures, such as flight controls, spoilers and fairings, are made of stiff light-weight honeycomb structure. This type of structure has a low resistance to impact damage. Therefore, it is most suited for parts that can be removed from the aircraft to be repaired. Most commercial aircraft program design teams have chosen a laminate type of structure for the fuselage and wing sections because it is rugged and impact resistant. Honeycomb structure typically uses only four plies for the facesheets. In a laminate structure,

Figure 3-2-13. An aft fuselage section manufactured as a one-piece part *Courtesy of Airbus*

Figure 3-2-14. One-piece fuselage manufacturing using automated tape-laying *Courtesy of Hawker Beechcraft*

a higher number of plies are used and the skin is reinforced with doublers, stringers and stiffeners to create a stiff panel much like an aluminum aircraft structure. Figure 3-2-11 shows a laminate skin with hat section stringers; and the integrated co-bonded stringers in the fuselage section of a Airbus A350 can be seen in the opening photo of this chapter. One disadvantage is that the laminate structure will be heavier than an equivalent panel of honeycomb sandwich construction.

In the most elementary form this type of design resembles an aluminum semi-monocoque aircraft design and is often called a "black aluminum" design. Skin sections, stringers, doublers and frame sections are manufactured as individual parts and assembled with fasteners or the parts are secondary bonded. More advanced structures such as the fuselage of the Airbus 350 XWB integrate stringers, stiffeners and doublers into the skin design. These parts are manufactured as one unit, which reduces the part count, the number of fasteners and bonded joints. The Airbus A350 uses four skin sections with integrated stringers to create a fuselage section. Figure 3-2-12 shows the four-panel design.

The Boeing 787 fuselage is manufactured on a mandrel with an automated tape laying process. The fuselage section has the stringers inte-

Figure 3-2-15. One-piece wing skin with integrated stringers *Courtesy of Airbus*

Figure 3-2-16. Automated tape laying manufacturing *Courtesy of MAG*

Step 1

Liquid resin and powder hardeners are combined in a computer-controlled mixer.

The mixture is poured into pans and frozen solid to stop the hardening process.

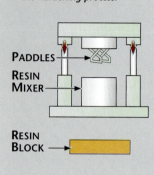

Step 2

The block of resin is melted in a machine that coats one side of a roll of paper with a thin resin film.

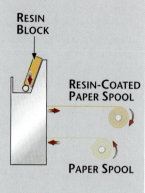

Step 3

Multiple threads of carbon fiber are pulled from bobbins on a creel and laid down in parallel to make a flat sheet of fibers.

Step 4

Fed into a resin-infusion machine, the fiber sheet is sandwiched between two rolls of the resin-coated paper. Heat and pressure transfer the resin from the paper to the fiber sheet. The resin-infused fiber sheet, with backing paper on one side, is rolled into a master roll.

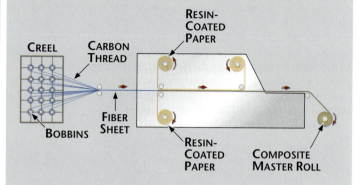

Step 5

The master roll of fiber tape is inspected and cut into smaller rolls to necessary specifications and delivered to the customer.

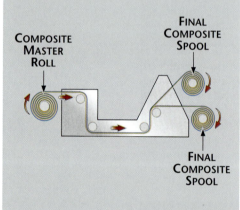

Step 6

Carbon-fiber tape is loaded into a robotic tape-laying machine. On a steel alloy platform (tool) shaped for the part being made, the machine places small strips of tape in multiple layers, following a pre-programmed pattern to build up a structure such as the vertical stabilizer's skin panel.

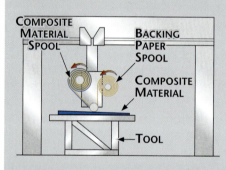

Step 7

The built-up part is placed in a vacuum bag, and all the air is removed so voids are not created in the composite part.

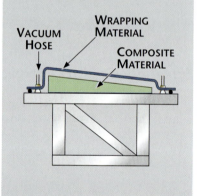

Step 8

The composite part is moved into an autoclave where the composite material is cured through a cycle of heat and pressure for about eight hours. The autoclave reaches a temperature of about 350° and a pressure of about 100 p.s.i. Normal pressure at sea level is about 14.7 p.s.i.

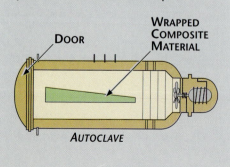

Step 9

After the autoclaving, the parts are unwrapped, trimmed, inspected, and painted.

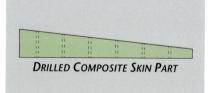

Step 10

The spars, ribs, and skins of the vertical stabilizer are assembled and the electrical and hydraulic systems are installed. The structure is assembled in a horizontal position using easily moveable equipment.

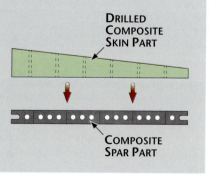

Figure 3-2-17. Boeing 777 vertical stabilizer manufacturing sequence

grated. Both the A350 and B787 use fasteners to install the frame sections into the aircraft fuselage sections. Figure 3-2-13 shows one piece of the A350 aft section with integrated stringers. Figure 3-2-14 shows the manufacture of a business jet using an automated tape laying process to create a one-piece fuselage section. The cutouts for windows and doors are accomplished after the initial manufacturing process.

Most modern aircraft wing designs utilize a box beam construction consisting of spars, ribs and skins with integrated stringers. The main advantage of a composite design is that the wing skins can be manufactured as one piece, eliminating the bolted joints common in metal aircraft.

The wing spars and ribs are typically installed using Hi-Lok® or lock bolt fasteners. Some aircraft still utilize aluminum parts in their wing design. For example aluminum wing ribs and composite wing spars and skin are used for the Boeing 787. Figure 3-2-15 shows a wing skin with integrated stringers.

Composite manufacturing of laminate structures can be automated and requires fewer parts and fasteners. Figure 3-2-16 shows an automated tape laying process for skin structures. This process is highly repetitive and produces high-quality parts.

Integrally Co-Cured Structures

Co-curing is a process wherein two parts are simultaneously cured. The interface between the two parts may or may not have an adhesive layer. Curing honeycomb sandwich panels often results in poor panel surface quality, but this can be prevented by using a secondary surfacing material co-cured in the standard cure cycle or a subsequent "fill-and-fair" operation. Co-cured skins may also have poorer mechanical properties, and this may require the use of reduced design values.

A typical co-cure application is the simultaneous cure of a stiffener and a skin. Adhesive film is frequently placed into the interface between the stiffener and the skin to increase fatigue and peel resistance. Principal advantages derived from the co-cure process are excellent fit between bonded components and guaranteed surface cleanliness.

Figure 3-2-17 shows the complete manufacturing process of a vertical tail section of a Boeing 777 aircraft. The process starts with the manufacturing of carbon fiber prepreg material that will be used in the vertical tail section. A tape laying process places the plies on the tool. Parts such as skins, ribs and stringers are assembled with bolts to produce the final product.

Section 3
Honeycomb Structures

Honeycomb sandwich construction is used extensively for the fabrication of aircraft parts because it is an extremely lightweight structural approach that exhibits high stiffness and strength-to-weight ratios. A sandwich construction is a structural panel concept that consists in its simplest form of two relatively thin, parallel facesheets bonded to and separated by a relatively thick, lightweight core.

The core supports the facesheets against buckling and resists out-of-plane shear loads. The core must have high shear strength and compression stiffness.

Composite sandwich construction is most often fabricated using autoclave cure, press cure or oven vacuum bag cure. Skin laminates may be pre-cured and secondarily bonded to the core, co-cured to the core in one operation, or attached to the core using some combination of these methods.

Honeycomb's beneficial strength-to-weight and stiffness-to-weight ratios compared to other materials and configurations are unmatched. Figure 3-3-1 shows a basic honeycomb sandwich construction. Film adhesive is often used to bond the facesheet to the core. Some of the aircraft parts that are made from honeycomb sandwich include:

- control surfaces such as ailerons, elevators, flaps, rudders, slats, spoilers and tabs
- powerplant items including cowls, nacelles and thrust reversers
- tail sections including empennages and stabilizers

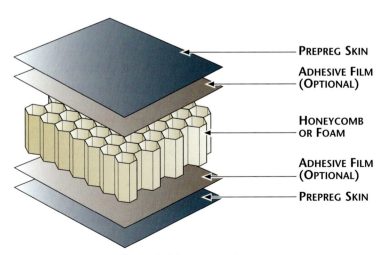

Figure 3-3-1. Honeycomb sandwich construction

- aircraft structures like doors and flooring
- fairings
- wing components including leading edges, struts and trailing edges
- radomes

Honeycomb Theory

The facing skins of a sandwich panel can be compared to the flanges of an I-beam, as they carry the bending stresses to which the beam is subjected. With one facing skin in compression, the other is in tension. The honeycomb core corresponds to the web of the I-beam.

The core resists the shear loads, increases the stiffness of the structure by holding the facing skins apart, and improving on the I-beam, it gives continuous support to the flanges or facing skins to produce a uniformly stiffened panel. The core-to-skin adhesive rigidly joins the sandwich components and allows them to act as one unit with a high torsional and bending rigidity. Figure 3-3-2 shows a comparison of a beam and sandwich construction.

Honeycomb Sandwich Design

Consider a cantilever beam with a load applied at the free end (Figure 3-3-3). The applied load creates a bending moment that is at its maximum at the fixed end and a shear force along the length of the beam. In a sandwich panel these forces create tension in the upper skin and compression in the lower skin. The core spaces the facing skins and transfers shear loads between them to make the composite panel work as a homogeneous structure.

The deflection of a sandwich panel is made up of bending and shear components. The bending deflection is dependent on the relative tensile and compressive moduli of the skin materials. The shear deflection is dependent on the shear modulus of the core (Figure 3-3-4). The total deflection is the sum of bending deflection and shear deflection:

Total Deflection = Bending Deflection + Shear Deflection

Failure Modes of Honeycomb Structures

Designers of sandwich panels must ensure that all potential failure modes are considered in their analysis. A summary of the key failure modes is shown below:

Strength. The skin and core materials should be able to withstand the tensile, compressive and shear stresses induced by the design load. The skin-to-core adhesive must be capable of transferring the shear stresses between skin and core, as shown in Figure 3-3-5.

Stiffness. The sandwich panel should have sufficient bending and shear stiffness to prevent excessive deflection (Figure 3-3-6).

Panel buckling. The core thickness and shear modulus must be adequate to prevent the panel from buckling under end compression loads, shown in Figure 3-3-7.

Shear crimping. The core thickness and shear modulus must be adequate to prevent the core from prematurely failing in shear under end compression loads (Figure 3-3-8).

Skin wrinkling. The compressive modulus of the facing skin and the core compression strength must both be high enough to prevent a skin wrinkling failure like the one seen in Figure 3-3-9.

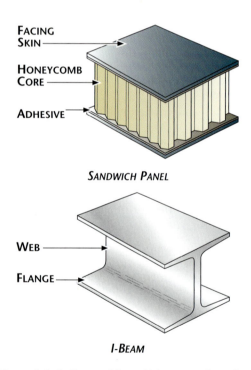

Figure 3-3-2. Comparision of I-beam and sandwich panels

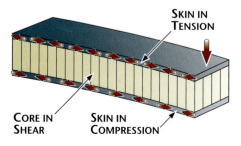

Figure 3-3-3. Bending and shear loads

Composite Structures | 3-11

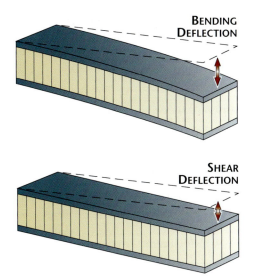

Figure 3-3-7. Panel buckling

Figure 3-3-8. Shear crimping

Figure 3-3-4. Deflection of honeycomb sandwich

Figure 3-3-9. Skin wrinkling

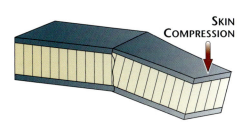

Figure 3-3-5. Skin compression failure

Figure 3-3-10. Intracell buckling

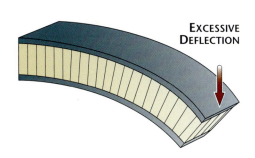

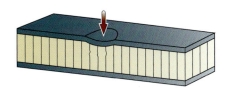

Figure 3-3-6. Excessive deflection

Figure 3-3-11. Local compression

Intracell buckling. For a given skin material, the core cell size must be small enough to prevent intracell buckling (Figure 3-3-10).

Local compression. The core compressive strength must be adequate to resist local loads on the panel surface as shown in Figure 3-3-11.

Properties of Honeycomb Structures

Sandwich construction has high bending stiffness at minimal weight in comparison to aluminum and composite laminate construction. Most honeycombs are anisotropic; that is, their properties are directional. Honeycomb L, W and T orientation are shown in Figure 3-3-12. The highest compressive and tensile strength

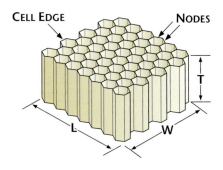

L = *Ribbon (or longitudinal) dimension*
W = *Dimension normal (or transverse) to ribbon direction*
T = *Thickness dimension*

Figure 3-3-12. Honeycomb core orientation and nomenclature

	SOLID METAL SHEET	SANDWICH CONSTRUCTION	THICKER SANDWICH
Relative Stiffness	100	700 (7 times more rigid)	3700 (37 times more rigid)
Relative Strength	100	350 (3.5 times as strong)	925 (9.25 times as strong)
Relative Weight	100	103 (3% increase in weight)	106 (6% increase in weight)

Table 3-3-1. Comparison of solid laminate and honeycomb sandwich structural stiffness

of honeycomb is in the T direction; other directions are substantially weaker. Honeycomb provides shear strength in the L and W directions. For the hexagonal-cell configuration, the shear strength and modulus are greatest in the L direction. The shear strength is nearly equivalent in the L and W directions in both the rectangular and the square cell configurations. The cross-core cell configuration is designed to have good structural properties in two directions.

As shown in Table 3-3-1, sandwich construction, especially honeycomb core construction, is extremely structurally efficient, particularly in stiffness-critical applications. Doubling the thickness of the core increases the stiffness more than 7 times with only a 3 percent weight gain, while quadrupling the core thickness increases stiffness more than 37 times with only a 6 percent weight gain.

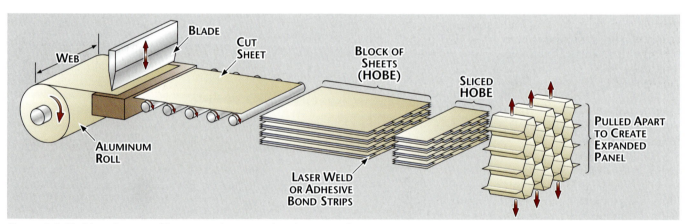

Figure 3-3-13. Manufacture of honeycomb cores using the expansion process

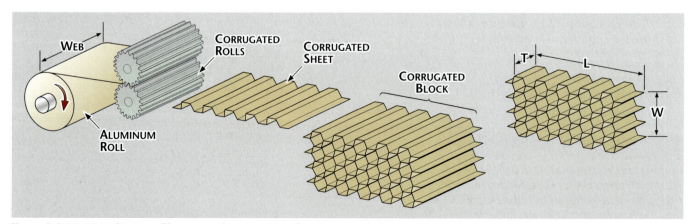

Figure 3-3-14. Manufacture of honeycomb cores using the corrugated process

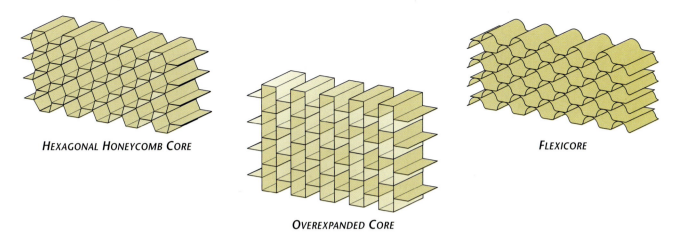

Figure 3-3-15. Honeycomb core cell shapes

Honeycomb Sandwich Manufacturing

Honeycomb is made primarily by the expansion method. The corrugated process is most common for high-density honeycomb materials.

Expansion Method

The honeycomb fabrication process by the expansion method begins with stacking of sheets of the substrate material on which adhesive node lines have been printed. The adhesive lines are then cured to form a HOBE® (Honeycomb Before Expansion) block.

The HOBE block itself may be expanded after curing to give an expanded block. Slices of the expanded block may then be cut to the desired T dimension. Alternately, HOBE slices can be cut from the HOBE block to the appropriate T dimension and subsequently expanded. Slices can be expanded to regular hexagons, under expanded to six-sided diamonds and over expanded to nearly rectangular cells. The expanded sheets are trimmed to the desired L dimension (ribbon direction) and W dimension (transverse to the ribbon). Figure 3-3-13 illustrates the expansion process.

Corrugated Process

The corrugated process of honeycomb manufacture is normally used to produce products in the higher density range. In this process adhesive is applied to the corrugated nodes, the corrugated sheets are stacked into blocks, the node adhesive cured, and sheets are cut from these blocks to the required core thickness. Figure 3-3-14 illustrates the corrugated process.

Types of Honeycomb Cell Structures

Figure 3-3-15 shows different types of honeycomb cell structures. Typical cell structures used are hexagonal, flexicore and over expanded core. Each type of cell structure will have distinct advantages and disadvantages and the designer must carefully choose the type of cell structure for the intended application. Figure 3-3-16 shows information that is provided by vendors for ordering purposes.

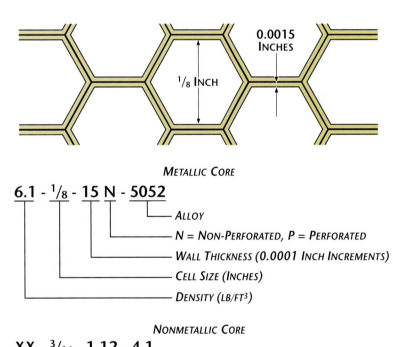

Figure 3-3-16. Sample vendor designations of honeycomb core

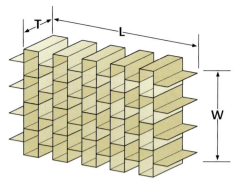

Figure 3-3-17. Overexpanded honeycomb core

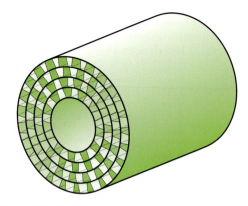

Figure 3-3-19. Tube-core honeycomb

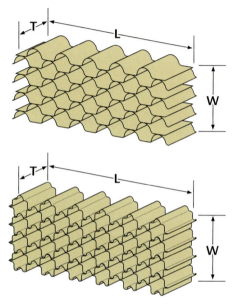

Figure 3-3-18. Flexible honeycomb cores

Hexagonal honeycomb core. Hexagonal honeycomb core is the most common geometry available. This product is primarily made by strip gluing sheets of material into a block and slicing the block into the desired sheet thickness. The block is then mechanically expanded into a sheet of honeycomb. Hexagonal honeycomb can also be manufactured through the corrugation process. The corrugation process does not require expansion and is often used to produce higher density hexagonal honeycombs.

Over expanded honeycomb core. Over expanded honeycomb core is extended in the W direction to create rectangular, rather than hexagonal, cells (Figure 3-3-17). This cell shape facilitates forming to contours in the L direction. Shear properties are increased in the L direction but decreased in the W direction when compared to hexagonal honeycomb.

Flexible core. Flexible core cell configuration (Figure 3-3-18) results in excellent formability in compound curvatures with reduced anticlastic (potato chip) curvature and cell wall buckling. When formed into tight radii, this type of core provides higher shear strengths than hexagonal cores of equivalent density. Flexible core is available in a variety of cell shapes and can be manufactured in most of the materials used for hexagonal honeycomb.

Tube-Core®. Tube-Core configuration (Figure 3-3-19) provides a uniquely designed energy absorption system when the space envelope requires a column or small diameter cylinder. The design eliminates the loss of crush strength that occurs at the unsupported edges of conventional honeycomb. Tube-Core is constructed of alternate sheets of flat aluminum foil and corrugated aluminum foil wrapped around a mandrel and adhesively bonded. Outside diameters can range from $1/2$ in. to 30 in. (1.3 to 76 cm) and lengths from $1/2$ in. to 36 in. (1.3 to 91 cm).

Honeycomb Sandwich Materials

Honeycomb is available in several kinds of materials. Metallic and nonmetallic materials are used in combination with carbon fiber, fiberglass and Kevlar facesheets. Aluminum honeycomb is available in four alloys—aerospace grades 5052 and 5056 and commercial grades 3104 and 3003. Nonmetallic materials used are: fiberglass-reinforced honeycombs, NOMEX and KOREX. The following list states the advantages and disadvantages of several core materials. Figure 3-3-20 illustrates several types of core materials.

Kraft paper. Kraft paper has relatively low strength and good insulating properties. It is available in large quantities and at the lowest cost compared to other core materials.

Thermoplastics. Thermoplastics have good insulating properties, good energy absorption and/or redirection, smooth cell walls, moisture and chemical resistance, and they are environmentally compatible, aesthetically pleasing and relatively low cost.

Aluminum. Aluminum has the best strength-to-weight ratio and energy absorption among core materials. It has good heat transfer properties, electromagnetic shielding properties, the thinnest cell walls and it is smooth, machinable and relatively low cost.

Steel. Steel is strong with good heat transfer properties, electromagnetic shielding properties and heat resistance.

Specialty metals. Speciality metals such as titanium have a relatively high strength-to-weight ratios, good heat transfer properties, are chemical resistant and heat resistant to very high temperatures.

Aramid fiber. Aramid fiber is flame resistan and fire retardant with good insulating properties, low dielectric properties and good formability.

Fiberglass. Fiberglass has tailorable shear properties by lay-up, low dielectric properties, good insulating properties and good formability.

Carbon. Carbon has good dimensional stability and retention, high-temperature property retention, high stiffness, a very low coefficient of thermal expansion, tailorable thermal conductivity, relatively high shear modulus and is very expensive.

Ceramic. Ceramic is heat resistant to very high temperatures, has good insulating properties, is available in very small cell sizes and is very expensive.

Figure 3-3-20. Honeycomb core materials

Mechanical Performance

Honeycomb strength and stiffness (compression and shear) is proportional to its density. Relative performance of the material types compared to PVC foam is shown in Figure 3-3-21.

Foam Cores

Foam cores include a wide variety of liquid plastic materials that are filled with chemically released or mechanically mixed gas bubbles to produce rigid forms. Several types of foam core are available including polyvinyl chloride (cross-linked and uncross-linked), polyurethane, ebonite, polyimide, polymethacry-

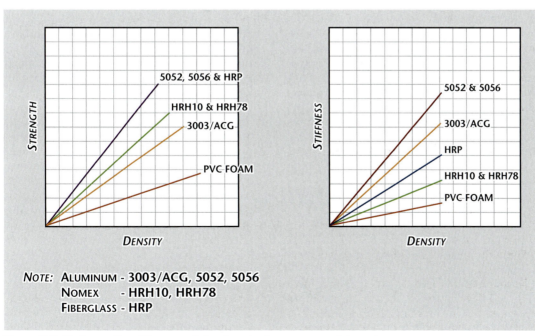

Figure 3-3-21. Strength, stiffness and density vary by core material used.

Figure 3-3-22. Cirrus aircraft with foam core composite structures

limide and Styrofoam. Carbon foam, a notable core material used for medium- to high-temperature applications, is made from coal.

The mechanical properties of foam cores vary in an approximately linear fashion with material density. Foams tend to have lower mechanical properties than honeycomb, for a given weight, but are often less expensive. Closed cell foams do not absorb moisture and are an excellent choice for applications in wet or humid environments. Figure 3-3-22 shows a Cirrus aircraft that uses a fiberglass/foam sandwich structure for the fuselage and wings.

End-Grain Balsa Wood Core

End-grain balsa wood core has been used in aircraft for many years. Balsa is a natural wood product with elongated closed cells. It is available in a variety of grades that correlate to the structural, cosmetic and physical characteristics. The density of balsa is less than half the density of conventional wood products. However, balsa has a considerably higher density than the other types of structural cores. Modern aircraft floor panels, galley structures and wardrobes may be fabricated from sandwich panels of balsa core faced with fiberglass or aluminum.

Infusible Core

Recent industry interest in the resin infusion process has ushered in a new variety of core materials. These cores are made primarily from polyester and are available in several geometries. Infusible cores are formed with channels or holes through which resin can flow and are available in several thicknesses and with many cell (or hole) sizes.

Facing Materials

Most honeycomb structures used in aircraft construction use aluminum, fiberglass, Kevlar® or carbon fiber facesheets. Carbon fiber facesheets cannot be used with aluminum honeycomb core material because it will cause the aluminum to corrode. Titanium and steel are used for specialty applications in high temperature constructions.

The facesheets of many components such as spoilers and flight controls are very thin—sometimes only three or four plies. Field reports have indicated that these facesheets do not have a good resistance against impact. Figure 3-3-23 shows a honeycomb sandwich structure with aluminum facesheets and aluminum core.

Adhesive Bonding of Honeycomb

Supported film adhesives are normally used to bond composite structural honeycomb assemblies. The primary considerations for select-

Figure 3-3-23. Honeycomb sandwich structure with aluminum facesheets and core

ing an adhesive system are strength requirements, service temperature range and ability to form a fillet at the cell wall ends. Sandwich panels are typically used for their structural, electrical and energy absorption characteristics, or a combination thereof.

Secondary bonding utilizes pre-cured composite detail parts. Honeycomb sandwich assemblies (Figure 3-3-24) commonly use a secondary bonding process to ensure optimal structural performance. Laminates co-cured over honeycomb core may have distorted plies that have dipped into the core cells. As a result, compressive stiffness and strength can be reduced as much as 10 and 20 percent, respectively.

While secondary bonding avoids this performance loss, care must be exercised prior to bonding in order to ensure proper fit and surface cleanliness. In some applications, aluminum foil layers or an adhesive sandwiched between two layers of polyester release film is placed into the bonded joint.

The assembly is then bagged and run through a simulated bonding cycle using the same temperatures and pressures as those in the actual cycle. The foil or film is removed, and its thickness is measured. Based upon these measurements, additional adhesive can be added to the bond line to ensure proper fit; or detail parts can be reworked to eliminate interference fits.

Advanced composite skins are bonded to the honeycomb cell walls using adhesive to form a fillet bond resulting in a sandwich assembly.

Honeycomb Processing

Honeycomb processing before adhesive bonding includes perimeter trimming, mechanical forming, heat forming, core splicing, contouring and cleaning.

Trimming. The four primary tools used to cut honeycomb to planned dimensions are the serrated knife, razor blade knife, band saw and die. The serrated and razor knives and die cutter are used on light-density cores, while heavy-density cores and complex-shaped cores are usually cut with a band saw.

Forming. Metallic, hexagonal honeycomb can be roll- or brake-formed into curved pans. The brake-forming method will crush the cell walls and increase the density in the inner radius. Over-expanded honeycomb can be formed to a cylindrical shape on assembly. Flexcore usually can be shaped to compound curvatures on assembly.

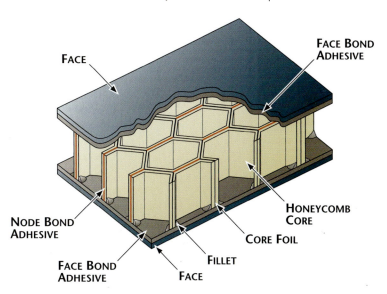

Figure 3-3-24. Components of a honeycomb panel

Nonmetallic honeycomb can be heat formed to obtain curved parts. Usually the core slice is placed in an oven at high temperature for a short period of time. The heat softens the resin and allows the cell walls to deform more easily. Upon removal from the oven, the core is quickly placed on a shaped tool and held there until it cools.

Splicing. When large pieces of core are required, or when complex shapes dictate, smaller pieces can be spliced together to form the finished part. This is usually accomplished with a foaming adhesive. Core splice adhesives normally contain blowing agents that produce gases (e.g., nitrogen) when heated to provide the expansion necessary to fill the gaps between the core sections. Different core types, cell sizes, or densities can be easily interconnected in this manner.

Machining. In many sandwich panel applications, such as airfoils, honeycomb must have its thickness machined to some contour. This is normally accomplished using valve-stem-type cutters on expanded core.

Occasionally, the solid honeycomb block is machined using milling cutters. Typical machines used for contour machining (carving) are the gantry, apex, three-dimensional tracer, or numerically controlled (NC) five-axis.

With five-axis NC machining, the cutting head is controlled by a computer, and almost any surface that can be described by x, y and z coordinates can be produced. These machines can carve honeycomb at speeds of up to 50 in/s (1.27 m/s) with extreme accuracy. A standard contour tolerance of an NC machine is ±0.005 in (±0.13 mm). Figure 3-3-25 shows a five-axis

Figure 3-3-25. Five-axis NC for cutting honeycomb

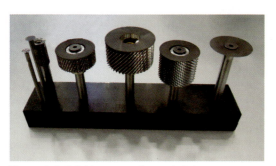

Figure 3-3-26. Honeycomb sandwich cutters

NC. Figure 3-3-26 shows special cutters for honeycomb sandwich core material. The bottom of the tool slices the honeycomb and the teeth of the tool remove excess material. These tools need to run at 15,000 to 20,000 r.p.m.

Cleaning and drying. It is preferable to keep honeycomb core clean during all manufacturing operations prior to adhesive bonding. Aluminum honeycomb core can be effectively cleaned by solvent vapor degreasing.

Nonmetallic core, such as Nomex® or Korex® (aramid), fiberglass and graphite core, readily absorbs moisture from the atmosphere. Similar to composite skins, nonmetallic core sections should be thoroughly dried prior to adhesive bonding. A further complication is that since the cell walls are relatively thin and contain a lot of surface area, they can reabsorb moisture rather rapidly after drying.

Basic Honeycomb Sandwich Production Methods

Honeycomb sandwich components may be produced using any of three well-established methods:

- A heated press is generally used for the production of flat board or simple preformed panels.
- Vacuum bag processing is used for curved and complex form panels.
- Matched mold processing is used generally for batch production of finished panels.

Heated Press

Ideally the panels should be assembled ready for curing as a single shot process. This method is suitable for metallic and prepreg facing skins. Alternatively prepreg facing skin materials may be pre-cured using a press and subsequently bonding with a film adhesive layer. Figure 3-3-27 shows the theory of operation of a heated press.

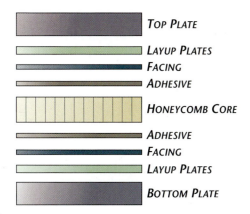

Figure 3-3-27. Theory of operation of a heated press

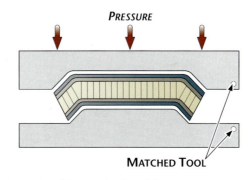

Figure 3-3-29. Matched mold process

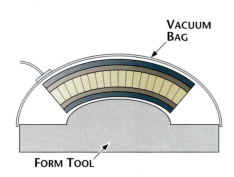

Figure 3-3-28. Vacuum bagging process

Figure 3-3-30. Edge closeout methods for sandwich panels

Vacuum Bag Processing

The component should be assembled for cure as a single-shot process. The necessary consolidation is obtained using a vacuum. This can be cured in an oven, and additional pressure can be applied if an autoclave is used. This method is suitable for items with prepreg or preformed composite or metallic facing skins. When flexible or formed honeycomb core and film adhesives are used complex items may be produced. Figure 3-3-28 shows the vacuum bag process.

Matched Mold Processing

This method is most suited to the single shot cure process where a key objective is to achieve production items with high levels of tolerance and surface finish. The heat and pressure cure cycle in this case is applied using a variety of methods.

Typical methods are the use of heated tools with external mechanical pressure or non-heated tools placed in a press or oven to achieve the full cycle. Using a room temperature curing adhesive cold bonding may be considered if the sandwich construction is too large to be processed using other methods or if heating equipment is unavailable. Figure 3-3-29 shows the matched mold process.

Sandwich Panel Edge Closure Design

When designing sandwich panels it may be necessary to consider methods of closing or sealing the edges. Exposed edge areas are a potential weakness in the design as they may be susceptible to local impact or environmental damage. Edge closures may also provide local reinforcements, attachment points, or simply meet aesthetic requirements. Figure 3-3-30 shows a number of methods commonly used to close sandwich boards.

4

Manufacturing Processes

There are many different manufacturing processes for composites. The process chosen will depend on the desired quality, speed of operation and costs. This chapter discusses hand lay-up, ply cutting operations, vacuum-assisted resin transfer molding (VARTM), filament winding, textile preforming, resin transfer molding (RTM), resin film infusion, automated tape laying, fiber placement, pultrusion, integrally co-cured structures and assembly operations

Learning Objective

REVIEW
- manual, hand lay-up manufacturing processes
- vacuum-assisted resin transfer process
- resin infusion process

DISCUSS
- tape laying automated manufacturing process
- fiber placement automated manufacturing process

EXPLAIN
- vacuum bagging molding process

Section 1

Hand Lay-Up

Two types of hand lay-up methods are often used in the aerospace industry to manufacture composite parts. *Wet lay-up* processes are mostly used for nonstructural applications and the repair of damaged composite structures. The mechanical properties of wet lay-up processes are less than the prepreg hand lay-up processes. The prepreg lay-up method is used in aircraft structural applications and for the repair of damaged structure. Hand lay-up greatly depends on the skill of the technician/laminator who will lay-up the woven or unidirectional plies on the tool (mold).

The placement accuracy is more difficult to achieve with hand lay-up compared to automated lay-up techniques and a tolerance of 1 mm and 2° is accepted. Currently hand lay-up processes are the most used methods for the manufacture of aerospace parts.

A disadvantage of this method is that it is labor intensive. The lay-up process for wet lay-up

Left: Many modern aircraft are manufactured with significant composite structures.

and prepreg is similar and will be briefly discussed. The lay-up process comprises the following five stages: part design, ply cutting, lay-up, debulking and curing.

Part Design

During the initial design phase, the design-engineering team will determine part shape and required mechanical properties. When designing for the manufacturing process, engineers will start with an analysis of the part to determine the number of plies and ply orientations. Often this analysis is accomplished with computer software like CATIA.

Software programs enable the designer to draw the tool, and virtually lay-up the plies to determine the best way to make the lay-up. After the part is created, an analysis can be performed to determine mechanical properties, the best way to lay-up the plies, and where to make cuts and darts in the plies to make them fit on the tool.

The software will also create a flat layout of a complex part and this data can be sent to a ply cutting table. The ply cutting table will quickly cut the required plies. It will also reduce waste materials by determining the most efficient way to cut materials.

The same software program is also used to generate computer code that will be sent to a computer numerically controlled (CNC) mill for tool manufacturing. The data generated can also be used to operate laser projection equipment that will outline where the laminator needs to place the plies.

Ply Cutting

The target for cutting operation is to minimize waste. Purchase cost and disposal cost is extremely high, even for low cost fiberglass prepregs. Hand cutting with rotary cutters (pizza cutters) or utility knives is utilized for small projects and automated cutting tables are utilized for more complex ply cutting operations.

The automated cutting tables use data generated by the design program to cut the plies accurately. Automated cutting tables use the material more efficiently and generate less waste material due to the capability to nest the plies closely.

All layup tables and tools that are used for cutting uncured material, including rulers, scissors, utility knives, templates and straight-edges must be cleaned with acetone or a similar approved solvent. For marking on uncured carbon fiber prepreg materials, use a graphite pencil only. Avoid unnecessary marking on any fabrics or prepregs. Mark on release papers, films or template material.

Yarns, rovings, fabrics and prepregs should be cut and trimmed using clean, sharp tools. Due to the abrasiveness of composite materials, conventional tools tend to dull rapidly. Cutters with tungsten-carbide cutting edges are recommended. Cutting and trimming aramids can be aided with several types of special tools, as illustrated in Chapter 5.

Lay-Up

Laminators will place the prepreg or wet lay-up plies on the tool and use their fingers or spreading tools to force the material into the corners of the tool. Then they smooth it over the flat or gently curving areas (Figure 4-1-1).

Hot air blowers are sometimes used locally to lower the viscosity of the prepreg resin so that it can be conformed into tight recesses. Even with a fully precut kit, the laminator has to trim plies with a blade at the component edges since, for double curvature components, each layer of prepreg is unique in terms of how the plies shear.

It is very important that the laminator retains the ply orientation during the lay-up process to retain the mechanical properties of the component. After the layup is complete a vacuum

Figure. 4-1-1. Manual lay-up process

bag is used to consolidate it. The vacuum bag process requires a vacuum bag, release films, bleeder, breather, peel ply and sticky tape.

These essential stages or features of the lay-up process help to achieve acceptable, quality moldings:

- A release agent (mold release) must be applied to the tool surface to prevent bonding during cure. A solvent or a water-based formulation is wiped onto the tool with a cloth. One coating of release agent is applied to each molding and three or more layers to a new or repaired tool.

- The prepreg must be at room temperature before it is used. Prepreg is hard to position when not properly thawed. If moisture is introduced to the layup, voids can result. The tack level is dependent on the resin formulation itself, its out-life (the resin becomes harder with time at room temperature) and the lay-up room temperature.

- It is important that no bridging of prepreg occurs across tool corners. This prevents the bagging materials from fully compressing the prepreg to the complete surface of the tool with no air pockets or resin filled corners during cure.

- All air must be removed from the layup. This is called debulking. This ensures that no air pockets are trapped between the plies since these may remain throughout the lay-up and cure resulting in delamination.

- The laminator should prevent wrinkling or folding of the layup. The stiffness and strength of the component is dependent on the fibers being as straight as possible along the main load paths. Wrinkles also act as stress concentrations and may cause failure below design-limit strain.

- Prevent the inclusion of backing materials or contaminants. These may prevent bonding, cause wrinkling, or produce gas during cure. Backing materials are especially easy to include in the layup. These backing materials are often bright yellow, red, blue or green for easy detection. Many inclusions are undetectable by non-destructive examination and may become partly bonded.

- Laser projection techniques are available that help the laminator place the plies in the correct position on the mold. Laser projection is a clever, yet essential and effective tool that greatly reduces lay-up time and improves quality. Instead of a laminator following a drawn outline, a

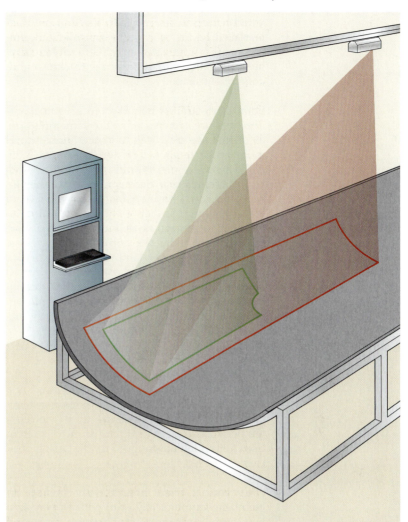

Figure 4-1-2. Laser projection equipment for hand lay-up processes

laser and mirror device causes very rapid projection of a laser point around the ply outline, which produces a static, bright red line.

The line is produced by a suspended laser projector connected to a computer, which converts ply outline data with data on the tool curvature to provide the true ply edge. The technician simply lines up the plies with the laser outline projected on the tool. Figure 4-1-2 illustrates the use of laser projection equipment.

Debulking

Debulking or consolidation is the process of removing air. It is necessary when parts are made from several layers of prepreg because large quantities of air can be trapped between each prepreg layer.

This trapped air can be removed by covering the prepreg with a perforated release film and a breather ply, and applying a vacuum bag for 10 to 15 minutes at room temperature or elevated temperature. Typically the first ply that is placed on the tool face is consolidated and this process is repeated after every three or five layers depending on the prepreg thickness and component shape.

Some parts are hot debulked in an autoclave. The pressure is increased to the same pressure as during the cure cycle, and the temperature is increased to about 180°F (82°C) for a 350°F (177°C) cure cycle. At this temperature the resin becomes less viscous and it is easier to remove air.

Another advantage of de-bulking is that the lay-up is consolidated to a thickness very close to that of the finished laminate. Consequently, when the fully laminated component is cured in an oven or autoclave, the outer plies should remain unwrinkled. Without de-bulking stages, the outer plies tend to wrinkle as the layup underneath compresses.

Curing

Wet lay-ups can, depending on the resin system, be cured at room temperature or an elevated temperature. An elevated temperature is often used for wet lay-ups to speed up the curing process.

Oven curing, a heat bonder with blankets or heat lamps are typically used with wet lay-ups and prepregs. Prepregs for structural parts are normally cured in an autoclave at 350°F (177°C) and 85 p.s.i. New out-of-autoclave prepregs can be cured in an oven using vacuum pressure only.

Wet Lay-up

The wet lay-up process is commonly used to repair damaged composite structures in the aviation industry. Wet lay-up manufacturing and repair processes often use fiberglass for non-structural applications.

Carbon and Kevlar® dry fabric could also be used with a wet lay-up resin system. Continuous fibers and chopped fibers are used depending on the required mechanical properties of the part or structure.

For instance, during the wet lay-up process of the repair of a damaged aircraft structure a dry fabric is impregnated with a low-viscosity resin. The resin system is mixed just before the repair is going to be made. The technician lays out the repair plies on a piece of fabric, then impregnates the fabric with a resin system. Then the repair plies are cut, stacked in the correct ply orientation and vacuum bagged.

The advantages of room temperature wet lay-up are:

- Many resin systems can be used with the wet lay-up process
- The layups cure at room temperature
- The layups are easy to accomplish
- The materials can be stored at room temperature for long times.

The disadvantages of room temperature wet lay-up are:

- It is difficult to control fiber fraction volume
- The possibility exists for resin-rich and dry areas
- It will not restore the strength and durability of original structure or parts that were cured at 250°F to 350°F (121°C to 177°C) during manufacturing.

Some wet lay-up resins use an elevated temperature cure and have improved properties. In general, wet lay-up properties are less than properties of prepreg material. Epoxy resins used for wet lay-up process may require refrigeration until they are used. This prevents the aging of the epoxy. The label on the container will state the correct storage temperature for each component. The typical storage temperature is between 40°F and 80°F (4°C and 27°C) for most epoxy resins.

Prepreg Lay-up

Prepreg is a fabric or tape material that is impregnated with a resin during the manufacturing process. The resin system is already mixed and is in the B stage cure. The prepreg material needs to be stored in a freezer below 0°F (-18°C) to prevent further curing of the resin.

The material is typically placed on a roll and a backing material is placed on one side of the material so that the prepreg will not stick together. The technician has to remove the prepreg from the freezer and let it thaw, which might take eight hours for a full roll.

The prepreg materials are stored in a sealed, moisture-proof bag that should not be opened until the material is completely thawed. This prevents contamination of the material by moisture. After the material is thawed and removed from the bag, it can be cut in repair plies, stacked in the correct ply orientation and vacuum bagged.

Do not forget to remove the backing material when stacking the plies. Prepregs need to be cured at an elevated cure cycle and the most common temperatures for the epoxy resins are 250°F and 350°F (121°C and 177°C). An autoclave, curing oven or heat bonder can be used to cure the prepreg material.

During the lay-up, resin tack and conformability characteristics of fabric determine the difficulty of manipulating the prepreg into tool recesses. For complexly shaped parts, a highly drapable, high-tack resin is preferred to produce a fully consolidated lay-up. For flat or single curvature parts, a less drape-able fabric such as plain weave with a low tack resin is better suited.

Section 2
Automated Processes

VARTM

Vacuum-assisted resin transfer molding (VARTM) is a variant of the traditional RTM process. It is a vacuum-only process for the manufacture of composite parts, typically using single-sided molds in combination with a specific vacuum bag set-up, providing both resin distribution and consolidation functions.

The process has advantages over conventional RTM in that it eliminates the need for costly matched tooling and allows impregnation and cure to be conducted at low (i.e., atmospheric) pressure. Consequently, simple ovens can be used for processing rather than expensive press or autoclave equipment.

Vacuum infusion was developed as an alternative to open-mold hand lay-up and spray-up techniques. Developments in the technology have shown that vacuum infusion can also be an alternative to prepreg compression molding and prepreg vacuum bagging with autoclave cure.

In the VARTM process, the preform is usually fabricated directly onto the tool. Each layer of reinforcement is applied and held in place using a binder or tackifier. Resin inlet tubes are positioned above the part in optimum locations to enable the resin to fully wet out the part prior to the resin gel.

Vacuum tubes connected to a vacuum manifold are positioned around the perimeter of the part. The part is vacuum bagged with conventional nylon vacuum bagging film and sealant tape, allowing the resin and vacuum lines to penetrate the bag along its edges.

Vacuum is applied to the part, the bag is positioned so as to prevent bridging, and a leak test is performed. The resin lines are inserted into an open container of mixed liquid resin. When the lines are opened the resin is forced through the part by the pressure differential between the resin and the vacuum bag.

After it is fully wetted out, the part is allowed to initially cure at room temperature or at an elevated temperature in a convection oven. The part is then removed from the tool, the process materials are removed, the part is post cured (if required) and finally trimmed.

Alternate methods of cure including ultraviolet, electron beam and microwave have also been employed. Other proprietary VARTM processes include the Marco Method, Paddle Lite, Prestovac, Resin Injection Recirculation Molding (RIRM), Ultraviolet VARTM, Seemann Composite Resin Infusion Molding Process (SCRIMP), and Sterkenburg, Futch, Garwood Vacuum Repair (SFG-VR). Figure 4-2-1 shows a basic VARTM process.

Resin systems formulated for wet lay-up are often not suitable for the VARTM process because the viscosity is too high and the gel time is too short. Due to the popularity of the VARTM process, many new specialized one and two-component VARTM resins have been developed that enable the operator to impregnate large complex shapes effectively.

Both room-temperature-cure and elevated-temperature-cure resin systems are available. VARTM resins are available from all major resin groups such as epoxy, BMI and benzoaxiam.

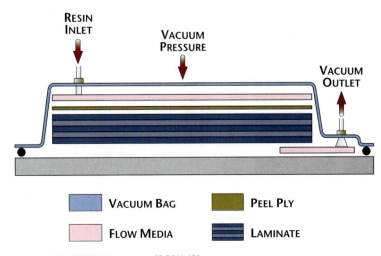

Figure 4-2-1. VARTM process (SCRIMP)

4-6 | Manufacturing Processes

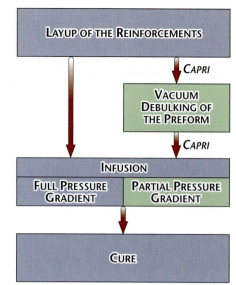

Figure 4-2-2. Flowchart showing SCRIMP and CAPRI process.

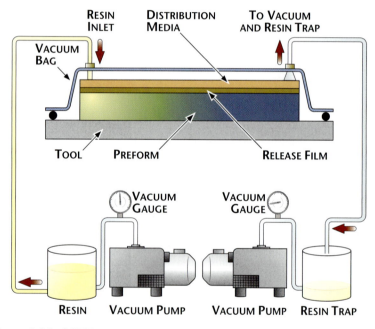

Figure 4-2-3. CAPRI process

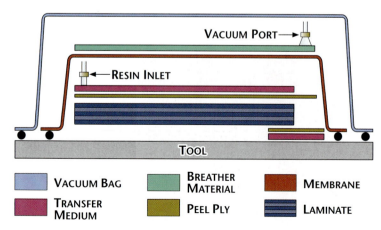

Figure 4-2-4. Membrane-based VARTM processing (VAP) process

Advantages and Disadvantages

Advantages of VARTM over RTM:

- Larger parts are possible, particularly large-surfaced components, such as wind blades and fuselage panels
- Out-of-autoclave cure—Simple oven cure in conjunction with vacuum
- VARTM uses simple, single-sided molds, compared to relatively costly matched-mold tooling for RTM
- Lower-cost infrastructure and tooling because lower pressures are used in VARTM processes. Lightweight foam cores can easily be incorporated into the layups.
- The absence of large forces on the mold compared to RTM
- The VARTM process can greatly reduce the emission of styrene when used with a polyester or vinyl-ester resin system.

Disadvantages of VARTM over RTM:

- The major disadvantage of using VARTM is the sensitivity to leakage. A leak will result in air flowing into the mold. This often leads to void-rich areas in the cured part. Leaks can be eliminated by using a double back process as used in the SFG-VR process.
- Waste is another disadvantage. Many ancillary materials often are used only once (foil, sealant tape, tubes, hoses, valves) and discarded after de-molding.
- Only specially formulated low-viscosity resin systems can be used or the resin must be preheated to lower the viscosity.

CAPRI

Boeing's Controlled Atmospheric Pressure Resin Infusion (CAPRI) VARTM process is a variation of the basic Seeman Composites Resin Infusion Molding Process (SCRIMP) VARTM process. The process uses differential pressure. As shown in Figure 4-2-2, the resin pot is also under a vacuum pressure although the vacuum in the resin pot is lower than the vacuum pulled at the vent side.

Controlling the vacuum difference pressure has certain advantages including increased fiber volume fraction, and reduced pressure, thickness and fiber volume fraction gradients. Disadvantages include a decrease in fabric permeability, an increase in flow times, and an increase in lead length. Figure 4-2-3 illustrates a basic CAPRI process.

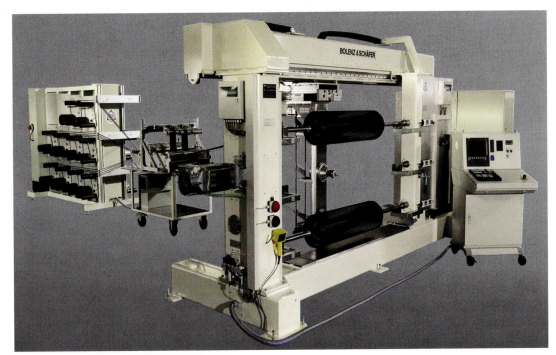

Figure 4-2-5. Filament winding process

Courtesy of EHA

Vacuum-Assisted Process

Membrane-based VARTM processing is another approach. It impregnates a dry preform with liquid resin using a vacuum-assisted processing (VAP) system (Figure 4-2-4). This system also uses a transfer medium to distribute the resin on top of the laminate.

The resin flow is through the thickness of the material. It differs from other processes in that it uses a membrane that allows air and volatiles to escape during the VARTM process but does not allow the resin to escape.

A second vacuum bag is used to apply pressure to the preform. The second bag also makes this process less prone to vacuum leaks. Industry feedback has shown that this process does not perform well for complex shapes that require draping of the membrane.

Filament Winding

Filament winding is an automated process in which a continuous fiber bundle or tape, either pre-impregnated or wet impregnated with resin, is wound on a removable mandrel in a pattern. The filament winding process consists of winding onto a male mandrel that is rotating while the winding head moves along the mandrel.

The speed of the winding head in relation to the rotation of the mandrel controls the angular orientation of the fiber reinforcement. Figure 4-2-5 shows a filament winding machine.

The construction of the mandrel is critical to the process and the materials of choice are dependent upon the use and geometry of the finished part (Figure 4-2-6). The mandrel must be capable of withstanding the applied winding tension and retaining sufficient strength

Figure 4-2-6. Filaments are wound onto a mandrel to create a large fuselage subassembly.

during intermediate vacuum compaction procedures.

In addition, if the outer surface of the part is dimensionally critical, the part is generally transferred from the male winding mandrel to a female tool for cure. If the internal surface of the part is dimensionally critical, the part is usually cured using the male winding mandrel as the cure tool.

Metal is used in segmented collapsible mandrels or in cases where the domes are removed to leave a cylindrical part. Other mandrel material choices are low melt alloys, soluble or frangible plaster, eutectic salts, sand and inflatables.

The following general steps are used for filament winding:

1. The winder is programmed to provide the correct winding pattern.

2. The required number of dry fiber or prepreg roving/slit tape spools for the specified band width are installed on the winding machine.

3. For wet winding, the fiber bundle is pulled through the resin bath.

4. The fiber bundle is pulled through the eye and attached to the mandrel. The winding tension is set and the winding program is initiated.

5. When winding is complete, the mandrel is disassembled as required and removed from the part if the part is to be cured on a female tool. Otherwise the part is trimmed and prepared for cure on the male mandrel.

6. Elevated temperature cure of thermoset resin parts is usually performed in an oven or autoclave; room temperature cure resin parts are usually placed under vacuum to provide compaction during cure. During cure the male mandrel or female tool is often rotated to maintain resin distribution.

7. After cure the mandrel is removed from the part.

Advantages and Disadvantages

Filament winding advantages:

- The most important advantage of filament winding is its lower cost, which is less than the prepreg cost for most composites. The reduced costs are possible because a relatively expensive fiber can be combined with an inexpensive resin to yield a relatively inexpensive composite. Also, cost reductions accrue because of the high speed of fiber lay-down.

- Highly repetitive and accurate fiber placement from part to part and from layer to layer. The accuracy can be superior to that of fiber placement and automated tape-laying machines.

- The capacity to use continuous fibers over the whole component area, without joints and to orient fibers easily in the load direction. This simplifies the fabrication of structures such as aircraft fuselages and reduces the number of joints for increased reliability and lower costs.

- Elimination of the capital expense and size restrictions of an autoclave and the recurring expense for inert gas. Thick-walled structures can be built that are larger than any autoclave can accommodate.

- Capability to manufacture a composite with high fiber volume

- Mandrel costs can be lower than other tooling costs because there is usually only one tool, the male mandrel, that sets the inside diameter and the inner surface finish.

- Lower cost for large numbers of components because there can be less labor than many other processes. It is possible to filament wind multiple small components, leading to sharply reduced costs compared to flag rolling. Costs are eliminated for bagging and disassembly of the bagging materials, as well as the recurring costs of these materials.

- Costs are relatively low for material since fiber and resin can be used in their lowest cost form rather than as prepreg.

Disadvantages of filament winding:

- Need for mandrel, which can be complex or expensive.

- Requires a component shape that permits mandrel removal. Long, tubular mandrels generally do not have a taper. Unless non-uniform shapes can be mechanically disassembled, mandrels must be made from a dissolvable or frangible material. Different mandrel materials, because of differing thermal expansion and differing composite materials and laminate lay-up percentages of hoops versus helical plies, will demonstrate varying amounts of difficulty in removal of the part from the mandrel.

- Difficulty in winding reverse curvature

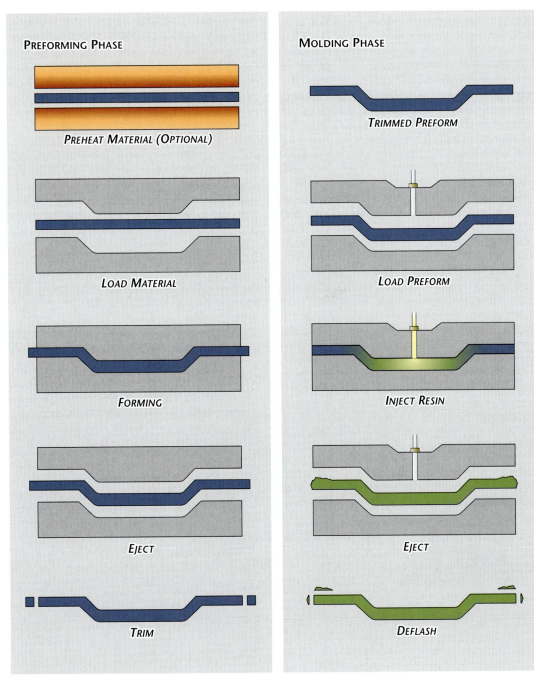

Figure 4-2-7. Resin transfer molding process

- Inability to change fiber path easily in one lamina
- Poor external surface finish, which may hamper aerodynamics or aesthetics

It is important to note that most of the disadvantages are application-specific and, in many cases, have been circumvented by innovative design and equipment modifications.

Resin Transfer Molding

Resin transfer molding (RTM) is a process which combines a dry fibrous reinforcement material or mixture of materials, generally referred to as a preform, with liquid resin during the molding process, whereby the combined materials are cured to produce a three-dimensional component (Figure 4-2-7). RTM is a broad term that describes a number of variations of this general manufacturing approach throughout the aerospace and non-aerospace industries.

The variations encompass extremely different results in terms of the quality of the end product. The conventional RTM process employs closed, "hard" tooling, similar to that used for injection molding, which completely encloses the preform and precisely controls all surfaces of the component.

RTM is a cost-effective means by which to produce a component due to its use of constituent materials in their simplest, and thus least expensive forms. Furthermore, the nature of conventional closed-mold RTM, permits the fabrication of extremely complex shapes and three-dimensional load paths. This enables the designer to combine what would otherwise be numerous individual components produced by alternative processes, thereby reducing overall part count and minimizing the cost of the end product.

The conventional RTM process begins with the fabrication of the preform. The fibrous reinforcement material or materials are formed and/or assembled to produce the geometry and load paths warranted by the application.

These fibrous materials may be woven into broad goods, braided into tubular goods or applied directly onto tooling, or otherwise combined with additional materials such as binders or tackifiers. This defines the geometry of the reinforcement in the end product. Likewise, three-dimensional reinforcements may be incorporated into the preform as part of the weaving or braiding process or as secondary processes such as stitching or alternative fiber insertion techniques.

The preform is placed on the tooling or into the mold and impregnated with the liquid resin. It is then cured while contained within the tooling to produce the as-molded geometry of the end product. Depending on the resin used and the desired end product material properties, the cure cycle may require elevated temperatures.

Many RTM resins for aerospace applications use one-component systems, which eliminates mixing and the defects potentially caused by personnel incorrectly mixing the two component resin. The cured component is then removed from the tooling for trimming, machining, finishing and final inspection as applicable.

The RTM process can be run and controlled by computer software (Figure 4-2-8). The following general steps are employed for any RTM process:

1. Produce the fibrous reinforcement preform (weaving, braiding, cutting, forming and assembling).
2. Locate the preform onto the tooling or into the mold. This may entail further assembly of preforms or reinforcement materials.
3. Impregnate the preform with liquid resin. This may require preheating the assem-

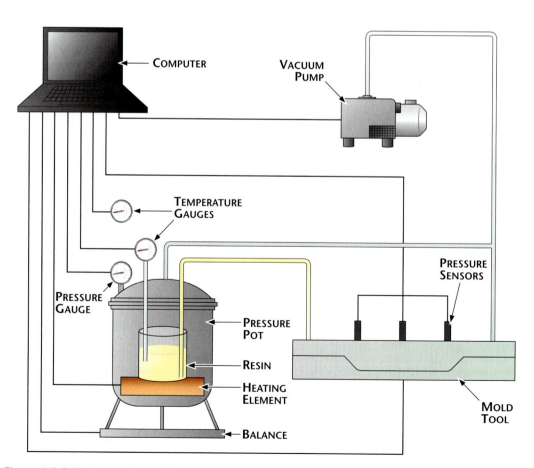

Figure 4-2-8. Resin transfer molding process

Figure 4-2-9 Automated tape laying equipment *Courtesy of Airbus*

bled tooling and preform, heating the resin and application of vacuum and pressure.

4. Cure using room temperature, elevated temperature, or alternative cure techniques.
5. Remove the cured component from tooling for further processing.
6. Post cure, if required.

Resin Film Infusion

Resin film infusion (RFI) is a type of RTM in which resin is placed against the preform. Resin form and placement vary with the resin and tool.

Parts have been fabricated using resin in the form of tiles, films and liquid, with placement either above or below the preform. Generally, parts are bagged and cured using procedures similar to the autoclave cure process.

During autoclave cure, the resin melts and vacuum and autoclave pressure is used to draw the liquid resin up through the tool to impregnate the preform. Once the infiltration cycle is complete, the temperature is raised to the cure temperature and the part is cured.

The advantages of RFI are:

- Particularly suitable for large composite structures
- Very fast deposition rates achievable
- Adaptable for a wide range of textile forms including two- and three-dimensional woven non-crimp fabrics
- Full infusion of thick reinforcements
- Flexibility to use non-autoclave processing

Automated Tape Laying

Composite tape lamination machines have been in use in the industry for about 20 years. Automated tape laying (ATL) has proven to be a very efficient and cost-effective manufacturing process for large contoured composite parts. For maximum efficiency of the machines, engineers tailor the part design to the machine capabilities. This tailoring results in reduced scrap lays, minimizes manual operations, and ensures an affordable manufacturing process.

ATL utilizes a single, wide, unidirectional reinforced, slit tape to layup simple, gentle contours or flat parts. The tape used is either 3, 6 or 12 in. wide. ATL machinery lays fiber down in the form of prepreg unidirectional tape or continuous strips of fabric rather than single tows.

Tape lay-up is versatile, allowing breaks in the process and easy changes in the direction of fiber orientation. ATL systems can be adapted for both thermoset and thermoplastic materials.

Typically the material is applied via a robotically controlled five-axis control head. The head includes a spool or spools of tape, a winder, winder guides, a compaction shoe, a position sensor and a tape cutter or slitter. In either case, the head may be located on the end of a multi-axis articulating robot that moves around the tool or mandrel to which material is being applied, or the head may be located on a gantry suspended above the tool.

Figure 4-2-10. Automated tape lay-up of a contour skin showing the integrated contour tooling

Courtesy of Airbus

Alternatively, the tool or mandrel can be moved or rotated to provide the head access to different sections of the tool. Tape or fiber is applied to a tool in courses, which consist of one row of material of any length at any angle.

Multiple courses are usually applied together over an area or pattern. The courses are defined and controlled by software programmed with numerical input derived from part design and analysis. The head also contains an infrared (IR) type of tape heater that heats the prepreg tape as it is laid down. Figure 4-2-9 shows tape laying equipment for wing skin production.

Examples of parts made from flat laminates are empennage structural parts such as spars, ribs, stringers, C-channel and I-beam stiffeners on the Boeing 777 and the Airbus A330/340. Examples of contour tape-laid parts include horizontal and vertical stabilizer skins on the Boeing 777 and the Airbus A330/340; wing skins on F-22 fighters; V-22 Osprey tilt rotor wing skins and Eurofighter upper and lower wing skins.

Tape laying is also used for the Boeing 787 fuselage and wings, the Airbus 350 fuselage panels and Bombardier C series aircraft. Figure 4-2-10 shows a tape laying machine applying tape to a contoured tool.

Advantages and Disadvantages

Advantages of ATL:

- Tape layers compact plies of graphite-epoxy tape with exceptional consistency and greatly reduce fabrication costs compared to hand lay-up. The bigger the part and plies, the more productive are tape layers.

- Tape layers have ±190° of head rotation; therefore, fiber angles are not limited. Any ply angle can be laid up. Cut angles range from 0° to 85°.

Disadvantages of ATL:

- Highly contoured parts are not suited for tape laying because the tape tends to buckle and bridge at plane transitions.

- Small plies lower the productivity of the tape layer.

Automatic Fiber Placement

Automatic fiber placement (AFP) places multiple, individual, pre-impregnated tows onto a mandrel from multiple spools at high speed. It uses a numerically controlled placement head to dispense, clamp, cut and restart each tow (tape) during placement (Figure 4-2-11 and Figure 4-2-12).

The machine collimates the material into a band up to 6 in. wide, which is a function of the individual tow width, the number of tows a particular machine can process, and the width that the part geometry can accommodate. The material is laminated onto a work surface (tool). Some machine heads are capable of adding or dropping individual tows as each band is placed to either widen or narrow the bandwidth.

This capability, allowing a true fiber orientation to be maintained on a contoured surface, is unique to the fiber placement process. The process allows material to be placed only where needed thereby greatly reducing material scrap. Minimum cut length, the shortest tow length

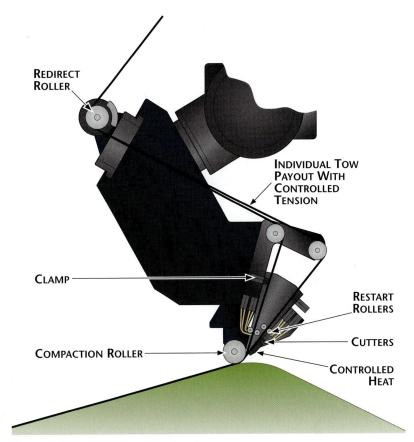

Figure 4-2-11. Fiber placement head

Figure 4-2-12. Automated fiber placement (AFP) system

Courtesy of MAG

a machine can lay down, is the essential ply-shape determinant. The fiber placement head can be attached to an existing gantry system.

Fiber Placement Process

The following general steps are taken with the AFP process:

1. Preparation of the tool or mandrel surface that the material will be applied to
2. Loading and aligning the mandrel into the fiber placement machine
3. Preparation of the machine by loading material, threading the tows through the delivery system and loading the computer path programs for the part being built
4. Machine collation or automated fiber placement of the tows included in a particular ply or layer
5. Inspecting/reworking defects after each ply is placed
6. Continuation of machine collation until all plies are placed
7. Preparing the part for cure
8. Bagging and curing the part. Some parts are cured right on the placement tool and other may require transferring the part to a cure tool. Autoclave or curing ovens could be used to cure the part.

After cure, the part is unbagged and removed from the tool. The bagging, cure, part removal and finishing steps are identical to those required for hand lay-up. This workflow may vary depending on the application. For example, some parts have other materials introduced during fabrication, such as core or alternate fibers, and interim compaction steps may occur.

Advantages and Disadvantages

Advantages of AFP:

- Material scrap for hand lay-up can be as high as 30 to 50 percent. Fiber placement has a typical material scrap of two to seven percent.
- Equipment is very accurate and maintains a tighter tolerance than the hand lay-up process.
- Reduction of labor cost by as much as 50 percent compared to hand lay-up process

The high initial investment for expensive equipment is the major disadvantage of AFP.

Pultrusion

Pultrusion is an automated process for the continuous manufacture of composites with a constant cross-sectional area. A continuous reinforcing fiber is integral to the process and the finished product. Pultrusion can be dry, employing prepreg thermosets or thermoplastics, or wet, where the continuous fiber bundle is resin-impregnated in a resin bath.

The wet-resin process was developed around the rapid-addition reaction chemistry exhibited by thermoset polyester resins, although advances in resin and catalyst systems have made the use of epoxy systems commonplace. Figure 4-2-13 illustrates product forms that can be made using the pultrusion process.

In pultrusion the material is cured in a continuous process that can provide large quantities of high-quality cured shapes. The material is drawn through a heated die that is specially designed for the shape being made.

The tool is designed such that the volume of the cavity for cure causes the resin pressure to build, allowing consolidation of the material to occur.

Figure 4-2-13. Products made with pultrusion process

(A) Courtesy of General Composites, Ltd.,
(B) Courtesy of China Fiber

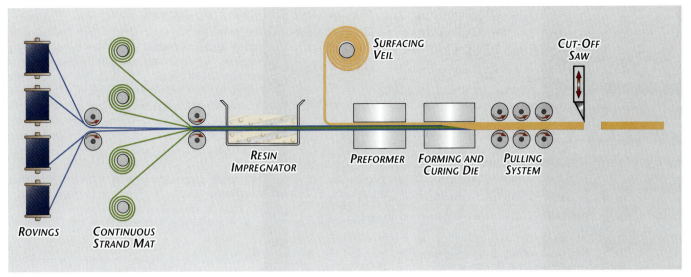

Figure 4-2-14. Pultrusion process

This cure cavity pressure is built up against the cured material downstream of it, and induced by the new material upstream that is continuously being drawn into the cavity. As a result this process can be very sensitive to variation in the tow and rate used for pultrusion.

The resins used for pultrusion are also very specialized. There is little time for volatile removal, consolidation and other activities that can take considerably longer using other cure processes. The resin must be able to cure very rapidly, sometimes in less than a second, when exposed to the proper temperature. The resin must also be very consistent.

Disruptions to this process can be very time consuming and expensive. Like most continuous processes, much of the operating expenses are associated with starting up and stopping the line.

The key elements in the process consist of a reinforcement delivery platform, resin bath (for wet pultrusion), preform dies, a heated curing die, a pulling system and a cut-off station. A wide range of solid and hollow profiles can be produced by the process and stitched fabrics, random mats and bidirectional reinforcements can be used in the process.

The die employs a bell section opening to help reduce hydraulic resin pressures that build up in the die. The die is also plated to help eliminate die-wall adhesion and is also hardened to counteract the abrasive action of the fibers.

In general the following process is used:

1. The reinforcements are threaded through the reinforcement delivery station.

2. The fiber bundle is pulled through the resin bath (if using a wet process) and die preforms.

3. A strap is used to pull the resin-impregnated bundle through the preheated die.

4. As the impregnated fiber bundle is pulled through the heated die, the die temperature and pulling rate are controlled such that the cure of the product, for thermosets, is completed prior to exiting the heated die.

5. The composite parts are cut off by the saw at the desired length as the continuous pultruded product exits the heated die.

The most critical process variable in pultrusion is the temperature control of the product. This is a function of the temperature profile of the heated die and the line speed. Temperature control is critical because the product must achieve full cure just prior to exiting the pultrusion die.

Other variables that affect cured properties are fiber tension, which directly influences the fiber alignment of the final product and resin bath viscosity, which contributes to the completeness of fiber wet-out and the uniformity of the fiber to resin ratio of the final product. Figure 4-2-14 shows the pultrusion process.

Section 3

Vacuum Bag Molding

Many of the processes discussed in this chapter use vacuum bag molding to consolidate the layup including manual lay-up, VARTM,

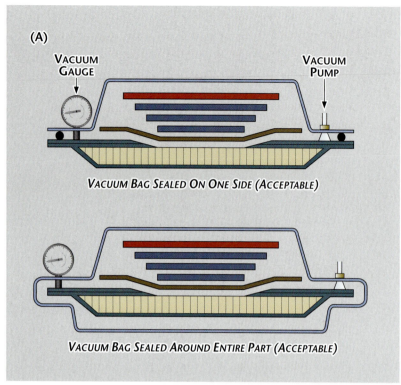

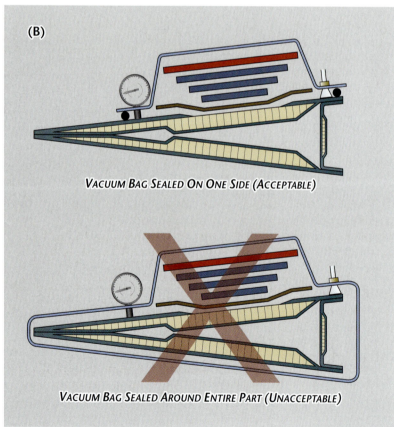

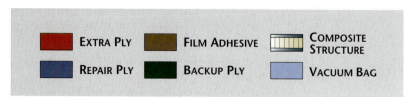

Figure 4-3-1. Vacuum bagging procedures, (A) Acceptable one side and acceptable envelope, (B) Acceptable one side and unacceptable envelope.

ATL, AFP, and filament winding. Vacuum bag molding is a process in which the layup is cured under pressure generated by drawing a vacuum in the space between the layup and a flexible sheet placed over it and sealed at the edges. In the vacuum bag molding process, the reinforcement is generally placed in the mold by hand lay-up using prepreg or wet resin. High-flow resins are preferred for vacuum bag molding.

The following steps are used in vacuum bag molding:

1. Place composite material for part into mold.
2. Install bleeder and breather material.
3. Place vacuum bag over part.
4. Seal bag and check for leaks.
5. Place tool and part in oven and cure as required at elevated temperature.
6. Remove part from mold.

Parts fabricated using vacuum bag molding can be cured with a heater blanket, oven, or autoclave. The main advantage is lower cost tooling than used with an RTM process.

The purpose of a vacuum bag molding process is twofold. First, it assists in the removal of entrapped air from wet lay-ups and prepreg materials. Removing air reduces porosity which makes the laminate stronger.

Second, the vacuum bag applies pressure. The pressure is created because the atmospheric pressure outside the bag is greater than the pressure inside the bag. The greater the difference in pressures, the greater the compacting force. When the layup is compacted, the different layers of fiber are pushed closer together, thus making a stronger laminate.

Vacuum Bag Process

When vacuum is applied to a vacuum-bagged part, air is removed from inside the bag to create a vacuum. To provide a path to draw off the air initially inside the bag, layers of fiberglass cloth or similar noncontaminating materials known as breather plies are placed inside the bag.

When prepreg is being cured as part of the repair, it is sometimes necessary to bleed off excess resin. To do this layers of fiberglass cloth or similar materials, known as bleeder plies, are placed over the prepreg. Some parts are made with a net resin prepreg that does not require bleeding and, therefore, does not require bleeder plies.

Porosity is the result of tiny air bubbles that are entrapped in the repair. When vacuum is applied, the air bubbles are drawn out of the repair plies into the bleeder or breather. Reducing the porosity increases the quality of the repair. Air leaks in a vacuum bag of greater than 1 in. Hg/min introduce air and negatively affect porosity.

Compaction, or clamping pressure, is applied by normal atmospheric pressure when the vacuum is applied. At sea level with maximum vacuum on a standard day (ideal), you can apply 14.7 p.s.i. that would be the equivalent of stacking 1,470 lbs. onto a 10 x 10-in. repair. In reality, pressures will vary between 10 and 15 p.s.i.

Small parts may be envelope bagged by enclosing the entire part in the bag. Larger parts with localized repairs can be bagged by sealing the surface around the part completely with sealing tape and applying the bagging material to the sealing tape (Figure 4-3-1A).

Envelope bagging can crush the structure and is should be determined that the part can withstand a vacuum pressure of 29.9 in. Hg before envelope bagging is used. Some flight controls with honeycomb panels, as shown in Figure 4-3-1B will be crushed if envelope bagging is used. Vacuum bag molding process bagging problems are shown in Figure 4-3-2.

Vacuum Bag Materials

Several processing materials are used for vacuum bagging a part. These materials do not become part of the repair and are discarded after the repair process.

Release agents. Release agents, also called mold release agents, are used so that the part will come off the tool or caul plate easily after curing.

Bleeder ply. The bleeder ply creates a path for the air and volatiles to escape from the part. Excess resin will be collected in the bleeder.

Bleeder material can be made of a layer of fiberglass or nonwoven polyester, or it can be a perforated Teflon® coated material. Thin laminates are more prone to bleeding than thick laminates. It is easy to remove too much resin from a thin laminate and this can result in voids and porosity.

Thick laminates tend to be too thick if they are bled from only one surface. Porosity in thick laminates have been observed in the surface plies, next to the bleeder pack, which can undergo severe overbleeding, while the center and tool plies of the laminate undergo no or minimal bleeding.

It is easier to trap air during ply collation of thick laminates because of their thickness and harder to remove it during debulking or processing. Furthermore, it is much more difficult to evacuate volatiles from the center of large, thick laminates where air and volatiles cannot escape horizontally to the edges.

Unidirectional laminates can be difficult to process. Unidirectional plies tend to nest and seal off at the edges, limiting the effectiveness of debulking. This leaves trapped air pockets in the laminate. In addition, it has been observed that volatiles will attempt to travel down the fiber lengths to evacuate out the edges. The term *linear porosity* has been coined to describe these microscopic tubes of porosity that run parallel to the fiber orientation.

In cross-plied laminates, several plies oriented in the same direction have the same effect. Internal ply drop-off areas also tend toward porosity. Many times voids are present at ply terminations. This is especially true in low-flow systems where the resin does not properly fill the gaps at ply terminations.

Peel ply. Peel plies are often used to create a clean surface for bonding purposes. A thin layer of fiberglass is cured with the repair part. Just before the part is bonded to another structure the peel ply will be removed. The peel ply is easy to remove, leaving a clean surface for bonding.

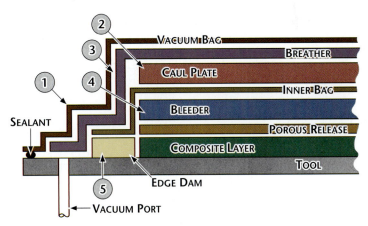

1. Vacuum bag ruptures at sharp corner or bridge causing pressure loss
2. Caul plate severs inner bag allowing resin to escape into breather pack
3. Caul plate bridges over top of dam causing low pressure area
4. Too much bleeder material overbleeds laminate
5. Improperly sealed dams allow resin to escape into breather pack

Figure 4-3-2. Vacuum bag problems

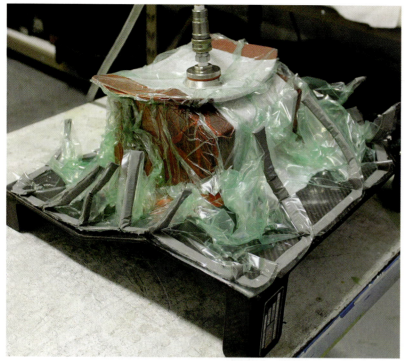

Figure 4-3-3. Vacuum bagging of complex part

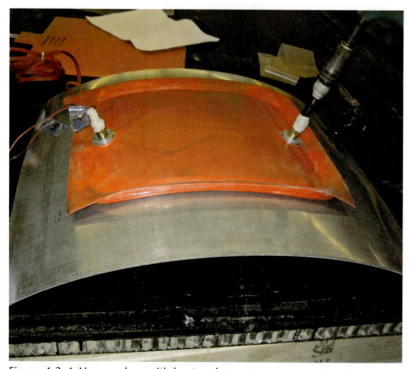

Figure 4-3-4. Vacuum bag with heater element

Peel plies are manufactured from polyester, nylon, fluorinated ethyl propylene (FEP) or coated fiberglass. They can be difficult to remove if overheated. Some coated peel plies can leave an undesirable contamination on the surface. The preferred peel ply material is polyester that has been heat-set to eliminate shrinkage.

Lay-up tapes. Vacuum bag sealing tape also called sticky tape is used to seal the vacuum bag to the part or tool. Most lay-up tapes can withstand 400°F (204°C). Always check the temperature rating of the tape before use.

Perforated release film. Perforated release film, also called parting film, is used to allow air and volatiles out of the part or repair. It also prevents the bleeder ply from sticking to the part or repair. It is available with different size holes and hole spacing to accommodate the amount of bleeding required.

Solid release film. Solid release films are used so that the prepreg or wet lay-up plies will not stick to the working surface or caul plate. Solid release film is also used to prevent the resins from bleeding through and damaging the heat blanket or caul plate if they are used.

Breather material. Breather material is used to provide a path for air to get out of the vacuum bag. The breather must contact the bleeder. Typically polyester is used in either 4 oz. or 10 oz.—4 oz. is used for applications below 50 p.s.i. autoclave pressure and 10 oz. is used for 50 to 100 p.s.i. autoclave pressure.

Vacuum bag. The vacuum bag material provides a tough layer between the repair and the atmosphere. Vacuum bag material is available in different temperature ratings so always ensure that the material used for the repair can handle the cure temperature.

Most vacuum bag materials are made for one-time use but material made from flexible silicon rubber is reusable. Two small cuts are made in the bagging material so that the vacuum probe valve can be installed. The vacuum bag is not very flexible and plies need to be made in the bag if it is to be used on complex (Figure 4-3-3).

Sometimes an envelope-type bag is used but the disadvantage of this method is that the vacuum pressure might crush the part. Reusable bags made from silicon rubber are available that are more flexible, and some have a built-in heater blanket that simplifies the bagging task (Figure 4-3-4).

Vacuum equipment. A vacuum pump is used to evacuate the air and volatiles from the vacuum bag so that atmospheric pressure will consolidate the plies. A dedicated vacuum pump (Figure 4-3-5) is used in a repair shop. For repairs on the aircraft a mobile vacuum pump can be used (Figure 4-3-6). Most heat bonders have a built-in vacuum pump.

Special air hoses are used as vacuum lines, because regular air hoses might collapse when a vacuum is applied. The vacuum lines that are used in the oven or autoclave also need to be able to withstand the high temperatures in the heating device. A vacuum pressure regulator is sometimes used to lower the vacuum pressure during the bagging process.

Vacuum compaction table. Vacuum compaction tables (Figure 4-3-7 and Figure 4-3-8) are convenient tools for de-bulking composite layups with multiple plies. Essentially a reusable vacuum bag, a compaction table consists of a metal table surface with a hinged cover. The cover includes a solid frame, a flexible membrane, and a vacuum seal. Repair plies are laid up on the table surface and sealed beneath the cover with vacuum to remove entrapped air. Some compaction tables are heated but most are not.

Types of Bleed-Out Techniques

Bleed-out techniques include vertical, controlled, no bleed out and edge bleed out.

Vertical (or top) bleed out. The traditional method of bleeding out using a vacuum bag technique involves a perforated release film and a breather/bleeder ply on top of the repair. The holes in the release film allow air to breath and resin to bleed off over the entire repair area. The amount of resin bled off depends on the size and number of holes in the perforated release film, the thickness of the bleeder/breather cloth, the resin viscosity and temperature and the vacuum pressure.

Controlled bleed out. This method allows a limited amount of resin to bleed out in a bleeder ply. A piece of perforated release film is placed on top of the prepreg material, a bleeder ply is placed on top of the perforated release film and a solid release film is placed on top of the bleeder. A breather and a vacuum bag are used to compact the repair.

The breather allows the air to escape. The bleeder can only absorb a limited amount of resin, and the amount of resin that is bled can be controlled by using multiple bleeder plies. Too many bleeder plies can result in a resin-starved repair. Always consult the maintenance manual or manufacturer tech sheets for correct bagging and bleeding techniques.

No bleed out. Prepreg systems with 32 to 35 percent resin content are typically no-bleed systems. These prepregs contain exactly the amount of resin needed in the cured laminate; for this reason resin bleed-off is not desired. Bleed out of these prepregs will result in a resin-starved repair or part.

Many high-strength prepregs in use today are no-bleed systems. No bleeder is used and the resin is trapped/sealed so that none bleeds away. A sheet of solid release film is placed on top of the prepreg and taped off at the edges with flash tape. Small openings are created at the edges of the tape with fiberglass yarns so that air can escape.

A breather and vacuum bag are installed to compact the prepreg plies. The air can escape on the edge of the repair but no resin can bleed out. Figure 4-3-9 shows a no-bleed lay-up.

Figure 4-3-5. Stationary vacuum pump

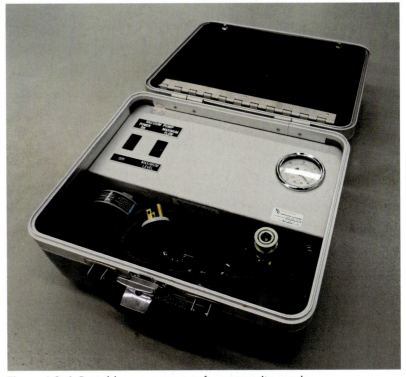

Figure 4-3-6. Portable vacuum pump for composite repair

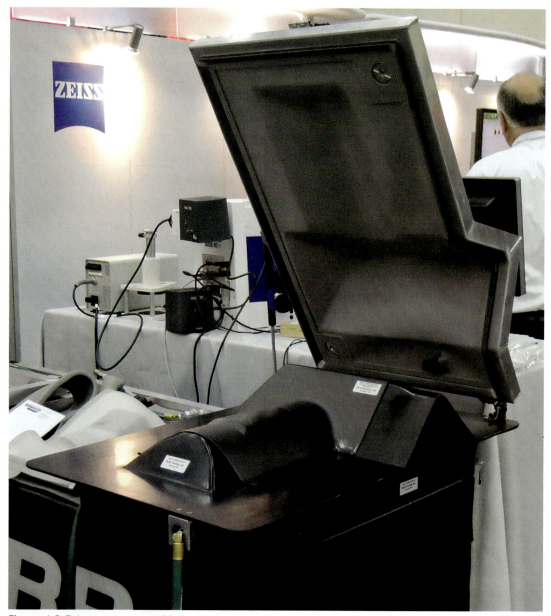

Figure 4-3-7. Large vacuum table

Horizontal (or edge) bleed out. This method is sometimes used for small room-temperature wet lay-up repairs. A 2-in. strip of breather cloth, called an edge breather, is placed around the repair or part. There is no need for a release film because there is no bleeder or breather cloth on top of the repair. The part is impregnated with resin and the vacuum bag is placed over the repair. A vacuum is applied and a squeegee is used to remove air and excess resin to the edge breather.

Debulking Operations

Debulking or compaction is primarily performed in production to ensure a high-quality structure. Debulking operations usually depend on the geometry and the thickness of the part. The process is used with prepreg materials and not with wet lay-ups, although sometimes wet lay-up repairs are made with the double vacuum debulk (DVD) process, which uses compaction and debulking.

The debulking process removes most of the entrapped air that occurs between plies as they are laid up and also minimizes wrinkles and wrinkle propagation. For repair, this process can be used in limited cases where vacuum bag processes alone do not produce adequate repairs.

Some materials are compacted every other ply whereas other materials require compaction after every three, four or even five plies are laid up. The difference is sometimes due to the resin being used and other times due to the product form, such as different styles of fabric or unidirectional tape prepreg materials. Also, the time the stack up is exposed to vacuum pressure can vary from 1 to 5 minutes.

A room temperature debulk or compaction must take place if a structure of more than five plies is being manufactured. The time under pressure could vary from 1 to 30 minutes depending upon the type of materials used. A heated debulk or compaction should be done whenever 10 plies or more compose the part.

When doing this, the general theory is to apply pressure with an autoclave, vacuum bag or physical force, elevate the temperature to a level that will soften the resin and allow it to flow, hold for a time to compact and remove air, and then cool again. Generally, 150°F to 180°F (66°C to 82°C) is the maximum temperature used unless materials with a cure temperature of 350°F (177°C) or higher are being processed. The heated debulking process must be accomplished in the fastest possible manner to minimize advancement of the resin system.

Debulking Procedure

If compaction is required, perform the following:

1. Place the perforated separator film over the laid up plies.
2. Place the breather material over the separator film.
3. Close the lid of the compaction table or make a vacuum bag and apply full vacuum. When a full vacuum is achieved, hold the vacuum on the plies for a minimum of 5 minutes.
4. Remove the vacuum and uncover the ply layup area. If, after debulking, the compacted plies do not conform to the tooling or the part, repeat the previous step.

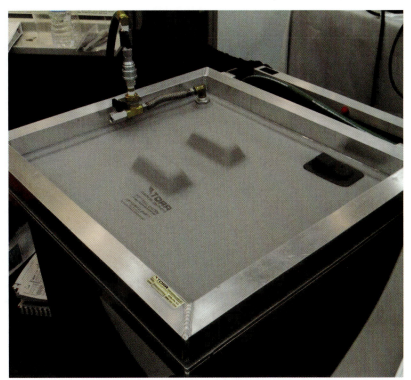

Figure 4-3-8. Vacuum table

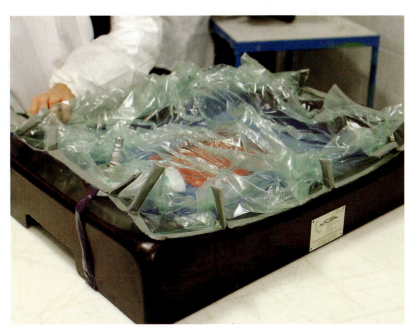

Figure 4-3-9. Vacuum bagging using a no bleed out process

5
Tool and Mold Making

Tooling is an essential part of composite manufacturing, and it is a necessary and expensive part of the manufacturing process. Most aircraft parts are not flat and have complex shapes. The tool or mold is required to support the complexities of the part during the lay-up and curing process.

Tools can be made from several different types of materials ranging from inexpensive foams and aluminum to very expensive alloys and composite tooling. Every tooling material has advantages and disadvantages and the manufacturer will have to make a choice between costs, accuracy and quality.

Learning Objective

REVIEW
- types of tools and molds used for parts manufacturing in aerospace industry

DESCRIBE
- materials used in tool and mold manufacturing

EXPLAIN
- how to make tools and molds using wet lay-up and prepreg materials

Section 1
Tooling Design

Master Tool

During development and production, aircraft master models are painstakingly constructed and stored in climate-controlled areas, as seen in Figure 5-1-1. The use of computer-aided design/computer-aided manufacturing (CAD/CAM), also known as three-dimensional, or 3-D, engineering technologies have helped to eliminate many of the conventional tooling methodologies once widely practiced up until about 1990.

Conventional tooling methods include hand fairing plaster or plastic faces over aluminum lofting templates. Master models are fabricated and then secondary control tools are produced from reverse splashes. This process is being replaced with elec-

Left: Composite propellers, like those shown here on an ATR72, are made using a complex molding process to achieve the curved shape.

Figure 5-1-1. Master tools are frequently stored on open racks allowing easy access.

tronic master models that exist in a computer-generated engineering tooling model.

The 3D engineering models provide all the control surfaces and coordination points to fabricate tooling associated with the engineering part.

The 3D engineering part model provides the tooling fabricator with the ability to design, plan and program the data as needed. Often these data are fed into recognition databases that support numerically controlled fabrication and inspection work centers, including multi-

Figure 5-1-2. An Invar tool machined on five-axis gantry machining center. *Courtesy of Coast Composites*

axis machining and cutting centers and high-precision measurement systems.

Developments in computers and computer-assisted drafting and manufacturing programs have resulted in a more automated method to design and fabricate master models. Often the master model now is based on an electronic image machined directly from design data.

The data set can be updated or modified easily in the CAD/CAM program and the part interfaces matched up to the mating parts of the assembly. Virtual fit and function checks can be made before a part is made. This has eliminated the large plaster master models that were kept in climate controlled, expensive storage facilities.

This method is often used at manufacturers and repair stations. The tool is designed in the CAD program and the tool paths for computer-controlled milling machines are generated in the CAM programs. Using this method eliminates the expense of artisans manually building a master and the long-term cost of storage. This method usually requires a large, five-axis milling machine to directly machine the mold surfaces as shown in Figure 5-1-2.

Depending on the number of parts that need to be manufactured, the production tooling can be made directly or a physical master tool is made using computer numerically controlled (CNC) machining centers or robots. These master tools are used to produce the production tooling. Figure 5-1-3 shows a master tool made using a computer numerically controlled machining center.

Figure 5-1-3. A master tool generated using a computer-controlled machine.

to craft a tool with reasonable surface acuity at an affordable price. New board materials have improved in their machinability, durability, thermal stability and surface quality. Figure 5-1-4 shows a master tool made from tooling board.

Production Tools

Production tooling is made from the master tool and is used to manufacture the part or component. For large production runs, multiple production tools could be made. Production tools are made from metal and composite materials depending on the number of parts to be made on the tool, part surface quality and cost. If the production tool is damaged it can be replaced with a new production tool made on the master tool.

Metal production tools could be directly made from the CAD model; however, carbon fiber composite production tools are made on a physical master tool. The master tool is often made from high-temperature tooling board.

Tooling board is supplied in a range of standard sizes, shapes and thicknesses. These sheet materials can be cut, adhesively bonded into large 3-D blocks and shaped with conventional hand tools or automated machining equipment. This provides a fast, simple means

Figure 5-1-4. A master tool made from tooling board.

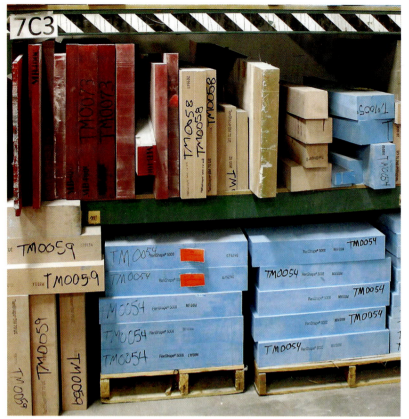

Figure 5-1-5. Tooling materials

Tooling Materials

Materials for master models are undergoing rapid evolutionary changes. Plaster and high-density woods are being replaced but are still being used. A wide variety of machinable plastics is available in sheet and castable forms.

Lightweight chemical foams formed by expansion and cut in slabs or mixed and poured in place are available off the shelf from composite suppliers. Denser resin systems filled with lightweight fillers such as micro-balloons or heavier solid spheres are sold in slabs or pour systems. Mass cast systems are available that can be poured near shape and machined or cast exactly to the finished shape.

A popular system used by many composite tooling shops is tooling board material. This epoxy or polyurethane material is available in many different hardnesses and temperature ranges. It is easy to machine compared to steel, Invar or aluminum.

If highly contoured parts need to be made, a tooling board master mold is most suitable. This material is available in sheet material that can easily be bonded together to build up the rough shape of the material.

A five-axis CNC mill is used to fabricate the part to close tolerance. The aircraft industry has traditionally used metallic tooling to produce composite airframe parts. The type of tooling material chosen depends on several factors.

Selection of the tooling material is typically based on, but not limited to, the coefficient of thermal expansion, expected number of cycles, end-item tolerance, desired or required surface condition, method of cure, glass transition temperature of the material being molded, molding method, matrix, cost and a variety of other considerations. Figure 5-1-5 shows several composite tooling board materials for the fabrication of master tools.

Metallic tooling made from Invar (a low-expansion iron-nickel alloy), steel, aluminum and electroplated materials is becoming more popular for production composite cure tools. Metallic tools generally cost more than a composite wet or prepreg lay-up tool, but offer some advantages by eliminating the need for control/transfer tools, by extending service life, and by providing higher durability.

If the mold is to be made of a metal, the metal tool can be directly machined to the desired shape and size using CAD data or a drawing of the finished part. If the mold will be going through a cure cycle, the differences of the coefficient of thermal expansion (CTE) will have to be taken into account when selecting the material and defining the size of the mold.

Aluminum Tooling

Aluminum is a relatively lightweight material, easy to machine and has good thermal conductivity; however, the CTE is much greater than carbon fiber and therefore not very useful to cure carbon fiber products at elevated temperatures.

Aluminum is most useful for flat caul plates to make flat sheets or for curing room-temperature wet layup parts. Aluminum is softer than

Figure 5-1-6. Aluminum tooling

most tool steels and easily scratched or damaged during production operations. Aluminum tools are sometimes used to make trapped tools because the large CTE is effectively used so that the tool can be released after the cure.

The production of a carbon fiber tube can be accomplished on an aluminum rod if the primary fiber orientation of the carbon fiber is in the hoop direction. During the cure, the aluminum will expand and so will the carbon fiber material. When the matrix of the carbon fiber product reaches the glass transition temperature it is set.

When the cure is complete the aluminum will return to its original size but the carbon fiber will not shrink too much because the fibers are in the hoop direction. The carbon fiber tube will release from the part as long as the CTE of the aluminum is larger than the shrinkage of the resin. If the fiber is placed with the fiber along the length of the aluminum tool the tool will not release because the carbon fiber resin will shrink more than the CTE of the aluminum. Figure 5-1-6 shows an aluminum tool.

Steel Tooling

An advantage of steel tooling is that it is very durable and could last a lifetime. Invar and tool steel are often used in the aerospace industry for making large molds for the production of fuselage and wing skin panels.

Invar tooling. The aerospace industry has traditionally used Invar tooling to manufacture large aircraft sections. Invar, a 36 percent nickel-steel alloy, is a very good tooling material due to its very low CTE, nearly the same as that of carbon-epoxy. Because an Invar tool expands and shrinks at the same rate as the composite material, no stresses are imparted to the molded composite part.

Disadvantages of Invar tooling are the high weight of the tool and cost. The Airbus A350's outer surface, including the forward fuselage, wings, center wing box and sections of mid- and aft-fuselage as well as some stringer and nacelle tools, are made from Invar. The Airbus A350 uses steel or aluminum for trim tools and other tool types. These metal tools do not need a master tool because the digital model-based tool design is transferred directly to the shop, where Invar sheets are welded or materials are machined to form the tool face.

Invar tooling as seen in Figure 5-1-7, can be made from sheets of metal that are welded together or they can be made from cast material. Both processes require that the surface need to be machined after assembly.

Figure 5-1-7. Large Invar tool for aircraft production

Courtesy of Airbus

Figure 5-1-8. Carbon foam cross section

An advantage of casting a tool skin over traditional bump forming and welding is that with a press-shaped metal tool face that is welded, there is always the potential for leak paths. Casting can create complex tool geometry in one piece, with no welding required. However, metal castings also can have porosity due to trapped gases or turbulence in the metal during the casting process.

Nickel Vapor Deposition tools. Nickel vapor deposition (NVD) tools are made by combining ground nickel powder with carbon monoxide gas in a reactor. The resulting vapor is condensed into a liquid and pumped to a deposition chamber, where it is reheated and vaporized.

Solid nickel then deposits at a thickness of 0.010 in. (0.254 mm) per hour onto a CNC-machined aluminum mandrel, and forms a thin uniform shell tool face. The thickness of the nickel shell is controlled by the length of time in the chamber and can be any thickness specified, regardless of mold size. Although the CTE of NVD tools is about the same as tool steel, its thermal conductivity is three times higher for faster thermal cycling. NVD autoclave bonding tools are used for the Boeing 787 Dreamliner's vertical tail fin leading edge.

Composite Tooling

Graphite-epoxy or high-temperature glass cure tools generally fall into three categories: wet lay-up tooling, prepreg tooling and carbon-foam tooling.

Advantages of composite tooling:

- Lighter than metal tooling
- Lower thermal mass results in more desirable heating and cooling rates than metals
- A composite tool heats and cools more evenly than metal tools
- Carbon-fiber reinforced tool laminates have a very low CTE that match the CTE of a carbon-fiber part more closely.

Disadvantages of composite tooling:

- Composite tools have less durability and damage tolerance than metal tools. Due to the many cure cycles in production, micro-cracks can develop that will result in vacuum or pressure leaks. Operator error such as using sharp objects on the tool could create fine scratches at the surface of the mold.
- Composite tools are easily damaged during operation or transportation.
- Composite tools cannot easily be adjusted or altered like metal tooling. Extra details in metal tooling are quite possible but with composite tools this will result in vacuum or pressure issues. The only way to alter the tool is to alter the master tool and make a new production tool.

Carbon Foam Tooling

This low-density, machinable material has a low CTE compatible with carbon composites. CFOAM is produced from powdered bituminous coal, which is pressed into tray molds and processed under high heat and pressure in an autoclave. Foam panels are bonded to form a near net-shape billet, which is machined to the desired shape.

A tool face is formed by applying a composite material, such as Hexcel's HexTool matte material. After cure of the tool face, the CFOAM tool is CNC-machined to the final profile, wet sanded, sealed and prepared for part production. Figure 5-1-8 shows a cross section of a carbon foam tool.

Many of these tools use resistive-heated foam elements just beneath the tool face to cure the part and an autoclave is not required. Advantages of these tools are low CTE, no need for a physical master tool, reduced manufacturing time, very accurate tool dimensions and high quality tool surface. On the other hand, these tools are more expensive than prepreg composite tooling and if tool is damaged a new tool needs to be made that is much more expensive than making a new composite tool on the master mold. If the resistive heating elements are faulty the tool becomes useless.

Other Design Considerations

Trapped Tools

Trapped tools are used to provide support on the inside walls of hollow parts. Tool removal can be difficult, but leaving the tool in place can compromise part weight and function. Multipiece tooling, silicon bladders, fiber-reinforced shape-memory polymers (SMP), washout mandrels and water-soluble materials are some of the solutions used to make hollow parts.

Fiber-reinforced SMPs are used as a trapped tooling solution for aerospace applications and other markets. In this process a fiber-reinforced SMP, also known as a smart mandrel, is formed into hollow tubing and placed into a two-part mandrel mold and heated to soften the blank. When softened, the mandrel is pushed against the mold contours with air pressure. After it is cooled, the SMP becomes rigid and maintains the molded shape.

The rigid mandrel is then coated with a mold release and used for layup of a composite part. The part, during cure, is heated to 250°F (121°C) which is below the mandrel's transition temperature. Then, the mandrel is reheated to above its softening temperature (more than 250°F). It resumes its original tube shape and can be extracted from the cured part. This process is shown in Figure 5-1-9.

Some warm-water washout mandrels for trapped tooling and traditional single-sided tools use ceramic microspheres mixed with water-soluble inorganic binders. These lightweight tools are produced via a vacuum molding process in a few days, a process that is speeded by making molds for the mandrels and masters for single-sided tools using an additive manufacturing process, fused deposition modeling. The mandrels and tools have a low CTE and low thermal mass.

Spring-In Tools

Engineers and technicians that have experience working with aluminum know that it will spring back when it is formed on a sheet metal brake. They also are aware that the flanges of a part typically need to be bent approximately 3° more than required. If a part needs 90° flanges, then it needs to be bent approximately 93°. The material springs back 3° after the bending operation.

A similar phenomenon happens with composite parts; however, the reasons are different. Composite flanges will actually spring in after the part comes off the mold. Spring-in is caused

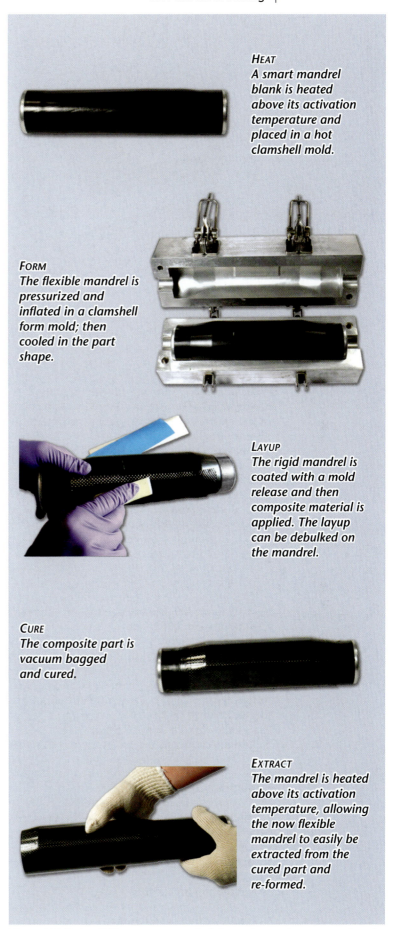

HEAT
A smart mandrel blank is heated above its activation temperature and placed in a hot clamshell mold.

FORM
The flexible mandrel is pressurized and inflated in a clamshell form mold; then cooled in the part shape.

LAYUP
The rigid mandrel is coated with a mold release and then composite material is applied. The layup can be debulked on the mandrel.

CURE
The composite part is vacuum bagged and cured.

EXTRACT
The mandrel is heated above its activation temperature, allowing the now flexible mandrel to easily be extracted from the cured part and re-formed.

Figure 5-1-9. An SMP, or smart mandrel, is used to make a trapped tool.
Courtesy of Smart Tooling

5-8 | Tool and Mold Making

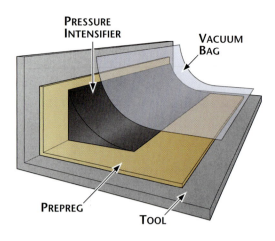

Figure 5-1-10. The pressure intensifier prevents the accumulation of resin in corners and high-void-content areas

by segregation and shrinkage of the resin to one side in an area with a large change in radius.

Because of differences in thermal expansion, residual stresses arise during the manufacturing process. When the part is removed from the tool, the part deforms to the state governed by the residual stress rate. For example, spring-in results in a 1 or 2° change in the L-section and the tool needs to compensate for the spring-in. For example, if 90° flanges are required, the tool needs to have an included angle of 88 to 89°. Some experimentation is required to get it right.

Coefficient of Thermal Expansion

Differences in the coefficients of thermal expansion (CTE) between the tool and the part are significant. Most forming processes involve complaint material being placed on the tool at room temperature with a subsequent rise in temperature to cure or consolidate the material. From this stress-free point, the part and mold are cooled to room temperature and differential shrinkage occurs.

This shrinkage could result in damaged parts, but this difference can also be used as a means to release a part, as with graphite/epoxy tubes on an aluminum or steel mandrel; however, the CTE of the tube in the hoop direction must be sufficiently smaller than that of the mandrel. In this way tubes with reinforcement in the hoop direction easily release from the mandrel, whereas highly longitudinally aligned tubes do not.

To provide better dimensional stability, the CTE of the tool is matched to that of the structural component in many high-performance aerospace applications. In most cases it is important to match the CTE of the tool to the CTE of the part. Therefore Invar and composite tooling are often used.

Pressure Intensifiers

Pressure intensifiers are used in corners of deep draw molds to apply pressure. Often the vacuum bag will bridge in these female corners and prevent the autoclave or vacuum pressure from consolidating the composite layup. This could result in resin-rich and high void-content areas. Some pressure intensifiers are made of silicon and are placed inside the vacuum bag (Figure 5-1-9) in the corners of the layup. These pressure intensifiers are especially important for out-of-autoclave prepregs that are cured with vacuum pressure only.

Field Repair Issues

Composite aircraft may require repair in the field. This requires modifying some of the typical manufacturers techniques.

For repair of minor local damage if a premade contoured patch blank is not available, splash tooling is often the only option. Splash molds have traditionally been pulled off plaster masters and used to produce families of tooling. The family of tooling may include lay-up molds, trim fixtures, drill jigs and assembly fixtures.

Without a master in the field, it is possible to use an existing undamaged part to make a mold in which a repair patch can be produced. Depending on the contour and materials, used shrinkage may be a significant issue. It may be necessary to make the contour larger by offsetting the surface with calendared adhesive-backed sheet wax.

Section 2
Tooling Construction Techniques

Wet Lay-Up Tooling

This section describes the method for manufacturing composite tools. The Airtech toolmaster system is described but many other systems are available. The Airtech system is not endorsed but used as an example of a wet lay up tool system.

Figure 5-2-1. Master model

Tool preparation. Lightly sand surface if required and remove previous release agents. Wipe down the master model surface (Figure 5-2-1) using solvent. Wear a mask and gloves for this operation. Thoroughly clean the master model.

Verify vacuum integrity of tool surface by creating a vacuum bag over the area where the layup will take place. Place a vacuum gauge on the vacuum valve. A vacuum loss of 1 Hg in 5 minutes is acceptable. If a greater loss occurs the tool surface will require sealing.

Apply a strip of 1-in. (2.5-cm) flashbreaker tape to the perimeter area of the master model that will be used for application of vacuum bag sealant tape at a later stage. The flashbreaker tape will prevent mold release agent application on these perimeter areas. Outside the flashbreaker tape mark the layup directions 0/90° on tool surface using masking tape.

Apply release agents per the manufacturer's instructions and best shop practice.

Apply a strip of adhesive-backed cork tape dam material to the master model surface following the proposed perimeter of the wet layup.

- Cover the cork tape dam with a layer of 1-in. (2.5-cm) wide Teflon pressure sensitive tape.
- Position the Teflon tape on the resin dam so that the Teflon tape extends down onto the face of the master model by about 0.25 in. (0.64 cm). Apply masking tape to the top of the Teflon covered resin dam to act as a mask to prevent a buildup of surface fill on the resin dam. This masking tape strip will be peeled away after application of the surface fill to give a clean surface to the Teflon covered resin dam. Figure 5-2-2 shows the application of sealant tape.

Application of Toolmaster surface fill.

- Trim a 2-in. (5-cm) wide natural-bristle paintbrush so the bristles are approximately 0.5 in. (1.3 cm) in length.
- Cut the bristles to give a slightly uneven line so that the applied surface fill will have a textured, grainy finish.
- Estimate the required quantity of Toolmaster surface fill on the basis of 1 oz. (30 g) of mixed surface fill for each square foot of master model surface area.

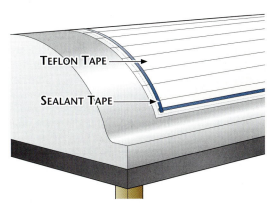

Figure 5-2-2. Application of sealant tape

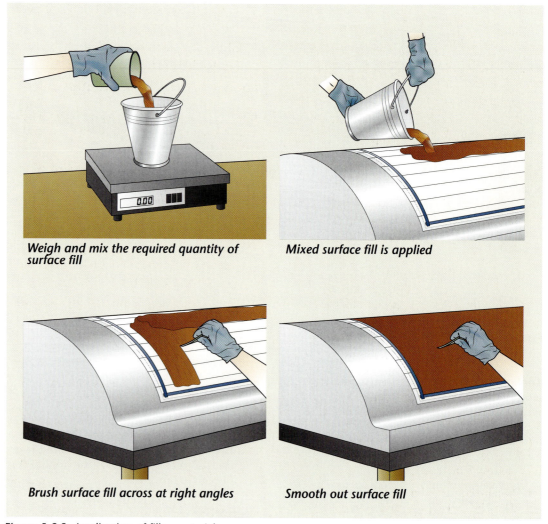

Figure 5-2-3. Application of filler material

Weigh and mix the required quantity of Toolmaster surface fill per manufacturing instructions.

- When the surface fill has been thoroughly mixed, transfer the mix to a new container and mix again with a clean mixing stick to ensure all the material around the edges of the container has been thoroughly mixed.

- Apply the surface fill to the master model surface using the trimmed paintbrush. Apply the surface fill in one direction only covering all surfaces including the sidewalls of the Airdam 1 perimeter resin dam. The surface fill should be applied in sufficient thickness so that the master model surface just cannot be seen through the surface fill. Take care to avoid buildup of surface fill in the angle between the master model surface and the Airdam 1 resin dam. For this application stage, the paintbrush should be held in an upright position in relation to the master model surface.

- Taking a clean 2-in. (5-cm) wide natural-bristle paintbrush (full-length bristle–not trimmed) draw the brush across the surface fill at right angles to the direction of the first-stage surface fill application. For this operation the brush should be held at a shallow angle to the master model surface. The reason for this second light brush stroke operation is to remove air bubbles from the surface fill coating and ensure an even surface fill distribution. Figure 5-2-3 illustrates the application of filler material.

- The surface fill-coated master model can now be left for approximately 16 hours (overnight) at room temperature to allow the surface fill to tack dry. This tack-dry condition can be defined as the stage when the surface fill feels tacky to the fingertip touch, but will not lift off or transfer to the gloved finger.

Cutting of dry fabric.

- Unroll dry fabric on table and precut all ply sizes and orientation. It is most com-

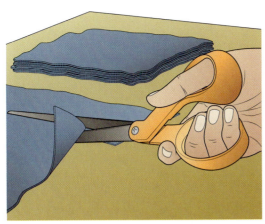

Figure 5-2-4. Cutting rectangles for lay-up

mon to cut rectangles of 10 x 6 in (25 x 15 cm). The smaller rectangles are easier to lay-up than a few large plies. Figure 5-2-4 shows the ply cutting process.

- Pieces should be cut so the long side of the rectangle corresponds to the warp direction of the fabric and the short side of the rectangle corresponds to the fill direction of the fabric.

Wet lay-up procedure.

- Mix the resin and hardener to the manufacturer's instructions.
- Prepare an area on a table to accommodate the largest ply and cover the table with plastic.
- Place the first ply of material on top of the plastic and pour a small amount of resin over the ply.
- Using a plastic squeegee, work the resin into the dry fiber ply until completely saturated, as seen in Figure 5-2-5.
- Carefully lift ply off plastic and place on surface fill.
- The long side of the rectangular pieces for the first ply of the layup is aligned with a direction on the master model we define to be the 0° direction.
- Using a plastic squeegee, remove air from under the ply and evenly spread the resin. Be careful not to distort fibers. Continue this process until the first ply lay-up is completed.
- All plies throughout the layup are to be overlapped by a minimum of 0.5-in. (1.3 cm) at all the joints.
- When applying fabric in female corner areas do not carry the fabric around the female corner but cut the fabric into the corner to form a butt joint or slight overlap in the corner radius.
- At the completion of the first ply perform a vacuum bag compaction/debulk.

Vacuum bag compaction (debulk).

- Cover the entire layup with a layer of perforated release film extending the over the resin dam edge strip.
- Remove the masking tape applied to the perimeter area of the master model and apply a strip of vacuum bag sealant tape to the perimeter area.
- Apply a layer of breather material over the whole layup (on top of the perforated release film), terminating at the perimeter of the vacuum bag sealant tape.
- Place a layer of vacuum bagging film over the entire assembly allowing sufficient material to enable the vacuum bag to conform fully to the contours on the bag face of the layup.
- Place vacuum valves in the layup where required to the bagged assembly. To avoid vacuum valve mark off on the Toolmaster

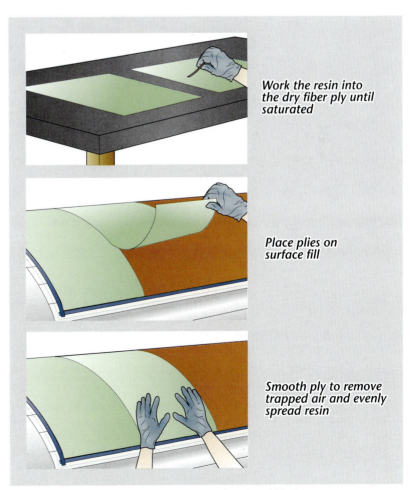

Work the resin into the dry fiber ply until saturated

Place plies on surface fill

Smooth ply to remove trapped air and evenly spread resin

Figure 5-2-5. Lay-up of rectangles on tool surface (filler)

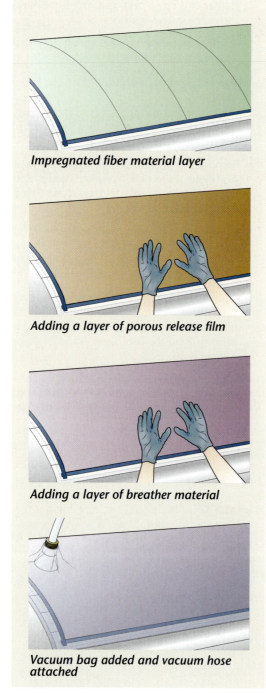

Impregnated fiber material layer

Adding a layer of porous release film

Adding a layer of breather material

Vacuum bag added and vacuum hose attached

Figure 5-2-6. Debulk

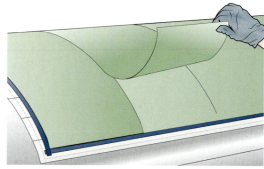

Figure 5-2-7. Application of additional wet layup plies

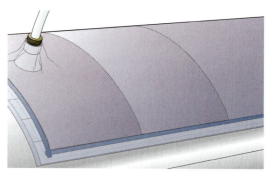

Figure 5-2-8. Final vacuum bag procedure

laminate surface, place the vacuum valve in a folded ear of breather or in the excess area of the layup.

- Seal the vacuum bag and apply full vacuum. Hold for 30 to 60 minutes at ambient temperature.
- During this step as seen in Figure 5-2-6 excess resin will flow through the perforated release film and collect in the bleeder. This step removes air pockets from the layup and compacts the first ply to the surface fill.

Wet lay-up procedure second ply application. The second (2) ply will have the long side of the rectangular prepreg pieces aligned with the 90° direction marked on the tool. Use this alternating pattern throughout the remainder of the laminate ply buildups. Debulk every four plies to improve compaction. Some tools need many plies to achieve the required tool thickness. Figure 5-2-7 shows the application of additional plies.

In general, the alternating 0/90° ply orientation pattern is recommended for most tools manufactured with Toolmaster graphite or fiberglass fabric. However, for some tool designs, particularly those having relatively large flat areas with little or no tool contour, the tool designer may decide that a quasi-isotropic ply layup is necessary involving 45° plies in addition to the 0/90° degree plies.

Take care to stagger the joints of successive plies throughout the layup so that the joint lines of each fabric layer do not coincide with joint lines of previous plies.

When finished with lay-up, cover wet laminate with a peel ply.

Final vacuum bag. Upon completion of the wet layup, a final vacuum bag is applied as seen in Figure 5-2-8.

Prepreg Tooling

During the tool design phase engineers consider certain conditions such as service temperature of the part, vacuum/pressure requirements, production rate (number of parts or uses required) and engineering dimensional tolerances for the final part or assembly. These conditions will govern the decision as to what materials and processes are used when building a tool laminate.

The tool designer should determine the most efficient way to stiffen the design and often bathtub type of flanges are incorporated to add stiffness. Adding reverse flanges about the periphery so that the tool laminate does not directly sit on the edge will increase its durability.

The actual tool laminate construction, including thickness, ply count and fiber orientations are determined by the size and shape of the tool as well as the static and dynamic loads that will be applied to the tool in service. The designer should carefully consider how to remove the part from the mold without causing damage to the mold.

Many composite tools, especially larger ones, need a secondary structure to support the composite tool surface. Light tubular, wood or steel structures, honeycomb or "egg crate," structures are utilized. Some tools have vacuum bag plumbing and locator pins integrated in the design.

Special low-temperature curing prepregs for high-temperature service have been developed that can be used to make high-quality carbon fiber composite tooling. These prepregs can often be cured at initial low cure temperatures followed by an elevated temperature post-cure cycle.

The post-cure is usually done after the substructure has been attached and the tool laminate is removed from the model or pattern. This is called a *free-standing post-cure*. Because the resin system is weak and not entirely cross-linked prior to post-cure, it can easily be damaged if flexed or impacted at this time. For this reason, extreme care should be taken to prevent excessive force on the tool laminate when removing from the mold.

The following paragraphs comprise a general discussion about how to make a prepreg tool. Always follow the prepreg/tooling system manufacturer's instructions because the requirements for a given system may differ.

Prepare the master tool. A master tool containing all the details of the part or component

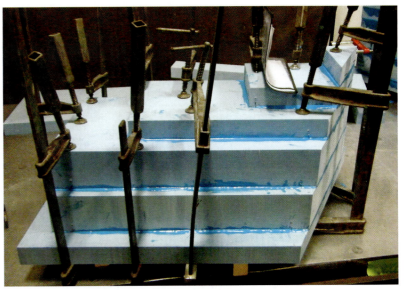

Figure 5-2-9. Tooling board stock material

needs to be built. A CAD/CAM program like CATIA is used to design the tool. The master tool is made from a stack of tooling board as seen in Figure 5-2-9. Figure 5-2-10 shows the tool after the machining process. After machining, the tool needs to be wet sanded and a release system, consisting of sealer and release coats, will be applied. A pre-lay-up vacuum and/or pressure check needs to be conducted to assure that the model surface will hold vacuum or pressure before the lay-up process is started.

Layup prepreg. Special prepreg low-temperature cure epoxy-based resin systems are used to make the composite tool. These prepreg systems may be post-cured to produce high-temperature composite tools. The majority of composite tooling is made from carbon fiber

Figure 5-2-10. Completed master tool

prepreg. Typically long-fiber fabrics are used instead of unidirectional or short fibers.

Most common fabric styles are plain, twill, or satin weaves, with the choice depending on how drape requirements for the tool surface. Satin weave is more drapable than plain weaves. Another disadvantage of plain-weave fabrics compared to the satin weaves is that they have a greater number of open areas at the intersecting yarns that are either void-filled or resin-rich.

The typical ply layup for most composite tools are quasi-isotropic, symmetrical and balanced. The prepreg is cut in smaller rectangles (6 x 10-in., or 15 x 25-cm, tiles) that can be laid up much easier than lager plies. An additional advantage is that a construction of tiles is more vacuum and pressure proof than a tool made of larger ply sizes.

The first layer of tiles is laid up on the tool and it is common practice to overlap the face plies (first layer) approximately 0.08 to 0.4 in. (0.2 to 1.0 cm) at all splice joints. The subsequent layers are butt-spliced but the laminator should offset the subsequent plies at least 1 in. (2.5 cm). The laminator should prevent bridging of the fiber in corners. An accepted practice is to cut the continuous fibers and make splices at or near the corner.

Vacuum debulking of first layer. After the first layer of tiles is placed on the tool, the layup needs to be debulked to consolidate the layup and remove air between the tool surface and the first ply. Sealant tape is placed around the perimeter of the tool and a vacuum bag is placed over the layup. The vacuum bag consists of a layer of porous release film, a bleeder/breather and vacuum bag.

A vacuum port is installed and the air is evacuated. Debulking can be conducted at room temperature or at an elevated temperature (hot debulk). Debulking times range from several minutes to several hours. After the debulking is completed the vacuum bag and materials are removed. The layup is inspected and corrected if necessary before the second ply is laid up. The debulking process is sometimes repeated for every ply or repeated every three or four plies depending on the prepreg tooling system manufacturer's instructions.

Final vacuum bag. Some tools require many plies to achieve the desired tool build-up, and after all plies are laid up on the master tool and have been debulked, the final vacuum bag is applied. Many prepreg manufactures make net resin prepregs that do not need to be bled but older, high-resin content prepreg systems still require a vacuum bag with a bleeder to collect excess resin during the cure.

Prepreg systems with a net resin require a nonporous release film over the complete part and flash tape is used to secure the release film to the master mold. A thick layer of breather material is placed on top and the vacuum bag and several vacuum ports are installed. High-resin systems require a porous release film, bleeder, nonporous release film, breather and vacuum bag with vacuum ports. Most prepreg systems require an autoclave cure to achieve a high tool quality.

Curing of the prepreg composite tool. Consult the prepreg or resin manufacturer's instructions when writing the cure cycle recipe. Incorrect curing operations can lead to a loss of structural or thermal properties in the tool laminate. Accelerating the cure with higher than recommended temperatures can also be detrimental. Generating an exothermic reaction in excess of the resin capabilities can lead to excessive shrinkage, reduced cross-linking, or micro cracking within the laminate.

Most tooling prepregs can be cured at an initial low curing temperature so that the master tool will not be overheated. After the initial cure is completed the tool is removed from the master tool and if necessary the substructure is attached. The tool is placed in the autoclave again for a freestanding high-temperature cure. This post-cure improves the mechanical properties of the tool.

Trimming of cured composite tool. After the tool is cured it needs to be trimmed to the correct size. Often the edges require trimming. Most trimming is accomplished with

Figure 5-2-11. Completed carbon-fiber tool

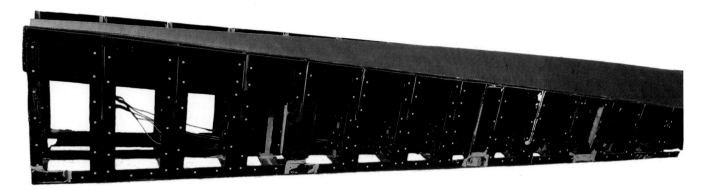

Figure 5-2-12. Tool with substructure

diamond coated high-speed cutting wheels or a water jet followed by sanding with sandpaper. Sometimes additional holes for locator pins need to be drilled in the tool before it is ready for production. Figure 5-2-11 shows the completed trimmed carbon fiber tool.

Inspection and dimension checks. After the tool is complete an inspector will inspect the tool for defects. This inspection method could be visual, coin tap, or ultrasonic. A vacuum and pressure check is performed to check the tool for leaks. The dimensions of the tool need to be checked carefully to ascertain that they fall within the required tolerance.

Substructure design. Most larger tools need a substructure to support the tool. Wood panels or beams, laminated particle wood, metal or composite tubular and beam structures, and even honeycomb panels are used to build a substructure. Figure 5-2-12 shows a carbon fiber box beam structure.

The choice of substructure is driven by cost and cure temperature. If the tooling is used at elevated temperatures the substructure needs to be to withstand the cure cycle. The thermal expansion of the tool needs to be matched to the substructure or provisions such as free-floating attachment points must be made to compensate for thermal expansion. It is important to reduce the weight of the substructure as much as possible. A heavy tool would be a big heat sink and could cause the part to lag significantly behind the autoclave temperature.

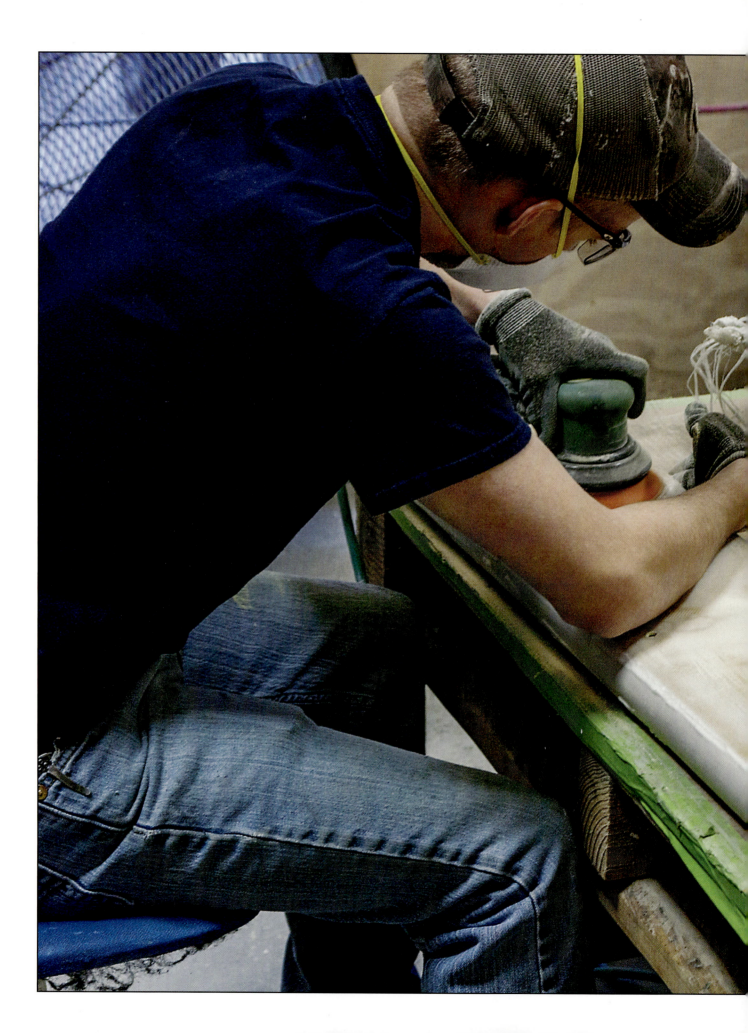

6

Assembly Operations

One of the primary advantages of composite designs is their ability to achieve part-count reductions of up to 60 percent compared to equivalent metallic designs. However, even with these significant reductions, almost all composite structures require some type of post-processing and/or assembly operations. Since both of these can add to the total cost of the product, it is advantageous to minimize these operations when possible.

In addition, many of the post-processing and assembly operations, such as trimming, drilling and fastening, are more expensive for composites than metals. Trimming requires greater care because dull tools or incorrect feeds can cause heat damage or delaminations. Drilling is complicated by the abrasive nature of carbon fibers that can result in accelerated tool wear and splintering of the surface plies. During assembly, composites tend to delaminate if excessive force is used to line up parts often encountered during assembly.

Learning Objective

REVIEW
- machining processes such as machining, drilling, countersinking, reaming and sanding
- special fasteners used in composite material manufacturing
- manufacturing and safety equipment for composite material machining

DESCRIBE
- bonding operations and bonded joint types

EXPLAIN
- mechanical fastening procedures for composite materials

Section 1

Machining Operations

Some general guidelines for machining of carbon-epoxy composites:

- Carbon-epoxy is abrasive by nature. Therefore, precautions should be taken to ensure that the carbon-epoxy dust and particles do not get into precision machine/ground ways of the machine tool, because this could initiate premature tool and machine wear as well.

Left: A technician sands the surface of a composite structure to prepare it for painting and final assembly.

Figure 6-1-1. CNC milling equipment automates many machining operations

- Carbon-epoxy dust can cause electrical components to short out or malfunction. All electronic components should be tightly sealed and have filter systems installed to prevent problems. Since thermoplastic composites generally form chips rather than particulates, electrical problems have not been experienced with these materials.

- Machining processes can be completed dry (with vacuum) or wet. When machining dry, a vacuum system must be used to collect the dust to prevent them from becoming airborne. Enhanced tool life results when these operations are accomplished wet. Typical coolants are tap water or commercially available specialty products.

- It is extremely important for programmers and operators to be familiar with the geometry of plated or brazed diamond tool shapes, because the geometry of the tool will determine feed and speed and quality of the hole.

- Never exceed the length of the cutting edge because this will put too much load on the tool and the tool can fail. If intricate part shapes are involved, use of carbide tooling may be necessary.

Figure 6-1-2. CNC milling tools

Milling

Carbon-epoxy can be milled with conventional and computer numerically controlled (CNC) milling equipment. The tools required for this process need to have a high wear resistance due to the abrasive nature of the carbon epoxy. Face milling, peripheral milling and slot machining processes are all used. See Figure 6-1-1.

The most common tool materials are: solid carbide; relatively inexpensive tool but with short tool life; diamond coated carbine tools, which provide better tool life than solid carbide but are more expensive; and polycrystalline cutting tools which are expensive but experience good tool life and offer higher feed rates than other tool materials. Figure 6-1-2 shows CNC milling tools.

Section 2
Drilling Operations

Hole drilling in composite materials is different from drilling holes in metal aircraft structures. Different types of drill bits, higher speeds and lower feeds are required to drill precision holes. Structures made from carbon fiber and epoxy resin are very hard and abrasive and special flat-flute drills or similar four-flute drills are required.

Aramid fiber (Kevlar®) epoxy composites are not as hard as carbon but are difficult to drill unless special cutters are used the fibers tend to fray or shred unless they are cut clean while embedded in the epoxy. Special drill bits with "clothes pin" points and "fish tail" points have been developed that slice the fibers prior to pulling them out of the drilled hole. If the Kevlar®-epoxy part is sandwiched between two metal parts, standard twist drills can be used. Always use a vacuum dust collection system when drilling composite materials.

Peck drilling (Figure 6-2-1) is a method that uses hard tooling and a power-feed drill motor with lock-in type nose bushings. Peck drilling is a repetitive process of the drill advancing to ever-increasing depths and then withdrawing from the hole to clear the debris and dissipate heat. This "wood-pecking" action continues until the hole is complete.

For deep holes, the drill can be rapid advanced almost to the surface to be cut, then slowed to the preset drilling feed rate to complete another peck cycle. The rapid advance reduces the drilling time, and stopping the rapid advance short prevents damage to the drill, which extends drill life. Peck drilling can be advantageous for drilling through material stack-ups as thick as 1.5 in. (4 cm).

Drill Material

Standard twist drill bits cannot be used for drilling composite structures. Standard high-speed steel drill bits are unacceptable because they dull immediately, generate excessive heat and cause ply delamination, fiber tear-out and unacceptable hole quality. Drill bits used for carbon fiber and fiberglass are made from diamond-coated material or solid carbide because the fibers are so hard.

Drill Types

Typically twist drills are used but brad point drills are also available. The hole quality can

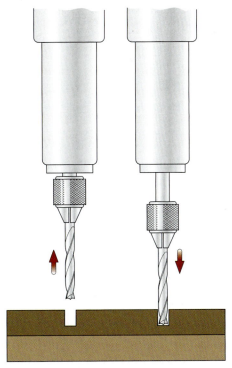

Figure 6-2-1. Peck drilling operation

Figure 6-2-2. Dagger bit

be poor if standard drill bits are used. The preferred drill style for aramid fiber is the dagger (Figure 6-2-2), spade (Figure 6-2-3) or brad point (sickle-shaped Klenk) drill (Figure 6-2-4).

The spade drill was originally developed for reinforced solid laminates and honeycomb sandwich panels with clean entrance and exit surfaces without sacrificial backing. It can easily be resharpened. Carbide or cobalt is generally the drill material of choice as they hold a sharp cutting edge significantly longer than HSS.

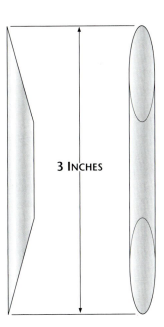

Figure 6-2-3. Spade drill

Figure 6-2-4. Klenk point bit for aramid (Kevlar®) fibers (brad point)

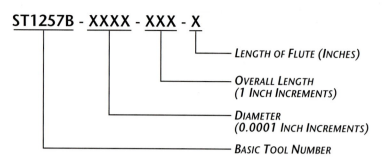

Figure 6-2-5. Typical drill reamer

The sickle-shaped Klenk drill will first pull on the fibers and then shear them which results in a better quality hole. This type of drill bit is best when drilling aramid materials as it minimizes fiber fuzz.

Larger holes can be cut with diamond-coated hole saws or fly cutters, but only use fly cutters in a drill press and not in a drill motor. Carbide or diamond-coated drill bits should be used to minimize backside damage to composites. Use a backup plate, if possible, when drilling.

A straight-fluted carbide drill reamer (Figure 6-2-5) has been found to cut high-quality holes, with minimum backside breakout, in graphite/epoxy and fiberglass materials. These last significantly longer than any other bit except for diamond-coated drills and counter-sinks. Drill reamers are expensive; however, they can be resharpened by tool manufacturers. The sharpening process will render them about 0.001 inches smaller than their original diameter.

Before using sharpened reamers, ensure the smaller diameter will be within tolerance for the fasteners you are installing. Diamond-coated drill bits last the longest and are the preferred drill bit for drilling holes in boron-reinforced composites.

Drilling Equipment

Composite materials are drilled with drill motors operating between 2,000 and 20,000 r.p.m., and a low feed rate is required. Drill motors with a hydraulic dash pod or other type of feed control are (Figure 6-2-6) preferred because they restrict the surging of the drill as it exits the composite materials. This reduces break-out damage and delaminations.

Parts made from unidirectional (tape) products are very susceptible to break-out damage; parts made from fabric material have experienced less damage. The composite structure needs to be backed with a metal plate or sheet to avoid break-out. Holes in composite structures are often pre-drilled with a small pilot hole, enlarged with a diamond-coated or carbide drill bit and reamed with a carbide reamer to final hole size.

Back counterboring is a condition that can occur when carbon-epoxy parts mate metal sub-structure parts. The back edge of the hole in the carbon-epoxy part can be eroded or radiused by metal chips being pulled through the composite. The condition is more prevalent when there are gaps between the parts or when the metal debris is stringy rather than small chips. Back counterboring can be minimized or eliminated by changing feeds and speeds, cutter geometry, better part clamp-up adding a final ream pass, using a peck drill operation, or a combination of these.

When drilling composite parts with metal parts, the metal parts may govern the drilling speed. For example, even though titanium is compatible with carbon-epoxy material from a corrosion perspective, slower drilling speeds are required in order to ensure no metallurgical damage occurs to the titanium. Titanium is drilled with a slow speed and high feed. Drill bits suitable for titanium might not be suitable for carbon or fiberglass.

Drill bits that are used for titanium are often made from cobalt-vanadium and drill bits used for carbon fiber are made from carbide or are diamond-coated to increase drill life and to produce an accurate hole. Small diameter HSS drills, such as the No. 40 drills that are used to manually drill pilot holes, are typically used because carbide drills are relatively brittle and are easily broken. The relatively low cost of these small HSS drills offsets the limited life expectancy. High-speed steel drills may last for only one hole.

Figure 6-2-6. Drill motor with feed control

The most common problem with carbide cutters used in hand-drill operations is handling damage (chipped edges) to cutters. A sharp drill with a slow constant feed can produce a 0.004 in. (0.1 mm) tolerance hole through carbon-epoxy plus thin aluminum, especially if a drill guide is used. With hard tooling, tighter tolerances can be maintained.

When the structure under the carbon-epoxy is titanium, drills can pull titanium chips through the carbon-epoxy and enlarge the hole. In this case a final ream operation may be required to hold tight-hole tolerances.

Carbide reamers are needed for holes through carbon-epoxy composite structure. In addition, the exit end of the hole needs good support to prevent splintering and delaminations when the reamer removes more than about 0.005 in. (0.13 mm) on the diameter. The support can be the substructure or a board held firmly against the back surface.

Typical reaming speeds are about one-half of the drilling speed. Cutting fluids are not normally used or recommended for drilling thin (less than 0.25 in., or 6.3 mm thick) carbon-epoxy structure. It is good practice to use a vacuum while drilling in composite materials to avoid that carbon dust will freely float around the work area.

To obtain good quality holes, portable drill stands or drill guides should be used. Drill motors equipped with feed-rate-limiting surge control are recommended. Steady pressure keeps the drill cutting at a constant rate. When drilling without depth sensors, extra care is needed to control hole depth. The drill should be turning before it contacts the laminate and also as it is being withdrawn from the completed hole. Reduce pressure and avoid tilting the drill, driving the drill chuck into the work or ramming the drill point into hidden material. Just before the drill breaks through the back of the material, reduce the pressure to prevent splintering or fuzzing of fibers on the back face of the laminate.

The drilling process must also be performed incrementally, beginning with a pilot hole. Thus, several sizes of drill bits are required for a drilling operation (e.g., pilot holes, $1/64$-inch undersized and final hole size). Do not continue to use a dull drill bit. If you do, the drill motor slows down, much more force and energy are required, the drill bit will most likely snap, and the resin can overheat.

All of these symptoms can damage, sometimes severely, the composite structure. As soon as any of these symptoms begin, stop and replace the drill bit with a sharp one. Generally, a high-speed, slow-feed method works best. If too much pressure is applied at high speeds, the excessive heat generated can damage the resin causing delamination or fracturing.

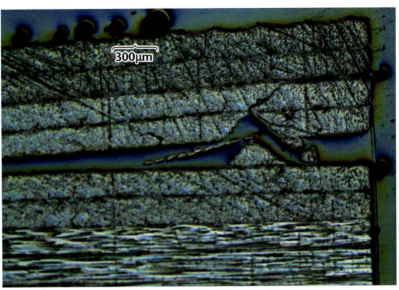

Figure 6-2-7. Hole delamination due to improper drilling

When drilling or reaming, backup material should always be used to prevent delamination, splintering or fraying. Several backup materials have been used successfully, including fiber-board, wood and fiberglass laminates. Clamp the part securely to prevent gaps between the laminate and the backup material or between multiple layers being drilled.

Hole Quality

The quality of the drilled hole is critical; therefore, each hole should be visually inspected to ensure correct hole size and location and proper normality, as well as the absence of unacceptable splintering or fiber breakout, fiber pullout, delaminations, back counterboring, evidence of heat damage and microcracking.

Delamination, separation of bonded composite plies, may occur at the drill entrance due to too fast of a feed rate for the speed, or at the drill exit due to too much feed force on unsupported materials. Splintering or fiber breakout conditions, fibers that break free from the surrounding resin matrix, may occur at the drill entrance or exit, especially in unidirectional material.

Fiber/resin pullout is a tear or breaking out of fibers or resin within a hole or machined edge. Microcracking is the creation of small cracks in the resin surrounding the fibers. Visual discoloration or partial melting of material surrounding a hole (usually worst on the drill exit side) is an indication of heat damage. Figure 6-2-7 shows what can happen when drilling a hole. The drill bit causes the plies to deliminate.

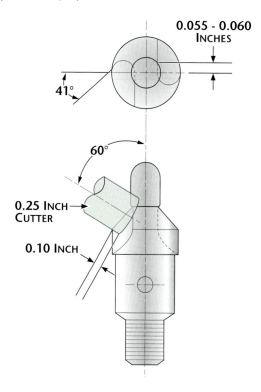

Figure 6-2-8. Countersink for aramid laminates

Countersinking

Countersinking a composite structure is required when flush head fasteners are to be installed in the assembly. For metallic structures, a 100°-included-angle shear or tension-head fastener has been the typical approach. In composite structures, two types of fasteners are commonly used: a 100°-included-angle tension-head fastener or a 130°-included-angle head fastener.

The advantage of the 130° head is that the fastener head can have about the same diameter as a tension head 100° fastener with the head depth of a shear head 100° fastener. For seating flush fasteners in composite parts, it is recommended that the countersink cutters be designed to produce a controlled radius between the hole and the countersink to accommodate the head-to-shank fillet radius on the fasteners. In addition, a chamfer operation or a washer may be required to provide proper clearance for a protruding head fastener's head-to-shank radii. Whichever head style is used, a matching countersink/chamfer must be prepared in the composite structure.

Carbide cutters are used to produce a countersink in carbon-epoxy structure. The countersink cutters usually have straight flutes similar to those used on metals. For Kevlar® fiber-epoxy composites, S-shaped positive rake cutting flutes are used. If straight-fluted countersink cutters are used, a special thick tape can be applied to the surface to allow for a clean cutting of the Kevlar® fibers, but this is not as effective as the S-shaped fluted cutters.

Use of piloted countersink cutters is recommended because it ensures better concentricity between the hole and the countersink with less chance of gaps under the fasteners due to misalignment or delaminations of the part.

Four-flute solid carbide, carbide tipped and polycrystalline diamond insert-type countersinks with pilots should be used for all composites except for aramids, for which fuzzing is not allowed. To prevent fuzzing, aramids require a special grind on the carbide to shear the fibers. Aramid countersinks should have two very sharp flutes with sickle-shaped cutting edges. A tool of this type with a positive rake in the radial direction will prevent peripheral fuzzing. See Figure 6-2-8 for aramid countersink geometry.

A microstop countersink gauge (Figure 6-2-9). should be used to produce consistent countersink wells Do not countersink through more than 70 percent of the skin depth because deeper countersink wells will reduce material strength. When a piloted countersink cutter is used, the pilot must be periodically checked for wear, as wear can cause reduction of concentricity between the hole and countersink. This is especially true for countersink cutters with only one cutting edge.

For piloted countersink cutters, position the pilot in the hole and bring the cutter to full r.p.m. before beginning to feed the cutter into the hole and preparing the countersink. If the cutter is in contact with the composite before triggering the drill motor, splintering may result.

Figure 6-2-9. Microstop countersink

Other Tool Types

Counterbores

Conventional counterbores do not generally produce acceptable holes in composite materials; they have a full-diameter cutting surface that produces abrasive debris that dulls the cutting surfaces and generates excessive heat. Diamond coated circular saws are a better choice.

Reamers

When acceptable hole tolerances cannot be maintained from a hole-drilling process, a reaming operation is needed. High-speed steel reamers are not recommended for any composite as the cutting edge will break down rapidly. Solid carbide reamers are recommended for most applications. Reaming boron requires diamond-coated reamers.

In addition, the exit end of the hole needs good support to prevent splintering and delaminations when the reamer removes more than about 0.005 in. (0.13 mm) on the diameter. The support can be the substructure or a board held firmly against the back surface.

Typical reaming speeds are about one-half of the drilling speed. When the reamer removes about 0.005 in. (0.13 mm) or less on the diameter and surge control is used, the hole can be reamed without backup with little or no splintering or fiber breakout, especially if the composite parts have woven materials as outer layers or if there are bonded-on shims.

Hole Saws

Diamond abrasive hole saws (Figure 6-2-10), used between 100 to 500 r.p.m., are the best choice for cutting fiberglass, boron and graphite-reinforced composites. Traditional hole saws work well on aramid-reinforced composite materials only when used in the reverse cutting direction.

When drill motors are used for damage removal, they are most often used with a diamond-coated hole saw for graphite, fiberglass and boron materials. A toothed hole saw run in reverse is appropriate for cutting aramids and polyethylenes.

A hole saw can easily remove damage from 1 to 3.5 in. (2.5 to 9 cm) in diameter in a very neat, uniform manner. The material being cut should be well supported and firmly backed up with wood or an aluminum plate to prevent backside breakout. Hole saws may also be used to cut through core for damage removal, but only when the damage removal cut is to be made perpendicular with the skin.

Figure 6-2-10. Diamond coated hole saws

When using a hole saw and access to the backside of the structure is available, do not cut the hole all the way through the skin of a sandwich structure unless backup material is used. Failure to use a backup material means a high potential for additional damage on the backside of the structure. The backside skin can easily be delaminated and separated from the core.

If access to the backside skin from the outside is not possible, extreme care must be taken to minimize any damage to the backside skin. Slowing the feed rate down considerably near the moment of penetration can minimize the damage potential.

Use of hole saws. The following practices are recommended with the use of hole saws on graphite composite materials:

- The speed of the motor should remain between 100 and 500 r.p.m.
- The tool should be kept perpendicular to the surface to allow the hole to be machined uniformly.
- The cutter should be dipped in water prior to use for lubrication and cooling.
- Light feed pressure should be applied.
- A backup should be used or the hole should be cut from both sides.
- Fuzz accumulated around the hole should be removed by light wet sanding.

Inspect the hole to ensure no edge delaminations exist or additional backside damage has been created during the cutting operation. If additional damage exists, consult a system-specific technical manual for damage assessment.

Section 3
Sanding and Trimming Operations

Many types of tools are used to trim the edges of composite parts. Personnel protection is very important when sanding and trimming. When trimming edges of laminates, determine the trim line and mark on the part using a suitable pen. Sand the edge of the part to the trim line using either the abrasive sleeve and sanding drum or the 1 in. diameter diamond coated router bit. The 1 in. diameter carbide router bit while not the preferred cutter is a suitable alternate. Do not exceed a feed rate of 15 inches per minute. Break sharp edges after trimming by hand sanding with 150 to 240 silicon carbide abrasive paper. Figure 6-3-1 shows tools for trimming.

Figure 6-3-1. Drills and saw blades used for composite repair

Down- or Side-Draft Booth Tables

For paint removal and machining of cured composite materials, facilities separate from the bonding and curing area are required. Tables and booths with forced ventilation remove harmful materials from the air.

A downdraft table is an efficient and economical device for protecting workers from harmful dust caused by sanding and grinding operations. The tables are also useful housekeeping tools as the majority of particulate material generated by machining operations is immediately collected for disposal.

Downdraft tables should be sized and maintained to have an average face velocity between 100 and 150 cubic feet per minute. The downdraft table will draw contaminants like dust and fibers away from the operators' material. Downdraft tables should be monitored and filters changed on a regular basis to provide

Figure 6-3-2. Down-draft table (center) in a side-draft booth

Figure 6-3-3. Waterjet cutters are well suited to composites.

maximum protection and particulate collection. Figure 6-3-2 shows a down-draft table in a side-draft booth.

Tools

Waterjet

For industrial applications the abrasive waterjet is the preferred method for trimming carbon-epoxy composites. Cut quality and trim accuracy are best controlled using this method. The system uses an abrasive material such as a No. 80 garnet grit that is introduced into the waterjet after the primary jet is formed.

Waterjet cutting produces less cutting force than most of the mechanical machining methods and generally requires only clamping to secure the part, virtually eliminating the need for intricate fixturing methods.

In addition, the waterjet produces no heat-affected zone and can dwell in one spot for some time without widening the cut width. However, the process is quite noisy (requiring ear protection), requires good filtration equipment for the water, must be carefully monitored for jet wear, and has a tendency to produce trail back, especially in thicker materials. This trail back or deflection results in an angled cut on the edge of the work piece but can usually be decreased to acceptable levels with a slower feed rate. Figure 6-3-3 shows a typical waterjet for cutting smaller parts.

Router

A router, as seen in Figure 6-3-4, is a portable, high-speed cutting tool equipped with a base and a guide. It may be used for machining both skin and core material. Normally, the router is used with a template that ensures a smooth and regular cut.

A router is often used for nonround holes or on round holes where access to the back side is limited and the material cannot be backed up to prevent splintering. A router is preferred for core removal operations.

When a router is to be used for damage removal, a template should be fabricated to guide and control the tool accurately and ensure uniform and neat cuts. The template should be config-

Figure 6-3-4. Routers are portable cutting tools.

Figure 6-3-5. Router bits for composite materials

Figure 6-3-6. Die grinders (90° and straight), drill and router

Figure 6-3-7. Orbital sander

ured to take into account the setback of the router guide and the required depth of penetration. If the part surface is curved, the template must be fabricated from a flexible material. Templates may also be necessary to control the depth of the damage removal.

If only the skin is to be removed, the template must follow the contour of the skin. The router should be set to cut through the skin only, leaving the adhesive on the core. If the core is to be removed through to the opposite skin of a non-uniform thickness sandwich, the core near the opposite skin should be cut by hand with a core knife. The skin-to-core bond can be easily broken with peeling action. Cutters $1/4$ in. in diameter may be preferred to $3/8$-in. cutters because of easier tool handling. Tungsten-carbide tools can be used for most applications.

Router bits. Router bits made from carbide work well when cutting all reinforcing fibers except boron. Special angle grinds are available for aramids, graphite and fiberglass. Boron requires diamond-coated router bits and a supply of approved coolant, either water- or alcohol-based.

Aramid routing is done with a split-helix router bit with either two or four helical flutes. Pin router tables should use a $1/4$-in. bit with a template or guide system. Cut in the direction the cutter turns and keep the cutter clean and sharp. Figure 6-3-5 shows a set of router bits for CNC operations.

Die Grinder

The die grinder is a high-speed motor with either a 90° or in-line head. When it is equipped with a silicon-carbide abrasive disc, it is useful for the removal of partial thickness damage to composite laminates and tapering (scarfing) the perimeter of the damage removal areas.

The die grinder is also used for partial depth removal of damaged core. Grinders (direct-drive) with abrasive discs are not recommended for paint removal. The use of nonoscillating grinders to remove coatings can remove too much material resulting in substrate damage.

Orbital-type sanders and hand sanding are the recommended methods for paint removal. Figure 6-3-6 shows straight and 90° die grinders.

Saws

Oscillating saw. An oscillating saw equipped with a diamond cutter blade is the quickest way to cut damaged laminates. The tool is easy to control, produces uniform cuts, and has a rapid material removal rate. The main disadvantage of the oscillating saw is that its use is limited to straight cuts or cuts with very slight curves.

Reciprocating saws. Saws that reciprocate the blade, commonly known as saber saws should be avoided because the constant changing blade direction imposes forces on the surface plies that tend to delaminate composites. These saws can be either air or electric powered.

Sanders

Sanding can be performed either by hand or with power tools such as the pneumatic right-angle die grinder, dual action (DA) sander or jitterbug-type sanders. Figure 6-3-7 shows an orbital sander.

Utility Knives, Scissors and Rotary Cutters

Utility knives and rotary cutters are commonly used for cutting prepregs and wet laminates. Utility knives with quick-change, retractable blades are preferred because blades must be changed often. Quick-change retractable utility knives provide increased productivity and enhanced safety. Scissors are used to cut dry fabrics. Figure 6-3-8 shows a series of hand tools and Figure 6-3-9 shows a series of electric cutters.

Ultrasonic Knives

An ultrasonic knife is a hand-held, portable instrument designed for cutting and trimming composite prepregs and other hard-to-cut materials.

Ultrasonic knives provide pattern shape versatility and produces precise cuts that do not disturb the fiber orientation. Hand and arm fatigue associated with knives and shears can be eliminated. Speeds should be governed by the material type and thickness.

Abrasives

Abrasives are miniature cutting surfaces combined to form a tool. They are derived from abrasive grains—hard crystals either natural or manufactured.

The most commonly used abrasive materials are aluminum oxide, silicon carbide, cubic boron nitride and diamond. Other materials such as garnet, zirconia, glass, and even walnut shells are used for some applications. Three-dimensional abrasive medium such as Scotch-Brite™ are very useful for preparing bonded areas. Figure 6-3-10 shows different types of sandpaper.

Figure 6-3-8. Utility knives, scissors and rotary cutters

Figure 6-3-9. Electric cutters

Figure 6-3-10. Abrasives such as sandpaper and Scotch-Brite™

Figure 6-3-11. Cutoff wheel

Figure 6-3-12. Sanding discs

Cutoff Wheels

Cutoff wheels for composites are of two main types: fiber reinforced abrasive wheels and steel wheels with a diamond-grit coated edge. The fiber discs can wear rapidly, and if they bind in the cut, the disc can fracture. Fiber reinforced abrasive cutoff wheels that have been fractured can explode when run up to a high r.p.m. (20,000 r.p.m.). It is better to use diamond cutoff discs. They cost much more than fiber-reinforced abrasives, but if used properly, they can last for years and are safer to use. Figure 6-3-11 shows a die grinder with cutoff wheel.

Coated Abrasive Discs

Coated abrasive discs (Figure 6-3-12) have an abrasive mineral bonded to a paper or fiber backing. Aluminum oxide and silicon carbide are the two abrasives most commonly used for aerospace applications. Silicon carbide is the preferred type of abrasive media because it stays sharp longer than aluminum oxide. Coated abrasive discs are the most frequently used discs for machining composite repair joints. These discs are usually mounted on a 90° die grinder motor, but other tools may be used when conditions merit. Various grit sizes are required (80 to 150 grit for rough sanding and 150 to 240 grit for finish sanding).

Bristle Discs

Bristle discs (Figure 6-3-13) are round discs with many individual bristles on their working face. These bristles have embedded abrasive material that provides the cutting power of the disc. The abrasive bristles provide sharp abrasive media as the individual fingers wear down. The bristles also prevent clogging of the abrasive by coatings, sealants or adhesives. Bristle discs are available in a variety of grit sizes and disc diameters.

Surface Conditioning Pads and Discs

Surface conditioning pads and discs (Figure 6-3-14) differ from abrasive discs in that the abrasive media is bonded to an open synthetic mesh. The advantage of this type of disc is that it more readily conforms to contoured surfaces and is less likely to be clogged with paints or sealants during the coating removal process. Surface conditioning pads are less efficient at material removal; therefore, they are not recommended for repair joint machining. Surface conditioning pads are excellent for preparing bare metal surfaces for bonding.

Figure 6-3-13. Bristle disc

Figure 6-3-14. Surface conditioning pad

Band Saw

Band saws (Figure 6-3-15) are used to trim composite parts and to cut all materials necessary for the production of tooling. The main difference between band saws used in wood and metal shops is the blade. A traditional blade with teeth cannot be used for cutting composite materials because the teeth will wear very quickly. A special blade with a toothless diamond cutting edge is used. These blades cut composites easily and produce a fine cut.

Composites are cut at high speed and low feed rates to produce the best possible cut. The band saw in the shop should be used only for cutting composites because cutting other materials with the toothless diamond blade can damage the blade. If contour cuts are required, a blade with a smaller width must be installed. A blade width of $1/4$-inch is often utilized for contour cutting. A vacuum system should be used to collect carbon fiber or fiberglass dust. Always wear safety glasses and keep your hands away from the blade by using push tools.

Table Saw

Table saws (Figure 6-3-16) are often used in composite shops to cut a wide range of materials for the fabrication of tooling. Always select the correct blade for the material. Wood and some tooling boards and foams require a blade with teeth.

Figure 6-3-16. Table saw

If composite materials are cut on a table saw, change to a toothless diamond blade. Use great care around this equipment. Always use the safety devices installed on the table saw and wear safety glasses.

Section 4

Mechanical Fastening and Adhesive Bonding

It would be difficult to conceive of a structure that did not involve some type of joint. Joints often occur in transitions between major composite parts and a metal feature or fitting.

In aircraft, such a situation is represented by articulated fittings on control surfaces as well as on wing and tail components that require the capability to pivot the element during operation. Tubular elements such as power shafting often use metal end fittings to connect to power sources or for articulation where changes in direction are needed. In addition, assembly of the structure from its constituent parts will involve either bonded or mechanically fastened joints or both.

Joints represent one of the greatest challenges in the design of structures in general and in composite structures in particular. The reason for this is that joints entail interruptions of the geometry of the structure and, often, material

Figure 6-3-15. A band saw with the proper blade works well for cutting composites.

discontinuities, which almost always produce local highly, stressed areas, except at certain idealized types of adhesive joints such as scarf joints between similar materials.

Stress concentrations in mechanically fastened joints are particularly severe because the load transfer between elements of the joint has to take place over a fraction of the available area. For mechanically fastened joints in metal structures, local yielding, which has the effect of eliminating stress peaks as the load increases, can usually be depended on.

Such joints can be designed to some extent by the *P over A* approach—that is by assuming that the load is evenly distributed over load bearing sections so that the total load (P) divided by the available area (A) represents the stress that controls the strength of the joint. In organic matrix composites, such a stress reduction effect is realized only to a minor extent, and stress peaks predicted to occur by elastic stress analysis have to be accounted for, especially for onetime monotonic loading.

In the case of composite adherents, the intensity of the stress peaks varies with the orthotropy of the adherend in addition to various other material and dimensional parameters that affect the behavior of the joint for isotropic adherends.

In principle, adhesive joints are structurally more efficient than mechanically fastened joints because they provide better opportunities for eliminating stress concentrations; for example, the ductile response of the adhesive reduces stress peaks. Mechanically fastened joints tend to use the available material inefficiently.

Sizeable regions exist where the material near the fastener is nearly unloaded, and these must be compensated for by regions of high stress to achieve a particular average load. As mentioned above, certain types of adhesive joints, namely scarf joints between components of similar stiffness, can achieve a nearly uniform stress state throughout the joint.

Mechanically fastened joints differ from bonded composite joints in one further aspect: the presence of holes ensures that the joint strength can never exceed the local laminate strength. Indeed, after years of research and development, it appears that only the most carefully designed bolted composite joints will be even half as strong as the basic laminate.

The simpler bolted joint configurations will attain no more than a third of the laminate strength. In many cases, however, mechanically fastened joints cannot be avoided because of requirements for disassembly of the joint for replacement of damaged structure or to achieve access to underlying structure.

In addition, adhesive joints tend to lack structural redundancy and are highly sensitive to manufacturing deficiencies, including poor bonding technique, poor fit of mating parts

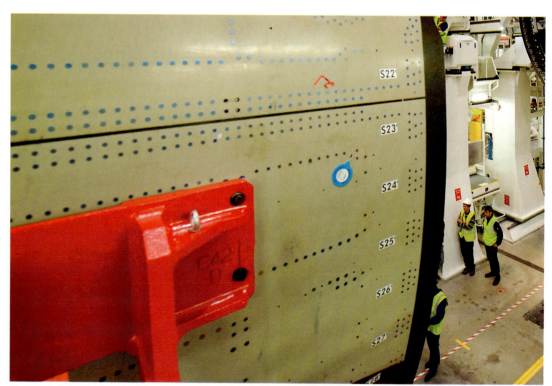

Figure 6-4-1. Final assembly of composite structures may involve mechanical fasteners. *Courtesy of Airbus*

and sensitivity of the adhesive to temperature and environmental effects such as moisture. Assurance of bond quality has been a continuing problem in adhesive joints; while ultrasonic and X-ray inspection may reveal gaps in the bond, there is no present technique that can guarantee a bond that appears to be intact does, in fact, have adequate load transfer capability.

Surface preparation and bonding techniques have been well developed, but the possibility that lack of attention to detail in the bonding operation may lead to such deficiencies needs constant alertness on the part of fabricators. Thus mechanical fastening tends to be preferred over bonded construction in highly critical and safety-rated applications such as primary aircraft structural components, especially in large commercial transports, since assurance of the required level of structural integrity is easier to guarantee in mechanically fastened assemblies.

Bonded construction tends to be more prevalent in smaller aircraft. For non-aircraft applications as well as in non-flight-critical aircraft components, bonding is likewise frequently used.

Mechanical Fastened Joints

Aircraft are made from several major sections that are often joined with mechanical fasteners. Figure 6-4-1 shows the major parts of an aircraft joined during final assembly. The behavior of composites in bolted joints differs considerably from what occurs with metals.

The brittle nature of composites necessitates more detailed analysis to quantify the level of various stress peaks as stress concentrations dictate part static strength to a larger extent than in metals (no local yielding). As a result, composite joint design is more sensitive to edge distances and hole spacings than metal joint designs.

Low through-the-thickness composite laminate strength has led to specialized fasteners for composites and eliminated the use of rivets (Figure 6-4-2). The special fasteners feature larger tail footprint areas that improve pull-through and bearing strengths. Galvanic corrosion susceptibility between carbon and aluminum has all but eliminated the use of aluminum fasteners.

Mechanically-fastened joints can be divided into single-row and multi-row designs. Typical lightly loaded non-critical joints require a single row of fasteners. The root joint of a wing, or a control surface, is an example of a highly loaded joint, where the entire load accumulated on the aerodynamic surface is off-loaded into another structure. The bolt pattern design,

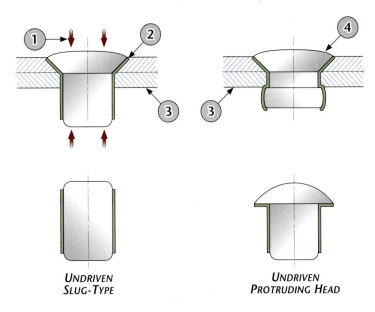

1. Optimum sleeve expansion inside hole provided by equal area on both ends of rivet for upset force.
2. Sleeve is a corrosion barrier
3. Carbon-epoxy structure, aluminum structure, or combinations of titanium and steel
4. Rivet head milling after installation is not required

Figure 6-4-2. Sleeved rivets have a corrosion barrier between the rivet and the composite material

consisting of several rows, distributes the load for more efficient transfer.

Load sharing in mechanically fastened joints is strongly dependent on the number, the diameter and the material of the bolts and the stiffness of joining members. For a single in-line row of bolts, the first and the last bolt will be more highly loaded if the plates are of uniform stiffness. This is illustrated in Figure 6-4-3 in which, in addition to the equal stiffness members (configuration 2), other combinations of fastener diameters/plate configurations are shown, which can alter the bolt distributions appreciably.

Clamp-up forces have been shown to have a significant effect on laminate failure, particularly under fatigue loading. Clamp-up can suppress delamination failure modes, and changes the fastener head restraint.

This effect cannot be included in the two-dimensional analysis methods described above. Before taking advantage of the beneficial effects of clamp-up, long-term relaxation of the laminate stresses should be considered. Because of this effect, minimum clamp-up (if possible) should be used when conducting bolt bearing tests, that is finger tight or 10 to 20 in.-lbs. (1 to 2 N-m) torque up on a $1/4$ in. (6.4 mm) diameter bolt. This may not be the normal torque installation of the fastener.

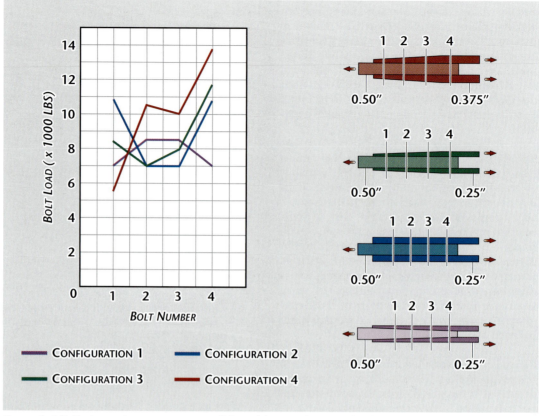

Figure 6-4-3. Fasteners in a row may not all be subject to the same load.

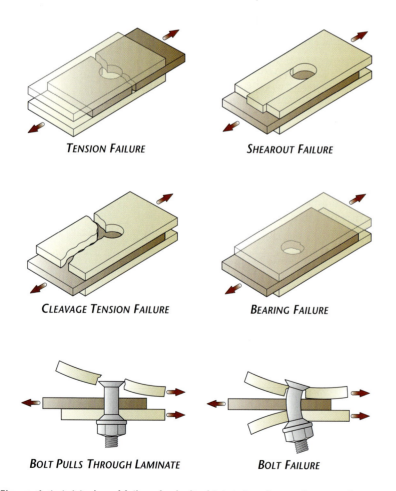

Figure 6-4-4. Modes of failure for bolted joints in advanced composites

Failure Criteria

The design of a mechanically fastened joint must assure against all possible failures of the joint. These are illustrated in Figure 6-4-4. Accepted design practice is to select edge distances, plate thicknesses and fastener diameters so that of all the possible failure modes probable failures would be net section and bearing.

Highly loaded structural joints should be designed to fail in a bearing mode to avoid the catastrophic failures associated with net section failures. Although this is a commendable goal, particularly for single-bolt joints, it is impractical in most cases, as the increase in edge distances adds weight to the structure. For usual width-to-bolt diameter ratios of six, both net and bearing failures are possible, and the stress engineer is satisfied if he or she can show a positive margin against both failure modes.

The engineer does not try to get a higher margin for net failure than for bearing failure. Steering the joint design to have bearing failures by having large bearing allowables may result in in-service problems of bolt hole wear, fuel leakage and fastener fatigue failures. Furthermore, net tension failure is unavoidable for multi-row joints. Figure 6-4-5 shows the problem with flush fasteners used in composite fittings.

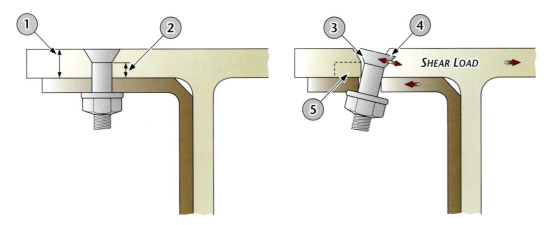

1. Full thickness that would have been available for bearing on a protruding head fastener
2. Reduced effective bearing area for countersunk fastener
3. Fastener moves out of contact underneath countersunk head
4. Contact here aggravates bearing load on shank
5. Primary bearing area on shank of bolt must fail before contact under the head can be re-established

Figure 6-4-5. Problems associated with flush fasteners in composite structures

Fasteners Used with Composite Laminates

Many companies make specialty fasteners for composite structures and several types of fasteners are commonly used—threaded fasteners, lock bolts, blind bolts, blind rivets and specialty fasteners for soft structures such as honeycomb panels. The main differences between fasteners for metal and composite structures are: the materials and the footprint diameter of nuts and collars.

Corrosion Precautions

Neither fiberglass nor Kevlar® fiber-reinforced composites cause corrosion problems when used with most fastener materials. Composites reinforced with carbon fibers, however, are quite cathodic when used with materials such as aluminum or cadmium, the latter of which is a common plating used on fasteners for corrosion protection.

Fastener Materials

Titanium alloy Ti-6Al-4V is the most common alloy for fasteners used with carbon fiber-reinforced composite structures. Austenitic stainless steels, superalloys such as A286, multiphase alloys such as MP35N or MP159, and nickel alloys such as alloy 718 also appear to be very compatible with carbon fiber composites.

Fastener System for Sandwich Honeycomb Structures

The adjustable sustain preload (Asp®) fastening system provides a simplified method of fastening composite, soft core, metallic or other materials that are sensitive to fastener clamp-up or installation force conditions. Clamping force can be infinitely adjustable within maximum recommended torque limits and no further load is applied during installation of the lock collar. The fastener is available in two types: the Asp has a full shank and the 2Asp has a pilot-type shank. Figure 6-4-6 shows the Asp system and Figure 6-4-7 shows the installation sequence.

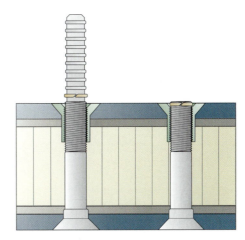

Figure 6-4-6. Asp fastener system for honeycomb sandwich structures

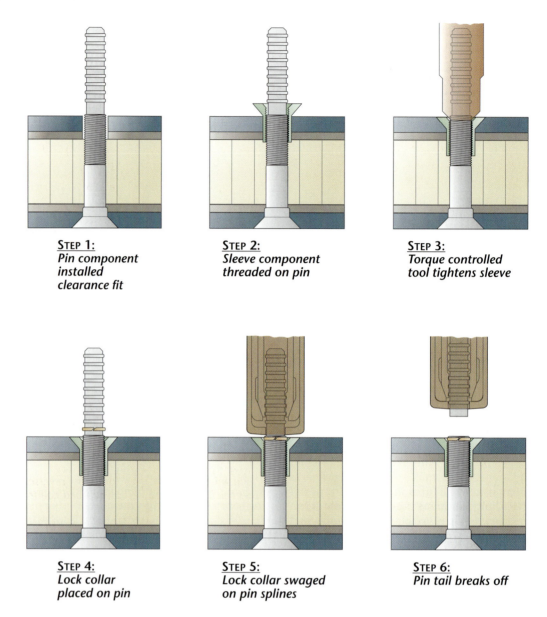

Figure 6-4-7. Asp fastener system installation sequence

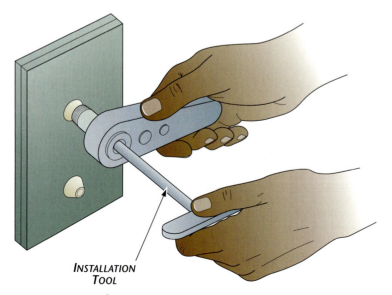

Figure 6-4-8. Hi-Lok® bolt installation

Hi-Lok® and LockBolt Fasteners

Most composite primary structures for the aircraft industry are fastened with Hi-Loks (manufactured by Hi-Shear Corp.), or LockBolts, (from Huck International, Inc.), for permanent installations. The Hi-Lok® is a threaded fastener that incorporates a hex key in the threaded end to react the torque applied to the collar during installation. The collar includes a frangible portion that separates at a predetermined torque value. Figure 6-4-8 shows the installation technique for Hi-Loks.

The LockBolt incorporates a collar that is swaged into annular grooves. It comes in pull-type and stump-type models. The pull-type is the most common, where a frangible pintail is used to react the axial load during the swaging of the collar. When the swaging load reaches a

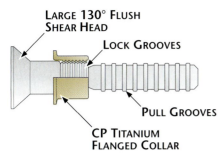

Figure 6-4-9. HUCKCOMP LockBolt

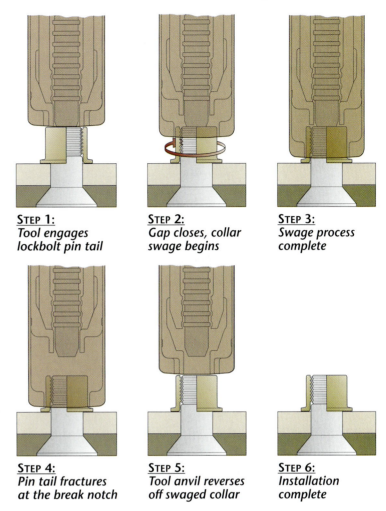

Step 1: Tool engages lockbolt pin tail

Step 2: Gap closes, collar swage begins

Step 3: Swage process complete

Step 4: Pin tail fractures at the break notch

Step 5: Tool anvil reverses off swaged collar

Step 6: Installation complete

Figure 6-4-10. HUCKCOMP LockBolt installation sequence

predetermined limit, the pintail breaks away at the breakneck groove.

The installation of the Hi-Lok® and the pull-type Lockbolt can be performed by one technician from one side of the structure. The stump-type Lockbolt, on the other hand, requires support on the head side of the fastener to react the swage operation. This method is usually reserved for automated assembly of detail structure where access is not a problem.

The differences in these fasteners for composite structure in contrast to metal structure are small. For the Hi-Lok®, material compatibility is the only issue; aluminum collars are not recommended. Standard collars of A286, 303 stainless steel and titanium alloy are normally used.

The LockBolt requires a hat-shaped collar that incorporates a flange to spread the high bearing loads during installation. The LockBolt pin designed for use in composite structures has six annular grooves as opposed to five for metal structure. Figure 6-4-9 shows a Lockbolt and Figure 6-4-10 shows a LockBolt installation technique.

Eddie-Bolt® Fasteners

Eddie-Bolt® fasteners (Alcoa) are similar in design to Hi-Loks and are a natural choice for carbon fiber composite structures. The Eddie-Bolt pin is designed with flutes in the threaded portion, which allows a positive lock to be made during installation using a specially designed mating nut or collar. The mating nut has three lobes that serve as driving ribs.

During installation, at a predetermined pre-load, the lobes compress the nut material into the flutes of the pin and form the locking feature. The natural advantage for composite structure is that titanium alloy nuts can be used for compatibility and weight saving without the fear of galling. The nuts spin on freely, and the locking feature is established at the end of the installation cycle. Figure 6-4-11 shows Eddie-Bolt® fasteners.

Figure 6-4-11. Eddie-Bolt® fasteners
Courtesy of Alcoa Global Fasteners, Inc.

Cherry's E-Z Buck® Hollow Rivet

The Cherry hollow-end E-Z Buck® rivet (Figure 6-4-12) is made from titanium-columbium alloy and has a shear strength of 40 k.s.i. The E-Z Buck® rivet is designed to be used in a double-flush application for fuel tanks.

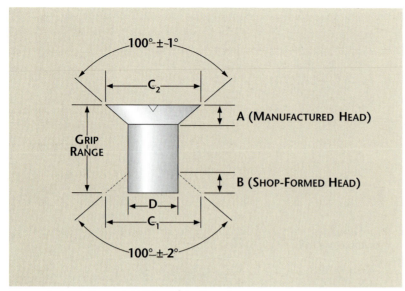

Figure 6-4-12. Cherry's E-Z Buck® hollow rivet

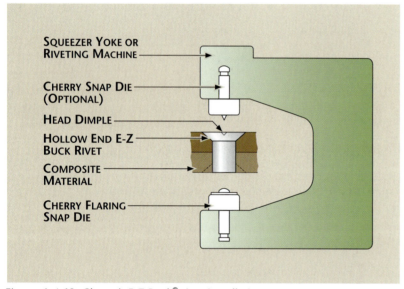

Figure 6-4-13. Cherry's E-Z Buck® rivet installation process

The main advantage of this type of rivet is that its installation takes less than half the force of a solid rivet of the same material. The rivets are installed with automated riveting equipment or a rivet squeezer, as shown in Figure 6-4-13. There are also optional dies that ensure that the squeezer is always centered during installation and won't damage the structure.

Blind Fasteners

Composite structures do not require as many fasteners as metal aircraft because stiffeners and doublers are often co-cured with the skins. The size of panels on aircraft has increased in composite structures which causes backside inaccessibility. Therefore blind fasteners or screws and nutplates must be used in these areas. Many manufacturers make blind fasteners for composite structures and a few are discussed below.

Blind bolts. The Cherry Maxibolt® (Figure 6-4-14) is available in titanium for compatibility with composite structures. The shear strength of the Maxibolt is 95 k.s.i. The Maxibolt can be installed from one side with a pneumatic-hydraulic installation tool. The Maxibolt is available in 100° flush head, 130° flush head and protruding head styles.

The Alcoa UAB™ blind bolt system is designed for composite structures and is available in titanium and stainless steel (Figure 6-4-15). It is available in 100° flush head, 130° flush head and protruding head styles.

The Accu-Lok™ Blind Fastening System is designed specifically for use in composite structures where access is limited to one side of the structure. It combines high joint preload with a large-diameter footprint on the blind

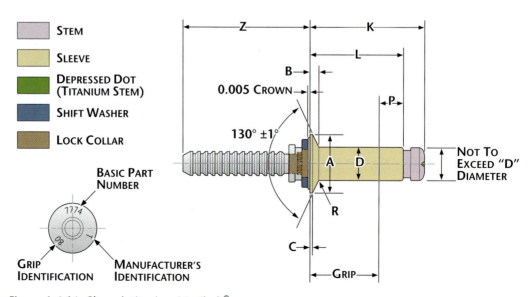

Figure 6-4-14. Cherry's titanium Maxibolt®

side. The large footprint enables distribution of the joint preload over a larger area, thus virtually eliminating the possibility of delaminating the composite structure. The shear strength of the Accu-Lok™ is 95 k.s.i., and it is available in 100° flush head, 130° flush head and protruding head styles. A similar fastener is designed by Monogram and is called the radial lock.

Screws and Nutplates in Composite Structures

The use of screws and nutplates in place of Hi-Loks or blind fasteners is recommended if a panel has to be removed periodically for maintenance. Nutplates used in composite structures usually require three holes—two for attachment of the nutplate and one for the removable screw—although rivetless nut plates and adhesive bonded nutplates are available that do not require drilling and countersinking two extra holes.

Adhesive Joints

Adhesive bonding is a reliable, proven and widely established technique for joining metals, plastics, composites and many other substrates. Bonding eliminates the need for holes and avoids subjecting the joint to welding temperatures that weaken metals. The cured adhesive, unlike rivets or bolts, ensures even distribution of stresses, leading to improved fatigue performances.

Because of a lack of reliable inspection methods and a requirement for close dimensional tolerances in fabrication, aircraft designers have generally avoided bonded construction in primary structure. Figure 6-4-16 shows a comparison of a mechanical and bonded joint.

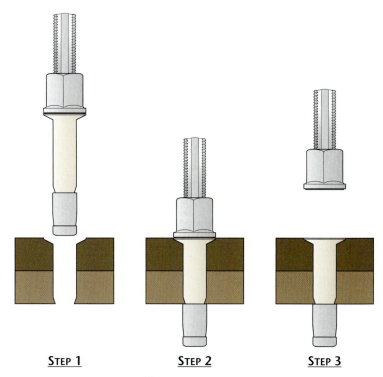

Figure 6-4-15. The Accu-Lok™ installation sequence

The riveted joint is highly stressed in the vicinity of the rivets (as shown by the arrows in Figure 6-4-16) and failure tends to initiate in these areas of peak stress. A similar distribution of stress occurs with spot welds and bolts. The bonded joint, however, is uniformly stressed. A continuous welded joint is likewise uniformly stressed but the metal in the heated zone will have undergone a change in performance.

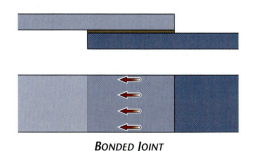 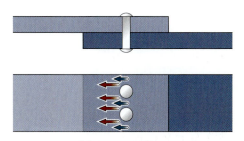

Figure 6-4-16. Comparison of mechanical and bonded joints

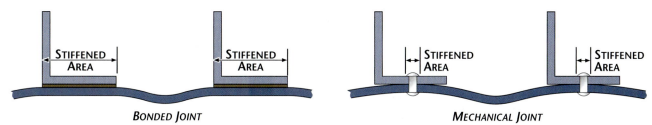

Figure 6-4-17. Bonded joints stiffen the structure differently than mechanical joints.

TENSION

COMPRESSION

SHEAR

CLEAVAGE

PEEL

Figure 6-4-18. Stresses in a bonded joint

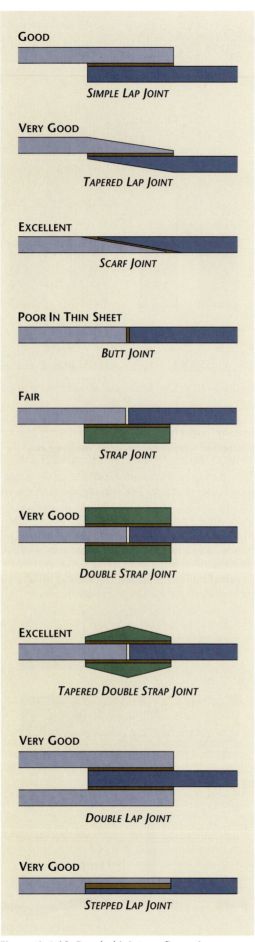

Figure 6-4-19. Bonded joint configurations

Figure 6-4-17 shows how a joint may be designed to take advantage of the stiffening effect of bonding. Adhesives form a continuous bond between the joint surfaces. Rivets and spot welds pin the surfaces together only at localized points. Bonded structures are consequently much stiffer and loading may be increased (by up to 30 to 100 percent) before buckling occurs.

Bonded joints may be subjected to a range of stresses including tensile, compressive, shear, peel or a combination of these. Figure 6-4-18 illustrates the range of stresses.

Adhesives perform best in shear, compression and tension. They behave relatively poorly under peel and cleavage loading. A bonded joint therefore needs to be designed so that the loading stresses will be directed along the lines of the adhesive's greatest strengths.

The basic types of bonded joints are shown in Figure 6-4-19. In practical structures two or more basic types may be used in combination and the relative dimensions of the joints may vary from those. In most cases the stress distribution throughout the joint can be improved by leaving intact the small amount of resin squeeze-out (fillet) and tapering the overlap to remove the sharp, right-angle ends.

Large sheets of thin-gauge material (metal or composites) may be stabilized by bonded stiffeners made of the same material in similar gauge. Figure 6-4-20 shows a "top hat" stiffener. Towards the edge of the sheet, the stiffener may be cut away (as shown) in order to reduce stress concentrations. The effect is similar to that of the scarf joint shown in Figure 6-4-19.

Figure 6-4-21 shows a series of typical bonded joint configurations. Adhesive joints in general are characterized by high stress concentrations in the adhesive layer. These originate, in the case of shear stresses, because of unequal axial straining of the adherends, and in the case of peel stresses, because of eccentricity in the load path.

Considerable ductility is associated with shear response of typical adhesives, which is beneficial in minimizing the effect of shear stress joint strength. Response to peel stresses tends to be much more brittle than that to shear stresses, and reduction of peel stresses is desirable for achieving good joint performance.

From the standpoint of joint reliability, it is vital to avoid letting the adhesive layer be the weak link in the joint. This means that, whenever possible, the joint should be designed to ensure that the adherends fail before the bond layer.

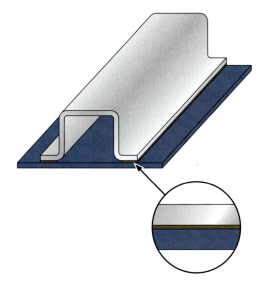

Figure 6-4-20. Bonded top-hat sections are used to stiffen panels

Failure in the adherends is fiber controlled, while failure in the adhesive is resin dominated, and thus subject to effects of voids and other defects, thickness variations, environmental effects, processing variations, deficiencies in surface preparation and other factors that are not always adequately controlled. This is a significant challenge, since adhesives are inherently much weaker than the composite or metallic elements being joined. However, the objective can be accomplished by recognizing the limitations of the joint geometry being considered and placing appropriate restrictions on the thickness dimensions of the joint for each geometry.

Figure 6-4-22 shows a progression of joint types that represent increasing strength capability from the lowest to the highest in the figure. In each type of joint, the adherend thickness may be increased as an approach to achieving higher load capacity.

When the adherends are relatively thin, results of stress analyses show that for all of the joint types in Figure 6-4-22, the stresses in the bond will be small enough to guarantee that the adherends will reach their load capacity before failure can occur in the bond. As the adherend thicknesses increase, the bond stresses become relatively larger until a point is reached at which bond failure occurs at a lower load than that for which the adherends fail. This leads to the general principle that for a given joint type, the adherend thicknesses should be restricted to an appropriate range relative to the bond layer thickness.

Because of processing considerations and defect sensitivity of the bond material, bond layer thicknesses are generally limited to 0.005 to

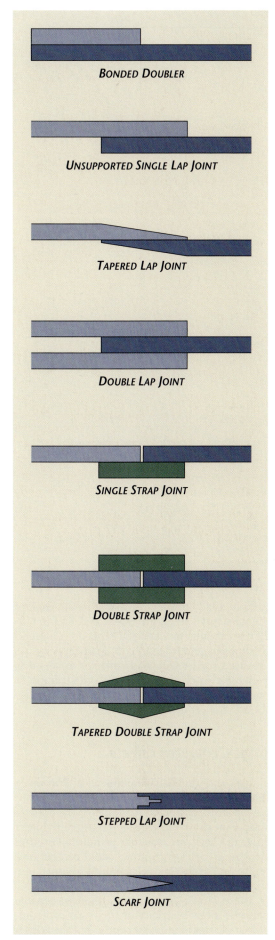

Figure 6-4-21. Adhesive joint types

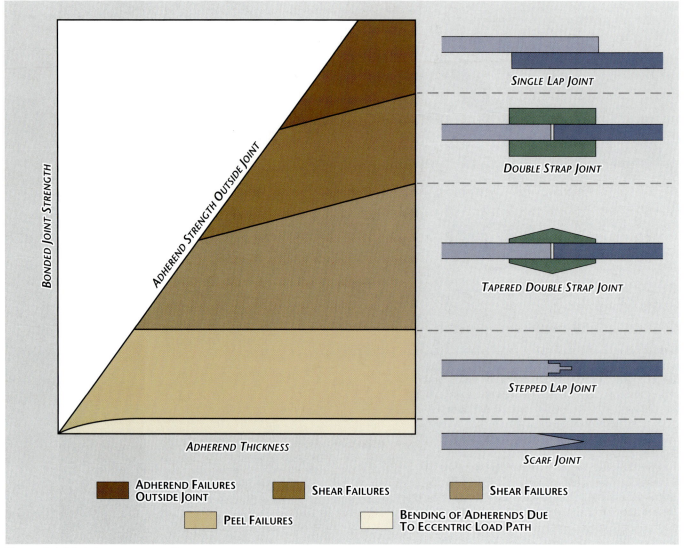

Figure 6-4-22. Joint geometry effects

0.015 in. (0.125 to 0.39 mm). As a result, each of the joint types in Figure 6-4-21 and Figure 6-4-22 corresponds to a specific range of adherend thicknesses and, therefore, of load capacity. As the need for greater load capacity arises, it is preferable to change the joint configuration to one of higher efficiency rather than to increase the adherend thickness indefinitely.

Joint Geometry Effects

Single- and double-lap joints with uniformly thick adherends, such as the unsupported single-lap joint, the double-lap joint and the double-strap joint shown in Figure 6-4-21, are the least efficient. They are suitable primarily for thin structures with low running loads (load per unit width, i.e., stress times element thickness).

Of these, single-lap joints are the least capable because the eccentricity of this type of geometry generates significant bending of the adherends that magnifies the peel stresses. Peel stresses are also present in the case of symmetric double-lap and double-strap joints and become a limiting factor on joint performance when the adherends are relatively thick.

Tapering of the adherends, as illustrated by the tapered lap joint and the tapered double-strap joint in Figure 6-4-21, can be used to eliminate peel stresses in areas of the joint where the peel stresses are tensile, which is the case of primary concern. No tapering is needed at ends of the overlap where the adherends butt together because the transverse normal stresses at that location is compressive and rather small.

Likewise, for double strap joints under compressive loading, there is no concern with peel stresses at either location since the transverse extensional stresses that do develop in the adhesive are compressive in nature rather than tensile; indeed, where the gap occurs, the inner adherends bear directly on each other and no stress concentrations are present there for the compression loading case.

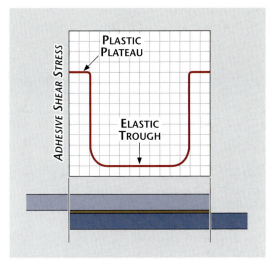

Figure 6-4-23. Typical bond line shear stress distribution

For joints between adherends of identical stiffness, scarf joints (Figure 6-4-20) are theoretically the most efficient, having the potential for complete elimination of stress concentrations. In practice, some minimum thickness corresponding to one- or two-ply thicknesses must be incorporated at the thin end of the scarfed adherend leading to the occurrence of stress concentrations in these areas.

In theory, any desirable load capability can be achieved in the scarf joint by making the joint long enough and thick enough. However, practical scarf joints may be less durable because of a tendency toward creep failure associated with a uniform distribution of shear stress along the length of the joint unless care is taken to avoid letting the adhesive be stressed into the nonlinear range. As a result, scarf joints tend to be used only for repairs of very thin structures.

Scarf joints with unbalanced stiffnesses between the adherends do not achieve the uniform shear stress condition of those with balanced adherends, and are somewhat less structurally efficient because of rapid buildup of load near the thin end of the thicker adherend.

Stepped lap joints (Figure 6-4-21) represent a practical solution to the challenge of bonding thick members. This type of joint provides manufacturing convenience by taking advantage of the layered structure of composite laminates. In addition, high loads can be transferred if many short steps of sufficiently small "rise" (i.e., thickness increment) in each step are used, while maintaining sufficient overall length of the joint.

If the distribution of the shear stresses in the bond line is not uniform the stresses peak at the ends of bonded joint. Simply making the overlap larger does not necessarily mean that the total bond strength will improve. The high stresses at the end of the joints will initiate failure at these locations. Tapering the ends of the adherends will decrease the shear stresses at the ends of single-lap joints. Figure 6-4-23 shows the bond line shear stress distribution for a single-lap joint.

Figure 6-4-24 shows how the high shear stresses at the end of the bonded joint can be controlled. Figure 6-4-24A shows a step joint in which the shear stresses are made more uniform by making several small bond areas.

This type of joint will have improved bond. Figure 6-4-24B shows a scarf joint and in theory it is possible to design such a joint in a way that the stress is uniform.

Effects of Bond Defects

Defects in adhesive joints that are of concern include surface preparation deficiencies, voids and porosity and thickness variations in the bond layer. Of these, surface preparation deficiencies are probably the greatest concern.

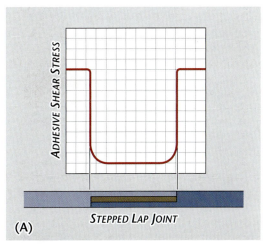

(A) STEPPED LAP JOINT

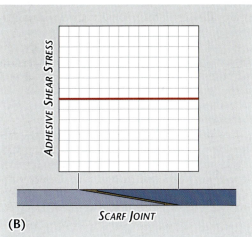

(B) SCARF JOINT

Figure 6-4-24. Stress distribution is affected by joint design

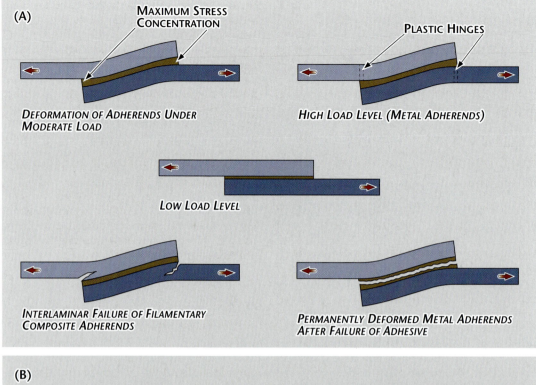
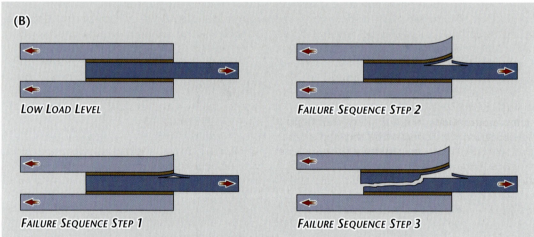

Figure 6-4-25. Failure modes of different types of single-lap joint bonded joints

These are particularly troublesome because there are no nondestructive evaluation techniques that can detect low interfacial strength between the bond and the adherends.

Bond thickness variations usually take place in the form of thinning due to excess resin bleed at the joint edges, leading to overstressing of the adhesive near the edges. Inside tapering of the adherends at the joint edges can be used to compensate for this condition. Bond thicknesses should be limited to ranges of 0.005 to 0.01 in. (0.12 to 0.24 mm) to prevent significant porosity from developing, although greater thicknesses may be acceptable if full periphery damming or high minimum viscosity paste adhesives are used.

During heating under pressure the adhesive will tend to squeeze out from a joint. Some film adhesives contain either a lightweight fabric "carrier" or microspheres that automatically ensure an optimum minimum bond line thickness. This is useful for bonding small areas to prevent excessive squeeze-out. A properly designed bonded joint should not fail in the adhesive, and Figure 6-4-25 shows several types of bond failures that can occur besides the failure of the adhesive.

Peel Stresses

Peel stresses (that is through-the-thickness extensional stresses in the bond) are present because the load path in most adhesive joint geometries is eccentric. It is useful to compare the effect of peel stresses in single- and double-lap joints with uniform adherend thickness, since peel stresses are most severe for joints with uniform adherend thickness.

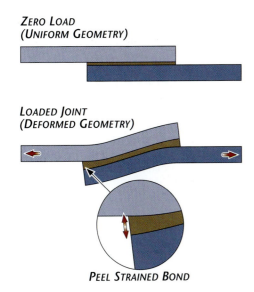

Figure 6-4-26. Peel stress can develop easily in single-lap joints

The load path eccentricity in the single-lap joint (Figure 6-4-26) is relatively obvious due to the offset of the two adherends, which leads to bending deflection as in Figure 6-4-26. In the case of double-lap joints shown in Figure 6-4-27, the load path eccentricity is not as obvious. There may be a tendency to assume that peel stresses are not present for this type of joint because, as a result of the lateral symmetry of such configurations, there is no overall bending deflection. However, while the load in the symmetric lap joint flows axially through the central adherend prior to reaching the overlap region, there it splits in two directions, flowing laterally through the action of bond shear stresses to the two outer adherends.

Eccentricity of the load path is also present in this type of joint. It is important to understand that peel stresses are unavoidable in most bonded joint configurations. However, they can often be reduced to acceptable levels by selecting the appropriate adherend geometry.

Surface Preparation of Metallic and Composite Materials

Surface preparation of a composite or metallic material prior to bonding is one of the most important steps in the process. Adhesive durability and longevity depends greatly on the surface preparation.

In general, high-performance structural adhesive bonding requires that great care be exercised throughout the bonding process to ensure the quality of the bonded product. Adhesive compatibility with original structure, surface preparation, fit up, tooling and the curing process are all required steps to produce high quality aerospace products.

Whenever structural components are to be produced using adhesive bonding, the condition of the adherend surfaces must be considered. They are likely to be contaminated with materials that could affect adversely the performance of the resultant joint.

Surface pretreatment will be necessary if optimum performance is to be achieved. If good environmental or thermal durability is required, it is vital. Dependent on the substrate, surfaces are prepared by one of the following pretreatment procedures. (For many substrates, this list is in increasing order of effectiveness.)

1. Degrease only
2. Degrease, abrade and remove loose particles
3. Degrease and chemically pretreat

Carefully avoid contaminating the surfaces during or after pretreatment. Contamination may be caused by finger marking, by cloths that are not perfectly clean, by contaminated abrasives, or by substandard degreasing or chemical solutions. Contamination may also be caused by other work processes taking place in the bonding area.

Particularly to be excluded are oil vapors from machinery, spraying operations (paint, mold release agents, etc.) and procedures involving powdered materials. Whatever the pretreat-

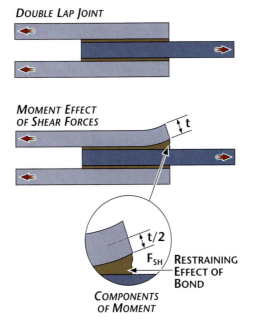

Figure 6-4-27. Peel stress development in double-lap joints

WATER BEADING (HIGHLY CONTAMINATED)   **BLOTCHY AREAS (UNEVENLY CONTAMINATED)**   **SINGLE WELL-DEFINED LINE OR NO LINE (CLEAN)**

Figure 6-4-28. Example of the water break test

ment procedure used, it is good practice to bond the substrates as soon as possible after completion, that is when the surfaces are most "active" and surface properties are at their best.

Testing of Bonding Surface

The water-break test (Figure 6-4-28) is a simple method to determine whether the surface to be bonded is clean. It is best suited to metals. If a few drops of distilled water applied to the adherend wet and spread—or if, on drawing the substrate from out of an aqueous medium—the water film does not break up into droplets the surface may be assumed to be free of contamination.

Uniform wetting of the surface by water indicates that it will probably be likewise wetted by the adhesive. However certain plastics, even when clean, may not be wetted by water but will be wetted by the adhesive. Furthermore, satisfactory wetting gives no information as to the potential bond strength. At best, it is a necessary—but not sufficient—requirement for achieving of high bond strengths.

Preparation of Composite Surface

The first step in the preparation of a composite surface is drying the surface. Composite materials absorb moisture easily, and if moisture is not removed before bonding, it could result in weak bonds, porosity or voids in the adhesive bond line during curing. If honeycomb is used in the structure, moisture can turn to steam during curing resulting in node bond failures or blown core.

Thin laminates up to $1/8$ inch can be dried in an air-circulating oven or with a heater blanket for repair at 250°F (121°C) for four hours minimum. Drying cycles for thicker laminates should be developed empirically using the actual adherend thicknesses. After drying, the surface should be prepared for bonding and then the actual bonding operation conducted as soon as possible.

With wet lay-up, RTM or RIM components or laminates prepared from prepregs, it may be possible to design the laminating process so that one peel ply of fabric is placed on the surface to be bonded. This peel ply becomes part of the laminate on curing. The peel ply is a woven nylon or polyester material that is cured with the laminate.

After the cure the peel ply is torn off of the laminate, leaving a rough surface that is ready for bonding. Most of the time it is advisable to abrade (sand) the surface with a Scotch-Brite™ pad, 180-grit sandpaper or low-pressure grid blasting. Figure 6-4-29 shows the application of peel ply.

The use of peel plies on composite surfaces to be structurally bonded deserves careful consideration. Factors to be considered include:

- Chemical makeup of the peel ply (e.g., nylon versus polyester) as well as its compatibility with the composite-matrix resin,
- Surface treatment used on the peel ply (e.g., silicone coatings that make the peel ply easier to remove also leave residues that inhibit structural bonding)
- Final surface preparation (e.g., hand sanding versus light grit blasting) employed

Nevertheless, peel plies are very effective at preventing gross surface contamination that can occur between laminate fabrication and secondary bonding.

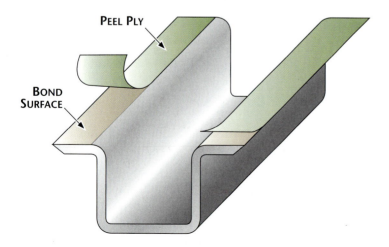

Figure 6-4-29. The application of peel ply for surface preperation

A typical cleaning sequence would be to remove the peel ply and then lightly abrade the surface with a dry grit blast at approximately 20 p.s.i. (138 kPa). After grit blasting, remaining residue may be removed by dry vacuuming or wiping with clean, dry cheesecloth.

Although hand sanding with 120- to 240-grit silicon carbide paper can be substituted for grit blasting, hand sanding is not as effective in reaching all of the impressions left by the weave of the peel ply on the composite surface. In addition, the potential for removing too much resin and exposing the carbon fibers is actually higher for hand sanding than it is for grit blasting.

If it is not possible to use a peel ply on a surface requiring adhesive bonding, the surface may be precleaned prior to surface abrasion with a solvent such as methyl ethyl ketone (MEK) to remove any gross organic contaminants (Figure 6-4-30). In cases where a peel ply is not used, some type of light abrasion is required to break the glazed finish on the matrix resin surface. The use of solvents to remove residue after hand sanding or grit blasting is discouraged due to the possibility of recontaminating the surface.

Another method can be used to avoid abrasion damage to fibers. When the graphite composite is first laid up, a ply of adhesive is placed on the surface where the secondary bond is to take place. This adhesive is then cured together with the laminate. To prepare for the secondary bond, the surface of this adhesive ply is abraded with minimal chance of fiber damage; however, this sacrificial adhesive ply adds weight to the structure.

Surface treatment of thermoplastic polymers. Thermoplastic polymeric substrates vary in the ease with which they can be bonded. Significant factors are the type and grade of polymer, the compounding ingredients and the molding conditions. Tests may be needed to determine bond strength under a given set of conditions.

Many of the surface pretreatments for such plastics as: ABS, acetals, polyamides (nylons), polycarbonates, polyesters, poly (meth) acrylates, polyolefines, polytetrafluoroethylene, polyethersulphones, polyurethanes and others have been, traditionally, chemical in nature. Currently, novel techniques such as flame, corona and plasma treatments are producing pretreated surfaces capable of supporting bonds with excellent strength properties.

Surface treatment for aluminum honeycomb. Unless there are obvious signs of contamination, aluminum honeycomb does

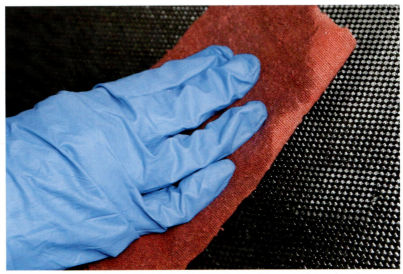

Figure 6-4-30. Preclean the composite surface prior to surface abrasion to remove contaminants.

not require pretreatment prior to bonding. However, if oil or grease contamination is evident, then the affected slice should be immersed in the vapor of a suitable hydrocarbon solvent in a vapor degreasing unit. After immersion, allow sufficient time for the honeycomb core to drain dry. This is particularly important as liquid solvent held in the corners of the honeycomb cell can be very difficult to detect and must be removed before bonding.

Surface treatment of aluminum sheet. Due to the relatively high ductility of aluminum, it is not recommended that such adherends are pretreated by any abrasion methods. Far better is a vapor and/or alkaline degrease followed by an acid etch (pickling) or by a suitable anodizing process. A controlled film of active, aluminum oxide, highly suitable for structural bonding, is grown on the surface of the aluminum. Its thickness depends on the chemical process and the alloy used. Bonding should take place within 2 to 8 hours of pretreatment.

Method 1: Chromic/Sulphuric Acid Pickling (CSA)

A suitable pickling solution of sodium dichromate in sulphuric acid can be made up as follows:

water – 1.500 liters

concentrated sulphuric acid (Sg: 1.83) – 0.750 liters

sodium dichromate ($Na_2Cr_2O_7 \cdot 2H_2O$) – 0.375 kg

(or chromium trioxide [CrO_3] – 0.250 kg)

water to make up to 5.0 liters

WARNING: *Handle concentrated sulfuric acid with care using all the recommended* *personal protection equipment; always add to water.*

Chromium trioxide is a powerful oxidizing agent and is highly toxic; particular care is essential when handling this chemical. It, or the chromate, should be dissolved in diluted sulfuric acid. Regulate the pickling bath at 140°F to 149°F (60 to 65°C) and then immerse the substrate to be pretreated, for 30 minutes. Remove the substrate and immerse in a tank of water at ambient temperature. Follow this with a spray-rinse with cold water. The pretreated components can then be air-dried, preferably in an air-circulating oven whose air temperature is no greater than 113°F (45°C). Bonding should take place within 8 hours

Method 2: Chromic Acid Anodizing (CAA)

A thicker, more robust oxide film can be grown by using chromic acid anodizing. Here, the pickled aluminum substrates (under certain circumstances it may be sufficient to use only an alkaline degrease before anodizing) are clamped to the anode of a standard anodizing bath and are immersed in a solution of chromic acid, at 104°F (40°C), of the following composition:

chromium trioxide (CrO3) – 0.500 kg

water – 10.0 liters

The anodizing voltage is raised over a 10-minute period to 40 V, held for 20 minutes, raised over a 5-minute period to 50 V and held for 5 minutes. At the end of this cycle the components are removed and immersed in a tank of water at ambient temperature. This is followed by a spray-rinse with cold water. The anodized components can then be air-dried, preferably in an air-circulating oven whose air temperature is no greater than 113°F (45°C). Bonding of the unsealed components should take place within 4 to 6 hours.

Method 3: Phosphoric Acid Anodizing (PAA)

To obtain a more open oxide film but thinner than that produced by CAA, aluminum adherends can be anodized in phosphoric acid. The anodic oxide contains bound phosphate that will impart some degree of durability to the final adhesive joint. Here, the pickled aluminum substrates (under certain circumstances it may be sufficient to use only an alkaline degrease prior to anodizing) are clamped to the anode of a standard anodizing bath and immersed in a solution of phosphoric acid, at 77°F (25°C) of the following composition:

"syrupy" orthophosphoric acid (Sg: 1.65) – 1.0 liters

water – 16.6 liters

(The concentration of phosphoric acid is 75 g/l.)

The anodizing voltage is raised to 10 to 15 V (preferably 15 V) and is held for 20 to 25 minutes. The adherends are removed and immersed in a bath of water at ambient temperature. This is followed by a spray-rinse with cold water. The anodized adherends can then be air-dried, preferably in an air-circulating oven where the air temperature is no greater than 113°F (45°C). Bonding of the unsealed components should take place within 2 to 4 hours.

Surface treatment of titanium and titanium alloys. Degrease and then either abrade, ideally by grit blasting, or etch and then anodize in chromic acid as follows:

Pre-etch, at ambient temperatures, for 10 to 20 minutes in a solution of:

concentrated nitric acid (Sg: 1.42) – 4.5 liters

hydrofluoric acid (Sg: 1.17) – 0.450 liters

water – 10.0 liters

WARNING: *Both acids are highly corrosive and toxic. Particular care is essential when handling these chemicals; use all the recommended personal protection equipment.*

Do not use glass equipment with hydrofluoric acid; polythene or polypropylene containers are suitable. Remove from the bath and then, under clean, cold, running water, brush off any black deposit with a clean, stiff-bristle, nylon brush. Clamp the etched substrates to the anode of a standard anodizing bath (anode-cathode ratio of approximately three to one) and immerse, at 104°F (40°C) in chromic acid of the following composition:

chromium trioxide (CrO3) – 0.700 kg

water – 10.0 liters

WARNING: *Chromium trioxide is a powerful oxidizing agent and is highly toxic; particular care is essential when handling this chemical.*

Raise the voltage to 20 V over a 5-minute period and hold (dependent on alloy type) for 5 to 30 minutes; the titanium should have developed a distinctive blue coloration. Remove from the anodizing bath, spray-rinse with cold water and air dry, preferably in an air-circulating oven whose air temperature does not exceed 113°F (45°C).

Thermoplastics Processing and Joining

True (or dry) thermoplastics, in which there are no chemical changes during processing, can be rapidly heated, remelted, shaped, consolidated and cooled. These relatively rate-insensitive process parameters lend themselves to innovative lay-up, forming and joining techniques that in certain applications slash process times from hours to minutes. A wing for an Airbus A350 XWB constructed using this method is shown in Figure 6-4-31. These processes are still under development and not yet widely used in the aerospace industry.

Material Options

Since advanced thermoplastic composites possess high-melt viscosity resins and high-volume fractions of continuous inelastic fibers, traditional thermoforming methods that rely on material flow during softening, such as injection molding, blow molding, compression molding, resin transfer molding, vacuum forming, and so on, cannot be used. Rather, these advanced material forms must either be placed directly to final shape or stacked in such a manner that individual plies can slip to shape during thermal forming. Further complicating manufacture is the fact that most thermoplastic parts are designed for weight-critical applications by tailoring thickness throughout to match loading requirements. Unlike metals, where material is machined or chemically milled away after processing to achieve a desired thickness, advanced composites require individual oriented plies to be cut to shape and sequentially stacked in precise locations.

Figure 6-4-31. An Airbus A350XWB wing constructed using thermoplastic processing and joining.

Courtesy of Airbus

7

Heating and Curing

Section 1

Heating and Curing Equipment

Most composite manufacturing and repair processes require heat to cure. In addition, heating equipment is also used to dry out composite laminate and honeycomb sandwich constructions. Common types of equipment used are autoclave, curing oven, heat bonder, curing lamps and hot-air units.

Heat Bonder

A *heat bonder* is a temperature control unit that is most often used with heat blankets, but may be used with other heating devices to control the cure temperature. A thorough understanding of the heat bonder's programming features is necessary to effectively cure a repair. Figure 7-1-1 shows a full size heat bonder and a mini bonder used for small field repairs.

Program. Program the cure in accordance with the heat bonder manufacturer's directions. To ensure the proper cure is obtained, you must know how the heat bonder selects the control thermocouples and how the alarms are triggered.

Monitor. To prevent damage to parts, equipment, aircraft, or repair facilities, heat bonders must be monitored. Anytime a vacuum bag is used to hold a heat blanket in place, the low-pressure alarm must be used. If the heat bonder is not equipped with a low-pressure alarm, a technician must visually verify the integrity of the vacuum bag every two minutes. Monitor the heat bonder during all heating cycles. Personnel

Learning Objective

DESCRIBE
- how to use a heat bonder and heat blanket
- the ultraviolet curing process

EXPLAIN
- the operation and application of an autoclave for curing composite materials
- the operation and application of a curing oven for curing composite materials
- the use of curing lamps and hot air modules

Left: Autoclaves are the most versatile and the most common equipment used to produce laminates for the aviation industry.
Courtesy of Coast Composites, LLC

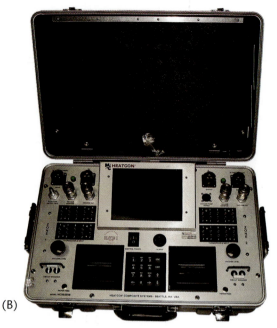

Figure 7-1-1. (A) Mini heat bonder used for field repairs, (B) Full-size heat bonder for shop

may move away from the heat bonder provided the controller has an audible alarm, the alarm is tested prior to the heating cycle and is serviceable, qualified personnel remain within hearing distance of the alarm, and qualified personnel periodically perform a visual check of the heat bonder and repair.

Temperature Control. Temperature control is accomplished by comparing the programmed temperature ramps and holds (the set points) to the temperatures measured by control thermocouples at the repair location. Typically, three options for control are available:

1. A thermocouple may be assigned as a single control thermocouple (not recommended).

2. An average of a specified set of thermocouples may be assigned to control the heat cycle.

3. Control may be established by either the leading (hottest) thermocouple or lagging (coldest) thermocouple automatically. It is typically used when one does not want to either exceed a temperature value (leading) or when one wants to ensure a minimum temperature is obtained in the entire repair area (lagging). This method is highly dependent upon thermocouple placement, which should be determined by a thermal survey of the repair area.

Alarm. A heat bonder provides the operator with the capability to set an alarm condition in which the actual measured temperature or vacuum varies from that specified in the programmed cure cycle. In most cases, this alarm will put the controller into a hold situation until the alarm condition is corrected.

Heat Blanket. Heat blankets (Figure 7-1-2) are a common method used to apply heat for repairs in the field. Heat blankets may be controlled manually; however, they are usually used in conjunction with a heat bonder. Heat is transferred from the blanket via conduction.

Consequently, the heat blanket must conform to and be in 100 percent contact with the part. This is usually accomplished using vacuum bag pressure. Lack of contact between the heat blanket and the area to be cured will result in inadequate heating of the repair area and an overheating of the heat blanket.

Figure 7-1-2. Heat blankets are available in multiple sizes.

For example, excessive height in a core plug being bonded into place causes an air gap at the edges of the core plug and correspondingly inadequate heating at the plug's edge. In addition, heat loss occurs around the outer perimeter of the heat blanket, causing the temperatures on the outer portion of the repair area to be less than that at the center.

Inspection. Prior to heat blanket use, perform the following inspections:

1. Inspect the wires, connectors and heating pad for loose or frayed wires or silicone cracking.
2. Energize the heating pad and ensure all areas of it are working. It is possible for a defective heating pad to heat one side or area and be cool elsewhere.

Follow the manufacturer's guidelines and the following:

1. Ensure the heat blanket overlaps the repair by a minimum of 2 in. (5cm) on each side to ensure even heating of the repair. This is necessary as temperatures on the edges of the heat blanket, especially constant watt density blankets, can be as much as 50°F (6°C) cooler than the rest of the heat blanket. A smaller overlap may only be used if a thermal survey has been performed and actions taken to ensure even heating of the repair. For structures thicker than 0.10 in.(0.25 cm), an overlap greater than 2 in. (5 cm) may be required.
2. Hot or cold spots caused by uneven heating within the heat blanket can be mitigated by placing a thin copper or aluminum sheet under the heat blanket. The sheet metal may conduct the heat more evenly. Ensure the sheet metal matches the contour of the part being repaired to eliminate air pockets and ensure even distribution of pressure. Annealed metal is preferred.
3. When using heat blankets in a hazardous environment such as Class 1, Division 1 or Division 2, use heat blankets designed for such areas. Heat blankets designed for these areas often have a secondary safety device that ensures the heat blanket does not reach the auto-ignition temperature of aviation fuel.
4. Do not use heat blankets on components that have a radius smaller than 0.5 in. (1.3 cm). Too tight a radius will damage the heat blanket.

Figure 7-1-3. Portable vacuum pump

5. Handle heat blankets delicately; do not fold, crush or pinch them. Store flat or loosely rolled. Rough handling will lead to broken heating elements resulting in cold spots in the blanket.

Pressurization

Advanced composite structures and repairs are fabricated from materials that are processed using various temperatures and pressure profiles. Pressure is required to shape repair patches to a part contour, to remove volatiles and entrapped air from the repair patch and bond line and to hold the repair in place while it is being cured.

The type and level of pressure used can significantly alter the quality and resulting strength of a repair. There are two general types of pressure: positive and negative. Positive pressure is produced by physically exerting an external force onto an object (repair) such that it is compacted as it reacts against another object (tooling or the component being repaired) to resist the pressure. Negative or vacuum pressure when an object (the repair) is exposed to a confined vacuum environment (supported by a tool or component) while allowing the surrounding atmospheric pressure to exert a compaction force onto the object.

Most field level bonded repairs involve the use of vacuum pressure to compact as well as to remove volatiles and air from the repair. Figure 7-1-3 shows a portable vacuum pump for field repairs and small manufacturing projects.

Autoclave

Autoclave curing is the aerospace industry's most widely used method of producing high-

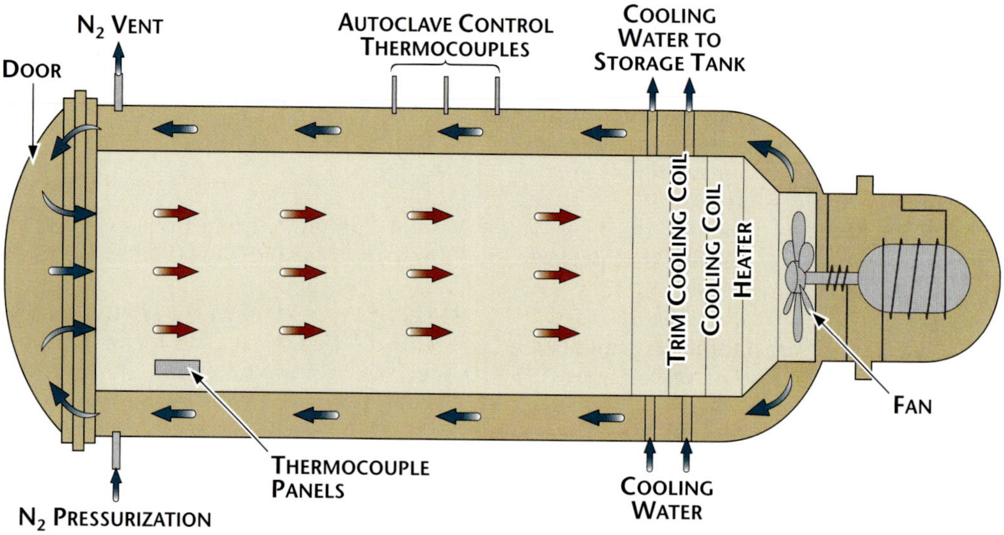

WORKING SPACE	12 ft. Diameter x 40 ft. Length
MAX TEMPERATURE	650°F
MAX PRESSURE	150 p.s.i.
HEATING	Electrical (3,120 kW)
AIR MOVEMENT	60,000 ft.³/min. at 600 r.p.m.
PART MONITORING	48 Vacuum Supply Outlets 24 Vacuum/Pressure Monitoring Outlets 108 Thermocouple Jack Outlets

Figure 7-1-4. A typical autoclave. Autoclaves are available in multiple sizes.

quality laminates. Autoclaves are extremely versatile pieces of equipment. Since the gas pressure is applied isostatically to the part, almost any shape can be cured in an autoclave. The only limitation is the size of the autoclave and the large initial capital investment for purchase and installation. A typical autoclave system, shown in Figure 7-1-4, consists of a pressure vessel, a control system, an electrical system, a gas generation system and a vacuum system.

An autoclave process produces the standard material properties to which all other processes are compared. Typically, 100 p.s.i. (690 kPa) pressure and 700°F (370°C) temperatures can be achieved. Autoclaves must be operated by trained professional personnel. Severe damage will occur with misuse.

Thermoset composite materials are generally processed at less than 100 p.s.i. (690 kPa) and at temperatures ranging from 250 to 400°F (120 to 200°C). Thermoplastic composites may require higher temperatures and pressures.

Due to the high temperatures in the autoclave during processing, the atmosphere within the vessel is generally purged of oxygen using an inert gas, such as nitrogen, to displace the oxygen thereby preventing thermal combustion or charring of the materials being cured. Two pressurization gases are typically used for autoclaves: air and nitrogen. Proportional inlet and vent valves allow autoclave pressures to be controlled and varied precisely. It is important that this very hot gas being introduced into the pressure vessel not impinge on the part load, because the gas stream could cause part damage due to thermal or mechanical shock.

Air is relatively inexpensive when supplied in the 100 to 150 p.s.i. (690 to 1,030 kPa) range and is acceptable for most 250°F (120°C) cures. The main disadvantage of air is that it sustains combustion and thus may be hazardous at temperatures above 300°F (150°C).

Nitrogen is the gas most commonly used in autoclaves. The liquid nitrogen is stored in cryogenic form and then vaporized at approximately 200 to 225 p.s.i. (1,400 to 1,550 kPa). Higher-pressure tanks and systems are available. Nitrogen suppresses combustion and diffuses well into the air when the autoclave is opened. However, nitrogen costs can be significant if many autoclaves in a plant are using nitrogen and if the autoclaves are large and operating at high pressure.

Materials that are to be cured in an autoclave are located onto tooling, which provides the eventual shape of the cured material. The tooling, frequently referred to as the mold, may comprise an assembly of mandrels or tool details to accommodate complex geometry. The mold may also include features such as locating devices, tooling tabs or net-molding details to enhance the subsequent processing of the final product or material.

Typically, an impervious layer of bagging film or a reusable elastic bladder is located over the material being cured and sealed against the mold. Vacuum is applied between the bagging material and the material being cured such that the plies of material are compressed through the thickness against the mold. In some instances, an autoclave or oven is used to apply heat and pressure to only a portion of the material being cured as an interim debulk step to enhance the quality of the finished product through improved consolidation.

As the temperature in the autoclave is raised, the viscosity of the curing material is generally lowered to a fluid state and the gasses within and between the layers escape as the material consolidates. A porous "bleeder" layer and/or a "breather" in the form of sheet, strips or strands may be utilized under the bagging material to enable the evacuation of gasses.

Surface films or in-mold coatings may also be included against the tool surface to improve the surface finish of the cured material. Rigid caul plates or intensifiers may also be incorporated under the bagging material to locally control the thickness and quality of the finished product. In some cases, pre-cured or stage-cured components may be co-cured or co-bonded with the material being cured in the autoclave.

Sources of Variability

The primary sources of variability in the autoclave curing process are:

Tooling or mold surface finish. Poor surface finish will transfer to finished product.

Tooling materials, density and spacing of tools in the autoclave. More tools closer together will act as a heat sink and affect the degree of cure.

Part geometry. The more complex the geometry, the more difficult it is to achieve uniform consolidation and to avoid wrinkling.

Lay-up symmetry. Non-symmetrical geometry or lay-up causes part warpage or springback.

Material location and alignment tolerances. Non-symmetrical lay-up causes part warpage.

Bagging technique and bagging materials including bleeder materials and cauls, etc. Vacuum bagging material movement or restriction from complete contact against curing material (i.e., bridging) causes non-uniformity in material compaction and resin flow affecting the quality of the finished product.

Number of interim debulk cycles and debulk time, temperature and pressure (vacuum). Insufficient debulking causes thickness and surface finish variability as well as wrinkles in the finished part.

Raw material variability (including batch-to-batch variability) and material shelf life. Materials are typically time and temperature dependent.

Moisture content of materials being cured or processed. Moisture in material affects laminate quality, causing porosity as it turns to steam during cure.

Number of vacuum ports, location of vacuum ports and vacuum integrity during cure cycles. Materials are consolidated through the thickness during cure as the resin flows and gels. Vacuum integrity affects the level of compaction.

Autoclave temperature, pressure and time. Variations in cure cycle affect the resin flow prior to cure, level of cure and finished product thickness.

Part thickness variations. Thickness variations may affect consolidation and curing uniformity.

Safety

It is usually standard to have redundant safety features on any autoclave because of the potential seriousness of any malfunction. Overpressure conditions are usually prevented by three different methods: a separate overpressure sensor and shutdown control; rupture disks designed to rupture at pressures above the operating pressure of the autoclave; and pop-off safety valves with the same function.

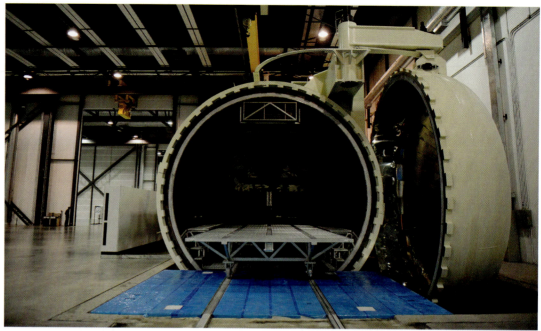

Figure 7-1-5. Autoclaves may be large or small.

Courtesy of Airbus

A standard autoclave has all three. Vessels are usually proof-tested to high margins of safety, but the danger posed by the possibility of a burst vessel cannot be overemphasized. Figure 7-1-5 shows an autoclave for composite manufacturing.

Over-temperature protection is not as critical from an injury standpoint, but such conditions could damage the interior systems of the autoclave; therefore, over-temperature controls are usually provided. The vessel shell, because of the internal insulation, may not be rated to the maximum operating temperature of the autoclave. The external surface of the autoclave should not exceed 140°F (60°C), except at penetrations.

Figure 7-1-6. Curing oven

Curing Oven

Composite material can be cured in ovens using various pressure application methods. Vacuum bagging can be used to remove volatiles and trapped air while atmospheric pressure provides consolidation. Another method of pressure application for oven cures is the use of shrink-wrapping or shrink tape. This method is commonly used with parts that have been filament wound because some of the same rules for application apply. The tape is wrapped around the completed layup, usually with only a layer of release material between the tape and the layup. Heat is applied to the tape, usually using a heat gun, to make the tape shrink, and this can apply a tremendous amount of pressure to the layup. After shrinking, the part is placed in the oven for cure.

High-quality parts can be made inexpensively using shrink tape, with a few limitations. First, the part must be of a configuration where the tape can apply pressure at all points. Second, flow of the resin during cure must be limited, because the tape will not continue to shrink in the oven. If the resin flows excessively, the pressure applied by the shrink tape will be reduced substantially.

Curing ovens are typically outfitted with vacuum outlets to supply vacuum pressure during the cure. Oven temperature is governed by an oven controller that can be programmed to run a cure recipe. The oven controller will use an oven air sensor or thermocouples placed on the part to control the part temperature. Figure 7-1-6 shows a walk in curing oven with vacuum.

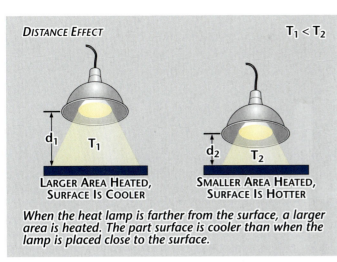
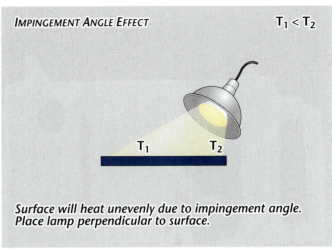
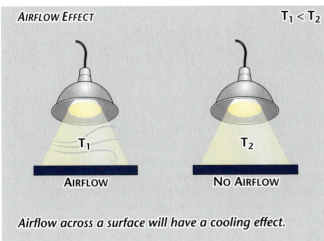
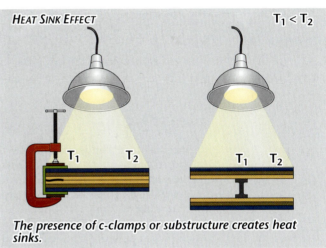
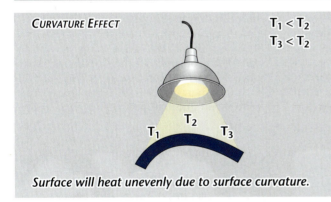
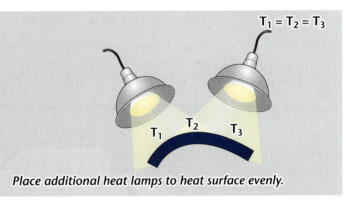
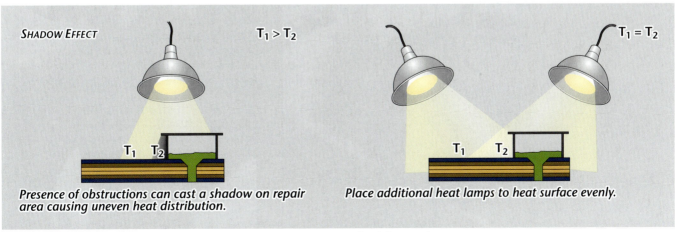

Figure 7-1-7. Heat lamps are configured according to the curing needs of the repair.

Figure 7-1-8. Hot-air unit (HAM) *Courtesy of Jet Solutions, LLC*

determine their heating characteristics. This is usually done by conducting a thermal survey. Figure 7-1-7 shows the use of heat lamps for curing of composites.

Hot-Air Unit

Hot-air Units (HAM) are generally controlled either manually or in conjunction with a heat bonder controller. They can be used to heat large areas of any contour or material. HAMs will supply controlled heat to over 900°F (480°C). HAMs lend themselves very well to heating and curing of materials that require noncontact such as paints and coatings. When using hot air for curing of composite laminates, care should be taken not to insulate the repair by using excessive breather materials. Figure 7-1-8 shows a portable HAM unit.

Heat Lamps

Infrared heat lamps can also be used for elevated temperature curing of composites if a vacuum bag is not utilized. However, they are generally not effective for producing curing temperatures above 150°F (66°C) or for areas larger than 2 ft^2. It is also difficult to control the heat applied with a lamp, and lamps tend to generate high-surface temperatures quickly. If controlled by thermostats (heat bonder), heat lamps can be useful in applying curing heat to large or irregular surfaces.

Heat lamps from different manufacturers produce different temperature profiles. Each heat lamp configuration must be evaluated to

Heat Gun

Thermostatically controlled heat guns can be used to cure small repairs. Most heat guns will supply air in the temperature range of 130 to 500°F (54 to 260°C). Heat guns are useful for warming materials, but overheating must be avoided. The use of heat guns must be restricted to areas free of fuel and other flammable materials.

UV Curing

Ultraviolet (UV) light is the range of shorter wavelengths adjacent to the visible-light spectrum. UV curing typically uses UVA light (320-400 nm) or short wave visible light (blue 400-450 nm). UV-cured materials contain what is known

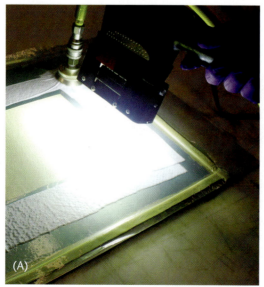
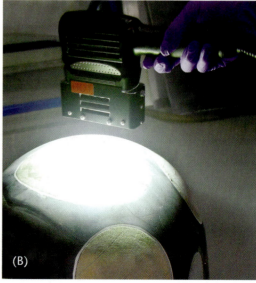

Figure 7-1-9. UV light is used to repair composite structures.

as photo initiators that start the curing reaction when exposed to a specific wavelength of light.

The intensity of the UV light source is measured in milliwatts per square centimeter (mW/cm^2) and the higher the light intensity of the proper wavelengths, the faster the curing occurs. The intensity of the UV light can also be affected by the distance from the light source to the target. Intensity decreases as the distance increases for both spot lamps and flood lamps.

Depth of cure is typically about 0.25 to 0.5 in. (0.6 to 1.3 cm) with special formulas capable of curing up to the depth of 1 in. (2.5cm). However, it may take three to four times longer to cure a product that is 0.5 in. in depth than a product that is only 0.25 in. deep.

Generally, once the UV-cured material changes from a liquid to a solid, it is considered cured. However, further testing can be performed to ensure that the material is providing the correct physical properties and that additional exposure to the UV light source will no longer improve the physical properties.

Figure 7-1-9 shows UV lights used for the repair of composite structures. Advantages of UV cure are that it is very fast and easy to accomplish. The disadvantages are that it can only be used with fiberglass. This technique does not work with carbon fiber.

Heated Press

A heated press is often used to make honeycomb panels. The press supplies the heat and pressure required for the cure. Heat presses can also be used in the laboratory for the manufacture of coupons and specimens. The heated press is also useful for parts using a thermoplastic resin system that requires high cure temperature and pressure. Figure 7-1-10 shows a heated press for the production of composite panels.

Thermocouples

A thermocouple (TC) is a thermoelectric device used to accurately measure temperatures. They may be connected to a simple temperature reading device or, more often, they are connected to a heat bonder, oven or other type of controller that regulates the amount of heat applied to the repair area.

TCs consist of a wire with two leads of dissimilar metals; the metals are joined at one

Figure 7-1-10. A heated press is used for making honeycomb panels.

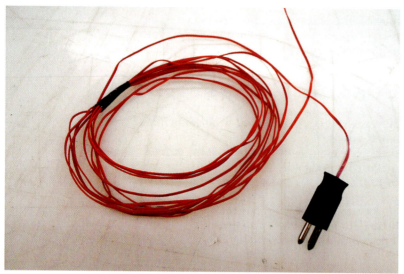

Figure 7-1-11. Thermocouples measure temperature

		THERMOCOUPLE COLOR (USA)	THERMOCOUPLE EXTENSION COLOR (USA)
J	Outer Sheath (Optional)	Brown	Black
	Positive (Iron)	+ White	+ White
	Negative (Constantan)	- Red	- Red
K	Outer Sheath (Optional)	Brown	- Yellow
	Positive (Nickel/Chromium)	+ Yellow	+ Yellow
	Negative (Nickel/Aluminum)	- Red	- Red

Table 7-1-1. Thermocouple identification

In some cases, TCs are required to be within a specified range of length to ensure their accuracy; consult the temperature monitoring equipment owner's manual for guidance. If no guidance exists, TCs should be between 10 and 50 ft. (3 to 15 m) long. TC wire color codes vary by nation (Table 7-1-1). Always check the label to ensure you are using the correct type. The industry standard in the United States is ANSI MC96.1. Sometimes, the TC wires used in the composite industry are supplied without the outer sheath to minimize the potential for vacuum leaks.

TCs may be locally manufactured. Welded TCs are less prone to problems and should be used when available. TC welders are available from most heat bonder vendors. Twisted TCs do not form as reliable a junction as a welded TC and their reliability decreases with repeated use. If necessary, a twisted TC may be made by overlapping the bare ends of the two TC wires $1/4$ in. (0.64 cm) and at 90° to each other. Tightly twist the wire four or five times and cut off the excess wire. The temperature reading will be measured at the twist closest to the TC monitor.

end. Heating the joint produces an electrical current, and this current is converted to a temperature reading with a TC monitor. Select the type of wire (J or K) and the type of connector (standard or miniature) compatible with the local temperature monitoring equipment (heat bonder, oven, autoclave, etc.).

TC wire is available with different types of insulation; check the manufacturer's product data sheets to ensure the insulation will withstand your highest cure temperature. Teflon-insulated wire is generally good for 390°F (199°C) and lower cures; Kapton-insulated wire should be used for higher temperatures. Figure 7-1-11 shows a thermocouple that is used with a heat bonder unit, oven, or autoclave.

Most TCs used for bonding are the J-type, which use one iron and one constantan wire. The K-type TC is used less often; it consists of one nickel and one chromium alloy for leads.

Section 2

Heating and Curing Operations

Thermal Survey

In order to achieve maximum structural properties in a bonded composite repair, it is essential to cure these materials within the recommended temperature range. Failure to cure at the correct temperatures can produce weak patches or bonding surfaces and can result in a repair failure during service.

A thermal survey should be performed prior to installing the repair to ensure proper and uniform temperatures can be achieved. The thermal survey determines the heating and insulation requirements as well as TC locations for the repair area. The thermal survey is especially useful for determining the heating method and monitoring requirements in cases where heat sinks (substructure for instance) exist in the repair area. It should be performed for all types of heating methods to preclude insufficient, excessive or uneven heating.

Bond line temperature estimation. During a cure, no TCs may be placed in the bond line; consequently, the only source of information during a cure is the TCs placed around the repair's perimeter. Because these TCs are not in the actual bond area, they may not accurately reflect the temperatures within the repair zone. Thermal survey data will allow repair technicians to accurately estimate internal patch and bond line temperatures by observing the perimeter TC readings.

Thermal variations. Thermal variations in the repair area occur for many reasons. Primary among these are material type, material thickness and underlying structure in the repair zone. For these reasons, it is important to know the structural composition of the area to be repaired.

Substructure in the repair zone will conduct heat away from the repair area resulting in a cold spot directly above the structure. Thin skins heat quickly and can easily be overheated. Thick skin sections absorb heat slowly and take longer to reach soak temperature. The thermal survey will identify these problem areas and allow the repair technician to develop the heat and insulation setup required for even heating.

Maximum temperature control. The heat generated by the heating source must be controlled so that it will not damage aircraft systems and degrade surrounding coatings, sealant and wiring. A thermal survey will help determine the maximum temperature required for a cure in order to overcome heat sinks in the structure.

Staging of aircraft, equipment and materials. Before performing the thermal survey, the aircraft or part should be positioned in the same location where the actual repair will be performed—usually an area that is thermally stable and wind free. If this is not possible, a temporary shelter should be erected to protect the area from the elements. The repair location should be convenient to electrical power, vacuum source and compressed air. If the repair location is not within easy reach of shop air and electricity, a generator and air compressor will be needed. When possible move the aircraft into a hangar, as shown in Figure 7-2-1.

General rules. General rules may vary for different manufacturers, but some basic rules for setting up the thermal survey are as follows:

- Use one TC for every 10 in.^{2} (65 cm2) of patch area, approximately. Use a minimum of three control TCs per patch.
- Place additional TCs near potential hot or cold spots.
- Use welded TC wire if available. If only twisted wire TCs are available, inspect the twisted ends to ensure they are firmly connected.

Process. Before beginning the thermal survey, all coatings have to be removed. If vacuum-bag processing will be used in the repair process, a vacuum integrity test should be performed before this process is conducted.

- Place flash tape below and above the TC tips to protect the control unit from electrical shorts.

Figure 7-2-1. Controlling the environment, like moving the aircraft into a temperature-controlled hangar, makes a thermal survey more accurate.

7-12 | Heating and Curing

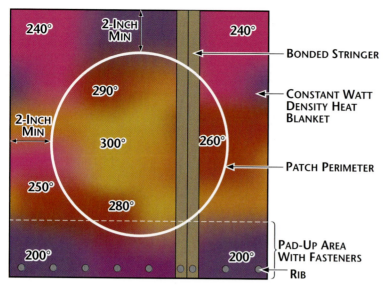

Figure 7-2-2. Temperature readings from a thermal survey

1. Place TCs in the bond line area on a 3- to 4-in. (8- to 10-cm) grid or strategically place the TCs over suspected heat sinks (e.g., stringers, spars, ribs, longerons) and hot spots.

2. Place additional TCs in the locations that would be used during an actual cure to control the heat. These must be placed around the patch perimeter (outside the bond line). Use these as control TCs on the heat bonder or temperature control equipment. Be sure to place the control TCs in the exact same location when performing the cure. Ensure TCs are installed away from the vacuum port.

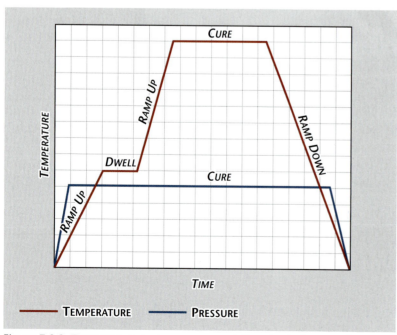

Figure 7-2-3. Temperature and pressure graph for a typical cure recipe

- Using clear Mylar film or other template material, create a map of the exact TC locations and proposed patch perimeter.

- Create a simulated patch made of appropriate material and temporarily attach it to the repair area. Ensure the simulated patch is in contact with the underlying structure.

- All TCs directly exposed to a heat lamp (infrared, quartz and other) must have a small piece of metallic foil tape placed over the flash breaker tape on the bare ends. The metallic foil tape prevents direct heating and erroneous readings of the TCs.

- Position the heat source in the same position and orientation that will be used during the actual repair.

- If the repair process requires a vacuum bag heat blanket cure, set up the vacuum bag (with breather, bleeder, peel ply, caul plates, etc.) exactly as it would be done during the repair. Apply vacuum.

- Heat the repair area to the cure temperature using the recommended ramp rate. Once the repair area has stabilized at the cure temperature, record the TC temperatures. The repair temperature has stabilized when there is no rise in the bond line temperature over 10 minutes.

- Examine the temperature readings in the bond line. If they are within the limits specified in the repair manual, the thermal survey is complete. If the system specific technical data does not specify an acceptable range, ensure the bond line TCs are ±20°F (±11°C). If they are not, do the following:

  1. If the temperature readings within the bond line vary more than ±20°F from the average, add insulation or heat. Repeat the thermal survey.

  2. If the temperature readings within the bond line are within ±20°F from the bond line average but they are lower than the acceptable cure temperature, raise the cure temperature setting on the heat bonder. Continue or repeat the thermal survey until satisfactory temperatures in the bond line are obtained in the thermal survey.

  3. Record the exact setup (Figure 7-2-2) to include the position and intensity of heat sources, insulation and heat bonder cure settings.

Cure Recipes

Cure cycles are directly related to the resin or adhesive system used. Failure to follow the prescribed cure cycle will result in a loss or lack of structural strength in the repair material as well as a loss of strength in the parent material.

Heat is never arbitrarily applied to a repair; it must be applied in a controlled manner to achieve the desired results without further damaging the part. Adhesives and resins can be cured in many ways. Some adhesives and resins can be cured at ambient temperatures with the simple addition of the curing agent; however, the cure time to achieve structural properties is typically days and the cured material typically will not stand up to environments that are hot, cold, or involve moisture or harsh fluids.

Most aerospace applications requiring bonded structural repairs involve processing the repair using heat while under pressure, typically vacuum pressure. In most cases, the repair is vacuum-bagged and uses a heat source and a heat bonder for control and monitoring of the temperatures and pressure within the vacuum bag.

In some cases, two to three temperature holds during ramp-up are required. The additional holds are for properly debulking, bleeding and consolidating the repair material. The final temperature hold is to complete the cure state of the adhesive or resin that provides the material with its structural properties.

A typical cure cycle is shown in Figure 7-2-3. The operator of an autoclave or curing oven must be aware, when programming the curing recipe, that the autoclave or curing oven temperature is not always the same as the part temperature. The reason for this is that large parts that require large tools or thick composite laminates require longer time to heat up.

Some large tools might lag more than an hour behind the oven or autoclave temperature. Therefore, the actual part temperature could lag significantly behind the autoclave or oven temperature. For this reason thermocouples are often placed on the part to measure part temperature.

Sometimes a dry run is accomplished to see how much the part temperature will lag and then the recipe is adjusted to achieve the correct temperature. Figure 7-2-4 shows a graph with the data from an autoclave cure. Figure 7-2-5 shows that by overshooting desired curing temperature with the autoclave temperature causes the part temperature to reach the desired curing recipe.

If the ramp rate of the part lags behind, the ramp rate of the autoclave could be increased to increase the ramp rate of the part. Remember that the temperature measured by the autoclave air sensor measures the air temperature in the autoclave and this is not always the same

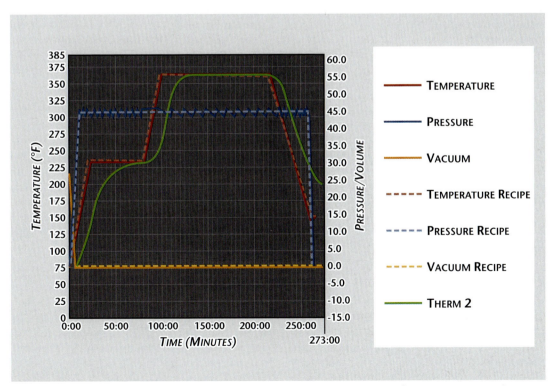

Figure 7-2-4. Standard autoclave recipe showing the resulting temperature lag

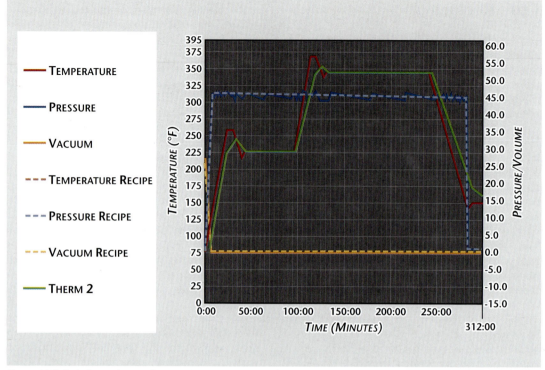

Figure 7-2-5. Adjusted autoclave recipe to account for temperature lag

as part temperature. Part temperature is what we should be concerned about.

Mechanics of Curing

The curing process is accomplished by the application of heat and pressure to the laminate. The resin will begin to soften and flow as the temperature is increased. At lower temperatures, very little reaction occurs. Volatile contaminants such as air and water are drawn out of the laminate with vacuum during this time.

The laminate is compacted by applying pressure, usually vacuum (atmospheric pressure); autoclaves (historically used by original equipment manufacturers) apply additional pressure, typically 50 to 100 p.s.i. (345 to 690 kPa). As the temperature approaches the final cure temperature, the rate of reaction greatly increases and the resin begins to gel and harden. The hold at the final cure temperature lets the resin finish curing and attain the desired structural properties.

Ramp Rates

Generally, parts and repairs must be heated and cooled slowly. If they are heated or cooled too quickly, previously cured laminates and some types of adhesives can be thermally shocked and lose structural integrity. Large structures, such as the tail cone in Figure 7-2-6, require careful planning. The *ramp-up rate* refers to how fast the repair is heated and is usually expressed in degrees per minute. The *ramp-down rate* refers to how fast an area is cooled.

Part temperature ramp rates range typically from 1 to 5°F (0.5 to 2.8°C) per minute. If temperature ramp-up and ramp-down rates are not specified, do not exceed 10°F (5.6°C) per minute. An exception to this would be for hot debulking, where the intent is to compact the laminate and remove volatiles. This generally is accomplished using the fastest rates possible for both heat up and cool down.

Pressure Ramp Rates

Ramp-up and ramp-down may also apply to pressure increases and decreases when an autoclave is used; however, they are seldom called out in field repairs. If a pressure ramp rate is not specified, full pressure is applied prior to the temperature ramp-up and then released after temperature ramp-down.

Cure Temperature

Some resins and adhesives have multiple cure cycles to choose from. For instance, some resins, according to the manufacturer's data sheet, can be cured at 200°F (93°C) for 220 minutes or 250°F (121°C) for 150 minutes or 300°F (149°C) for 130 minutes. The properties of the resin

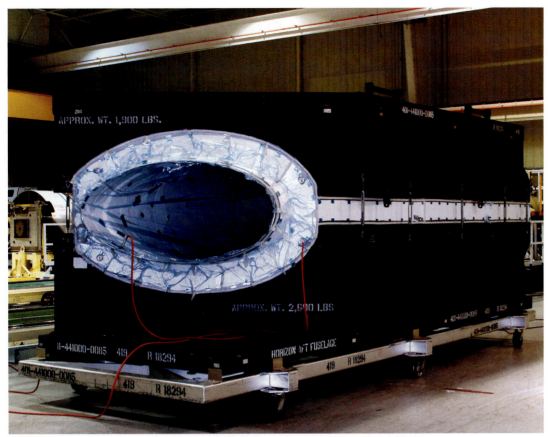

Figure 7-2-6. Large structures require careful planning when determining ramp rates.

are dependent on the final cure temperature; therefore, when a particular cure temperature is called for in the maintenance instructions it must be followed.

When you have the prerogative to choose between cure temperatures, you should use the highest cure temperature at which you can maintain a uniform temperature across the repair. If a temperature range is given, such as 240 to 260°F (116 to 127°C), ensure all areas of the repair are maintained between those temperatures. When no temperature range is given, ensure the lagging thermocouple (lowest temperature) reaches the given cure temperature and the leading thermocouple (highest temperature) is within 20°F (11°C).

If the difference between the leading and lagging thermocouples exceeds 20°F, seek engineering assistance.

For complex structures or where substructure exists in the repair area, a thermal survey must be performed prior to the bonding operation and corrective actions taken to ensure that a uniform cure temperature can be maintained.

Cure Time

Unless otherwise specified in the manufacturing or repair instructions, start the cure time when the lagging thermocouple reaches the cure temperature. Cure time is not the same as cure cycle. Cure cycle is the total time of the curing process, including cold debulk, ramp-up, hot debulk, cure time and ramp-down.

When a programmable heat source is used, the cure cycle must be determined in order to program the control unit. The cure cycle can be determined using the specified cure temperature and the desired ramp rate. If a nonprogrammable control unit is used, the cure cycle must be determined in order to know when to manually increase or decrease the power going to the heat source during ramp-up and ramp-down.

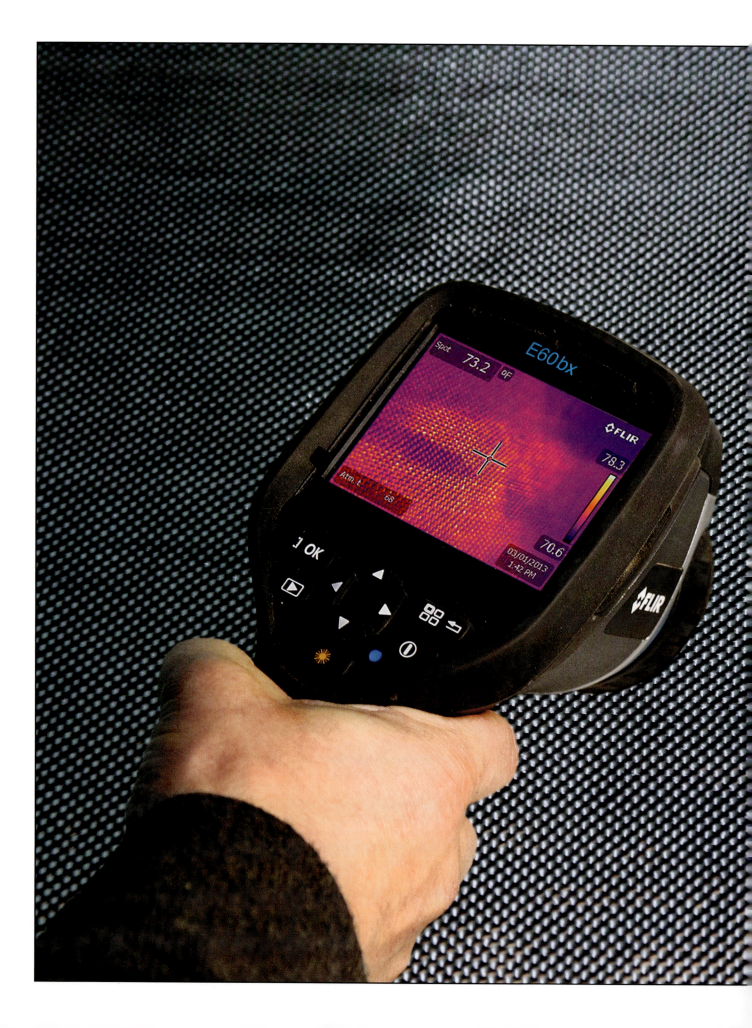

8

Inspection and Testing

Nondestructive Testing

Damage to composite components is not always visible to the naked eye and the extent of damage is best determined for structural components by suitable nondestructive test (NDT) methods, also called nondestructive inspection (NDI).

NDI methods range from simple visual inspections to very sophisticated automated systems with extensive data handling capabilities. In this chapter we will look at tests that include tap testing, ultrasonic testing and X-ray.

It should be noted that composites are generally more difficult to inspect than metals due to their non-homogenous nature (i.e., laminated structures containing multiple ply orientations with numerous ply drop-offs). It is important that technicians conducting NDI be trained and certified in the method they are using.

Visual

A visual inspection is the most common type of inspection method for metallic and composite aircraft structures. The trained eye of a technician can quickly scan large areas and determine if further, more detailed in-depth inspections are required (Figure 8-1-1). Consequently, visual inspection is performed routinely as a means of quality control and damage assessment.

Fortunately, most types of damage scorch, stain, dent, penetrate, abrade, or chip the composite surface making the damage visually verifiable. Once detected, the affected area will be inspected more closely with other more in-depth inspection methods. Flashlights, magnifying glasses, mirrors and borescopes are

Learning Objective

DESCRIBE
- visual inspection techniques
- coin tap inspection techniques

EXPLAIN
- nondestructive ultrasonic testing methods:
  pulse echo
  through transmission
  phase array
  bond testing
  X-ray
  thermography
  shearography

Left: Infrared detection is a commonly used type of thermal inspection. It scans the surface for defects by measuring heat energy applied to a structure.

Courtesy of Energistics, LLC

8-2 | Inspection and Testing

Figure 8-1-1. Visual inspection is usually the first step.

employed as aids in the visual inspection of composites. They are used to magnify defects that otherwise might not be seen easily and to allow visual inspection of areas that are not readily accessible.

Shining a flash light under an angle is a great aid to finding damage. Resin starvation, resin richness, wrinkles, ply bridging, discoloration (due to overheating, lightning strike, etc.), impact damage by any cause, foreign matter, blisters and disbonding are some of the discrepancies readily discernible by a visual inspection.

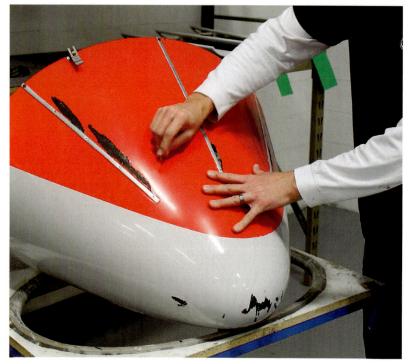

Figure 8-1-2. Coin tapping

The presence of dents requires a closer look and can be aided by using a straight edge over a suspected dent area and comparing the suspected dent area with the surrounding part. Visual inspection cannot find internal flaws in the composite, such as delaminations, disbonds and matrix crazing. More sophisticated NDT is needed to detect these, although an experienced technician can often surmise whether there is internal damage.

Additionally, tight surface cracks and edge delaminations may not be detected visually. Therefore, visual inspection techniques need to be supplemented by other methods of NDT. Because many of the defects associated with composites are hidden within the component's structure (i.e., within the ply lay-up or common to the honeycomb core), special techniques dealing with the analysis of sound attenuation are utilized to assure structural continuity within the composite.

Personnel who perform visual inspections should have good eyesight and should be familiar with the appearance of the defects they are expected to find. Also, surfaces to be inspected should be clean and free of all conditions that mask or obscure defects (e.g., dirt and paint).

Tap Testing

Sometimes referred to as audio, sonic or coin tap, this technique makes use of frequencies in the audible range (20 to 20,000 Hz). A surprisingly accurate method in the hands of experienced personnel, tap testing is perhaps the most common technique used for the detection of delamination or disbond.

Sandwich structures with low-density cores are particularly sensitive to impact damage; care shall be taken by the inspector to avoid causing further damage. Judicious tapping of suspected locations, along with careful observation, are the first approaches to damage assessment of bonded structures. Tap testing is widely used to evaluate the condition of laminated and bonded structures. The method (Figure 8-1-2) consists of lightly tapping the surface of the part with a coin or other suitable object.

The acoustic response of the damaged area is compared with that of a known good area. An acoustically flat or dull response is considered unacceptable. A dull sound is a good indication that some delamination or disbond exists, although a clear, sharp tapping sound does not necessarily ensure the absence of damage, especially in thick panels. The acoustic response of a good part can also vary dramatically with changes in geometry; therefore, the geometry and interior construction of the part must be known before performing the tap test. If results are questionable, the technician can compare the results to a tap test of like parts that are known to be good or use another inspection method. Figure 8-1-3 shows a calibrated sample. The entire area of concern must be tapped in order to map the damage.

Where multiple bond lines exist over the core, the core bond cannot be evaluated. In a honeycomb structure, the far-side bond line cannot be evaluated. Thus, two-side access is required for a complete inspection of honeycomb structures. Surfaces to be inspected should have all oil or grease removed and should be dry. A tap test hammer is illustrated in Figure 8-1-4.

Automated Tap Test

This test is very similar to the manual tap test except that a solenoid is used instead of a hammer. The solenoid produces multiple impacts in a single area. The tip of the impactor has a transducer that records the force versus time signal of the impactor. The magnitude of the force depends on the impactor, the impact energy and the mechanical properties of the structure.

The impact duration (period) is not sensitive to the magnitude of the impact force; however, this duration changes as the stiffness of the structure is altered. Therefore, the signal from an unflawed region is used for calibration, and any deviation from this unflawed signal indicates the existence of damage. The Mitsui Woodpecker device is shown in Figure 8-1-5.

Ultrasonic Inspection

Ultrasonic inspection has proven to be a very useful tool for the detection of internal delaminations, voids or inconsistencies in composite components not otherwise discernible using visual or tap methodology. There are many ultrasonic techniques (Figure 8-1-6), but each one uses sound wave energy with a frequency above the audible range.

A high frequency (usually several MHz) sound wave is introduced into the part and may be directed to travel normal to the part surface, or along the surface of the part, or at some predefined angle to the part surface. Different directions are used as the flow may not be visible only from one direction. The introduced sound is then monitored for significant damage as it travels its assigned route through the part. Ultrasonic sound waves have properties similar to light waves.

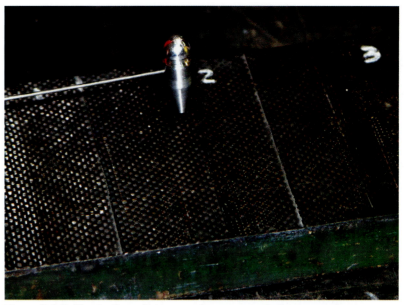

Figure 8-1-3. The testing often uses a known sample for comparison.

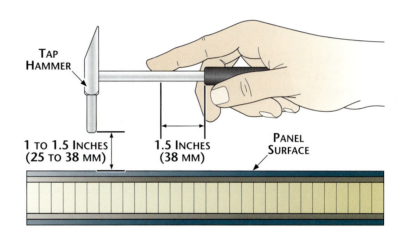

Figure 8-1-4. Tap testing using hammer

Figure 8-1-5. Automated tap testing using Mitsui Woodpecker device

Courtesy of Wavelength NDT/Marine Results

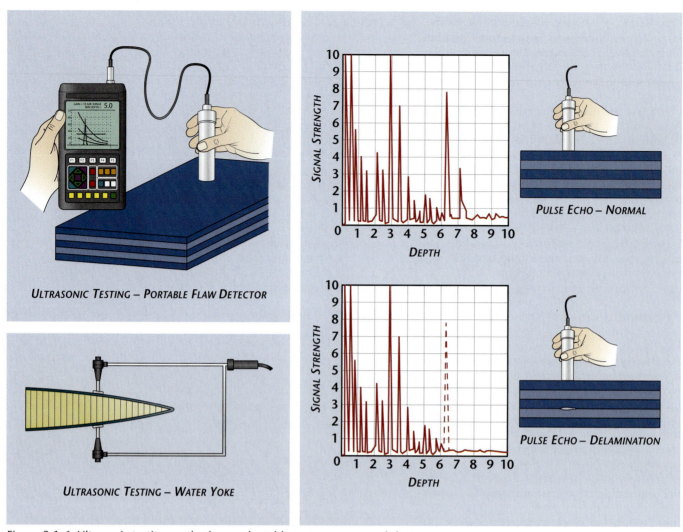

Figure 8-1-6. Ultrasonic testing methods are adaptable to many structural shapes.

When an ultrasonic wave strikes an interrupting object, the wave or energy is either absorbed or reflected back to the surface. The disrupted or diminished sonic energy is then picked up by a receiving transducer and converted into a display on an oscilloscope or a chart recorder.

The display allows the operator to comparatively evaluate the discrepant indications against those areas known to be good. To facilitate the comparison, reference standards are established and utilized to calibrate the ultrasonic equipment.

The repair technician must realize that the concepts outlined here work fine in the repetitious manufacturing environment, but are likely to be more difficult to implement in a repair environment given the vast number of different composite components installed on the aircraft and the relative complexity of their construction. The reference standards also have to take into account the transmutations that take place when a composite component is in-service over a prolonged period or has been the subject of repair activity or similar restorative action.

Through-Transmission Ultrasonic Inspection

High-frequency sound waves are transmitted into the test article through one surface. The sound energy travels through homogeneous materials with no appreciable loss until a discontinuity is encountered. The discontinuity attenuates the energy through a combination of reflection, refraction and absorption.

The variations in transmitted ultrasound are used to detect the presence of internal flaws. Required equipment includes a pulsed ultrasonic generator, sending and receiving transducers located on opposite sides of the test article, and a signal processing and display device.

Ultrasonic test results may be displayed in two basic ways. The A-scan presentation measures the amplitude of the transmitted and received energy. It reveals the presence of flaws and provides some indication of their relative size but does not locate its depth from the surface of the part.

The C-scan presentation requires automated scanning of the test article and the use of signal processing techniques. A persistent image display or paper recorder is used to display ultrasonic test responses.

The C-scan provides a plan view of the article, revealing the area of the flaw, but it provides no information relative to the flaw's depth or distance from the surface. Successive C-scans with signal gates set to various depths below the surface may be used to locate the flaw in a section.

Through-transmission ultrasonic testing (Figure 8-1-7) requires the sending and receiving transducers to be normally opposed to each other over the test article. A coupling medium is required. For contact testing methods a thin layer of fluid is generally used. This requires that the surface of the test article be clean and relatively smooth.

The requirement for surface contact is a disadvantage when large specimens must be scanned. A technique involving immersion of the article in a fluid is sometimes used to facilitate large area inspection. Through-transmission ultrasonic is effective in detecting internal flaws in a variety of materials, including parts with very thick sections. However, the flaws must be relatively perpendicular to the ultrasonic beam to be detected.

A disadvantage of ultrasonics for the detection of flaws in composite materials is the high attenuation caused by absorption in porous resin and scattering by the fibers. Hybrid configurations pose particular problems because the abrupt variations in acoustic impedance from one material to another tend to mask internal flaws.

Complex part geometry (variable surface contours, section thicknesses, wall thicknesses, etc.) make ultrasonic inspection difficult. Ultrasonic transmission requires access to both sides of the part, prohibiting its use in many on-aircraft applications.

Interpretation of ultrasonic test responses requires a reference standard containing flaws of known size and location for comparison purposes. For some types of tests, signal gates and sensitivities must be varied in the course of the test, placing a high demand on operator skill.

Unlike pulse-echo ultrasonic, the sound does not have to traverse the thickness of the part twice. Through-transmission ultrasonic testing is usually more sensitive to flaw detection in bonded assemblies. This technique is not able to determine defect depth or type.

Pulse-Echo Ultrasonic Inspection

Short, rapid pulses of high-frequency sound are transmitted into the test article through one surface. The sound energy travels through homogeneous materials with no appreciable attenuation, scattering or reflection. When an abrupt change in the conductive medium is encountered, a portion of the sound energy is reflected back toward the source.

Reflection is produced at the surfaces of the article, at interfaces between different materials, and at locations where internal discontinuities are present. The amplitude of the reflected sound wave can be used to measure the size of an internal defect. The travel time of the reflected wave can be used to measure the location of the defect from the surface of the article.

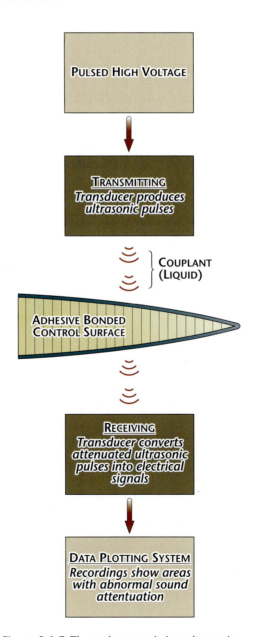

Figure 8-1-7. Through transmission ultrasonics

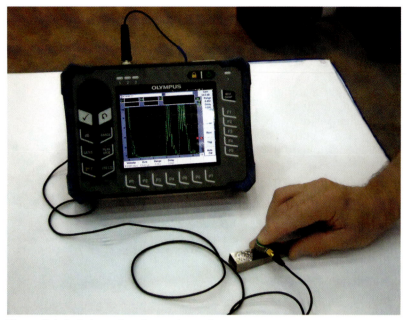

Figure 8-1-8. Pulse-echo ultrasonic equipment

complex geometries, the need for reliable reference standards, and the high dependency on operator skill. Pulse-echo NDI has the added disadvantage that flaws located close to the surface of the part are usually obscured by near-surface resolution losses.

One advantage of the pulse-echo method over through-transmission is that the A-scan presentation can be used to reveal both the presence of a defect and its location relative to the surface of the part. It also has the advantages of requiring access to only one side of the test article.

The major disadvantage of pulse-echo compared to through-transmission testing is that it is more affected by the acoustic attenuation properties of composites. Because the sound must traverse the material twice, it is more likely that flaws will be obscured by reflection and scattering.

Equipment required for pulse-echo ultrasonic testing (Figure 8-1-8) includes a pulsed ultrasonic generator, a transducer that acts alternately as a transmitter and receiver and a signal processing and display device. The A-scan and C-scan methods of presentation are also used to display pulse-echo information.

The pulse-echo technique suffers many of the limitations of the through-transmission ultrasonic technique—the need for coupling to the test article, the insensitivity to flaws that are not perpendicular to the beam, the difficulty of inspecting parts with hybrid configurations or

Resonance Ultrasonic Inspection

Continuous, compressional ultrasonic waves are transmitted into the test article from one surface. The sound waves are reflected back toward the source from the opposite surface.

The frequency of the sound waves is varied manually or automatically until a frequency is reached that causes the incident and reflected waves to be in phase. This produces standing waves within the material that cause it to vibrate or resonate. The resonant frequency is determined by the acoustic impedance of the material and its thickness.

Internal flaws and discontinuities are observed as changes in the strength and location of the resonance indications. Laminar discontinuities and bond separations are particularly sensitive to ultrasonic resonance NDI.

Required equipment includes a power supply and oscillator; detection, amplification and indicating circuits; and a transducer. Portable, self-contained, battery-operated units are produced for field work. The portable units generally use a meter, audible alarm and/or headphones to monitor resonance indications. Gating circuits can be used to detect resonant frequencies within a narrow range, thereby providing some discrimination capability with respect to flow size.

Resonance ultrasonics is useful primarily for the detection of interlaminar defects and disbonds. It is quite sensitive to these kinds of defects and can provide relatively good indications of their size and location in plain view. It is a poor method with respect to locating the depth of the defect below the surface.

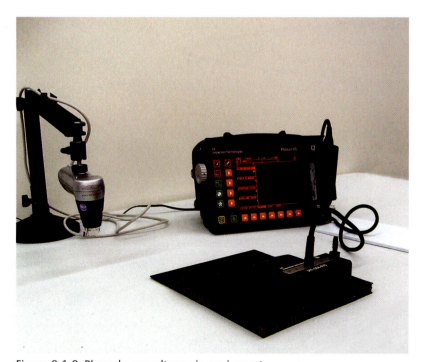

Figure 8-1-9. Phased-array ultrasonic equipment

Unlike through-transmission and pulse-echo ultrasonics, resonance testing is not significantly affected by laminar variations in the material, provided the lamina interfaces are intact. Resonance testing is generally not sensitive to fine cracks and other small defects that do not alter the natural frequency of the part.

Unlike through-transmission and pulse-echo methods, resonance ultrasonics is able to detect delaminations and disbonds close to the surface of the part. Contact with the part is required. Fluid couplant between the transducer and the surface of the part is needed for contact testing. Reference standards are necessary as they are with the other ultrasonic methods, and the dependency on operator skill is a factor.

Phased array. *Phased-array testing* is a specialized type of ultrasonic testing that uses sophisticated multi-element array transducers (Figure 8-1-9) and powerful software to steer high-frequency sound beams through the test piece and map returning echoes. This produces detailed images of internal structures similar to medical ultrasound images.

The principle of operation is the same as pulse echo testing, but it uses many sensors which speed up the process. It is used for inspection of aerospace composite structures. One of the disadvantages of this process like other ultrasonic methods is that there is a coupling agent required. This could be water, gel or a similar product.

Bond tester. Low-frequency and high-frequency *bond testers* (Figure 8-1-10) are used for ultrasonic inspections of composite structures. These bond testers use an inspection probe that has one or two transducers.

The high-frequency bond tester is used to detect delaminations and voids. It cannot detect a skin- to-honeycomb core disband or porosity. The minimum size of defects that can be detected is 0.5 in. (1.25 cm).

The low-frequency bond tester uses two transducers, and it is used to detect delamination, voids and skin-to-honeycomb core disbands. This inspection method will not detect which side of the part is damaged. The minimum size of defects that can be detected is 1 in. (2.5 cm).

Ramp checker. A *ramp checker* (Figure 8-1-11) is a miniature ultrasonic device that is used to check repairs made to composite structures in a field environment (the airport ramp). These ramp checkers can quickly determine whether the repair is airworthy. Typically defects found with these ramp checkers are voids in the bond line of the repair. Some of these devices are go no-go and simply indicate good or bad.

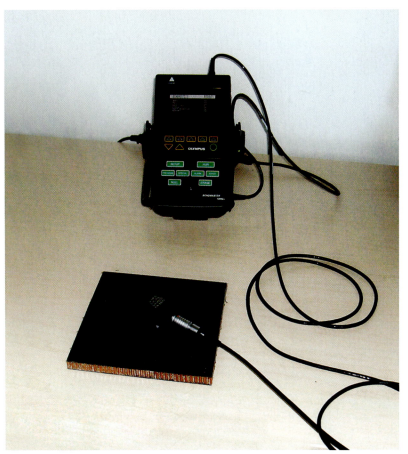

Figure 8-1-10. Bond tester

Radiography

Radiography, or X-ray as it is often referred to, is a very useful NDI method in that it allows a view into the interior of the part. This inspection method is accomplished by passing X-rays

Figure 8-1-11. Ramp checker

Figure 8-1-12. X-ray equipment can inspect interior areas

Figure 8-1-13. X-ray center for smaller parts

through the part or assembly being tested while recording the absorption of the rays onto a film sensitive to X-rays (Figure 8-1-12).

Low-energy X-ray, gamma ray or neutron emissions penetrate the test article. Variations in material thickness or density and the presence of flaws affect the intensity of the transmitted radiation. An internal image of the test article is recorded using a scintillation detector (radiometry), fluoroscope (fluoroscopy), photographic film (film radiography) or a closed-circuit television camera (video radiography).

Voids and other discontinuities attenuate the radiation to different degrees and are revealed as contrasting light and dark areas (shadows) on the recorded image. Defects less dense than surrounding material (such as voids in a composite laminate) absorb less radiation and are shown on X-ray film as darker areas.

Defects more dense than surrounding areas absorb more radiation (such as water in honeycomb sandwich assemblies) and are shown as lighter areas on X-ray film.

Fine-grain film offers the best radiographic sensitivity and provides a permanent record of defects for comparison with reference standards. Recent advancements in video radiography provide radiographic images equivalent to the best fine-grain films. With color television, variations in radiation intensity indicative of internal flaws and discontinuities are displayed as variations in color and color intensity.

The radiograph of a test article is a record of the differential attenuation of radiation as it passes through the material. Subtle variations in material density representative of interlaminar defects may not be detectable unless the flaw is nearly parallel to the direction of the radiation and of significant length. The need to precisely orient the test article to obtain adequate sensitivity to flaws may preclude the use of penetrating radiation for inspection of complex shapes.

Radiometry and fluoroscopy offer the advantage of real-time imaging of the test specimen but are relatively insensitive to small internal flaws and discontinuities, making them suitable only for quick scanning for gross defects and foreign objects. Radiation intensity, focusing and exposure times are critical, and highly specialized skills are required to set up tests and interpret test results.

Penetrating radiation techniques involve equipment that is relatively high in cost, and exposure to radiation may pose a safety hazard to personnel. Penetrating radiation methods are most practical for small parts that can be brought to a fixed facility (Figure 8-1-13). They are least practical for large, complex structures that require on-side inspection. However, because of safety concerns it is impractical to use around aircraft.

Operators should always be protected by sufficient lead shields, as the possibility of exposure exists either from the X-ray tube or from scattered radiation. Maintaining a minimum safe distance from the X-ray source is essential.

The following types of defects are detectable using radiographic techniques:

Voids in patch-to-part bond lines. Voids contain less material than the surrounding adhesive and show up as darker areas when compared to areas lacking voids.

Water entrapment in honeycomb sandwich assemblies. The water present is excess or added material for the X-rays to penetrate and appears lighter when compared to images of adjacent cells not containing water.

Honeycomb core damage. Damage to metallic core material, such as blown, crushed, corroded, fatigued, or distorted material, is best detected when the cell walls appear to be laid over on the X-ray film. (The area of interest should be offset from the central ray of the X-ray beam to allow viewing of the cell walls and determination of whether damage is present.)

Thermography

Thermography comprises all methods in which heat-sensing devices are used to measure temperature variations for parts under inspection. Common sources of heat are heat lamps and heater blankets.

The basic principle of thermal inspection consists of measuring or mapping surface temperatures when heat flows from, to or through a test object. All thermographic techniques rely on differentials in thermal conductivity between normal, defect-free areas and those having a defect.

Normally, a heat source is used to elevate the temperature of the article being examined while observing the surface heating effects. Because defect-free areas conduct heat more efficiently than areas with defects, the amount of heat that is absorbed or reflected indicates the quality of the bond.

The types of defects that affect thermal properties include disbonds, cracks, impact damage, panel thinning and water ingress into composite materials and honeycomb core. Thermal methods are most effective for thin laminates or for defects near the surface.

The most widely used thermographic inspection technique uses an infrared (IR) sensing system to measure temperature distribution. This type of inspection provides rapid, one-sided, non-contact scanning of surfaces, components or assemblies.

The heat source can be as simple as a heat lamp so long as the appropriate heat energy is applied to the inspection surface. The induced temperature rise is a few degrees and dissipates quickly after the heat input is removed. The IR camera (Figure 8-1-14) records the infrared patterns.

The resulting temperature data is processed to provide more quantitative information. An operator analyzes the screen and determines whether a defect was found. Because thermog-

Figure 8-1-14. An infrared camera is used to measure temperature distribution on a composite specimen.

Courtesy of Energistics, LLC

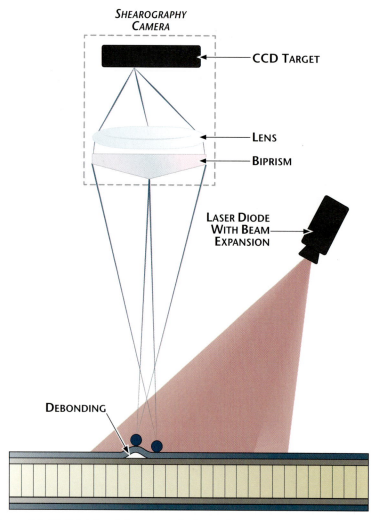

Figure 8-1-15. Priciple of shearography inspection system

raphy is a radiometric measurement, it can be done without physical contact.

Depending on the spatial resolution of the IR camera and the size of the expected damage, each image can be of a relatively large area. Furthermore, as composite materials do not radiate heat nearly as much as aluminum, and they have higher emissivity, thermography can provide better definition of damage with smaller heat inputs. Understanding of the structural arrangement is imperative to ensure that substructure is not mistaken for defects or damage.

Shearography

Shearography (Figure 8-1-15) is an optical NDI technique that detects defects by measuring the variations in reflected light from the surface of the object. Using a laser light source, an original image of the illuminated surface is recorded on video.

The part is subsequently stressed by heating, changes in pressure or acoustic vibrations during which a second video image is made. Changes in the surface contour caused by disbonding or delaminating become visible on the video display.

Shearography is being used in production environments for rapid inspection of bonded composite structure assemblies including carbon-epoxy skin and Nomex core sandwiches. This is accomplished by inducing stresses by partial vacuum. Partial vacuum stressing causes air content defects to expand, leading to slight surface deformations that are detected before and during stressing comparisons.

Display of the computer processed video image comparisons reveals defects as bright and dark concentric circles of constructive and destructive reflected light wave interference. Shearography is an ideal composite repair evaluation tool because it is not affected by the nonhomogeneity of the repaired structure. It also is able to detect and easily differentiate between crushed core and disbonding in most cored materials. Figure 8-1-16 shows a handheld shearography tester that uses vacuum and heat to find defects in composite structures.

Laser Vibrometer

Laser vibrometer (Figure 8-1-17) is another system under development that promises the capability to inspect large areas quickly. Stationary, robotic and hand-held systems are available. Laser vibrometers can be used

Figure 8-1-16. Hand-held vacuum and heat shearography unit

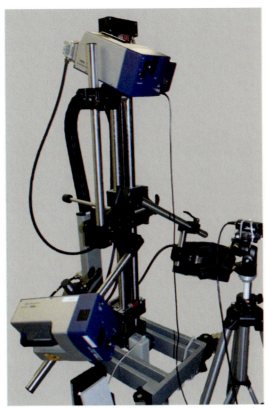

Figure 8-1-17. Experimental laser vibrometer set up

Figure 8-1-18. Automated ultrasonic testing equipment

to detect subsurface damage such as disbonds, delaminations and core crushing or cracking.

Linear and non-linear methods are currently investigated. The linear type finds changes in the linear behavior of the structure, and comparisons are made between healthy and damaged structures. The non linear approach is based on the theory that damage introduces nonlinearities to the composite structure in the vicinity of damage.

Automated Inspection Techniques

Automated ultrasound systems are increasingly used by industry to test aircraft structures. This method is reliable and relatively quick. The use of robots, as shown in Figure 8-1-18, will increase the reliability of the NDI process. Robots can be used with many different applications such as ultrasonics, X-ray and shearograhpy. The robot in Figure 8-1-18 is performing ultrasonic inspections.

9

Testing

Section 1
Materials Testing Methods

During the aircraft design phase mechanical tests of the composite structure are preformed to validate the design. Composite structures are tailored to handle stresses in very specific directions. It is important to verify that the finished structures meet the design criteria.

Failure analysis is also used in determining appropriate redesign if the original criteria is not met. The failure is examined and a structural change is engineered to prevent future failures.

This is accomplished by testing samples, often to the breaking point. A wide variety of test are available. These include tests such as tension, compression, shear, multi-axial, adhesive strength, microscopy, acid digesting, double cantilever beam and three- and four-point bending operations.

The testing process starts with small coupons followed by small panels, intermediate panels and large panels. Each subassembly design is tested. The subassemblies are combined into larger assemblies and tested. The final step in the testing process is full scale static and dynamic (fatigue) testing of the aircraft.

This insures that individual elements as well as complete assemblies achieve their designed structural strength. Figure 9-1-1 shows the building block approach and Figure 9-1-2 shows a static test of a Hawker Horizon fuselage.

Learning Objective

REVIEW
- laminate mechanical testing methods

DISCUSS
- testing methods for mechanical testing of specimens, components and aircraft structures
- test equipment used for mechanical testing of specimens, components and aircraft structures

EXPLAIN
- how to prepare test specimen for mechanical testing
- static testing
- fatigue testing

Left: A composite lug undergoes a mechanical test. *Courtesy of Wichita State University, National Institute for Aviation Research*

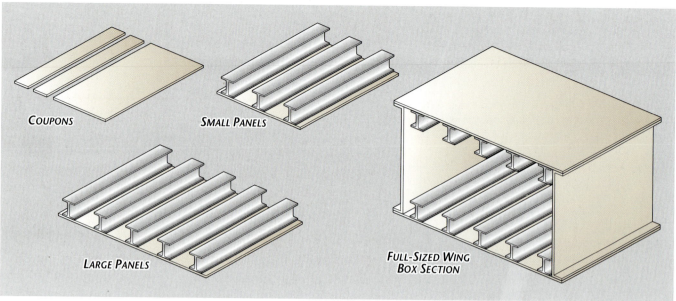

Figure 9-1-1. Building-block testing approach

Test Equipment

Several types of standard and specialized test equipment are used to test composite structures. The standard test machine in Figure 9-1-3 is used for tensile, compression, bending, double cantilever beam and other standardized tests.

The specialized test equipment in Figure 9-1-4 is used for multi-axial testing. The differential scanning calorimetry (DSC) testing equipment in Figure 9-1-5 could be used to test the glass transition temperature of a matrix system.

Test Specimen Preparation

Standardized tests are used to test composite specimens. These test standards include instructions on how to prepare the specimens used for the test. The American Society for Testing and Materials (ASTM) international testing standards are generally used for testing composite materials. This chapter discusses some of the commonly used test standards. Figure 9-1-6 shows an example of a test specimen prepared in accordance with ASTM D3039. These specimens could be made with or without tabs. Figure 9-1-7 shows examples of

Figure 9-1-2. A Hawker Horizon fuselage undergoes a static test.

Courtesy of Wichita State University, National Institute for Aviation Research

straight-edged specimens outfitted with strain gauges.

Specimen Fabrication. The general steps for specimen preparation are:

1. Lay up laminates in their desired orientations and cure based on the recommended cure cycle provided in the material technical datasheet.
2. Once the laminates are cured, square the edges of the laminates.
3. Scuff and clean the tab bonding areas on the laminates.
4. Cut long strips of tabbing materials to desired dimensions. Fiberglass boards can be used for this.
5. Bond the tabbing materials to the laminates using a two-part ductile epoxy adhesive.
6. Allow the adhesives to fully cure.
7. With a surface grinder, cut the laminates to specific dimensions for the test specimens.
8. Scuff and clean the surface where strain gauges are to be bonded.
9. Bond strain gauges in the desired directions.

Specimens used for the testing of composite materials have often tabs installed at the ends of the specimens. There are two reasons for using tabs: to protect the material from dam-

Figure 9-1-4. Multi-axial test equipment

Figure 9-1-5. DSC equipment for testing glass transition temperature

Figure 9-1-3. Universal test machine

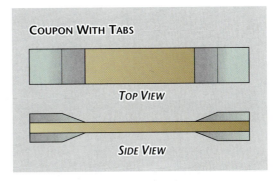

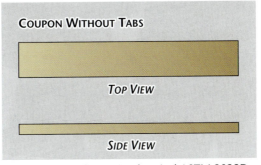

Figure 9-1-6. Schematic of typical ASTM 3039D test specimen geometry

Figure 9-1-7. Example of carbon fiber test specimen with tabs and outfitted with strain gauges

age from the grip clamping pressure and to increase the area of loading to reduce stress concentrations. Tabs are especially useful with unidirectional materials.

The following guidelines relate to applying tabs to tensile test specimen.

- Both the tabbing material and the adhesive should be as compliant (soft) as possible without losing the strength necessary to transfer loads from the grips to the specimen's gauge section. The gauge section is the specimen length unsupported by the loading grips. This always involves a trade-off because the softer materials will tend to exhibit lower strengths.

- The tabbing material should have toughness sufficient to withstand the harsh tearing action of the grip faces, which are typically serrated or roughened to dig into the tab surfaces and maximize the grips' holding power.

- Both the tabs and the adhesive layers act as cushioning materials. Increasing the thickness of both is beneficial, but a greater benefit comes from increasing the adhesive thickness because it is the layer closest to the surface of the test material. A ductile adhesive is preferred.

- Tab taper reduces the geometric discontinuity and, thus, reduces the stress concentrations in the tab termination regions. However, recent comparisons have shown that specimen with tabs with no taper but a ductile adhesive outperformed tapered tabs with a less ductile adhesive. Many testing methods do not use a tab taper.

- Plain-weave glass fabric/epoxy is an excellent tabbing material. A ductile adhesive that has the strength of typical epoxies is sufficient. A bond-line thickness of 0.02 in (0.5 mm) is usually adequate, although a thickness twice that or more is acceptable.

- If tensile specimen tabbing problems are encountered despite adherence to the preceding guidelines, the first consideration should be to reduce the specimen thickness if possible. This reduces the applied force required to cause specimen failure and thereby reduces the demands on the previously discussed testing parameters.

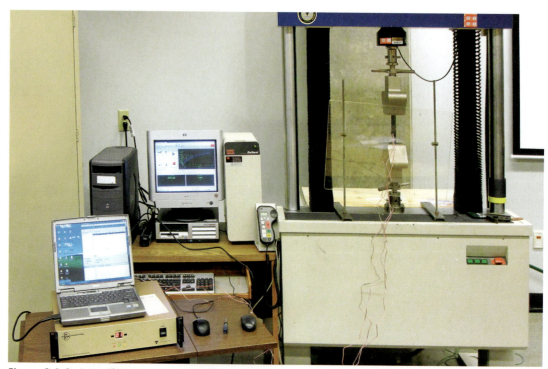

Figure 9-1-8. A tensile test set up includes monitoring and recording equipment.

Testing Methods

There are many standardized testing methods available. The following section will discuss the most commonly used methods: tensile test, compression test, shear test, double-cantilever beam test, bending tests and multi-axial tests. This text is not a substitute for ASTM International test standards and only provides examples of available testing methods. Always consult the test standards for your application. Further information about test standards is available from ASTM International.

Tensile Test

Perhaps the most commonly used test is the tensile or tension test. A test specimen is gripped at the ends and loaded in uni-axial tension until it fails. Load (force) and displacement (strain) are recorded by the test equipment. Figure 9-1-8 shows a typical tensile test setup, and Figure 9-1-9 shows a typical tension failure of multidirectional laminate using a tabbed coupon.

ASTM D3039/D3039M is the standard test method for straight-sided rectangular coupons. During this test method, a tensile stress is applied to the specimen through a mechanical shear interface at the ends of the specimen, normally by either wedge or hydraulic grips. The material response is measured in the gauge section of the coupon by either strain gauges or extensometers, subsequently determining the elastic material properties. Tabs are used to protect the specimen from the force of the grips and to distribute the load from the grips into the specimen with a minimum of stress concentration. Tabs are very useful but can be the cause of a premature failure if not correctly applied.

Testing of unidirectional materials is more sensitive than testing woven materials, especially specimens with fibers only in the 0° direction. A 1° misalignment of the fiber direction can result in a 30 percent testing error. Therefore, many times $[90/0]_{ns}$-type laminate specimens are prepared that are less sensitive for fiber misalignment error.

The unidirectional properties can be easily derived from this type of specimen. A straight-sided $[90/0]_{ns}$-type specimen is now generally believed to be the lowest cost, most reliable configuration for lamina tensile testing of unidirectional materials. The straight-sided configuration works equally well for non-unidirectional (woven fabric) materials and for other general laminates. Figure 9-1-10 shows unidirectional 45° and 10° specimens that were tested until failure.

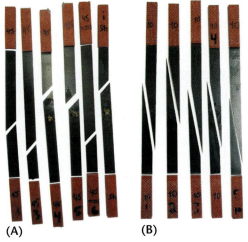

(A) (B)

Figure 9-1-10. Unidirectional specimens that failed during testing, (A) 45° specimen, (B) 10° specimen

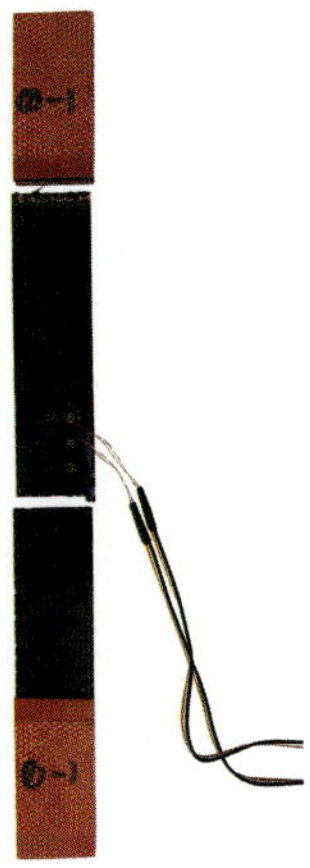

Compression Test

The objective of compression tests of composite materials is to determine the compressive modulus and the compressive strength of strain-at-failure. Test fixtures are necessary to prevent end crush, buckling of the specimen, and to introduce the stress uniformly in the specimen.

If thin relatively long specimens are not supported they will buckle, therefore, the specimens are short and supported by a fixture to reduce bucking failures. The specimens need to have tabs to introduce the load in the tabs and to prevent end crush. Compression test equipment is shown in Figure 9-1-11. Many test methods are available; two are discussed below.

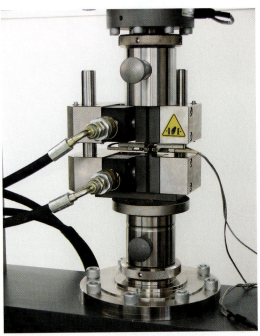

Figure 9-1-11. Compression test equipment and specimen
Courtesy of Zwick GmbH and Co. KG

Figure 9-1-9. Typical tension failure of multidirectional laminate using a tabbed coupon

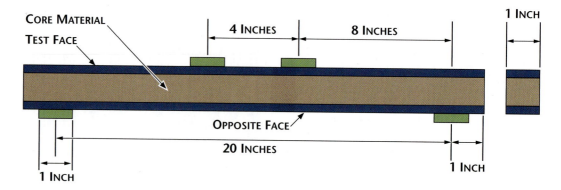

Figure 9-1-12. Typical sandwich beam compression specimen

- ASTM D3410, "Standard Test Method For Compressive Properties of Polymer-Matrix Composite Materials with Unsupported Gauge Section by Shear Loading" is an in-plane compression test method that can be used to generate the ultimate compression strength, strain-at failure, longitudinal modulus and Poisson's ration of [0], [90] and orthotropic specimens, over a typical thickness range of approximately 0.040 to 0.200 in (1 to 6 mm). Two different procedures are described in ASTM D 3410. In procedure B, the test specimen is typically tabbed, with a rectangular cross-section having recommended dimensions of 0.040 to 0.200 in (140 to 155 mm) long, 0.5 to 1.0 in (10 to 25 mm) wide, and with a 0.5 to 1.0 in (10 to 25 mm) gauge length. Specimens tested with this procedure have a minimum required thickness, specified as a function of gauge length, material modulus, and expected material strength, with an absolute minimum thickness of 0.04 in. (1 mm). The load that is applied to the fixture is transferred from the wedge grips to the specimen tabs through shear, and from the tabs to the test specimen through shear. The complex stress state in the tabbed region of the specimen changes to uni-axial compression in the specimen test section. Compression strength is determined from load at failure, while modulus and strain-at-failure are determined when strain gauges or extensometers are employed.

- ASTM D5467, "Standard Test Method for Compressive Properties of Unidirectional Polymer Matrix Composite Materials Using a Sandwich Beam" is limited to unidirectional material and uses a honeycomb-core sandwich beam that is loaded in four-point bending, placing the upper face-sheet in compression. Figure

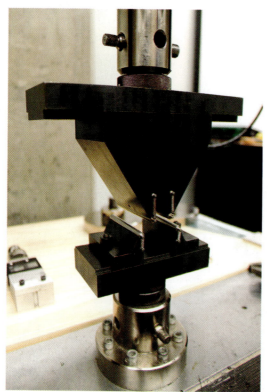

Figure 9-1-13. Four-point bending jig

Figure 9-1-14. Shear specimen with a 45° failure

9-1-12 shows the bending set up, Figure 9-1-13 shows the bending jig. The upper sheet is usually a six-ply unidirectional laminate. The lower facesheet is typically the same material, but twice as thick in order to drive failure into the compressive facesheet. The two facesheets are separated by and bonded to a deep honeycomb core, usually aluminum. Failure of the compressive face sheet enables measurement of compression strength, compression modulus, and strain-at-failure if strain gauges or extensometers are employed.

Shear Test

Testing of shear has proven to be very difficult and there is no single test that works with all material combinations. The proper test needs to be carefully selected. ASTM D3518/D3518M, "Standard Practice for In-Plane Shear Response of Polymer-Matrix Composite Materials by Tensile Test of a ±45° Laminate," is discussed here. This test uses a modified ASTM D3039 tensile test coupon with a lay-up of $[\pm 45]_{ns}$ to measure in-plane shear properties.

The in-plane shear stress in this coupon can be shown to be a simple function of the average applied tensile stress, allowing for straightforward calculation of the shear response of the material. This test method uses a simple test coupon, requires no fixturing, and measurement of strain can be performed using either extensometers or strain gauges. Figure 9-1-14 shows a failed shear specimen.

Panel shear test. Combined in-plane loaded composite materials test elements and methodology can be as simple as the rail-shear test

Figure 9-1-15. Picture frame used to test unidirectional test panel in shear

detailed in ASTM D4255. This test, also called a picture frame test, is used to obtain shear stress-strain curves to failure of simple, unnotched, unidirectional, or multidirectional laminates. A picture frame test setup shown in Figure 9-1-15 is used for testing notched and unnotched multidirectional laminates in shear.

Double Cantilever Beam Test

Fracture in structural materials is usually initiated by some crack or notch-like flaw that induces high stresses in its immediate vicinity. This section briefly discusses ASTM D 5528, "Standard Test Methods for Mode I Interlaminar Fracture Toughness of Unidirectional Fiber-Reinforced Polymer-Matrix Composites." The test, commonly referred to as a double-cantilever beam (DCB) test, is shown schematically in Figure 9-1-16.

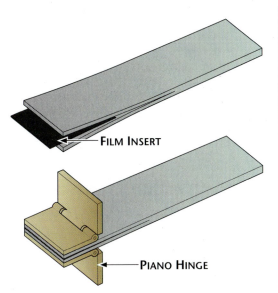
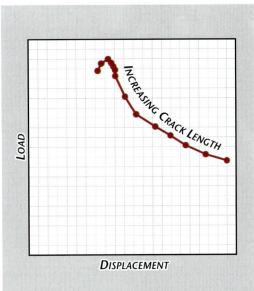

Figure 9-1-16. Double-catilever beam (DCB) test.

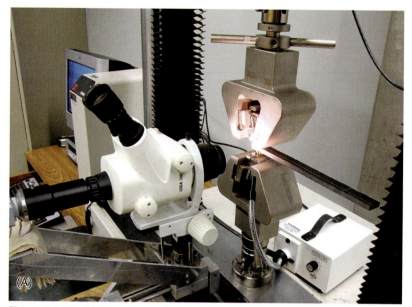
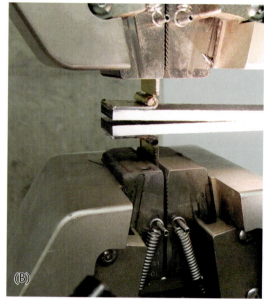

Figure 9-1-17. (A) Test set up of a double-cantilever beam test, (B) Closeup of DCB test

The specimen measures 5 in. (125 mm) long, 0.8 to 1 in. (20 to 25 mm) wide and 0.12 to 0.20 in. (3 to 5 mm) thick. It uses a non-bondable film insert placed at the specimen midplane during panel manufacture to create an initial crack length of approximately 2.5 in. (63 mm). The applied load, P, to the two arms; the corresponding displacement and typical load-displacement traces obtained are shown in Figure 9-1-16.

The numbers on these traces indicate results for various delamination lengths and are obtained as the delamination progresses. Figure 9-1-17 shows a DCB specimen during a test.

Multi-Axial Test

Multi-axial testing can evaluate material strengths and failure mechanisms under properly proportioned loadings that simulate actual service conditions. Such tests are usually combinations of compression and compression or tension and compression loading, each at 90° to the other. Figure 9-1-18 shows a bi-axial test setup. The load frame of this testing equipment can apply a load in two directions at the same time. Load cells and strain gauges are used to record data.

Figure 9-1-18. Bi-axial test equipment for testing honeycomb sandwich panels

Section 2
Testing of Adhesive Bonded Joints

Many composite structures are bonded and the evaluation of the bond integrity is very important. Bonded joints can fail in several ways and several tests are available to determine the integrity of the bonded joint. Some of these tests are discussed in this section. Table 9-2-1 shows the most common causes of bond failure. The bond failures need to be investigated after testing to determine the probable cause.

Bonding technology is a systemic joining technique that is based on a variety of interrelated processes. Besides the properties of the adhesive film, substrate materials and the stresses and loads on the joint, the fundamental factor for a bond to be effective is its geometric design.

Flaws in bonded structures are a common occurrence because key basic principles of bond design have been neglected. Even in the design phase of a component, special relationships must be taken into account. The principle requirement on a bond is to transmit forces and be able to withstand the stresses caused by these forces for a long period of time.

When designing bonds, two key requirements must be met in order to create a bond with good long-term stability (meaning in particular resistance to moisture): Firstly, a sufficiently large area must be available for bonding and, secondly, measures must be taken to prevent mechanical loads causing stress peaks in the bond.

Figure 9-2-1 shows the stresses that act on a bonded joint. Peel stress leads to near line-form, high stress on the adhesive in the bonded joint. This is often many times higher than the final strength of most adhesives. Being a planar joining technique, bonds must be designed to withstand shear stress. The substrates are pulled apart parallel to the bonding surface, meaning that the entire bonding area is subject to stress.

In general, the bonding area of bonded joints can be increased such that the stresses can be distributed over an area so large that the point collapse load is not exceeded. Tensile stresses act vertically to the plane of the joint. Bonded joints are not sensitive to compressive stress. The behavior of bonded joints under torsional stress is similar to their behavior under lap shear stress.

The choice of test method depends on the properties of the bonded joint in question. Bond strengths are determined using the lap shear test, peeling resistance using the floating roller peel test, or T-peel test and adhesion behavior using, for example, the wedge test.

In order to obtain information about the long-term stability of bonds, the samples are

FAULT	CAUSE	REMEDY
Bond fails leaving bare surface	• Surface not properly pretreated • Non-removal of film's protective covers	• Check that pretreatment procedures are correct • Ensure parts are not contaminated after pretreatment • Remove covers before assembly
Adhesive still soft after cure cycle	• Adhesive not properly cured	• Check recommended cure temperature of the adhesive is achieved throughout the curing cycle
Voids in bond line and thick bond line	• Bonding pressure too low • No follow-up pressure • Initial poor fit of parts	• Increase pressure • Check that there is a constant application of pressure as adhesive flows • Check for distortion or mismatch before assembly with adhesive
Wedge-shaped or tapered bond line	• Incorrect jigging	• Check for correct assembly of the component

Table 9-2-1. Causes of bond failure

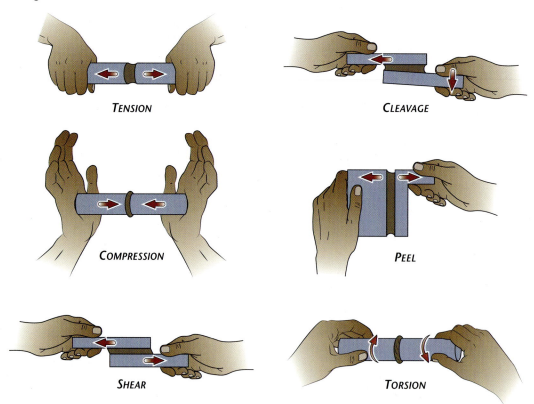

Figure 9-2-1. Bonded joints are subjected to different types of stress.

equilibrated under the likely conditions of the actual surroundings and are then subjected to mechanical tests. Common conditions are equilibration under hot, humid conditions; sweating test; salt spray test; cataplasma test; stability test under changing climatic conditions.

In the mechanical tests, the bonded joints are loaded to the point of fracture. The nature of the fracture (adhesive fracture, cohesive fracture, substrate fracture or a combination of these) provides information about the quality of the bond and about potential production errors. Regarding tests on samples equilibrated under controlled conditions, a cohesive fracture indicates that the adhesion remained stable despite the influences acting on the bond (e.g., moisture). In contrast, an adhesive fracture indicates that the bond has failed at its most sensitive point, the adhesion. This may indicate incompatibility between the substrate material and adhesive, inadequate surface pretreatment or processing/application errors. Possible processing/application errors are:

- Pot life/skinning time exceeded
- Surface too cold
- Adhesive too cold
- Adhesive stored for too long
- Mixing errors

Lap Shear Test

The lap shear test is the most commonly used standard test for determining the strength of medium-strength and high-strength bonds. The most common is the DIN EN 1465 test. DIN stands for the German name of the German

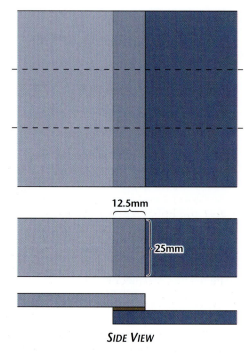

Figure 9-2-2. Schematic of lap shear specimen

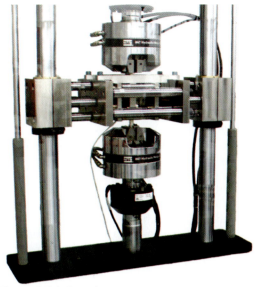

Figure 9-2-3. Lap shear test setup

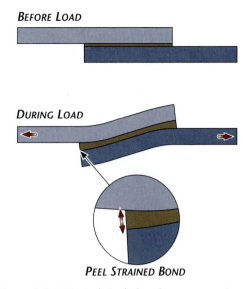

Figure 9-2-4. Typical single-lap shear test specimen

Institute for Standardization, another author of test standards.

The strength of bonded single-lap joints on subjecting the substrates to loads is determined by lap shear forces in the direction of the bonded joint. In accordance with the standard, the overlap corresponds to a width of 1 in. (25 mm) and a length of 0.5 in. (12.5 mm) as shown in Figure 9-2-2.

To prepare the specimen, first manufacture two plates. Bond the two plates together and then cut the panel into specimens 1 in. (25 mm) wide.

Each sample must be measured individually. To do this, a sample is clamped in the self-aligning jaws of the test unit so that the force acts in the center of the bonded layer (Figure 9-2-3).

The test is carried out in such a way that the period of time for separation of the substrates is 65 ± 20 s, with the speed of movement of the jaws being constant. The highest force (Fmax) that acts can then be read from the force gauge and recorded. The bond strength (tb) in N/mm2 is then calculated using the following equation:

$tb = F_{max}/A$

$A = L_U \times b$ where:

F_{max} = highest force in N

L_U = overlap length in mm

b = average sample width in mm

A = bonded area in mm^2

Adhesive bond strength is usually measured by the simple single-lap shear test, as shown in Figure 9-2-4. The lap shear strength is reported as the failure stress in the adhesive. This is calculated by dividing the failing load by the bond area. Since the stress distribution in the adhesive is not uniform over the bond area, the reported shear stress is lower than the true, ultimate strength of the adhesive.

While this test specimen is relatively easy to fabricate and test, it does not give a true measure of the shear strength due to adherend bending and induced peel loads. In addition, there is no method of measuring the shear strain and, thus, of calculating the adhesive shear modulus required for structural analysis.

To measure the shear stress versus shear strain properties of an adhesive, an instrumented thick-adherend test can be run where the adherends are so thick that the bending forces are negligible. However, the single-lap shear test is an effective screening and process control test for evaluating adhesives, surface preparations and for in-process control.

When testing or characterizing adhesive materials there are several important points that should be considered:

- Test conditions, such as surface preparation, the adhesive and the bonding cycle, must be carefully controlled.
- Tests should be run on the joint that will be used in production.
- In-service conditions that the adhesive will be exposed to during its service life must be evaluated, including temperature, moisture and any solvents or fluids.

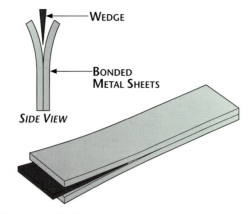

Figure 9-2-5. Wedge test

In order to carry out the wedge test, two metal sheets of a prescribed thickness and pretreated under production conditions are bonded to each other. A wedge is driven into the bond and the end of the crack that is produced is marked.

Thereafter the prepared sample is equilibrated under hot humid conditions, such as 75 minutes at 122°F [50°C] and 95 percent humidity, or in water. The bond that is under stress from the wedge is possibly forced further apart. After being equilibrated the progress of the crack is marked and measured, the bonded area is separated and the surface of fracture is evaluated. The advantage of this test compared to the lap shear test is that results are obtained relatively quickly and direct information is obtained about the effect of aging conditions on the adhesive layer when it is exposed to mechanical loads. The wedge test is shown in Figure 9-2-5.

The failure modes for all test specimens should be examined. For example, if the specimen exhibits an adhesive failure at the adherend-adhesive interface rather than a cohesive failure within the adhesive, it may be an indication of a surface preparation problem that will result in decreased joint durability.

Wedge Test

The DIN 65448 wedge test is one of the few methods that test the quality of bonds under the influence of mechanical, chemical and media loads.

Sandwich Peel Test

The sandwich peel test is performed to evaluate the bond strength of honeycomb structures. Figure 9-2-6 shows a setup for climbing drum peel testing in accordance with ASTM D 1781. This test literally peels one of the face sheets away from the core to establish the bond strength between the constituent materials.

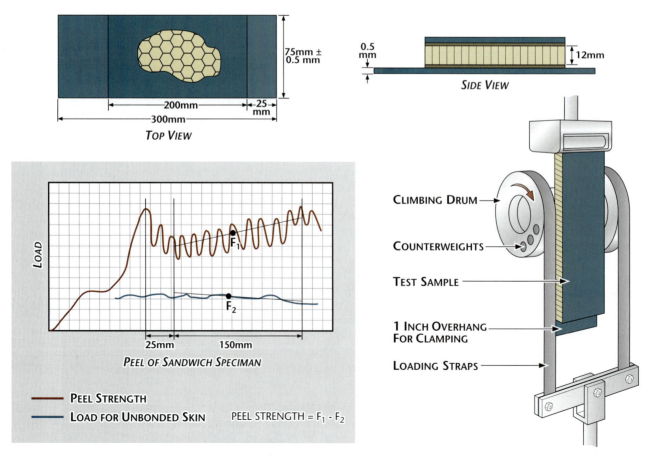

Figure 9-2-6. Honeycomb sandwich peel test

Section 3
Other Testing Methods

Microscopy

Microscopy is a valuable tool in materials investigations related to problem solving, failure analysis, advanced materials development and quality control. The most common use of microscopy for composites is determining void content, ply counts, delaminations and fiber orientations. It is also used to investigate failure mechanisms and for microstructural analysis. A microscope is used to study a prepared cross-sectional specimen. Specialized software is available to measure void volume directly when using an image analysis approach.

The most important step in microscopy is the preparation of a sample that can be viewed with the microscope. The following is a step-by-step approach.

Specimen sectioning. The composite part typically needs to be sectioned so that it is manageable for polishing. Use a surface grinder with a diamond blade or a band saw with a toothless diamond-coated blade. Rough grinding can be accomplished to size the cross-section to the correct size.

Mounting of the cross section. The cross section needs to be mounted in a little mold made of silicone rubber so that it can be polished on an automated polisher. The little cup is cleaned, treated with a mold release agent and filled with an epoxy resin.

The cross-section is placed in the resin filled cup and left to cure. A little clip can be used to ensure that the cross-section remains in place. After the resin is cured, the cross-section will be removed from the silicone mold. Figure 9-3-1 shows a prepared specimen.

Polishing. The easiest way to polish the specimen is to use a polisher, as shown in Figure 9-3-2. This type of polisher is outfitted with two rotating wheels and water is used for removal of polishing particles. The polishing process consists of several steps.

Silicon paper is used for initial rough polishing and subsequent finer grades of silicon paper are used. An example would be to start with 120-grit paper and proceed to 320- and then 600-grit paper.

After the silicon paper, a diamond platen is used. Final polishing is accomplished with 0.3 µm levigated alumina slurry (5 g AL_2O_3 to 1 L distilled water) on a silk cloth. Consult the equipment manufacturer information to determine optimum polishing steps and required materials.

Polishing steps:

1. Grind the specimen in order using 180-, 240-, 320- and 400-grit silicon paper.
2. Polish the specimen using 5 µm, 1 µm and 0.3 µm of levigated alumina slurry
3. Begin polishing in any direction and maintain the direction until the step is complete.
4. Rotate the specimen by 90° each time you change to a finer abrasive.
5. Rinse the specimen after each step to remove remaining grit.

Figure 9-3-1. Microscopy specimens

Figure 9-3-2. Polishing equipment

Viewing. There are many questions to consider when viewing a specimen. What are the fibers and what is the matrix? What are the capabilities of the microscope?

Viewing samples with a light microscope is the preferred start. In most cases, relevant detail may be resolved from 5x to 100x magnification. Epi-bright-field illumination is used more than 90 percent of the time and on all types of composites.

This method is particularly useful for imaging samples for void studies, fiber orientation verification, resin-to-fiber ratio determination and most microcrack studies. Figure 9-3-3 shows a typical microscope used for microscopy.

Void analysis of composite specimens can be performed using low-magnification (6x to 50x)

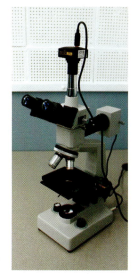

Figure 9-3-3. Microscope used for microscopy

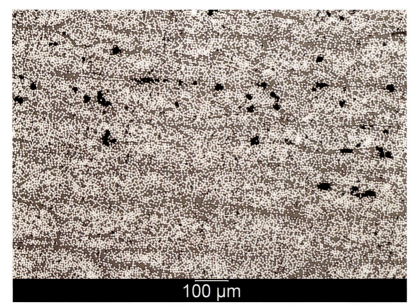

Figure 9-3-4. Microscopy analysis of a unidirectional composite specimen at 50x magnification showing voids in the cured structure.

bright-field illumination of the cross-section. An example of a unidirectional fiber polymer composite material containing a significant number of voids is shown in Figure 9-3-4. The voids show up as dark holes on the surface.

Acid Digestion

Most commonly, composites consists of one type of fiber and one type of resin. Determination of resin content, along with void content, is useful in characterizing cure and in evaluation of mechanical test results.

Resin-matrix composites may be analyzed using ASTM D 3171, "Fiber Content of Resin Matrix Composite by Matrix Digestion." The method employs standard techniques to digest or remove the resin matrix without dissolving the fiber. Method A, a hot nitric acid digestion, and method B, a sulfuric acid/hydrogen peroxide digestion, are commonly used on carbon fiber composites.

Method C is a sodium hydroxide digestion that is designed for aramid composites. Figure 9-3-5 and Figure 9-3-6 show the setup for acid digestion testing.

Acid digestion equipment includes:

- Rubber gloves and safety glasses
- Fume hood with a vacuum system
- Buchner funnel with filter
- A 0.042-quart (400mL) beaker
- Nitric acid
- Glass stirring rod
- Bunsen burner or electric heater
- Precision balance

The steps in the acid digestion testing process are as follows:

1. Prepare a 2 in. (9.5 cm) square specimen.
2. Weigh the specimen to determine the combined weight of the fiber and epoxy.
3. Place the specimen into a beaker filled with 30mL of 70 percent nitric acid.
4. Heat nitric acid to 176°F (80°C) and wait for all the epoxy to be digested by the nitric acid.
5. Once the nitric acid is digested, filter out the fibers and wash fibers with distilled water three times.
6. Dry the clean fibers in the oven with a minimum of 212°F (100°C).
7. Weigh the dried fibers to determine fiber weight.
8. Calculate results using the following equations.

Fiber Volume Fraction Equation:

$$V_f = \frac{\rho_m W_f}{\rho_f W_m + \rho_m W_f}$$

V_f = Volume fraction of fibers

W_m = Weight of the matrix

W_f = Weight of the fibers

ρ_m = Density of the matrix

ρ_f = Density of the fibers

The void content of the composite is assumed to be negligible.

EXAMPLE:

W_f = 3.06 g; W_m = 1.20 g
(weight of laminate minus weight of fibers)

ρ_f = 1.65 g/cm³ and ρ_m = 1.26 g/cm³

$$V_f = \frac{(1.26)(3.06)}{[(1.65)(1.20)] + [(1.26)(3.06)]}$$

Determination of Void Content:

Vf = 0.66

$$\rho_c = \frac{W}{V}$$

ρ_c = Density of the laminate

W = Weight of the laminate

V = Volume of the laminate

Consider the following assumption:

$V_f + V_m + V_v =$

V_f = Volume of the fibers

V_m = Volume of the matrix

V_v = Volume of the voids

$V_v = 1 \dfrac{[(W_f/\rho_f) + (W_m/\rho_m)]\rho_c}{W}$

W_m = Weight of the matrix

W_f = Weight of the fibers

ρ_m = Densities of the matrix

ρ_f = Densities of the fibers

EXAMPLE:

$V_v = 1 - \dfrac{[(W_f/\rho_f) + (W_m/\rho_m)]\rho_c}{W}$

W_f = Weight of fiber = 3.0671 g

W_m = Weight of matrix = 1.2071 g

ρ_f = Density of fiber = 1.65 g/cm^3

ρ_m = Density of composite = 1.505 g/cm^3

W = Weight of composite = 4.2742

$W_f + W_m = W$

3.0671 + 1.2071 = 4.2742

$V_v = 1 - \dfrac{[(3.0671/1.65) + (1.2071/1.265)]1.505}{4.2742}$

V_v = 0.00948

V_v = 0.9%

Analysis

In addition to grouping material property tests by building-block level, collections of material property test data can be grouped by purpose into the five categories of screening, qualification, acceptance, equivalence and structural substantiation.

Screening Data

The purpose of screening testing is initial evaluation of new material systems under worst-case environmental and loading test conditions. Test matrix results in small-sample mean values for various strengths, moduli and physical properties, and includes key properties at both lamina and laminate levels. It is designed to both eliminate deficient material systems from the material selection process and to reveal promising new material systems before planning subsequent, more in-depth evaluations.

Material Qualification Data

This collection of tests defines the requirements necessary for a material to meet a procurement specification. Ideally, material qualification testing is a subset of, or directly related to, the design allowables testing performed to satisfy structural substantiation requirements. The objective is quantitative statistics for key material properties. The resulting statistics are used in establishing material acceptance, equivalence, quality control and design basis values.

Acceptance Data

These tests are normally a subset of material qualification. They serve to verify material consistency by periodic sampling of material product and evaluation of key material properties. Test results from small sample sizes are statisti-

Figure 9-3-5. Test specimens in acid solution on heated plate under hood

Figure 9-3-6. Weighing of the dried fibers

Figure 9-3-7. An Airbus A380 wing undergoes a full-scale wing load test.
Courtesy of IABG Dresden

Figure 9-3-8. A wing undergoes a static test. *Courtesy of Wichita State University, National Institute for Aviation Research*

cally compared with control values established from prior testing to determine whether or not the material production process has changed significantly.

Equivalence Data

This testing category assesses the equivalence of an alternate material to a previously characterized material, usually for the purpose of using an existing design property database. In general, the alternate material is substantially the same as the known material, but may have minor process changes to the raw material or minor changes in the final end-object process due to processing at a different site by different equipment and operators. Key properties are tested in quantities large enough to provide an engineering conclusion, but small enough for significant cost savings (if equivalence is shown) as compared to generating an entirely new, self-sufficient database.

Structural Substantiation Data

These are all data used in the engineering assessment of the ability of a given structure to meet the requirements of a specific application. The development of design allowables, ideally derived or related to statistical data obtained during a material qualification task, is a subset of this category

Full-Scale Testing of Aircraft Structures

The aircraft structure and components are tested during the manufacturing phase of a new aircraft program. Static loads and fatigue tests are conducted to make sure that the aircraft structure will withstand the anticipated design loads that the aircraft will encounter during operation. The fuselage is pressurized to determine the effects of pressurization cycles and the wings are tested under static and dynamic loads to determine whether they will hold up. These tests are necessary and are required by the FAA for certification of the aircraft. The wings should hold up to at least 150 percent of the design limit load.

The full-scale test is one of the primary means of demonstrating how successfully a structure meets these structural performance requirements and is extremely important because it tests all combined relationships of the critical elements of the structure in the most realistic manner. In airframe production, the full-scale structural test is most often performed on one of the first three or four airframes manufactured. Typical full-scale tests are static, durability (fatigue) and damage tolerance, the last of which may not require a full-scale test.

Static Test

The full-scale static test is the most important test in qualifying composite structures because of their brittle nature, sensitivity to stress concentrations and insensitivity to fatigue cycling. Some manufacturers use cables attached to the top of the wing surface and others use hydraulic jacks positioned at the bottom of the wing surface to apply a load to the wing structure. The loading setup is controlled by computers, which control not only the loading applied by each hydraulic jack but also the rate of loading. They also check the displacement of the jack or the load cell to prevent overload of the specimen. Figure 9-3-7 shows a typical wing test setup, and in Figure 9-3-8, a static test is performed on a wing.

To meet FAA requirements, conventional metal structures are usually tested only to the limit load. This may also be true for composite structures if the manufacturer has had experience with similar composite structures; otherwise, testing to the ultimate load level is required. Various U.S. Department of Defense agencies require the ultimate load level for the static test in order to qualify most structures.

After completing the required testing, whether to limit or ultimate load, the manufacturer often picks the most critical condition and tests the article to destruction. This destruction test further validates not only the capability of the analysis to predict the load distribution but also the strength of the structure. .

The final step in the static test sequence is a review of the data obtained from the test and evaluation of its correlation with the stress analysis. The structure is also carefully inspected using nondestructive techniques to determine whether damage that has occurred cannot be readily detected visually. This is of particular importance to composite structures because many of their failure modes and sequences are interlaminar and thus may not be visible.

Fatigue Testing

The effects of cyclic loading on current carbon-epoxy composites have generally been shown to be noncritical, due to the static load sensitivity of composite structures to stress concentration. In addition, the load level threshold at which composites become sensitive to cyclic loading is a very high percentage of their static failure load.

Because this threshold is so high and most aircraft do not experience repeated loads that approach their ultimate loads, composite structures are not fatigue critical. Even if they were to experience loads near this threshold, or slightly above, there are so few of these high cycles in the spectrum life of the vehicle that no significant fatigue damage would occur that would affect structural capability.

During the fatigue test (Figure 9-3-9), the structure is repeatedly loaded and unloaded in a predescribed loading sequence. The fatigue-testing program will often cycle the loads to the equivalent of several times the expected service life of the aircraft. The methods of loading, attachment of load fixtures, instrumentation, data recording and checkout of the test setup are all similar to those used in static tests.

The fatigue test has the additional feature of inspection intervals throughout the test life. These inspections are conducted to determine whether any damage is progressing because of cyclic loading, to obtain fatigue performance of the structural details, and to catch a critical damage growth that could cause loss of the test article during load cycling.

Figure 9-3-9. A fatigue test is performed on a composite sandwich panel. *Courtesy of Wichita State University, National Institute for Aviation Research*

10

Types and Causes of Damage

Damage from many causes, such as scratching, gouging, impact, abrasion, erosion, local chemical attack or overheating, may affect only a few surface plies over a large area or a depth of many plies in a smaller area. Failure to use protective devices, such as padded fixtures and sacrificial plies, may cause additional damage.

Inadvertent or accidental impact may occur during the handling of parts during maintenance. The types of damage range from small surface scratches to more severe defects like punctures.

Once damage is identified, the extent of damage must be determined and then it can be classified to determine the disposition of the defective part. Improper damage removal and repair techniques can impart greater damage than originally sustained. Whenever damage is left unrepaired, damage growth becomes a concern.

A large amount of research has been directed toward the potential growth of undetected small damages. Growth of damage between advanced composite materials and metallic materials differ in several ways. Cracking in metal structures is similar to delamination in advanced composite structures. Penetration damage becomes critical in advanced composites due to the nonisotropic nature of the material design. Keep in mind that the potential for damage growth is peculiar to each aircraft type.

Many honeycomb structures such as wing spoiler, fairings, flight controls and landing gear doors have thin face sheets that have experienced durability problems. These could be grouped into three categories: low resistance to impact, liquid ingression, and erosion.

Learning Objective

REVIEW
- types of damage to composite structures
- causes of damage to composites
- repair qualification and authority

EXPLAIN
- composite damage assessment
- categories of damage to composites

Left: A tear, like the one in carbon fiber material shown here, is just one type of damage to which composites are subject due to impact, environment or extended use.

Figure 10-1-1. Dent in honeycomb sandwich structure

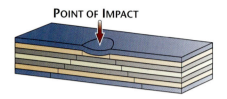

Figure 10-1-2. Delamination following impact on a monolithic laminate

Figure 10-1-3. Laminate splitting

Figure 10-1-4. Puncture in honeycomb sandwich structure

Figure 10-1-5. Heat and burn damage

These structures have adequate stiffness and strength, but low resistance to a service environment where parts are crawled over, tools dropped, and where service personnel are often unaware of the fragility of thin-skinned sandwich parts. Damages to these components, such as core crush, impact damages and disbonds, are quite often easily detected with a visual inspection due to their thin face sheets. However, sometimes they are overlooked, or damaged by service personnel, who do not want to delay aircraft departure or bring attention to their accidents, which might reflect poorly on their performance record. Therefore, damages are sometimes allowed to go unchecked, often resulting in growth of the damage due to liquid ingression into the core. Non-durable design details (e.g., improper core edge close-outs) also led to liquid ingression.

Section 1

Damage Types

Composite structures can be damaged in many ways. Damage type must be identified to determine a repair scenario.

Surface scratch. Damage considered a surface scratch does not damage fibers or the internal structure of a composite. Repair of such damage usually requires only blending or refinishing.

Dent. A dent is a hollow or low place usually caused by impact. It will usually have deformed fibers, but no broken fibers. It is detectable by visual inspection or straight-edge comparison. On solid laminates, the backside of the dented surface will usually show significantly more damage than the front side; therefore, technicians should always examine both the front and back sides. Figure 10-1-1 shows a honeycomb sandwich structure that has a dent.

Delamination. Delamination is the separation of plies caused by impact or inclusion causing a void in the material. Delaminations are typically repaired using a scarf repair. Underlying damage can extend to a much greater extent in laminate structures. Figure 10-1-2 shows the effects of impact damage causing delaminations.

Disbond. Disbond is adhesive failure at a bond line. It occurs between a honeycomb core and a face sheet or between adjacent bonded structures.

Laminate splitting. The damage does not extend through the full length of the part. The effects on mechanical performance depend on the length of split relative to the component thickness. Figure 10-1-3 shows the effects of laminate splitting.

Scratch and gouge. Damage where one or more plies are broken and the structure skin has not been fully penetrated.

Puncture. A puncture is any penetration of a structure. A puncture to a honeycomb sandwich structure is shown in Figure 10-1-4.

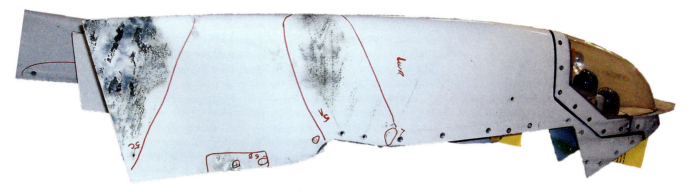

Figure 10-1-6. Erosion damage to wing tip

Heat/burn damage. Temperature exposure in excess of the part cure temperature can degrade matrix strength. Epoxy matrix materials that cure at 350°F (177°C) and that are exposed to temperatures above 400°F (204°C) but less than 600°F (316°C) can experience a marked degradation in properties and show little or no visual indication of damage to the laminate. However, if the laminate is painted, discoloration of the paint system provides an indicator that laminate damage may have occurred. For 350°F (177°C) curing epoxy matrix materials, exposures beyond 600°F (316°C) may result in visual blistering and pyrolyzation of the outer plies of the laminate.

For bonded composite assemblies, epoxy adhesives degrade at lower temperatures (typically 50°F [10°C] lower) than laminate matrix materials. Advanced composite materials and bonded composite assemblies exhibiting discolored paint or that are suspected of being exposed to excessive temperatures (above 400°F [204°C] for epoxy matrix composites or 500°F [260°C] for bismaleimide matrix composites) may have experienced heat damage.

These advanced composite materials and bonded composite assemblies are suspect. The matrix material beneath any blistered, delaminated or pyrotyzed plies are suspect as well. The suspect areas require evaluation and disposition by engineering to evaluate laminates, laminate-to-core bonds and laminate-to-substructure bonds. Heat damage could result in a local fracture with separation of surface plies. Its effect on the mechanical performance depends on the thickness of the part. Figure 10-1-5 shows the effect of excessive heat on a honeycomb sandwich structure.

Erosion damage. Erosion resistance capabilities of composite materials have been known to be less than that of aluminum and, as a result, their application in leading edge surfaces has been generally avoided. However, composites have been used in areas of highly complex geometry, though generally with an erosion coating. The durability and maintainability of some erosion coatings are less than ideal.

Another problem, not as obvious as the first, is that edges of doors or panels can erode if they are exposed to the air stream. This erosion can be attributed to improper design or installation/fit-up. On the other hand, metal structures in contact or in the vicinity of these composite parts may show corrosion damage due to: inappropriate choice of aluminum alloy, damaged corrosion sealant of metal parts during assembly, at splices, or insufficient sealant and/or lack of glass fabric isolation plies at the interfaces of spars, ribs and fittings. Figure 10-1-6 shows erosion damage to a wing tip.

Corrosion of lightning protection materials. Many fiberglass and Kevlar® parts have a fine aluminum mesh for lightening protection. This aluminum mesh often corrodes around the bolt or screw holes, as shown in Figure 10-1-7. The corrosion affects the electrical bonding of the panel, and the aluminum mesh must be removed and new mesh installed to restore the electrical bonding of the panel.

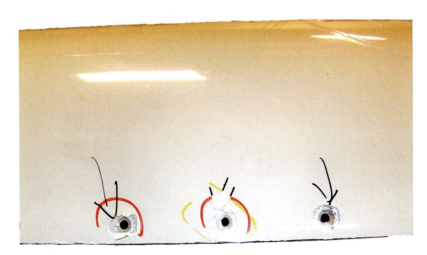

Figure 10-1-7. Corrosion damage to the lightning protection mesh

Moisture damage. The repair of parts due to liquid ingression can vary depending upon the liquid, of which water and Skydrol® (hydraulic fluid) are the two most common. Water tends to create additional damage in repaired parts when cured unless all moisture is removed from the part. Most repair material systems cure at temperatures above the boiling point of water, which can cause a disbond at the skin-to-core interface wherever trapped water resides. For this reason, core drying cycles are typically included prior to any repair. Some operators will take the extra step of placing a damaged but unrepaired part in the autoclave to dry so as to preclude additional damage from occurring during the cure of the repair.

Skydrol® presents a different problem. Once the core of a sandwich part is saturated, complete removal of Skydrol® is almost impossible. The part continues to weep the liquid even in cure such that bond lines can become contaminated and full bonding does not occur. Removal of contaminated core and adhesive as part of the repair is highly recommended. Figure 10-1-8 shows a nose radome of transport aircraft with multiple repairs.

UV damage. There has been a concern with ultraviolet (UV) radiation affecting composite structures. Composite structures need to be protected by a top coating to prevent the effects of UV light. Special UV primers and paints have been developed to protect composite materials.

Section 2
Damage Assessment

The damage assessment is the intermediate stage between inspection and repair and includes making a decision about if and how to repair a damaged structure, the nature of the repair (permanent or temporary), and the needed inspection after the repair and during the residual life of the repaired structure. This decision depends upon where the damage is detected, the accuracy of damage characterization, the means available in determining the severity of the damage and designing and performing an adequate repair.

Prior to actually beginning a repair, the damage should be assessed and then categorized to determine if the repair is required/feasible (Figure 10-2-1). Three types of damage are categorized below:

Negligible damage. Damage that because of its size, nature and location does not adversely affect the structural integrity of the part is defined as negligible. It may be allowed to exist without repair, or may only require a cosmetic repair to prevent further damage (such as further stripping of outer ply material). Refer to the part-specific Structural Repair Manual (SRM) for further guidance on what constitutes negligible damage.

Repairable damage. This is defined not only as damage requiring repair, but also damage that is within the repair capability of the maintenance organization at which the repair is to be performed. The location of damage, complexity of the repair procedure, repair weight limitations, availability of repair equipment and materials, repair time/cost, spare part availability, etc., are all factors in deciding whether a part is beyond the capability of maintenance (BCM) at that maintenance organization.

Figure 10-1-8. Radomes are sensitive to moisture and impact damage.

Types and Causes of Damage | 10-5

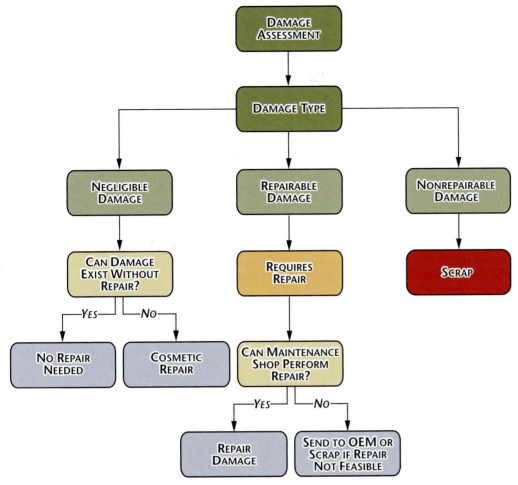

Figure 10-2-1. Damage assessment and categorization must be completed to determine if a repair is required and feasible.

In the field, the repair is limited to following the manufacturer's instructions. In a repair station and at the manufacturer's facilities, it can be extended, provided that engineering approvals and civil aircraft authority approvals, are obtained. For larger damages, experimental substantiation may be required.

Non-Repairable damage. Parts determined to be non-repairable must be scrapped.

Damage Assessment Methodology

Four steps are involved in assessing damage.

STEP 1

First, locate the damage. This is usually done by visual inspection. However, caution must be exercised as non-visible subsurface damage may exist beneath impact areas and areas suspected of having been impacted. Areas impacted (with or without visual indication on the part surface) or suspected of having been impacted must be further evaluated for delaminations and matrix cracks.

STEP 2

Once the damage has been located, the extent of the damage must be determined and the damage characterized. The depth of delamination and the presence of skin to core or skin-to-substructure disbonds (if applicable) should be determined to characterize the damage. Damage to honeycomb core should be characterized using radiographic or other techniques. Determining the extent of damage and characterizing the damage is an important part of the damage assessment process, as it will have a direct bearing on the repair procedures to be employed.

STEP 3

After the damage has been characterized and the extent determined, the repair zone in which the damage is located is determined using the part-specific Structural Repair Manual (SRM). Overlap of damage from one repair zone to another requires the damage limits for the worst-case zone

LOCATION	DAMAGE INFORMATION	DESIGN INFORMATION	REPAIR CAPABILITY	QUALIFICATION OF ASSESSOR	MANDATE OF ASSESSOR
In The Field	Limited	Limited, Manufacturer Instructions	Limited, Means and Time, Facility Conditions	Mechanic or Repairman	Limited to manufacturer repair manual
Repair Station	Partial, Varies according to station	Partial, manufacturer instructions and some functional and design information	Partial, Varies according to station	Mechanic or repairman and engineering support	Partial, Requires manufacturer and civil authority approval or military depot engineering deposition
Manufacturer	Complete, Equipment and know how available	Complete, Design information, analytical capabilities, knowledge and mandate for certification	All facilities, From complicated repairs to rework	Engineering and manufacturing team	Ample, Needs civil authority approval for changes to certified products

Table 10-3-1. Repair capabilities are dependent on the location and resources available

is used. If the damage limits for the repair zone in which the damage is located are exceeded, engineering support is needed from the aircraft manufacturer. If the damage lies in a non-repairable zone, the part must be removed and replaced with a new part.

STEP 4

Following damage removal, reinspect the damage area to ensure all the damage was in fact removed. Current nondestructive inspection (NDI) methods used to detect subsurface delaminations are capable of only finding the first delamination nearest the surface on which the probe was applied. Deeper delaminations can be masked by the first delamination. After removing what initially appears to be all the damage present, it is necessary to re-inspect the area to ensure no delaminations remain below the originally defined damage.

Section 3

Repair Qualification and Authority

The repair station or airline maintenance department engineering/technical personnel should have the technical background to understand the inspection results, to understand the available design information, be familiar with the repair capabilities and have the necessary skills and experience. The demands on its technical expertise vary according to the repair location, for example, FAR Part 65, Certification: Airman Other than Crew Members, prescribes the requirements for issuing Mechanics and Repairman certificates. The assessment of in field damage for civil aircraft are done by a certified mechanic, appropriately rated, with knowledge in composites and under the restrictions stated by the aircraft manufacturer in the Maintenance Manual and SRM. In a repair station and at the manufacturers site, the assessment should involve a team that includes engineering design and analysis.

It is the responsibility of the designer of the part (the airframe manufacturer) to define maximal damage that can be repaired in field conditions and the repair method based on his or her knowledge of the structure and knowledge of the inspection and repair capabilities of the user. For civil airplanes, this is required by FAA regulations, Part 43, which state that repair methods and personnel should be FAA approved. A standard repair manual should include the detection method, the maximum damage that can be left unrepaired, the maximum damage that can be repaired and the repair methods. See an example of this type of information in Table 10-3-1.

Damage Causes

Lightning Strikes

High-energy lightning strikes can cause substantial damage to composite surface structure. For civil aircraft and rotorcraft, the FAA regulations for lightning protection are FAR 25.581, 23.867, 27.601 and 29.610. Fuel system lightning protection requirements are in 25.954 and 23.954. System lightning protection requirements are in 25.1316. Advisory circulars AC20-53 and AC20-136 provide means of compliance with the regulations.

There are zones on the airplane with high probability of lightning strike occurrence. These zones are called lightning strike zones. Protection of composite structure by conductive materials is required on lightning strike zones and beyond them to enable conductivity of induced currents away from attachment zones (Figure 10-3-1). An all-composite wing may have to be completely covered by a conductive layer, even if the attachment zone is located near the wing tip.

At fasteners and connections, electrical resistance to current flow generated by lightning produces heat that causes burning and delaminations. Minor lightning attachment also can cause significant damage, particularly to the tips and trailing edges. The following are guidelines to reduce the repair requirement:

- Provide easily replaceable conductive material with adequate conductive properties.
- Provide protection at tips and along trailing edge spans.
- Make all conductive path attachments easily accessible.

Fatigue

Composite materials have higher fatigue threshold stresses than metals. Once this threshold is exceeded, composites show more scatter in fatigue than metals and might tend toward lower reliability performance if the composite structures were stressed that highly. Because of this high threshold stress, fatigue is not the limiting factor in the design of composite structures. Design criteria such as damage tolerance limit the stress levels in composite structures to such low values that fatigue does not generally represent a design constraint. However, this is not necessarily true for high-cycle fatigue (e.g., $n > 10^7$) dynamic system components in rotorcraft.

Fatigue performance of bolted composite joints is generally very good as compared to metal joints. Under maximum cyclic load level as high as 70 percent of the static strength, composite bolted joints have been observed to endure extremely long fatigue life with minimal reduction in residual strength. The predominant damage mechanism under cyclic loads is usually bearing failure in the form of hole elongation with net section failure for static residual test.

Permanent Repairs

Repair design criteria for permanent repairs are the same as the design criteria of the part

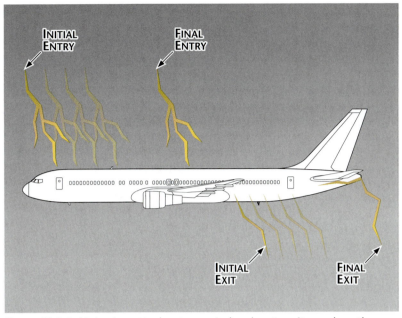

Figure 10-3-1. Lightning attaches to an airplane's extremity, such as the radome or a wing tip, and then travels along the conductive material in the structure and exits to the ground.

that is to be repaired. These are: restore stiffness of the original structure, withstand static strength at the expected environments up to ultimate load including stability (except for postbuckled structure), assure durability for the remaining life of the component, satisfy original part damage tolerance requirements and restore functionality of aircraft systems. Additionally, there are other criteria applicable in repair situations: minimize aerodynamic contour changes, minimize weight penalty, minimize load path changes and be compatible with aircraft operations schedule.

Any permanent repair must be designed to support applied loads at the ultimate design load level at the extremes of temperature excursions, moisture levels and barely visible damage levels. If the loads are not available, SRAM repair recommendations must be strictly adhered to. In SRAM repairs, there is an implicit assumption that the specific repairs meet all static strength and stability requirements.

Interim Repairs

Repair design criteria for temporary or interim repairs can be less demanding, but may approach that of permanent repairs if the temporary repair is to be on the airplane for a considerable time. Most users of aircraft and OEM's prefer permanent repairs, if at all possible, as the temporary repairs may damage parent structure and necessitate a more extensive permanent repair or part scrapping. All tem-

DAMAGE TOLERANCE ACRONYMS	
ADL	Allowable Damage Limit: *Damage size and state which reduces strength to design ultimate load*
BVID	Barely Visible Impact Damage
CDT	Critical Damage Threshold: *Damage size and state which reduces strength to design limit load*
Dll	Design Limit Load
DUL	Design Ultimate Load
MDD	Maximum Design Damage
RDD	Readily Detectable Damage *Damage of a size and state such that it will be detected within a small number of flights during routine aircraft servicing*

Table 10-3-2. Commonly used acronyms in damage tolerance assessment.

porary repairs have to be approved before the aircraft can be restored to operational status.

A special subset of temporary repairs are those associated with aircraft battle damage repair (ABDR) and other emergency repairs. In this situation repair design criteria will require sufficient strength, stiffness and functionality restoration to permit the aircraft to fly to a repair facility or sustain 100 hours of limited flight envelope, or in the ABDR scenario, to fly one more mission. In the military, there are ABDR manuals that suggest the types of repairs to be implemented. These repairs are usually required to be accomplished within 24 hours.

Cosmetic Repair

In this case inspection has determined that the damage has not affected the structural integrity of the component. A cosmetic repair is carried out to protect and decorate the surface. This does not involve the use of reinforcing materials.

Damage Tolerance and Fail Safe Design

Engineered structures must be capable of performing their function throughout a specified lifetime while meeting safety and economic objectives. These structures are exposed to a series of events that include loading, environment and damage threats. These events, either individually or cumulatively, can cause structural degradation, which, in turn, can affect the ability of the structure to perform its function.

In many instances, uncertainties associated with existing damage as well as economic considerations necessitate a reliance on inspection and repair programs to ensure the required structural capability is maintained. The location and severity of manufacturing flaws and in-service damage can be difficult to anticipate for a variety of reasons. Complex loading or structural configurations result in secondary load paths that are not accurately predicted during the design process.

Some manufacturing flaws may not be detectable until the structure is exposed to the service environment. For example, joints with contaminated surfaces during bonding may not be detectable until the weak bond further deteriorates in service.

The numerous variables associated with damage threats (e.g., severity, frequency, geometry) are rarely well defined until service data is collected. Moreover, established engineering tools for predicting damage caused by well-defined damage events often do not exist.

Economic issues can include both non-recurring and recurring cost components. The large number of external events, combined with the interdependence of structural state, structural response and external event history, can result in prohibitive non-recurring engineering or test costs associated with explicitly validating structural capability under all anticipated conditions. Moreover, large weight-related recurring costs associated with many applications rule out the use of overly conservative, but simpler approaches.

The goal in developing an inspection plan is to detect, with an acceptable level of reliability, any damage before it can reduce structural capability below the required level. To accomplish this, inspection techniques and intervals for each location in the structure must be selected with a good understanding of damage threats, how quickly damage will grow, the likelihood of detection and the damage sizes that will threaten structural safety. Table 10-3-2 lists common acronyms used in damage tolerance assessment and classification.

To avoid costs associated with excessive repairs, inspection methods should also quantify structural degradation to support accurate residual strength assessments. This concept of combining an inspection plan with knowledge of damage threats, damage growth rates and residual strength is referred to as "damage tolerance." Specifically, *damage tolerance* is the ability of a structure to sustain design loads in the presence of damage caused by fatigue, corrosion, environment, accidental events and other sources until such damage is detected, through inspections or malfunctions, and repaired.

Durability considerations are typically combined with damage tolerance to meet economic and functionality objectives. Specifically, *durability* is the capability of a structural application to retain adequate properties (strength, stiffness and environmental resistance) throughout its life to the extent that deterioration can be controlled and repaired, if there is a need, by economically acceptable maintenance practices.

As implied by the two definitions, durability addresses largely economic issues, while damage tolerance has a focus on safety concerns. For example, durability often addresses the onset of damage from the operational environment. Under the principles of damage tolerance design, the small damages associated with initiation may be difficult to detect, but do not threaten structural integrity.

Composite-Related Issues

All structural applications should be designed to be damage tolerant and durable. In using composite materials, a typical design objective is to meet or exceed the design service and reliability objectives of the same structure made of other materials without increasing the maintenance burden.

The generally good fatigue resistance and corrosion suppression of composites helps meet such objectives. However, the unique characteristics of composite materials also provide some significant challenges in developing safe, durable structure. The brittle nature of some polymer resins causes concern about their capability to resist damage and, if damaged, their capability to carry the required loads until the damage is detected. While the primary concerns in metal structure relate to tension crack growth and corrosion, other damages, such as delamination and fiber breakage resulting from impact events and environmental degradation are more of a concern in polymer matrix composites (Figure 10-3-2). In addition, composites have unique damage sensitivities for compression and shear loading, as well as tension.

In composite structure, the damage caused by an impact event is typically more severe and can be less visible than in metals. As a result of the increased threat of an immediate degradation in properties, another property, damage resistance, has been used for composite structures and material evaluation. *Damage resistance* is a measure of the relationship between parameters that define an event, or envelope of events (e.g., impacts using a specified impactor and range of impact energies or forces) and the resulting damage size and type.

Figure 10-3-2. Delamination is one common type of damage seen in composite structures.

Damage resistance and damage tolerance differ in that the former quantifies the damage caused by a specific damage event, while the latter addresses the capability of the structure to tolerate a specific damage condition. Damage resistance, like durability, largely addresses economic issues (e.g., how often a particular component needs repair), while damage tolerance addresses safe operation of a component.

Optimally balancing damage resistance and damage tolerance for a specific composite application involves considering a number of technical and economic issues early in the design process. Damage resistance often competes with damage tolerance during the design process, both at the material and structural level.

In addition, material and fabrication costs, as well as operational costs associated with inspection, repair and structural weight, are strongly influenced by the selected material and structural configuration. For example, toughened-resin material systems typically improve damage resistance relative to untoughened systems, which results in reduced maintenance costs associated with damage from low-severity impact events.

However, these cost savings compete with the higher per-pound material costs for the toughened systems. In addition, these materials can also result in lower tensile capability of the structure with large damages or notches, which might require the addition of material to satisfy structural capability requirements at limit load. This extra material and associated weight results in higher material and fuel costs, respectively.

General Guidelines

There are a large number of factors that influence damage resistance, durability and damage tolerance of composite structures. In addition, there are complex interactions between these factors that can lead to nonintuitive results. Often a change in a factor can improve one of the areas of damage resistance, durability, or damage tolerance, while degrading the other two.

It is important for a developer of a composite structure to understand these factors and their interactions as appropriate to the structure's application in order to produce a balanced design that economically meets all the design criteria. The following paragraphs outline some of the areas where significant and important interactions occur.

- An important part of a structural development program is to determine the damages that the structure is capable of carrying at the various required load levels (ultimate, limit, etc.). This information can be used to develop appropriate maintenance, inspection and real-time monitoring techniques to ensure safety. The focus of damage tolerance evaluations should be on ensuring safety in the event of "rogue" and "unanticipated" events, not solely on likely scenarios of damage.

- The damage tolerance approach involves the use of inspection procedures and structural design concepts to protect safety, rather than the traditional factors of safety used for ultimate loads. The overall damage tolerance database for a structure should include information on residual strength characteristics, sensitivities to damage growth and environmental degradation, maintenance practices and in-service usage parameters and damage experiences.

- Fiber and matrix materials, material forms and fabrication processes are constantly changing. This requires a strong understanding of durability and damage tolerance principles; the multitude of parameter interactions; and an intelligent, creative adaptation of them to achieve durability and safety goals. Also, new materials and material forms may have significantly different responses than those exhibited by previous materials and structures (i.e., "surprises" will occur). Therefore, the information and guidelines based on previous developments should not be blindly followed.

- Focusing strictly on meeting regulatory requirements will not ensure economical maintenance practices are established. For example, the ultimate load requirements for barely visible impact damage, (BVID) in critical locations (see FAR 23.573, AC 20-107A, etc.) result in insufficient data to define allowable damage limits (ADL) in higher-margin areas. Similarly, demonstrating compliance for discrete source damage requirements typically involves showing adequate structural capability with large notches at critical locations. Neither of these requirements ensures safe maintenance inspection practices are established to find the least detectable, yet most severe defect (i.e., those reducing structural capability to limit loads). As a result the supporting databases should not be limited to these conditions. An extensive residual strength database addressing the full range of damage variables and structural locations is needed to provide insights on ADLs for use in SRMs. For example, clearly visible damage may be acceptable (i.e., below the ADLs) away from stiffening elements and in more lightly loaded portions of the structure. A more extensive characterization of the residual strength curves for each characteristic damage type (impact, holes, etc.) will also help define damage capable of reducing strength to limit load.

- Well-defined inspection procedures that (a) quantify damage sufficiently to assess compliance with ADLs and, (b) reliably find damage at the critical damage threshold (CDT) will help provide maintenance practices that are as good as or better than those used for metal structure. Clearly defined damage metrics facilitate quantitative inspection procedures, which can be used to define the structural response of the detected damage.

- Currently, most initial inspections of composite structure have involved visual methods. Therefore, dent depth has evolved as a common damage metric. Development efforts should define the dent depths that correspond to the threshold of detectability for both general visual (surveillance in Boeing terminology) and detailed visual levels. The influence of dent-depth decay, which can come from viscoelastic and other material or structural behaviors, must be considered for maintenance inspection procedures and the selection of damage that will be used to demonstrate compliance.

- Another factor motivating a more complete characterization of damage and structural variables is that the internal damage state for a specific structural detail is not a unique function of the dent depth. It is a complex function of the impact variables (e.g., impactor geometry, energy level, angle of incidence, etc.). A range of these variables should be evaluated to understand the relationship between them and to determine the combinations that result in the largest residual strength degradation.

- Structure certified with an approach that allows for damage growth must have associated inservice inspection techniques that are capable of adequately detecting damage before it becomes critical. These inspection methods should be demonstrated to be economical before committing to such a certification approach. In addition, the damage growth must be predictable such that inspection intervals can be reliably defined.

Damage Tolerance

Damage tolerance provides a measure of the structure's ability to sustain design loads with a level of damage or defect and be able to perform its operating functions. Consequently, the concern with damage tolerance is ultimately with the damaged structure having adequate residual strength and stiffness to continue in service safely until the damage can be detected by scheduled maintenance inspection (or malfunction) and be repaired or until the life limit is reached. The extent of damage and detectability determines the required load level to be sustained. Thus, safety is the primary goal of damage tolerance.

Damage tolerance methodologies are most mature in the military and civil aircraft industry. They were initially developed and used for metallic materials, but have more recently been extended and applied to composite structure. The damage tolerance philosophy has been included in regulations since the 1970s. It evolved out of the "Safe Life" and "Fail Safe" approaches.

The safe-life approach ensures adequate fatigue life of a structural member by limiting its allowed operational life. During its application to commercial aircraft in the 1950s, this approach was found to be uneconomical in achieving acceptable safety, since a combination of material scatter and inadequate fatigue analyses resulted in the premature retirement of healthy components. The approach is still used today in such structures as high-strength steel landing gear. Due to the damage sensitivities and relatively flat fatigue curves of composite materials, a safe-life approach is not considered appropriate in composite applications.

The fail-safe approach assumes members will fail, but forces the structure to contain multiple load paths by requiring specific load-carrying capability with assumed failures of one or more structural elements. This approach achieved acceptable safety levels more economically, and, due to the relative severity of the assumed failures, was generally effective at providing sufficient opportunity for timely detection of structural damage.

Its redundant-load-path approach also effectively addressed accidental damage and corrosion. However, the method does not allow for explicit limits on the maximum risk of structural failure, and it does not demonstrate that all partial failures with insufficient residual strength are obvious. Moreover, structural redundancy is not always efficient in addressing fatigue damage, where similar elements under similar loading would be expected to have similar fatigue-induced damage.

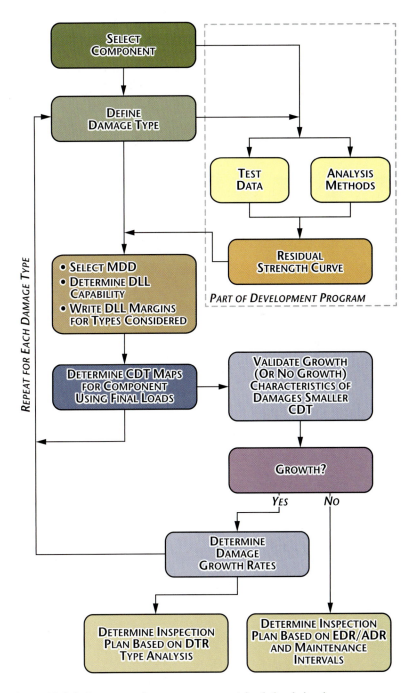

Figure 10-3-3. Damage tolerance assessment for fail-safe loads

11

Repair

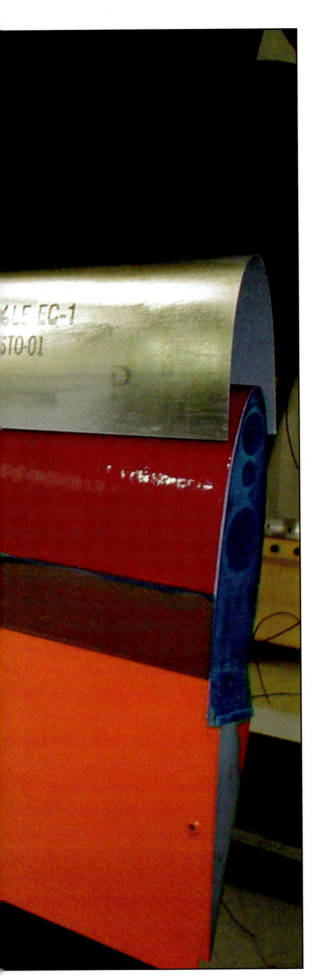

Once a composite structure is placed in service it is subject to wear and damage. In addition to repair of damage inflicted in service, rework is necessary if the component is damaged during manufacture or if a quality assurance check indicates that specifications are not met. The choice between repair or rejection depends on the ability to repair the structure effectively. This requires both access and proper procedures.

Clearly, a proper design would anticipate likely damage events, such as delicate areas being overstrained prior to final assembly or a tool drop on a composite surface. Poorly designed manufacturing processes yield a systematic flaw that may go undetected until the component is in the field.

All repairs of composite or bonded assemblies should be conducted per the instructions in the appropriate Structural Repair Manual (SRM). SRMs are prepared by the aircraft manufacturer and approved by the appropriate governing agency, such as the Federal Aviation Administration (FAA) for commercial aircraft. If the damage exceeds the limits specified in the SRM, it is imperative that a qualified stress engineer approves the repair procedure.

All personnel conducting structural repairs should be properly trained and certified in the repair procedure. The instructions in the repair manual must be followed to the letter. A repair that is done incorrectly can result in a second, more extensive and more complicated repair.

The first task of repair is to inspect the extent of the damage. The repair has the objective of restoring the damaged structure to a required capability in terms of strength, stiffness, functional performance, safety, service life and cosmetic appearance. Ideally, the repair will return the structure to original capability and appearance.

Learning Objective

REVIEW
- repair design criteria
- repair of honeycomb sandwich structures

DISCUSS
- bonded repair methods and processes for composite structures
- bolted repair methods and processes for composite structures

EXPLAIN
- moisture removal methods and processes for laminate and honeycomb sandwich structures
- curing process for composite repairs

Left: A technician repairs a composite helicopter main rotor blade. *Courtesy of Advanced Composite Structures*

To start the repair process the structural makeup of the component must be known and the appropriate design criteria should be selected. The continuity in load transfer is re-established in a damaged part by attaching new material by bolting or bonding thus bridging the gap or reinforcing the weakened portion. The repair is in reality a joint where a load is transferred from the parent material into and out of the patch. Figure 11-0-1 shows an aircraft repair flowchart used by aircraft maintenance technicians as a guide to conduct the repair.

Repair design criteria. Design is typically a compromise of conflicting requirements. This is particularly so with the design of composite structures. On one hand, there is the capability to produce very efficient structures that are lightweight and cost-effective to manufacture. On the other hand, in-service maintenance and repair often require a structure that does not have the best strength-to-weight ratio or stiffness-to-weight ratio and could be more complex and costly to fabricate. The final structure needs to be both production and structurally efficient and simple to maintain and repair.

Section 1
Introduction to Designing for Repairability

The use of bonded repairs for secondary structures is a well-established process and often the only viable option for the repair of honeycomb sandwich structures. Bolted repairs are seldom used to repair secondary structures. However, airframe manufactures like Boeing

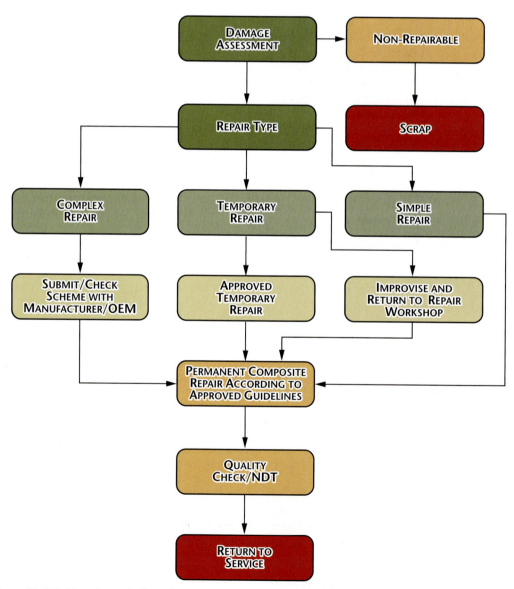

Figure 11-0-1. Aircraft repair flow chart

and Airbus use bolted repairs for some of the composite structures on their aircraft.

Boeing has used bolted repairs for the B777 stabilizers and floor beams and bolted repairs are also used for the repair of the primary structure of the B787. Users have two options for repairing the primary structure of a Boeing 787 aircraft: bolted repairs using titanium, composite, or aluminum repair doublers; and bonded repairs using prepreg or wet lay-up techniques.

The primary structure of the B787 was designed to allow bolted repairs. The ability to perform bolted repairs in composite structure has been service-proven on the 777 and offers comparable repair times and skills as employed on metallic airplanes. By design, bolted repairs in composite structure can be permanent and damage tolerant, just as they can be on a metal structure.

The choice to use bolted repairs instead of bonded repairs is not based on superior mechanical properties or because bonded repairs are often more efficient than bolted repairs, but because airline personnel often prefer bolted repairs because they are similar to the repair of an aluminum aircraft, are often easier and quicker to accomplish, and there is no need for high cure temperatures in a hangar like those required for bonded structural repairs.

In addition, airlines have the option to perform bonded composite repairs, which offer improved aerodynamic and aesthetic finish. These repairs are permanent, damage tolerant and do not require an autoclave. While a typical bonded repair may require 24 or more hours of airplane downtime, additional rapid repair techniques have been developed that require less than an hour. These rapid composite repair techniques offer temporary repair capability to get an airplane flying again quickly, despite minor damage that might ground an aluminum airplane.

Review of Joining Methods

The choice between a bolted or bonded repair of advanced composite structures often depends on how the component was designed. For instance, minimum-gauge control surfaces are lighter if bonded rather than bolted because there is no need for locally thickened seams to allow for countersunk fastener heads. Very thick primary structures, on the other hand, are best made by bolting or riveting together simple details that do not have the critical weaknesses due to laminate wrinkling that seems to be inherent in many integrally stiffened co-cured panels.

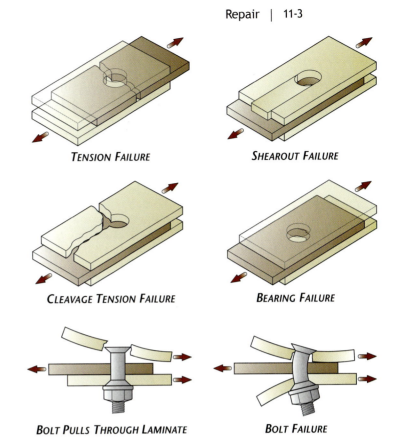

Figure 11-1-1. Failure modes of mechanically fastened joints

Bolted-Joint Failure Modes

The failure modes of mechanically fastened joints are illustrated in Figure 11-1-1. The individual mode of failure is dependent upon the joint geometry and the lay-up pattern. The strongest joint usually fails by tension through the hole at a particular width-to-diameter (wld) ratio. The width is the strip width or bolt pitch distance, and the diameter is that of the hole or fastener.

Bearing failures occur at lower total loads per unit width and at greater width-to-diameter ratios, where the bolts are further apart. Shearout failure is controlled by near quasi-isotropic laminate patterns and sufficient edge distances; whereas fastener-type failure is restricted by appropriate fastener diameter-to-component thickness ratios. It suffices here to state that in both original structure and repairs, the strongest joints are developed only by keeping the fastener loads low in comparison with both the rated shear strength and the laminate bearing allowable.

Adhesively Bonded Joint Failure Modes

The failure modes of adhesively bonded joints are illustrated in Figure 11-1-2. Adherend failure is the preferred failure mode, and the strength of the adhesive in cohesive shear must

Repair

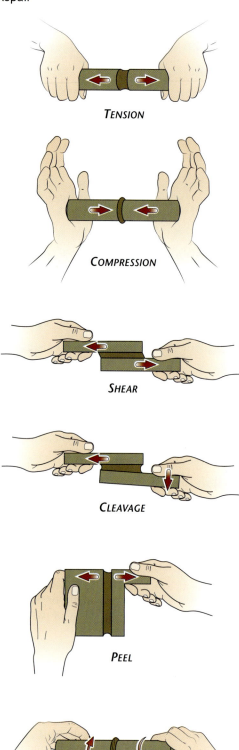

Figure 11-1-2. Failure modes of adhesively bonded joints

be designed to be at least half as much stronger than the adherends. Adherend and cohesive peel failure mode are controlled by detailed joint end design. Adhesive failure is excluded by specific and detailed attention to surface preparation.

Design of Composite Repairs

Unidirectional fibers (tape) have so little strength in the transverse fiber direction that it is necessary to include fibers in every direction for which some load condition exists. The need for fibers in every direction in a composite laminate is most pronounced around bolt holes.

The quasi-isotropic layup (0°, ±45°, 90°) with one quarter of the plies in each of the four directions lies in the middle of a plateau of bolt bearing strength on the plane of varying fiber patterns. Excessive deviation from that pattern involves substantial loss of bolted joint strength. It should be noted that there is a minimum requirement for about 12.5 percent of the fibers in each of the four directions.

In addition, a good balance of strength around the circumference of the bolt bearing area is achieved with a maximum of 37.5 percent of the fibers in any one direction. A limit of no more than 50 percent of the fibers in any one of the four directions is suitable for the mechanical repair of lightly loaded, minimum-gauge composite structures. Figure 11-1-3 shows a chart that is used to select suitable fiber patterns for bolted structures.

Repair design criteria were developed to assure that the structural integrity and functionality of the repaired part are the same as that of the undamaged part. The repair design criteria should be established by the original manufacturer. They are used to develop repairs found in the SRM. Repairs within the scope of the SRM need to follow the SRM to the letter.

When a repair is necessary that exceeds the limits of the SRM, the repairs must be substantiated and approved based on the specified repair criteria. SRM's for specific aircraft frequently "zone" the structure to show the amount of strength restoration needed or the kinds of standard repairs that are acceptable.

Zoning permits the use of simpler repairs in areas where large strength margins exist. Zoning also restricts repairs by airline or repair station personnel in areas where repairs are too complex and should be only repaired with original equipment manufacturer (OEM) involvement.

Repair design criteria for permanent repairs are to restore stiffness of the original structure, withstand static strength at the expected environments up to ultimate load including stability, except for post-buckled structure, assure durability for the remaining life of the component, satisfy original part damage tolerance requirements and restore functionality of aircraft systems. Additionally there are other criteria applicable in repair situations. These are to minimize aerodynamic contour changes, minimize weight penalty, minimize load path changes, and be compatible with the aircraft's operations schedule.

Part Stiffness

The first consideration in any repair is to replace structural material that is damaged. This means that for large repairs the stiffness and placement of repair material should match the parent material as closely as possible. This avoids any recalculations of the overall dynamic behavior of the component, such as flutter or structural load redistribution.

Many lightweight aircraft structures are designed to meet stiffness requirements that are more critical than their strength requirements. A repair made to a structure of this type must maintain the required stiffness so that deflections or stability requirements are met.

Fixed aerodynamic surfaces, such as wings and tails, are frequently designed to have bending and torsion stiffness that are adequate to prevent excessive deflections under aerodynamic loading. This is to prevent divergence and control surface reversal on parts such as ailerons. Moveable surfaces are frequently sensitive to aerodynamic flutter and their stiffness may have been carefully tailored to obtain natural frequencies for which flutter will not occur.

Increasing the stiffness of a control surface, especially the bending stiffness, can reduce the flutter speed to unacceptable levels; a decrease in stiffness can be equally damaging. Any significant change in stiffness must be evaluated for its effect on the dynamic behavior of the structure. Stiffness can also affect the deflections of actuated doors, such as landing gear doors. Reduction in stiffness can result in excessive deflections under aerodynamic loading. These reductions may increase drag or in extreme cases cause loss of the structure.

Static Strength and Stability

Every permanent repair must be designed to support applied loads at the ultimate design load level at the extremes of temperature ranges, moisture levels and barely visible damage levels. Load path changes are a special concern when designing repairs. When strength restoration is necessary, attention must be given to the effect of the stiffness of the repair on the load distribution in the structure.

If a patch has less stiffness than the original structure, the patch may not carry its share

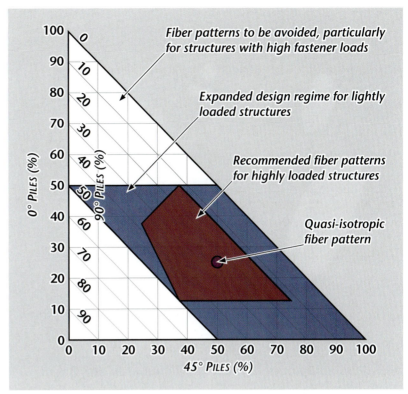

Figure 11-1-3. Selection of lay-up patterns for composite laminates

of the load, and this causes an overload in the surrounding material. This condition can be caused by a patch made from a less stiff material, or from fasteners that fail to transfer full load because of loose fits or fastener deformation.

Conversely, an overly stiff patch may attract more than its share of load, causing adjacent areas to be overloaded. Stiffness mismatch between parent material and the patch may cause peel stresses that can initiate debonding of the patch.

Structures loaded in compression or in shear, such as some wing skins, webs of spars or ribs, and fuselage structure, including both external skins and internal bulkheads, may be stability critical rather than strength critical at ultimate design load. Two types of stability failure are possible:

Panel buckling. The panel, such as a section of wing skin, buckles between its major supports, for example, spars and ribs. The repair must account for the stiffness of the panel and the amount of support provided by the attachment to the substructure. Some portions of structure are permitted to buckle below ultimate design load.

These types of structures develop specific post-buckling behavior that redistributes the load and allows the structure to carry ultimate load. Any repair of a stability-critical structure,

Figure 11-1-4. The leading edge of this Airbus A380 wing is an example of a critical zone where the smoothness of the surface is extremely important in minimizing drag.

and especially a structure that is permitted to buckle, should not affect its buckling and post-buckling modes. Matching of stiffness of the parent material is of utmost importance here.

Local crippling and buckling. This is buckling of the cross section of a member or its component, such as a spar cap, by distortion of the cross-section rather than the overall buckling along its length or width. Restoration of local crippling strength must be considered when making repairs to substructure.

Composite laminates under compressive load can fail when individual fibers or bundles of fibers buckle where delaminations or penetrations result in fibers with reduced support. Because of the danger of microbuckling or local ply buckling, resin injection repair that fills a delamination without adequately bonding the delaminated plies together could be unsatisfactory.

Durability

Although the parent composite structure may not be durability critical, structural repairs may be more susceptible to damage caused by repeated loads during their service lives. This is because the repair process is not as well controlled and the repairs themselves create solitary joints and discontinuities in areas that are exposed.

For bolted repairs, high bearing stresses on fastener holes should be avoided as they may elongate under repeated loading and lead to fastener fatigue. Bonded repairs should be well sealed as they can develop disbonds after being weakened by environmental effects. All delaminations exceeding the acceptance/rejection criteria of the SRM should be repaired as unrepaired delaminations may grow under compressive or shear loading. Bolted repairs of sandwich structure must be sealed.

Damage Tolerance

Composite structures are designed to be tolerant of accidental damage. In practice, this is accomplished by lowering design strains so that the structure with damage caused by impact can withstand ultimate load.

Repairs must also be capable of tolerating a predetermined level of impact damage. The level of impact damage is usually established by OEMs with concurrence of the certifying agency. When using metal for a large damage repair, damage tolerance requirements for metallic structure must be followed. Metallic doublers and parts also will require protection against galvanic corrosion and lightning strike.

Related Aircraft Systems

In addition to satisfying structural criteria, compatibility with related aircraft systems—fuel system, lightning protection system, mechanical system—may also be required of the repair. These systems include:

Fuel system. Structure is frequently used to contain fuel, as in the "wet" wings of many aircraft. A repair must seal adequately to prevent leakage of the fuel. The repair may also be subjected to fuel pressure loading. Repair material must be compatible with fuel.

Lightning protection system. Some composite structure has provision for conducting lightning strikes by use of flame-sprayed coatings, bonded metallic strips, wire mesh, etc. A repair to the structure must restore the electrical continuity as well as the structural strength. Bolted repairs around fuel tanks must avoid creating an electrical path.

Mechanical system. Components that are mechanically actuated, such as landing gear doors or control surfaces, must function correctly after repair. Clearances and fit-up to adjacent fixed structure may be critical. Re-rigging or rebalancing may be required after repair.

Aerodynamic Smoothness

High-performance flight vehicles depend on smooth external surfaces to minimize drag. During initial fabrication, smoothness requirements are specified, usually by defining zones where different levels of aerodynamic smoothness are required. Most SRM's specify smoothness requirements for repairs consistent with initial part fabrication.

The most critical zones typically include leading edges of wings and tails, forward nacelles and inlet areas, forward fuselage and overwing areas of the fuselage (Figure 11-1-4). The least critical zones typically include trailing edges and aft fuselage areas. In addition, intermediate zones may be specified.

For the most critical zones, forward-facing steps are usually limited to 0.005 to 0.020 in. (0.13 to 0.51 mm) at permanent butt joints. At removable panels, mechanical doors and major joints, forward-facing steps from 0.010 to 0.030 in. (0.25 to 0.76 mm) are typically allowed. At installed equipment, such as antennas and navigation lights, steps up to 0.020 to 0.040 in. (0.51 to 1.02 mm) are permitted. All sharp edges as the result of patch ply termination should be smoothed and feathered.

Whatever the requirements, each exterior repair should restore aerodynamic contour as accurately and smoothly as structurally and economically feasible. Trade-offs exists between accepting a slight reduction in performance in order to accept a repair that is more structurally sound and that is easier and quicker to accomplish.

Weight and Balance

Compared to the overall weight of the vehicle, the weight added by most repairs is insignificant. Exceptions may exist for very large repairs or for space vehicles. The weight of repair becomes a major concern when the repair changes the mass balance of components sensitive to dynamic response, such as moveable control surfaces, rotor blades and rotating shafts. In such cases, it may be possible to remove as much damaged material as will be added by the repair so that there is little change in weight and moments of inertia. If that is not possible, the part must be re-balanced after repair.

Operating Temperatures

Most aircraft experience extremes of temperature during use. Repairs to such aircraft must be acceptable for the temperature extremes for which the aircraft was designed. Low temperatures result from high-altitude flight or from extremes of ground storage in cold climates. Many aircraft are designed for a minimum service temperature of -65°F (-54°C).

Elevated-temperature requirements vary with the type of aircraft. The maximum temperature for commercial transport aircraft and most helicopters is 160°F (71°C) and generally occurs during ground soak on a hot day. However, components experiencing significant loads during takeoff and initial climb may require validation of design ultimate loads at temperatures up to 200°F (93°C).

Supersonic transport, fighter and bomber aircraft typically experience aerodynamic heating of up to 220°F (104°C) or, in special cases, as high as 265°F (130°C), especially on the leading edges of lifting surfaces. Components exposed to engine heat, such as nacelles and thrust reversers, may be required to withstand even higher temperatures in local areas.

Operating temperature influences the selection of repair materials: resin systems for prepreg repairs, resins for wet lay-up repairs and adhesives for bonded repairs. Materials that develop adequate strength at the required temperature must be selected. The combination of temperature extremes with environmental exposure, especially moisture, frequently is the critical condition for which the repair must be designed.

Environment

Repairs may be exposed to many environmental effects including:

- Fluids (salt water or salt spray, fuel or lubricants, hydraulic fluid, paint stripper and humidity)
- Mechanical loading (shock, acoustic or aerodynamic vibration and operating loads)
- Thermal cycling

Moisture is particularly critical to composite structures. At elevated temperatures absorbed moisture reduces the ability of the matrix to support the fibers, thereby reducing the strength of the laminate for compressive or shear loading. This effect is considered in the original design, and allowable loads are frequently limited by "hot-wet" conditions. The same considerations pertain to bonded repairs. Absorbed moisture can affect bonded repairs in three ways. These must be considered in the selection of a repair procedure.

BOLTED VS. BONDED REPAIR	BOLTED	BONDED
Lightly loaded structures - (Laminate thickness less than 0.1 inches)		X
Highly loaded structures - (Laminate thickness between 0.125 and 0.5 inches)	X	X
Highly loaded structures - (Laminate thickness greater than 0.5 inches)	X	
High peeling stresses	X	
Honeycomb structure		X
Dry surfaces	X	X
Wet and/or contaminated surfaces	X	
Disassembly required	X	
Restore unnotched strength		X

Table 11-1-1. Bolted vs. bonded design criteria

Parent laminate blistering. As a "wet" laminate is heated to cure a bonded repair, the absorbed moisture may cause local delaminations or blisters. Pre-bond drying at lower temperatures, slow heat-up rates and reduced cure temperatures all diminish the tendency to blister.

Blown skins/core of sandwich structure. Moisture in the cells of honeycomb sandwich structure expands when the part is heated to cure a bonded repair and develops sufficient pressure to separate the skin from the core, especially if the strength of the adhesive has been reduced by temperature and moisture. Similarly, this process may be sufficiently severe to rupture cell walls in the low-density core. Pre-drying is normally used to prevent bond line failure of this type.

Porosity in bond lines. As a repair is bonded to a "wet" laminate, the moisture tends to cause porosity in the bond line. This porosity can reduce the strength of the bond line. This problem can be minimized by pre-drying, reduced temperature cure and selection of moisture-resistant adhesives.

Surrounding Structure

In the course of the repair process it is imperative that the surrounding structure does not sustain any damage. The predominant sources of damage are dropped tools, scratches caused by prying of bagging material and the application of high temperatures during the cure of the repair. If there is a potential for the latter damage, resins should be selected that cure at sufficiently low temperature while still capable of hot, wet performance.

Bolted vs. Bonded Repairs

Bonded repair concepts have the advantage of not introducing stress concentrations by drilling fastener holes for patch installation and can be stronger than original part material. The disadvantage of bonded repairs is that most repair materials require special storage, handling and curing procedures.

The preferred bonded repair method is the scarf repair. In this repair method the parent material will be scarved to create a flush repair. However for thick structures this could result in very large repairs.

The general rule of thumb for scarfing is to remove 0.5 in.(13 mm) per ply. A 0.375-inch thick structure could be approximately 75 plies thick. By the standard rule of thumb, this would translate to a scarf area of about 37.5 in. (95cm). Scarf distance is measured not from the center of the damage but from the edge of the cleaned-up damaged area.

So if the damaged structure has a 6-in. (15.25 cm) hole in it after the damage is removed, then the outer diameter of the scarfed area would be 37.5 in. plus 6 in. plus 37.5 in., for a total diameter of 81 in. (202 cm). It is very difficult and time consuming to accurately scarf such a large area and in this case a bolted repair would be a better solution. An equivalent bolted repair with multiple rows of fasteners would approximately measure 12 in. (30 cm).

Bolted repairs are quicker and easier to fabricate than bonded repairs. They are normally used on composite skins thicker than 0.125 in. (0.32 cm) to ensure sufficient fastener bearing area is available for load transfer. They are seldom used in honeycomb sandwich assemblies due to the potential for moisture intrusion from the fastener holes and the resulting core degradation and low bearing area of thin face sheets. Bolted repairs are heavier than comparable bonded repairs limiting their use on weight-sensitive flight control surfaces.

Honeycomb sandwich parts often have thin face sheets and are most effectively repaired by using a bonded scarf repair. A bonded external step patch can be used as an alternative. Bolted repairs are not effective for thin laminates because of the low bearing stress of the composite laminate. Thicker solid laminates used on larger aircraft can be up to 1 in. (2.5 cm) thick in highly loaded areas and these types of laminates cannot be effectively repaired using a bolted repair. Table 11-1-1 indicates when a bonded repair is most effective:

Bolted Repairs

Bolted repairs can comprise an external or an internal patch that results in a single shear joint, or two patches, one on each side with a double shear joint. In both cases the load is transferred through the fasteners and the patch by shear forces, but in the case of the two-patch repair, transfer load eccentricity is minimized. The main disadvantage of bolted repairs is that the new holes created in the parent structure weaken the structure by creating stress concentrations that become damage initiation sites.

The external bolted patch is the easiest repair to fabricate. The patch overlaps the parent skin with sufficient area to install the required amount of fasteners to transfer the load. Figure 11-1-5 shows three different patch configurations that can be used.

For large repairs the patch may be stepped and different size fasteners may be used in different rows to ease the load transfer. The external patch thickness may be limited by aerodynamic considerations and by the induced load eccentricity due to neutral axis offset. However, this type of repair does not need backside access as the fasteners can be blind. It can be installed from one side only. If the external patch is unfeasible, an internal patch can be applied.

When backside access is not possible, the patch is split to allow insertion through an elliptical or circular cutout in the skin. In some cases the damage must be enlarged in the direction of the primary load to perform the repair. Because of hardware, internal bolted patches may have interference problems with substructure members.

The two-patch repair using external and internal patches is a desirable repair from the load transfer point-of-view; however, the repair is more complicated and is heavier. Figure 11-1-6 shows a SRM external repair illustration. Note that three rows of fasteners are used around the damaged area. This type of repair is very similar to repairs made to aluminum aircraft.

For complex repairs, multi-row fastener patterns will be required to gradually introduce the load from the part being repaired into the repair patch. It is virtually impossible to distribute the load evenly between all the fasteners in a multiple-row pattern, but careful design of patch geometry, fastener diameter and spacing can alleviate the high loads at the first fasten-

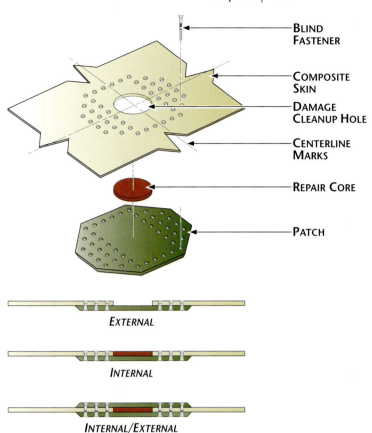

Figure 11-1-5. Basic repair joints

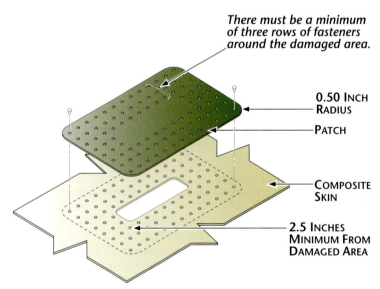

Figure 11-1-6. Bolted repairs

ers. Such complex repairs are not usually identified in the approved repair manuals or procedures and normally need engineering input for design.

Stringer repair. The primary structure of new generation composite aircraft is often composed of a laminate structure reinforced with stringers and frame sections. These stringers and frame sections are often repaired with a

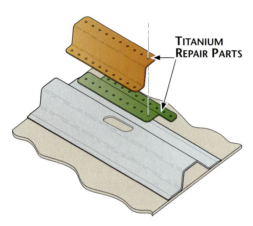

Carbon fiber hat section stringer co-cured to carbon fiber skin

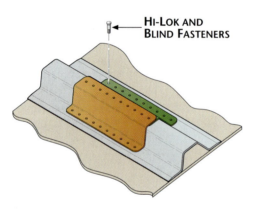

Figure 11-1-7. Stringer repair with metallic doubler

bolted repair as illustrated in Figure 11-1-7. A combination of pin type and blind fasteners are utilized to transfer the load from the original structure to the repair.

Repair Materials

For bolted repairs, there is only the need to select patch material and fasteners. Patches may be aluminum, titanium or steel, or pre-cured composite, carbon-epoxy or fiberglass epoxy. For aluminum patch repair on carbon parent material, a layer of fiberglass cloth is placed between them to prevent galvanic corrosion. For repair of highly loaded components, titanium or pre-cured carbon-epoxy patches are usually preferred. For repair of high-strain structure coupled with severe fatigue load environment, carbon-epoxy patches can be more effective.

Pre-cured carbon/epoxy patches will have the same strength and stiffness as the parent material as they are usually cured and inspected similarly. The major disadvantages of this type of patch are that they do not conform to curved or irregular surfaces and that warpage during pre-cure can result in a poor fit that requires shimming. The use of titanium patches is somewhat more flexible than pre-cured carbon patches, however, titanium is difficult to form to a double compound curved surface.

Titanium can be rolled with a power roller to a single curvature but cannot be formed with simple sheet metal tooling as easily as aluminum to perfectly fit a double curvature. Therefore in some situations aluminum could be the only practical solution.

For repair of composite parts the choice of fasteners is limited to titanium, Monel, or stainless steel. The choice of fastener type is strictly controlled by the SRM. There is a general misconception that bolted repairs require very little logistics support in terms of materials. This is false, as many types of fasteners with different grip lengths need to be stored.

As fasteners for composites are expensive, the inventory can be costly. If pre-cured carbon-epoxy patches are used, different patch sizes and thicknesses have to be available, as cutting to size requires specialized equipment.

Fastener selection. Engineers consider many factors when selecting fasteners for a particular application. These factors must be addressed for all the materials the fastener goes through. These factors include, but are not limited to:

- Strength (lap, shear, tension and bearing)
- Corrosion potential
- Removable or permanent
- Access for fastener installation or removal

Fastener features. Features common to most fasteners used in composites include:

- Non-hole filling (most fasteners that expand to fill the hole will damage composite parts)
- Large footprint (the back side needs a large shop head or footprint to prevent pulling through)
- Limited torque (over-torqueing fasteners damages composites)

- For sandwich panels, limited or adjustable clamp-up force; this prevents the core from being crushed

Fastener selection. There are a few rules of thumb that can be applied to fastener selection for composite parts.

- Consult the SRM. If information is not given in the SRM, request an engineering disposition.
- Use fasteners that are electrochemically compatible with the composite structure being repaired. For example, in graphite/epoxy, galvanic corrosion of the fasteners can be avoided by using fasteners made of titanium, Monel or CRES. Do not use cadium or aluminum.

Some criteria for mechanical fastener selection include strength, tolerance, galvanic compatibility and head geometry, which are explained in the following paragraphs.

The shear strength of the fasteners must be high enough to react fastener shear loads due to transfer of load from the part skin to the patch. The fastener single shear allowable load is used for external bolted patches and the fastener double shear allowable load is used for external/internal bolted patches.

Close-tolerance fasteners are required to provide greater load sharing of fasteners in multi-fastener patterns.

To prevent corrosion of the fasteners, they must be galvanically compatible with the composite skin and the repair patch material. Titanium is the material of choice for most bolted repair applications.

Flush, 100° or 130° shear head fasteners should be used for bolted repairs when mold-line protrusion occurs. Protruding-head fasteners should be used for those repair applications where mold line protrusion does not occur (such as for substructure repairs).

In general, use the following guidelines when selecting fasteners for bolted repairs:

- For repair of carbon fiber composites, do not use cadmium-plated steel fasteners, stainless steel fasteners, aluminum or aluminum-coated fasteners. Use only titanium or Inconnel fasteners with carbon fiber composites.
- Do not use cadmium-plated fasteners with titanium patches to keep from embrittling the titanium.

TYPE OF FASTENER	MANUFACTURER
TITANIUM STRUCTURAL SCREWS	Hi-Shear Corporation
TITATNIUM COMPOSI-LOK BLIND BOLT SYSTEM	Monogram Aerospace Fasteners
TITANIUM HI-LOK PIN FLUSH SHEAR HEAD FASTENER	Hi-Shear Corporation
TITANIUM HI-LOK PIN PROTRUDING TENSION-HEAD HEAD FASTENER	Hi-Shear Corporation
HI-LOK COLLAR	Hi-Shear Corporation
TITANIUM VISU-LOK BLIND BOLT SYSTEM	Monogram Aerospace Fasteners
ASP FASTENER FOR HONEYCOMB SANDWICH STRUCTURES	SPS Technologies Comp-Tite
TITANIUM HUCKCOMP LOCK BOLT	Huck Corporation
UAB™ BLIND BOLT SYSTEM	Alcoa Corporation
ACCU-LOK™ BLIND FASTENER SYSTEM	Monogram Aerospace Fasteners

Table 11-1-2. Typical fasteners used for composite repair

- Do not use interference-fit fasteners or expanding, hole-filling rivets in composites as they will cause damage to the fastener hole during installation.
- Do not use driven rivets or fasteners requiring rivet guns for installation. They can cause delamination of composite skins.
- Do not use fasteners made of composite materials. They have insufficient strength for repair applications.
- When blind fasteners are required, use a fastener with a large clamp-up side footprint such as a Composi-Lok fastener. This will prevent fastener pull through during installation.

Table 11-1-2 shows typical fasteners used for composite aircraft construction and repair.

Fastener materials and strength considerations. Titanium alloy Ti-6Al-4V is the most common alloy for fasteners used with carbon fiber reinforced composite structures. Ultimate tensile and shear strengths for Ti-6A1-4V are 160 and 95 k.s.i. (1,100 and 660 MPa), respectively. Ti-3Al-2.5V and commercially pure titanium are used for some components of fastening systems.

When higher strength is required, materials such as A286 or alloy 718 that have been strengthened by cold working can be used. Cold-worked A286 fasteners can be obtained with an ultimate tensile strength of 200 k.s.i.

(1,400 MPa) and an ultimate shear strength of 110 k.s.i. (760 MPa). The respective values for alloy 718 (cold worked) are 220 and 125 k.s.i. (1,515 and 860 MPa).

Multiphase alloys can be obtained with a tensile strength up to 220 k.s.i. (1,800 MPa). In the past, multiphase alloys were only used as blind fastener stems or core bolts where ultra-high strength was required for the fastener to function. Today, multiphase bolts are being considered to replace alloy 718 where loads are increasing due to growth of some aircraft models. However, in composite structure, it takes a very thick structure to warrant the high shear strength (F_{su} = 132 to 145 k.s.i. or 910 to 1,000 MPa, of multiphase alloys.

Repair Analysis

Analysis of a bolted repair is similar to the analysis of a bolted joint. In the following, the main steps will be presented, with emphasis on items specific for repairs.

Estimation of load transferred through the repair. The repair is a joint where load is transferred from the parent material into and out of the patch. The estimation of the transferred load through the repair is the first stage in the repair analysis.

The two situations where there is need for analyses of repair are during the writing of the SRM or when damage that exceeds the allowed SRM limits has to be repaired. The SRM is written by the manufacturer, who has all the needed information from the analysis of the undamaged structure. In the second case, the load information has to be obtained from the manufacturer.

In special occasions, especially for temporary repairs, loads can be approximated by reverse engineering, utilizing the known design of the parent structure. Care should be taken to use conservative approximations that are based on the maximum load that can be sustained by the geometry and lay-up of the parent structure.

Load sharing in the repair. After the load transferred through the repair is known, evaluate the distribution of this load between the fasteners, and then, in the region of each fastener between the parent structure, the patch and the fasteners.

Analysis of local failure. The parent structure, patch structure and fasteners should be examined.

The parent part of the joint may not be adequate to accommodate the mechanically fastened joint. It may not have the adequate thickness or the proper layup to provide the bearing resistance. As the lay up cannot be changed, the only recourse is to bond additional plies. However, care must be taken so as not to end up with a highly unsymmetrical layup.

Care must also be taken to properly estimate the bearing/bypass ratio and to consider all possible laminate failure modes, in order to avoid increasing the damage by failing the periphery of the repair. For the case of repairs to be incorporated into the SRM, a test program is usually performed to verify the analysis and substantiate the repair.

In the patch design there is freedom to select composite material, lay-up and thickness according to the analytical results. Patches can be prepared to provide the accurate strength, stiffness, edge distance and bolt spacing.

Fastener stiffness should be determined by test or analysis and subsequently used in the analysis of the overall repair. Fastener tensile and shear stresses should be determined as to their adequacy for static strength and for fatigue loading.

Repair Procedures

Bolted repair procedure consists of six distinct steps: patch preparation and pilot-drilling holes; laying out the hole pattern on the parent skin and pilot-drilling skin holes; the transfer of the holes in the skin to the patch if the patch covers some existing skin holes; drilling/reaming of patch and skin; patch and fastener installation; and sealing the repair.

The first step is to cut, form and shape the patch before attaching the patch to the damaged structure. In some cases repair patches are stocked pre-shaped and pre-drilled. If cutting is required, use standard shop procedures that are suitable for the patch material. Metal patches require filing to prevent crack initiation around the cut edges.

When drilling pilot holes in the composite, the holes for repair fasteners must be a minimum of four diameters from existing fasteners and have a minimum edge distance of 2-1/2 fastener diameters. This is different than for metals where the edge distance of two is standard practice. Specific pilot hole sizes and drill types to be used can be found in the SRM.

To locate the patch on the damaged area, two perpendicular centerlines are drawn on the part that defines the principal load or geometric directions. The hole pattern is then laid-out and the pilot holes in the skin are drilled.

The principal directions of the patch are then aligned between the patch and the parent structure. The edges of the patch are marked so that it can be returned to the same location. After the patch is removed, it is advisable to check whether there is sufficient edge distance between the patch perimeter and the outer holes. The pilot holes in the patch are then enlarged.

Composite skins should be backed-up to prevent splitting. The patch is then reattached through the interior fasteners so that the corner fastener holes can be enlarged. All holes are then reamed. A tolerance of +0.0025/-0.000 in. (+0.06/-0.00 mm) is usually recommended for aircraft parts. For composites this means interference fasteners are not used.

Once fastener holes are drilled full size and reamed, permanent fasteners are installed. Before installation the fastener grip length must be measured for each fastener using a grip length gauge. As different fasteners are required for different repairs, the SRM should be consulted for permissible fastener type and installation procedure. However, all fasteners should be installed wet with sealant and with proper torque for screws and bolts.

Sealants are applied to bolted repairs for prevention of water/moisture intrusion, chemical damage, galvanic corrosion and fuel leaks. They also provide contour smoothness. The sealant has to be applied to a clean surface. Masking tape is usually placed around the periphery of the patch parallel with the patch edges leaving a small gap between the edge of the patch and the masking tape. Sealing compound is applied into this gap.

Example of a Bolted Repair

External patch bolted repair of through penetration of the composite skin is used in Figure 11-1-8 as an example. The repair is applicable to repair holes up to 4 in. (10 cm) in diameter in a thick monolithic skin. A single metallic plate is used to span the hole and fastened to the skin by 40 blind fasteners. The repair assumes there is single-side access. A scrim cloth is used to prevent galvanic corrosion.

The applicability of this repair for specific application depends on loading conditions and laminate thickness. Figure 11-1-8A shows a typical bolted repair and Figure 11-1-8B shows a repair for a transport aircraft composite skin repair using titanium doublers. This type of repair is authorized to be used for Boeing 787 aircraft as an alternative for bonded repair methods. The maintenance departments of airlines might have a preference for this type

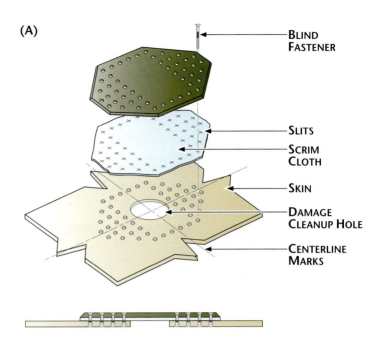

1. Fasteners must have a minumum spacing of 4D and a maximum spacing of 6D
2. Fasteners must have a minimum edge distance of 3D
3. Fasteners to edge of damage cleanup hole must be a minimum of 3D
4. Drill pilot holes in patch first. Enlarge holes to final size after transferring holes to composite skin.

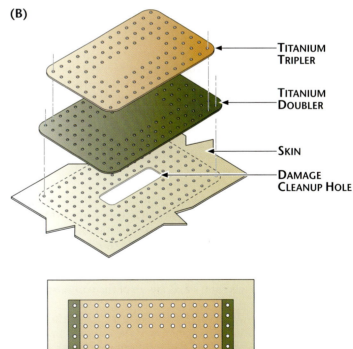

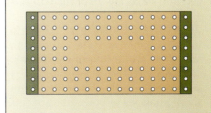

1. Corner radius - 0.5 inches
2. Rivet spacing - 1 inch
3. Fastener diameter - $^{3}/_{16}$ inch
4. Edge Distance - 3D
5. Rivet Spacing - 1 inch

Figure 11-1-8. (A) Example of a bolted repair, (B) Example of a skin repair using titanium doublers

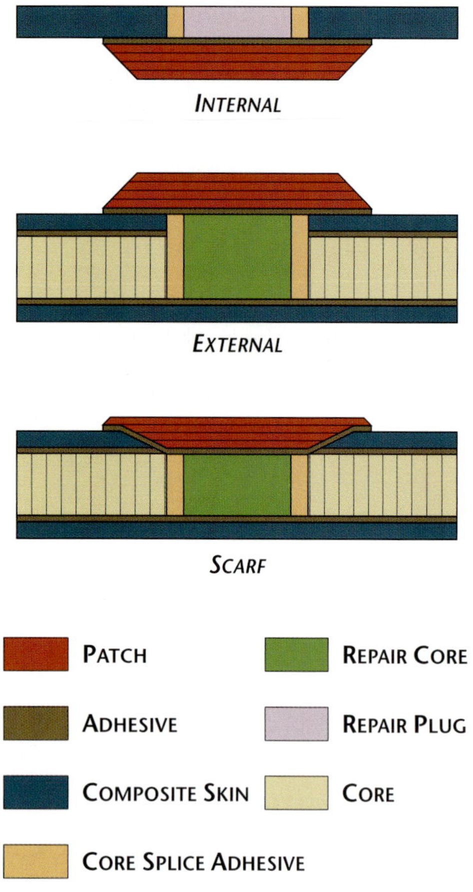

Figure 11-1-9. Bonded repair methods

Legend:
- Patch
- Adhesive
- Composite Skin
- Core Splice Adhesive
- Repair Core
- Repair Plug
- Core

(Illustrations labeled: INTERNAL, EXTERNAL, SCARF)

of repair because it is very similar to sheet metal repairs which they are familiar with. Additionally, it is a quick repair that does not require high temperature curing requirements.

Bonded Repairs

Bonded repairs have been used for many years for secondary structures such as flight controls, fairings and radomes, and are often the only option to repair honeycomb sandwich and thin laminates. Many different repair techniques have been developed using prepreg and wet lay-up. Both scarf type and external repairs are utilized.

Repair Concepts

The two most common bonded repairs use external patches or are internal patches that are made flush with the parent material. Combinations of both types of repairs are also common.

Although the external patches are usually stepped, the internal repair can be stepped or more commonly scarfed. The scarf angles are usually small to ease the load into the joint and to prevent the adhesive from escaping. This translates into a thickness-to-length ratio between 1:10 to 1:40.

The adhesive placed between the repair material and the parent material transfers the load from the parent material to the patch by shear.

The external patch repair concept is the easier of the two to accomplish. Its drawbacks are eccentricity of the loading, which causes peel stresses and protrusion into the air stream. The stress concentration at the edge of the patch can be reduced by stepping or tapering the patch. Because inspection of bonded repairs is difficult, bonded repairs require a higher commitment than bolted repairs to quality control, better trained personnel and cleanliness.

The scarf joint is more efficient from the viewpoint of load transfer as it reduces load eccentricity by closely aligning the neutral axis of the parent and the patch. However, this configuration has many drawbacks in making the repair.

First, to maintain a small taper angle, a large quantity of sound material must be removed. Second, the replacement plies must be very accurately laid-up and placed in the repair joint. Third, the curing of replacement plies can result in significantly reduced strength if an autoclave is not used. Fourth, the adhesive can run to the bottom of the joint creating a non-uniform bond line.

This can be alleviated by approximating the scarf with a series of small steps. For these reasons, unless the part is lightly loaded, this type of repair is usually performed at a repair facility, where if the part can be inserted into the autoclave, this type of repair can result in part strength equal to the original.

Although it may seem that there are only two common repairs, it is somewhat misleading as the two repair joints can be made by many different methods. The patch can be pre-cured and then secondarily bonded to the parent material. This procedure most closely approximates the bolted repair. The patch can be made from prepreg and then co-cured at the same time as the adhesive. Lastly the patch can be made using dry cloth and paste resin and co-cured. This latter repair is called "wet" lay-up repair. The curing cycle can also vary in length of time, cure temperature and cure pressure, thus increasing the number of possible repair combinations.

Repair Materials

Bonded repairs require selection of both the repair material and adhesive. The selection cannot be independent as the curing parameters of the adhesive and the repair material must be compatible for co-cured repairs. Bonded repairs also require materials that are used in the processing of the repair but do not remain with the repair.

Many materials used in bonded repairs require special handling, are storage time and temperature sensitive and may require controlled environment during the repair process. Metal patches for bonded repairs are constructed using sheet material that is bonded to each other to form a stepped patch.

The same method is used for pre-cured composite patches with sheets made of two or more unidirectional plies of fabric or tape. Because the pre-cured patches can be cured in an autoclave, they are made from composite materials that were used in construction of the original part. As shown in Figure 11-1-9, these patches are then attached to the primary structure.

Co-cured bonded repairs use parent material prepreg if the repair can be cured in the autoclave, or repair material prepreg, or dry fabric with paste resin (a "wet" lay-up repair). The prepreg provides a uniform distribution of resin in the composite, but requires refrigerated storage. The resin for the wet lay-up repair usually consists of two parts that do not require freezers. However, mixing the two parts and spreading the mixed resin on the dry fabric requires strict adherence to written protocol and experienced personnel to effect consistent repairs.

Two categories of adhesives that are used are films and pastes. Films come with and without mesh carrier cloth with typical thickness between 0.0025 to 0.01 in. (0.064 to 0.25 mm). The carrier cloth provides improved handling, results in more uniform bond line and helps reduce galvanic corrosion. Although films provide a more uniform bond line thickness than paste adhesives, repair part inaccessibility or a lack of refrigerated storage equipment sometimes necessitates use of paste adhesives.

Wet lay-up repairs almost always use paste adhesives as they are more compatible with paste resins in terms of curing characteristics. Like the paste resins, the paste adhesives consist of two parts that have a long shelf life. Conversely, film adhesives are more prevalent when prepreg is used to form repair patches as they usually require higher temperature and pressure for curing.

Bonding repairs require many ancillary materials. These materials do not become part of the repair and are removed and discarded after the repair is complete. They include items such as vacuum bag materials, scrim cloths, bleeder/breather materials, release films, tapes, wiping materials and solvents. The specifications for these materials are usually given in the SRM.

Repair Analysis

A bonded repair is from a structural point of view a bonded joint. As in a joint the load is transferred from the parent structure by the bond to a patch (single lap) bypassing the damaged portion of the parent structure. The geometry is usually two dimensional.

If a sandwich structure is repaired, the core repaired original or new replaced, forms a substrate that provides support for the out-of-plane loads. This is why bonded repairs are very efficient for sandwich structures. The repair analysis of a bonded repair follows similar guidelines as the analysis of a bonded joint. The main steps for bolted repairs are as follows:

Estimation of load transferred through the repair as for bolted repairs. See bolted repairs guidelines.

Load sharing in the repair. The load flow in a bonded repair is continuous. It depends on the elastic properties of the adherends and the adhesive and on-joint geometry. In some cases, the geometry can be approximated by the use of models of lap or strap joints. A two-dimensional finite element model can be used to calculate load distributions in the skin, patch and adhesive layer. A nonlinear solution can be used to account for the nonlinear stress-strain behavior of the adhesive.

Several specially developed computer applications can be used for analyzing bonded repairs. The PGLUE program contains an automatic mesher that creates a three-dimensional finite element model of a repaired panel containing three components: a plate with a cutout, a patch and an adhesive connecting the patch and the plate. Plasticity of the adhesive is considered in the analysis. However, the version available through ASIAC does not consider peel stresses, which can be critical. Traditional bonded joint applications, such as A4EI and ESDU8039, model only a slice through the repair and do not consider the two-dimensional effects of stiffening of the sides of the panel. Both bonded joint programs allow the patch to be stepped. A4EI considers plasticity in the adhesive shear stress but does not predict peel stress, while ESDU8039 predicts peel stress in the joint but does not consider plasticity. More advanced programs will likely improve the accuracy of analysis.

Analysis of local failure. As in the case of bolted repairs the parent structure is a given item in the repair design. The advantage of the bonded repair is that loads are introduced into the parent structure in a continuous way without inducing any stress concentrations in the parent structure. Thus there is no need for an increase in thickness in the joint region. After establishing the stress distribution in the parent structure, the stress and failure analyses are performed.

Patch structure. Patch structure is analyzed like the parent structure.

Adhesive. The joint should be designed in such a way that the adhesive layer is not the critical joint element. Peel and transverse shear stresses should be minimized by design (tapered or stepped adherends, filleting, etc.). Incorporation of nonlinear stress-strain behavior of the adhesive (usually approximated by elastic-plastic stress-strain curve). Dependence of the measured elastic mechanical properties of adhesive on its thickness. Change of adhesive properties as a function of the environment as well as long term degradation.

Repair Procedures

Bonded repairs require close control of the repair process and the repair environment. Structural integrity of the bonded joint is strongly dependent on the cleanliness of the work area and the ambient temperature and humidity. Other important factors are workmanship and geometrical fit of mating parts.

The four major activities to affect a bonded repair consist of patch and parent surface preparation, adhesive application, bagging and curing. Each of these activities may be different for the type of bonded repair being attempted, materials used and the part being repaired.

Size of the repair may be limited by the allowable out-time of the adhesive. A drawing of the patch is used to lay-up the composite tape or fabric, sheet metal or dry fabric materials. Standard shop procedures are used to make the composite patch laminate from prepreg. Dry fabric plies for wet lay-up are cut to size before impregnating with resin. This is done to minimize repair time.

Before adhesive application, the repair patch and the parent surfaces must be wiped clean with solvent and allowed to dry. At this point the composite surface should be abraded. A light grit blast gives a more uniform abrasion than hand sanding. The surface is then wiped dry with a clean, lint-free cloth.

Sheet metal patches have special surface preparation requirements depending on whether the patch is aluminum or titanium. They are specified in detail in the SRM and should be followed closely. Film adhesives are first attached to the patch, trimmed, and then applied to the damaged area.

Bagging encloses the repair for the curing operation. As most of the repairs are done outside the autoclave, the process described here will address only vacuum bagging. This allows the repair to be cured under atmospheric pressure. When the repair can be cured in an autoclave, additional pressure and higher, more uniform heat can be applied.

A typical bagging arrangement involves patch plies of prepreg co-cured with a layer of adhesive and a heating blanket to supply heat.

Starting from the top of the patch, the repair bagging assembly contains:

- Porous separator release film to prevent bleeder plies from sticking to the repair plies
- Bleeder plies to absorb extra resin (not applicable to net resin prepregs).
- A solid parting film
- Caul or pressure plate to help provide smooth finish to the repair
- Breather plies to provide for the air initially inside the bag to be drawn off by the vacuum source
- Rubberized vacuum bag

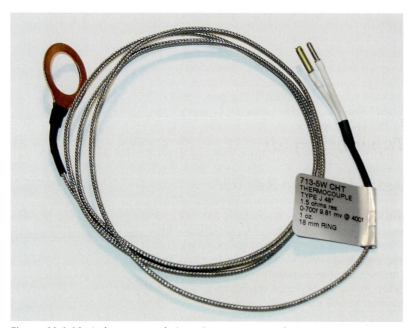

Figure 11-1-10. A thermocouple is an instrument used to measure temperature that consists of two wires of different metals joined at one end.

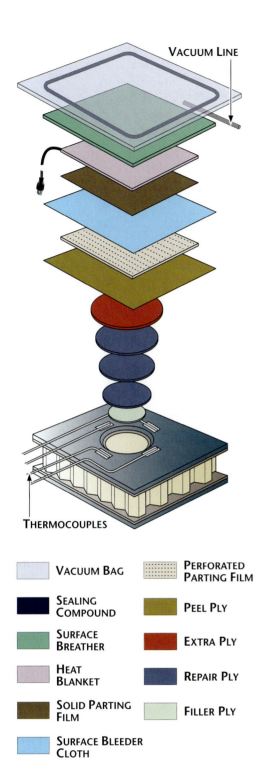

Figure 11-1-11. Vacuum bagging of a repair

Thermocouples on the part are needed to make sure that the part is not overheated. Figure 11-1-11 shows only one thermocouple wire.

For larger repairs, more thermocouples are needed to map the temperature distribution for the complete repair area. Distributing the heat evenly on the repair is one of the goals of proper bagging technique. In some cases a thin aluminum or copper sheet is inserted inside the bag for that purpose. Care must be taken not to puncture the bag.

The process of curing structural adhesives and composite resins is achieved by a chemical crosslinking accelerated by heat. Cure temperatures should be sufficiently high to achieve this, but care must be taken not to reach temperatures that may damage the original structure. Keeping the cure temperature as low as possible to affect cure is the safest policy.

The rate of heat-up is important as the resin and the adhesive undergo physical and chemical transformations. The resin and the adhesive must have compatible cure cycles and follow a prescribed time-temperature curve, (i.e., rate of increase in temperature, dwell temperature duration and rate of decrease in temperature). If the repair is an autoclave cure, pressure must be applied according to cure specifications.

The maximum thermocouple reading is usually used as a control on the maximum allowed temperature. Cure time is adjusted by monitoring the minimum thermocouple reading. After the cure is completed the repair assembly is cooled before vacuum pressure is relieved. Heat blankets, individual or integral with repair kits, are most commonly used to cure bonded repairs. Autoclaves, ovens and quartz lamps are other acceptable methods.

The vacuum bag is sealed on the periphery using tape. For a bonded repair with a metallic or pre-cured composite patch, bagging would still be needed to apply vacuum pressure to the adhesive but the setup would be more simple.

An integral part of the bagging process is the placement of the thermocouples (Figure 11-1-10) to monitor part and repair temperatures during cure. The more common practice is to place the heat blanket within the vacuum bag.

Section 2
Types of Repair

Resin Injection Repairs

Advanced composite structures often experience damage in the form of ply delaminations and matrix cracks. The damage may be either open or closed to an edge. Delaminations and cracks that are not open to an edge are difficult to repair via the injection method.

The method often suggested to repair this type of damage is to drill a series of holes around the cracked/delaminated area and inject those

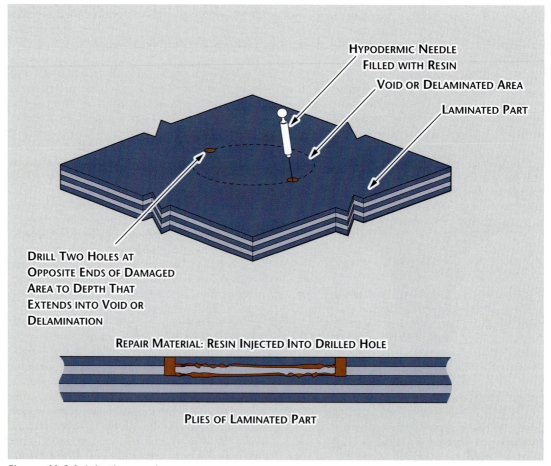

Figure. 11-2-1. Injection repair

holes with resin (Figure 11-2-1). This method is usually unsuccessful. Matrix cracks and delaminations are often too small and are not interconnected.

The currently available resin systems do not possess sufficient flow capability to infiltrate them. Hence, application of injection repair techniques is limited to delaminations that are either open to an edge or involve a clearly defined blister. Resin injection repairs are used on lightly loaded structures for small damages to a solid laminate due to delamination.

Two holes are drilled on the outside of the delamination area and a low-viscosity resin is injected in one hole until it flows out the other hole. Resin injection repairs are sometimes used on sandwich honeycomb structure to repair a facesheet disbond.

Disadvantages of the resin injection method are that the fibers are cut as a result of drilling holes, and it is difficult to remove moisture from the damaged area and to achieve complete infusion of resin.

The are two types of injection repair are: positive pressure injection and vacuum injection.

Positive pressure injection involves drilling holes into the delaminated area and injecting them with resin. It is used when a leak path exists, such as a delamination open to an edge or a blister.

The vacuum injection method involves using a vacuum to remove air from the delaminated area, allowing resin to flow into the void. It is used in areas where little or no airflow is possible and the delamination is too close to an edge to allow drilling injection holes, such as small-area delaminations in and around fastener holes.

Adhesive Characteristics

Injection repairs utilize a low-viscosity liquid adhesive to facilitate flow into tight matrix cracks and delaminations. The viscosity of most adhesives at room temperature is too high for successful injection.

Adhesive viscosity is reduced at higher temperatures; however, heating the adhesive causes an increase in the rate of polymerization, reducing the work life of the material. As the adhesive is mixed and brought up to temperature, the viscosity drops to its minimum value in about

20 minutes. After reaching minimum viscosity, gelation occurs rapidly. After about 10 minutes at 125°F (52°C), the resin becomes too viscous for successful injection to occur.

There is a trade-off between insuring a reasonable viscosity for injection and ensuring an adequate pot life to complete the injection. Heating the adhesive to its minimum viscosity temperature before injection may result in gelation occurring too quickly. Instead, heat the delaminated area to the minimum viscosity temperature prior to performing the injection to facilitate adhesive flow and ensure sufficient work life prior to adhesive gelation.

Damage Classification

NDI must first be performed on the component to determine location, depth and perimeter of the damage. The information obtained from NDI will determine which injection repair method should be used.

Positive Pressure Injection Repair

This method is used when positive airflow through the laminate is possible. The method involves drilling injection holes, heating the delaminated area to the minimum viscosity temperature of the adhesive, and injecting the resin into an injection hole using positive pressure.

The adhesive is injected into one hole until it flows out free of bubbles, either from another injection hole (in the case of a blister) or out of an open edge. A lack of bubbles indicates that the air in the delamination has been replaced by adhesive. The maximum time allowed for this to occur is the gel time of the adhesive. External pressure is then applied to the delaminated area, and the adhesive is cured. NDI is performed again after the repair is complete to insure successful injection.

Vacuum Injection Repair

This method is used when little or no airflow is possible, such as delaminations around fastener holes. The delaminated area is heated to the minimum viscosity temperature of the adhesive, and then adhesive is added to a vacuum chamber that has been placed over the delaminated area.

The adhesive is maintained at this minimum viscosity temperature under vacuum to allow outgassing of air and/or volatiles, then vented to atmosphere to force the resin into the delaminated area. The vacuum chamber is then

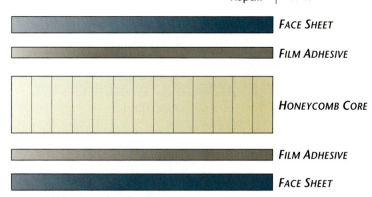

Figure 11-2-2. Sandwich construction

removed and a fastener or clamp is installed to provide positive pressure for curing the adhesive. NDI is performed on the delaminated area when the repair is complete to ensure successful injection.

Injected Foam Repair

Injected foam could be used to fill a repair area. After cure, the expanded foam is trimmed to match the part contour. In addition, syntactic two-part epoxy foams can be mixed and applied in areas as filler. Some of these products have the capability to be cured in 5 to 10 minutes and then sanded to contour. In some situations, a precured piece of foam can be placed in the repair area, similar to the core plug method used to repair honeycomb core, and bonded in place using an adhesive. In these repair methods, an overlay patch is typically placed over the repaired core area and bonded on with an adhesive.

Honeycomb Repair

A large proportion of current aerospace composite components are light sandwich structures (Figure 11-2-2) that are susceptible to damage. Sandwich structures consists of thin, high-strength skins that are separated by, and bonded to, lightweight honeycomb cores. The thicker the core the stiffer the panel with minimal weight increases.

Because sandwich structure is a bonded construction and the face sheets are thin, damage to sandwich structure is usually repaired by bonding. When repairing one face skin of the sandwich, remember that half of the in-plane load is transferred through that facesheet, and if the repair does not approximate in stiffness the undamaged face sheet extraneous bending moment could induce peel loads between the face sheets and core. Thus, external patch is usually applicable only for thin skin repairs while scarf concepts are used to repair thicker skins.

Figure 11-2-3. Three typical repair procedures used for honeycomb sandwich structures

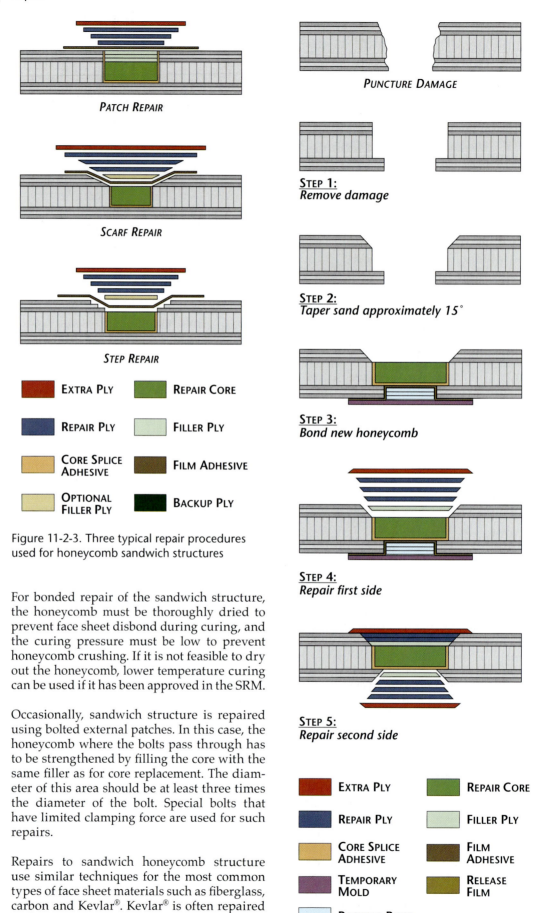

Figure 11-2-4. Double-sided repair

For bonded repair of the sandwich structure, the honeycomb must be thoroughly dried to prevent face sheet disbond during curing, and the curing pressure must be low to prevent honeycomb crushing. If it is not feasible to dry out the honeycomb, lower temperature curing can be used if it has been approved in the SRM.

Occasionally, sandwich structure is repaired using bolted external patches. In this case, the honeycomb where the bolts pass through has to be strengthened by filling the core with the same filler as for core replacement. The diameter of this area should be at least three times the diameter of the bolt. Special bolts that have limited clamping force are used for such repairs.

Repairs to sandwich honeycomb structure use similar techniques for the most common types of face sheet materials such as fiberglass, carbon and Kevlar®. Kevlar® is often repaired with fiberglass. Figure 11-2-3, and Figure 11-2-4 shows typical repair procedures used for honeycomb sandwich structures.

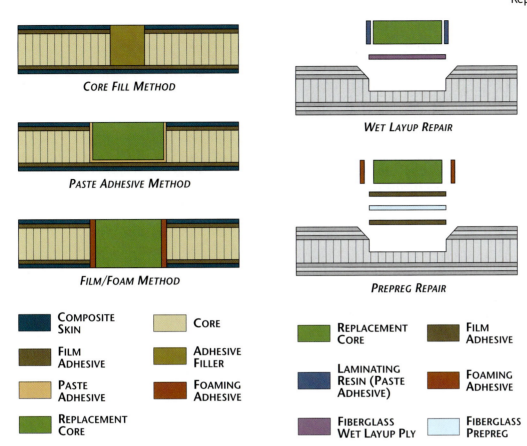

Figure 11-2-5. Core replacement methods

Figure 11-2-6. Partial depth core replacement

Core Damage

There are three common methods for core replacement: the core fill method, the paste adhesive method and the film/foam method. The three methods for full depth repair are shown in Figure 11-2-5.

Figure 11-2-6 illustrates partial depth core replacement for wet lay-up and prepreg repairs.

The core fill method replaces the damaged honeycomb with glass floc filled paste adhesive and is limited to small damage sizes. The weight of the repairs must be calculated and compared with flight control weights and balance limits set out in the SRM.

The other two methods can be used interchangeably depending on the available adhesives. However, the paste adhesive method results in a much heavier repair than the film/foam method, especially if the damage diameter is greater than 4 in. (10 cm).

The foaming adhesive required to utilize the film/foam method is a thin unsupported epoxy film containing a blowing agent that is liberated during cure causing a foaming action. The expansion process needs to be performed under positive pressure to become strong, highly structured foam.

Like film adhesives, foaming adhesives require high-temperature cure and refrigerator storage. Core replacement is usually accomplished with a separate curing cycle and can not be co-cured with the patch.

Minor Core Damage (Filler and Potting Repairs)

A potted repair can be used to repair damage to a sandwich honeycomb structure that is typically smaller than 0.5 in. (1.3 cm). The honeycomb material can be left in place or removed and then filled with a potting compound to restore some strength. Potted repairs do not restore the full strength of the part.

Potting compounds are most often epoxy resins filled with hollow glass, phenolic or plastic microballoons, cotton, flox or other materials. The potting compound can also be used as filler for cosmetic repairs to edges and skin panels.

Potting compounds are also used in sandwich honeycomb panels as hard points for bolts and screws. The potting compound is heavier than the original core and this could affect flight control balance. The weight of the repair must be calculated and compared with flight control weights and balance limits set out in the SRM.

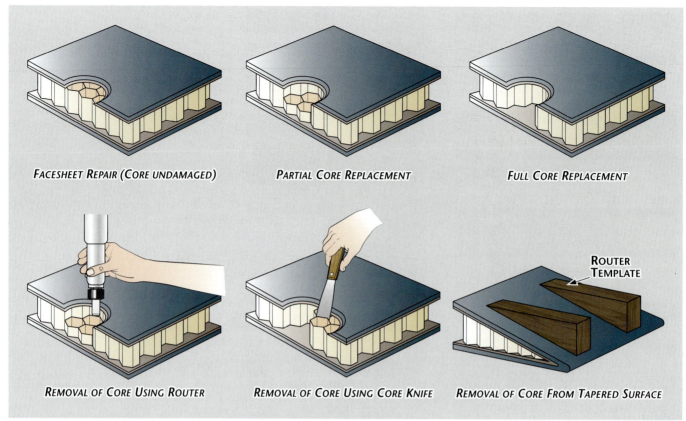

Figure 11-2-7. Honeycomb core is replaced based on the level of damage

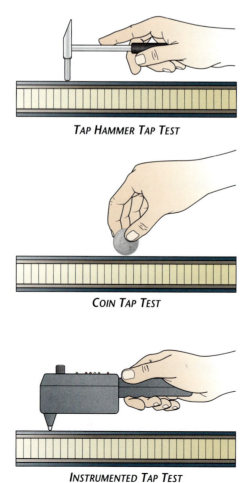

Figure 11-2-8. Tap testing techniques

Repair Example For Honeycomb Structure

Honeycomb structures are repaired based on the level of damage. Figure 11-2-7 shows some of the common repairs. The following steps are not a substitute for those found in the aircraft-specific SRM. Do not assume that the repair methods used by one manufacturer will be applicable to another manufacturer.

Inspect the damage. Thin laminates can be visually inspected and tap tested to map out the damage. Figure 11-2-8 shows some tap testing methods. Thicker laminates need more in-depth NDI methods such as ultrasonic inspection. Check in the vicinity of the damage for entry of water, oil, fuel, dirt or other foreign matter. Water can be detected with X-rays, back lighting, or a moisture detector.

Remove water from damaged area. Moisture has long been, and will continue to be, a problem in sandwich structure. Moisture, either present in the repair environment or absorbed by the parent structure or any of the materials used in the repair, is still the major source of trouble. Nonmetallic core is subject to rapid moisture absorption, which if present during the repair cure, can destroy adhesion of the laminate to the core surface by creating porosity in the repair material and bond line.

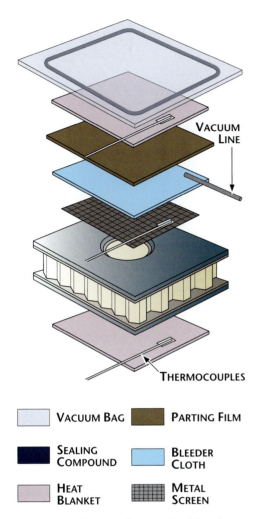

Figure 11-2-9. Vacuum bag method for drying parts

Water must be removed from the core before the part will be repaired, because if the water is not removed it will boil during the elevated-temperature cure cycle and the face sheets will blow off the core resulting in more damage. Water in the honeycomb core could also freeze at the low temperatures that exist at high altitudes, which could result in disbonding of the face sheets. Figure 11-2-9 shows on method of removing moisture.

Remove the damage. Trim out the damage to the face sheet to a smooth shape with rounded corners, or a circular or oval shape. Do not damage the undamaged plies, core or surrounding material. If the core is damaged, remove it by trimming to the same outline as the skin.

1. If the damage cleanup hole is 1.5 in. (3.8 cm) in diameter or less, remove damage down to undamaged core by sanding with a 90° degree router motor and a small sanding disk. Vacuum clean the repair area.

2. If damage cleanup hole is larger than 1.5 in. (3.8 cm) in diameter, completely remove damaged core.

3. Using a core slicer or core knife, carefully slice down the core cell walls to separate the core in the damage cleanup area from the remaining part core section. Use the damage cleanup hole in the skin as a guide. Slice along the part core cell axis. Ensure that the core slicer cutting edge is sharp.

4. If only one skin has been damaged, use the core slicer to separate the core. Then, completely remove separated core in the damage cleanup hole area down to the opposite skin's inner surface.

5. Low-density core can easily be removed (Figure 11-2-10) by causing cell wall failure using needle nose pliers and a gentle pulling and twisting motion. High- density core is sometimes more difficult to remove. Be careful not to delaminate the opposite skin during removal.

Use a 90° router motor and an 80-grit abrasive disk to remove the core and adhesive

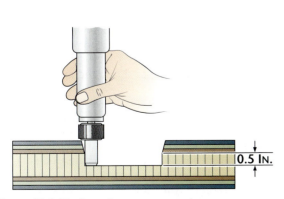
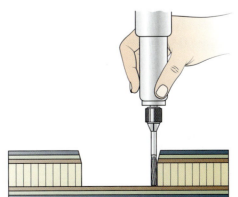

Figure 11-2-10. Core damage removal

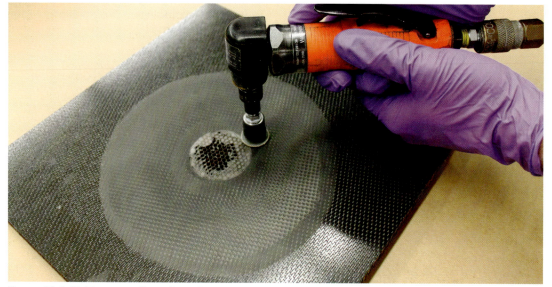

Figure 11-2-11. Taper sanding of repair area

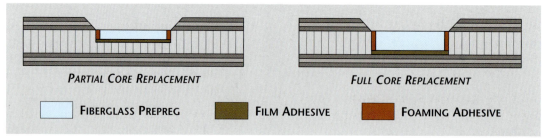

Figure 11-2-12. Core replacement

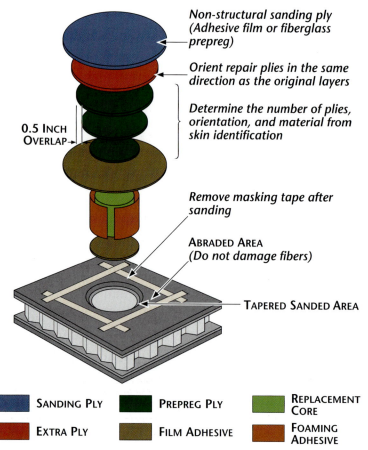

Figure 11-2-13. Installation or orientation of repair plies

from the inner surface of the opposite skin. It is acceptable to allow some adhesive to remain on the inner skin surface to avoid sanding into the laminate.

6. Vacuum core and sanding residue from repair area. Wipe inner skin surface using clean, dry Rymplecloth® to remove remaining sanding residue. Tape barrier material or release film over the area to prevent contamination.

Prepare the damaged area. Use a flexible disk sander or a rotating pad sander to sand a uniform taper (Figure 11-2-11) around the cleaned-up damage. Some manufactures give a taper ratio such as 1 to 40 and others prescribe a taper distance like a 1-in. (2.5-cm) overlap for each existing ply of the face sheet.

Remove the exterior finish, including conductive coating for an area that is at least 1 in. larger than the border of the taper. Remove all sanding dust with dry compressed air and a vacuum cleaner. Use a clean cloth moistened with approved solvent to clean the damaged area.

Install honeycomb core (wet lay-up). Use a knife to cut the replacement core. The core plug must be of the same type, class and grade of the original core. The direction of the core cells

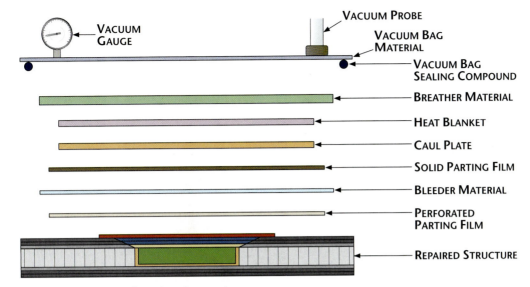

Figure 11-2-14. Vacuum bagging the repair

should line up with the honeycomb of the surrounding material. The plug must be trimmed to the right length and be solvent-washed with an approved cleaner.

For a wet lay-up repair, cut two plies of woven fabric that will fit on the inside surface of the undamaged skin.

Impregnate the fabric plies with a resin and place in the hole. Use potting compound around the core and place it in the hole.

For a prepreg repair, cut a piece of film adhesive that fits the hole and use a foaming adhesive around the plug. The plug should touch the sides of the hole. Line up the cells of the plug with the original material.

Vacuum bag the repair area and use an oven, autoclave or heat blanket to cure the core replacement. The wet lay-up repair could be cured at a room temperature up to 150°F (66°C). The prepreg repair must be cured at 250° to 350°F (121° to 177°C). Usually the core replacement will be cured with a separate curing cycle and not co-cured with the patch. The plug must be sanded flush with the surrounding area after the cure. See Figure 11-2-12.

Prepare and install the repair plies. Consult the repair manual for the correct repair material and the number of plies required for the repair. Typically, one more ply than the original number of plies is installed. Cut the plies to the correct size and ply orientation.

The repair ply must be installed with the same orientation as that of the original plies. Impregnate the plies with resin for the wet lay-up repair or remove the backing material from the prepreg material. See Figure 11-2-13.

The plies are usually placed using the smallest-ply, first-taper lay-up sequence, but an alternative method is to use the largest-ply-first lay-up sequence, where the first layer of reinforcing fabric completely covers the work area, followed by successively smaller layers, ending with an extra outer layer or two extending over the patch and onto the sound laminate for some distance.

Vacuum Bag the repair. Figure 11-2-14 shows a typical vacuum bag setup.

Cure the repair. The repair is cured at the required cure cycle. Figure 11-2-15 shows a

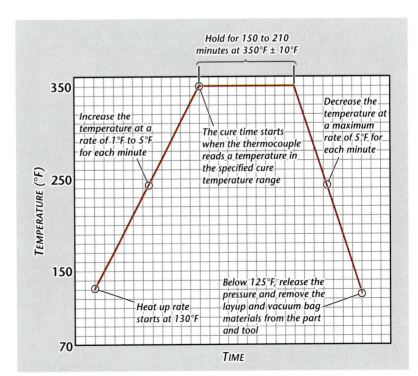

Figure 11-2-15. Cure cycle for heat blanket and hot bonder

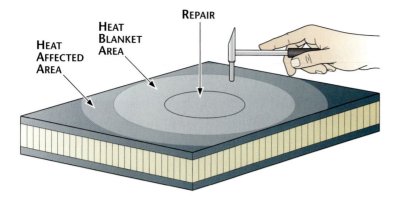

Figure 11-2-16. Post-repair inspection

sample cure cycle. Wet lay-up repairs can be cured at room temperature, but an elevated temperature up to 150°F (66°C) can be used to speed up the cure.

The prepreg repair needs to be cured at an elevated cure cycle. Parts that can be removed from the aircraft could be cured in a hot room, oven or autoclave. A heating blanket is used for on-aircraft repairs.

Remove the bagging materials after curing and inspect the repair. The repair should be free from pits, blisters, resin-rich and resin-starved areas. Lightly sand the repair patch to produce a smooth finish without damaging the fibers. Apply top finish and conductive coating (i.e., lighting protection).

Inspect the repair. Use visual, tap and/or ultrasonic inspection to inspect the repair after it has been completed (Figure 11-2-16). Remove the repair patch if defects are found.

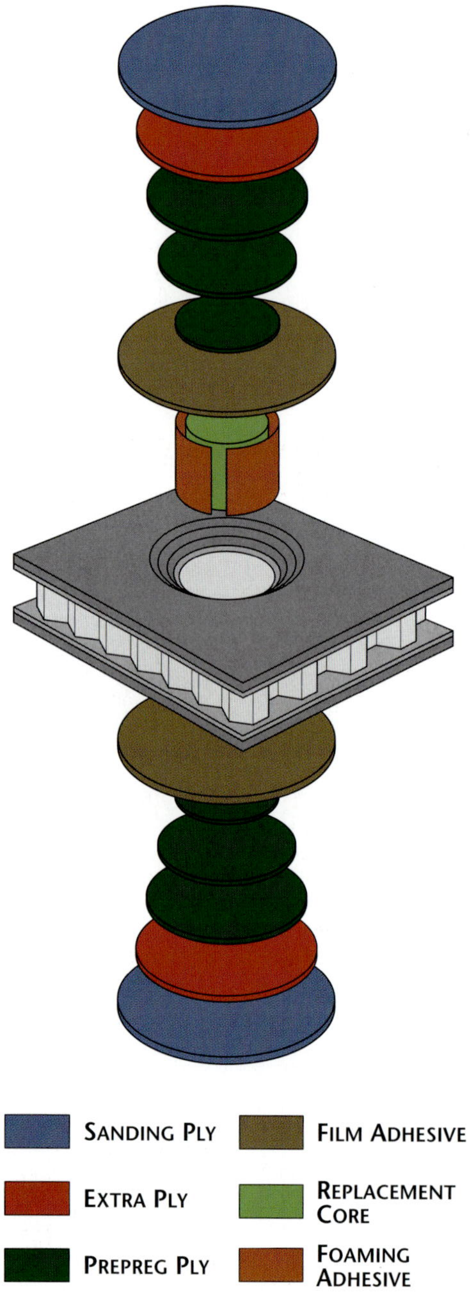

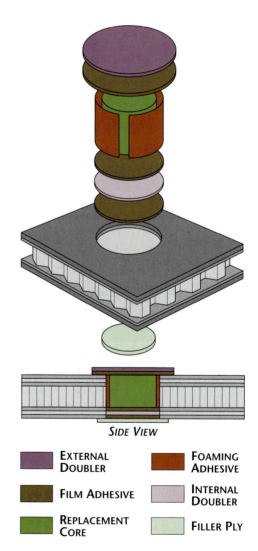

Figure 11-2-17. Repair procedure for damage to both face sheets and core

Figure 11-2-18. External repair procedure using a doubler

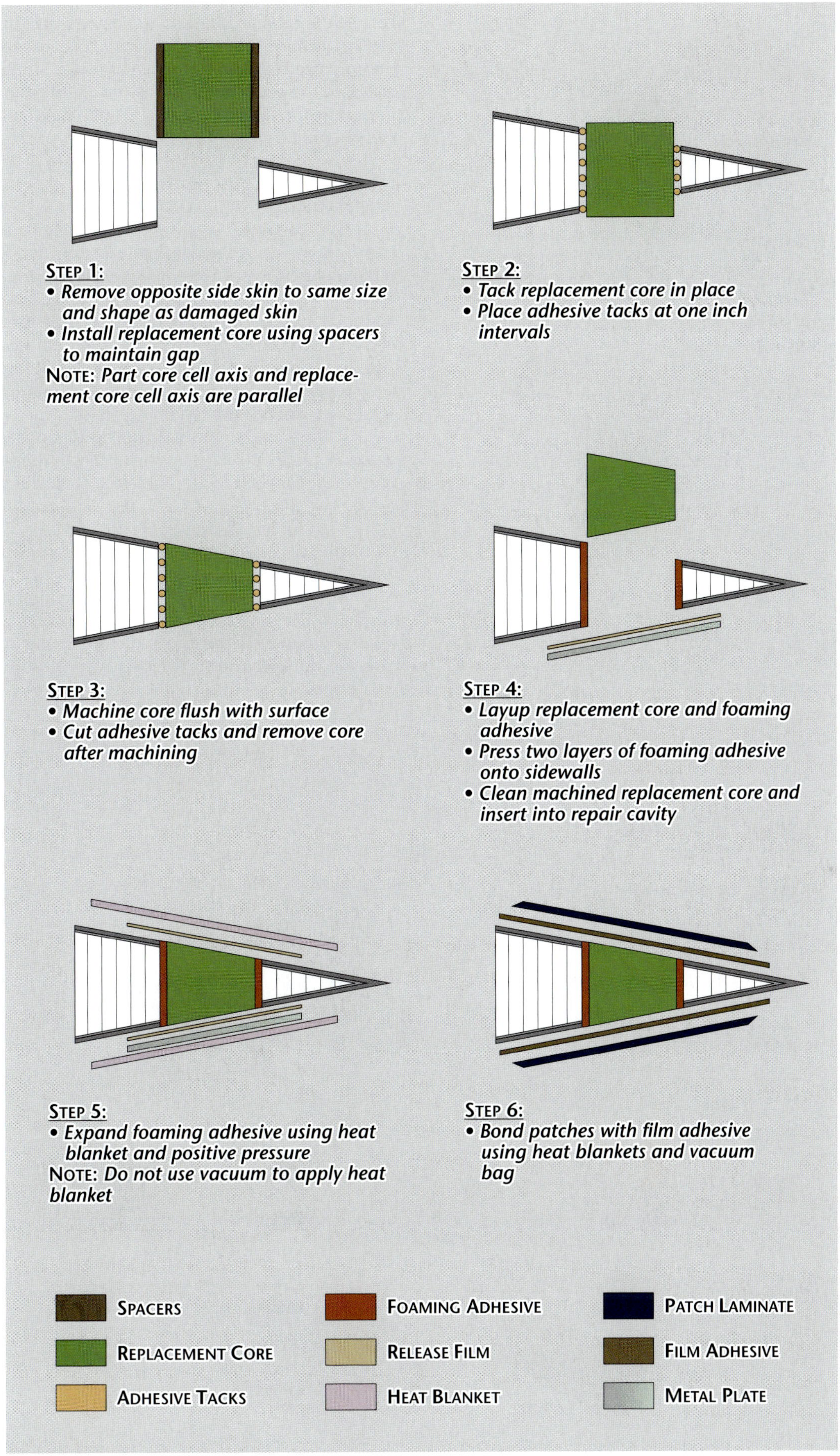

STEP 1:
- Remove opposite side skin to same size and shape as damaged skin
- Install replacement core using spacers to maintain gap

NOTE: *Part core cell axis and replacement core cell axis are parallel*

STEP 2:
- Tack replacement core in place
- Place adhesive tacks at one inch intervals

STEP 3:
- Machine core flush with surface
- Cut adhesive tacks and remove core after machining

STEP 4:
- Layup replacement core and foaming adhesive
- Press two layers of foaming adhesive onto sidewalls
- Clean machined replacement core and insert into repair cavity

STEP 5:
- Expand foaming adhesive using heat blanket and positive pressure

NOTE: *Do not use vacuum to apply heat blanket*

STEP 6:
- Bond patches with film adhesive using heat blankets and vacuum bag

Spacers	Foaming Adhesive	Patch Laminate
Replacement Core	Release Film	Film Adhesive
Adhesive Tacks	Heat Blanket	Metal Plate

Figure 11-2-19. Honeycomb flight control surface repair

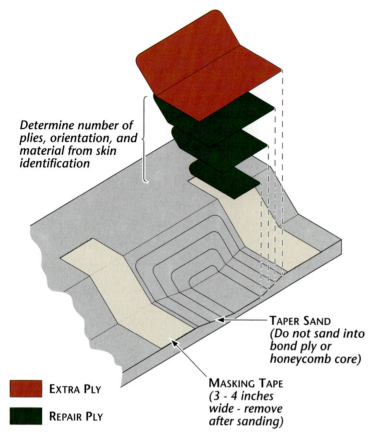

Figure 11-2-20. Damage to edge band and ramp

Perform a balance check if a repair to a flight control surface was made, and make sure that the repaired flight control is within limits stated in the SRM. Failure to do so could result in flight control flutter and safety of flight can be affected.

Common Repair Configurations

Example of double-side honeycomb sandwich repair. A double-sided repair is necessary if the damage has penetrated both sides of the honeycomb sandwich structure. First the core needs to be removed and replaced and the surfaces need to be scarf sanded before new repair plies could be laid up. The outer most plies are often fiberglass plies that can be sanded flush and smooth after the repair has cured. Figure 11-2-17 shows a typical repair procedure for damage to both face sheets and core.

Example of honeycomb sandwich repair using a pre-cured doubler (non flush). Aluminum, titanium and procure composite doublers are sometimes used to repair sandwich structure. These types of repair use an external doubler that is bonded with either a past adhesive or a film adhesive. The advan-

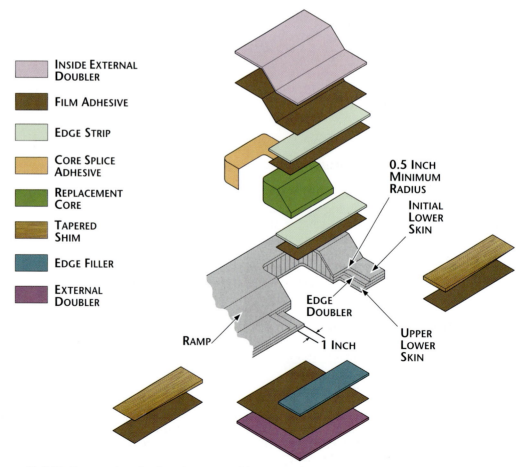

Figure 11-2-21. Damage to edge band, ramp and honeycomb core

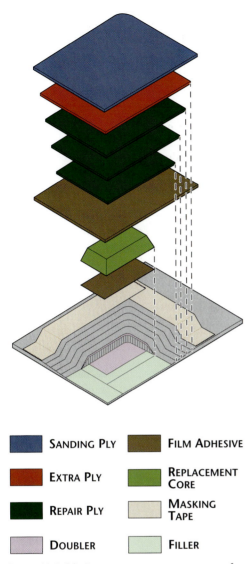

Figure 11-2-22. Damage to a corner ramp of a honeycomb sandwich panel

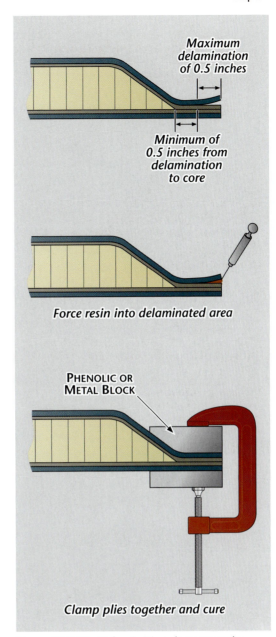

Figure 11-2-23. Delamination damage at the edge of a panel

tage of the external doubler repair is that is quicker.

A disadvantage is that if the doubler is not perfectly aligned with the honeycomb structure the bond line will vary in thickness and a weak bond can occur. This type of repair is not recommended for highly stressed skin. Figure 11-2-18 shows the repair procedure for using a doubler repair.

Repair example of honeycomb flight control surface. Figure 11-2-19 illustrates the full depth repair of a honeycomb flight control surface.

Repair of honeycomb ramp. Damage to the ramp of a honeycomb sandwich panel is a typical repair illustrated in SRMs. Figure 11-2-20 shows a repair where only the surface plies are damaged. The ramp area is scarf sanded with a 0.5 in. overlap and new repair plies are laid up. Figure 11-2-21 shows damage to the ramp and the honeycomb core. External doublers are used to repair the damage.

Repair of honeycomb ramp corner. The corners of honeycomb panels are often damaged during the operation of the aircraft. Figure 11-2-22 illustrates how to repair corner damage using prepreg and film adhesive. Similar repairs are also possible using wet lay-up repair techniques.

Example of repair to panel edge band. Delamination of the plies at the edge of a panel could be repaired if the damage is limited to the edge band only and no core damage is found. Figure 11-2-23 shows one example of this type of repair.

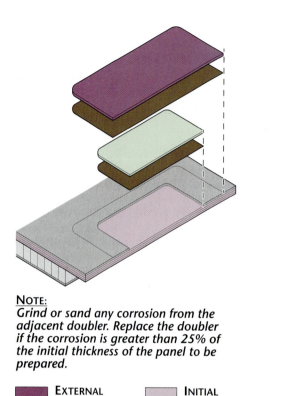

NOTE:
Grind or sand any corrosion from the adjacent doubler. Replace the doubler if the corrosion is greater than 25% of the initial thickness of the panel to be prepared.

- EXTERNAL DOUBLER
- FILM ADHESIVE
- INITIAL DOUBLER
- FILLER

Figure 11-2-24. Damage to plies at the edge of panel but no core damage

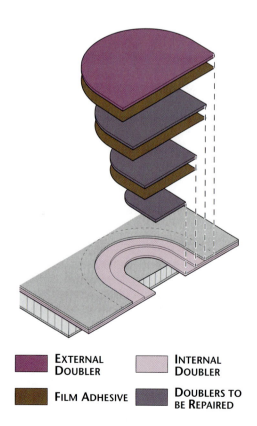

- EXTERNAL DOUBLER
- FILM ADHESIVE
- INTERNAL DOUBLER
- DOUBLERS TO BE REPAIRED

Figure 11-2-25. Edge band fully penetrated but no core damage

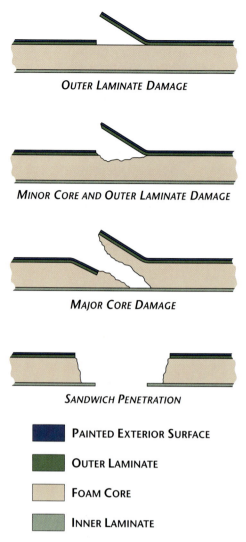

- PAINTED EXTERIOR SURFACE
- OUTER LAMINATE
- FOAM CORE
- INNER LAMINATE

Figure 11-2-26. Damage scenarios to a foam core sandwich structure

Example of damage at edge. If the plies are damaged at the edge of a honeycomb panel but there is no damage to the core, the panel could be repaired (Figure 11-2-24 and Figure 11-2-25). In these repair procedures the damage is removed and the void is inserted and bonded. An external doubler is used to restore the structural strength of the panel.

Repair of Foam Sandwich Structure

Some aircraft designs use a foam as the core in the sandwich construction instead of honeycomb. These structures can be repaired in a similar way as honeycomb sandwich structures.

Figure 11-2-26 shows the different damage scenarios for foam core sandwich structure. Figure 11-2-27 and Figure 11-2-28 show repair techniques to repair damage to facesheet and core.

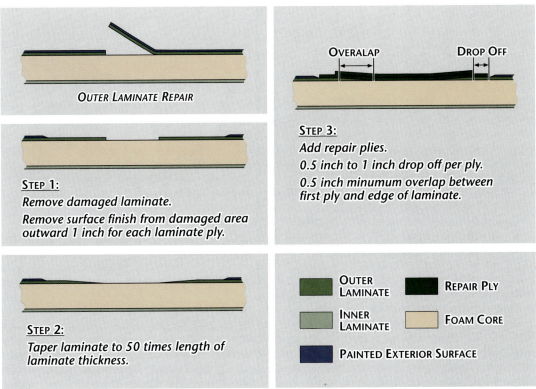

Figure 11-2-27. Damage repair procedure for damage to one facesheet and no core damage.

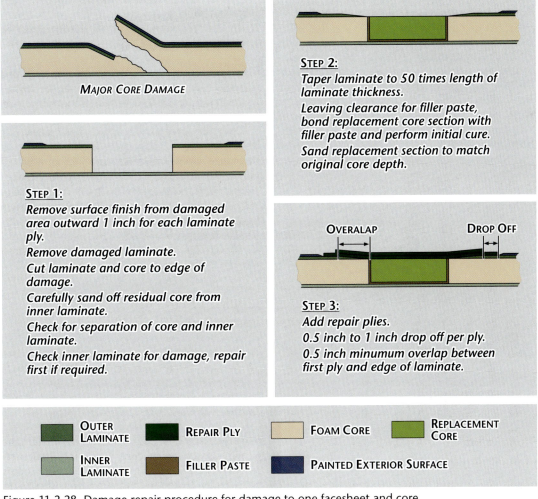

Figure 11-2-28. Damage repair procedure for damage to one facesheet and core

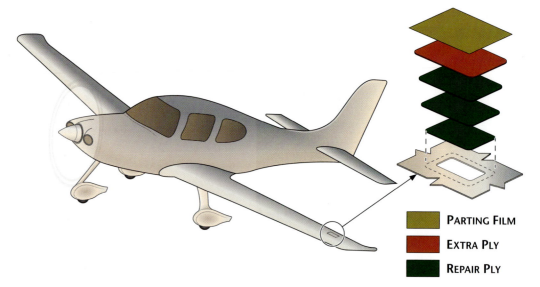

Figure 11-2-29. Ply layup on scarved surface.

Figure 11-2-29 illustrates the correct way to lay-up the repair plies on the scarf sanded original structure. Prepreg or wet lay-up techniques can be used. Wet lay up with low temperature cure resins is often the preferred way for smaller fiberglass aircraft.

Repair of Laminate Structure

Laminate structures resemble sheet metal structures and consist of a single laminate reinforced with stringers, frames and bulkheads. The stringers are often co-cured with the laminate. These laminate structures can be fairly thick, for example most of the B787 laminate structures consist of 20 plies, and some parts have 75 or more.

Both bolted and bonded repairs are used. Bonded repairs consists of patch (external), scarved (flush) and stepped (flush). The stringers could also be damaged and require repairs. Figure 11-2-30 shows a typical solid laminate repair scheme.

Patch repair. The top illustration in Figure 11-2-31 shows a typical external patch repair with prepreg material. Wet lay-up could be used as well.

Scarved repair. A scarved repair similar to that used to repair honeycomb sandwich structures is depicted in the middle illustration in Figure 11-2-31. The scarf angle is often between 1:10 and 1:70. If the structure becomes very thick this repair method will become impractical due to the large amount of good material that needs to be removed to create the shallow scarf angle.

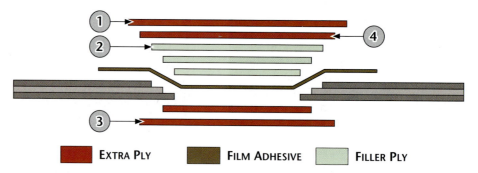

1. Orientation of outermost extra repair ply needs to be the same as the outermost layer of the laminate.
2. Component structure identification determines number of plies, orientation, and material.
3. Extra repair plies only necessary on this side if the damage penetrates through this surface.
4. Orientation of other extra repair plies is to be +45° to the extra repair ply immediately above it.

Figure 11-2-30. Example of solid laminate repair scheme

Stepped repair. A stepped repair is shown in the bottom illustration in Figure 11-2-31. The advantage of this method over the scarved repair method is that the adhesive will not run down during the cure. Disadvantages of this type of repair is that it is very difficult to accomplish precisely and it will be difficult to prepare repair plies that fit the prepared surface perfectly. For this reason, the scarved repair is more often used.

Section 3
Repair Processes and Procedures

Double-Vacuum Debulk Process

The double-vacuum bag processing concept was developed to improve the overall quality of composite laminate repair patches for thicker laminates. It has been shown that lower levels of porosity, improved resin distribution and improved resin dominated mechanical properties in prepreg repair patches can be achieved.

This process is also used to stage ambient storable prepreg repair patch laminates for later use in co-bonded field repair patch applications with the intention of performing the final cure on-aircraft using a single-vacuum bag process.

Debulking can be used with prepreg and wet lay-up methods. To fabricate wet lay-up repair laminates using the double-vacuum bag process, an additional step is required where the impregnated fabric is placed within the debulking assembly (Figure 11-3-1).

To begin the debulking process, air within the inner flexible vacuum bag is evacuated. The rigid outer box is then sealed onto the inner vacuum bag, and the volume of air between the rigid outer box and inner vacuum bag is evacuated.

Since the outer box is rigid, the second evacuation prevents atmospheric pressure from pressing down on the inner vacuum bag over the patch. This prevents air bubbles from being "pinched-off" within the laminate and facilitates air removal by the inner vacuum.

The laminate is then heated to a predetermined debulking temperature in order to reduce the resin viscosity and further improve the removal of air and volatiles from the laminate. The heat

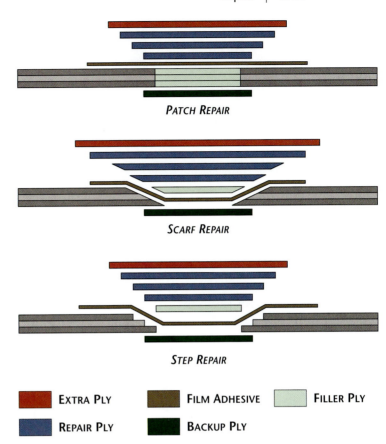

Figure 11-2-31. Three types of repair to laminate structure

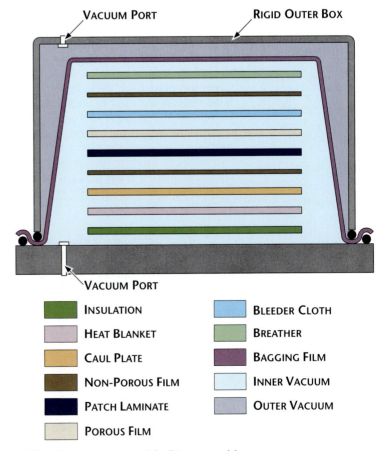

Figure 11-3-1. Double vacuum debulking assembly

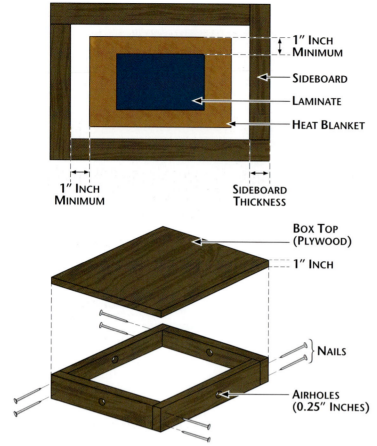

Figure 11-3-2. Wooden debulking box fabrication

ture to consolidate the plies. Upon completion of the compaction cycle, the staged prepreg laminate is removed from the assembly and is either prepared for storage or immediately cured.

The double-vacuum bag approach has been shown to produce repair laminates with low void content and compaction approaching that of autoclave-processed laminates. However, there are several limitations in application of the process due to the required use of a rigid outer vacuum box.

In the case of co-bonded applications, the patch laminate must be debulked, compacted and staged off-aircraft. As the staged patch remains formable, the patch can then be transferred to the aircraft, formed to contour and co-bonded in place using a single-vacuum bag process for the final cure. This two-step process is necessary since using the rigid vacuum box assembly on-aircraft creates a peeling load that may be sufficient to further damage the parent structure.

Likewise, the vacuum box assembly is difficult if not impossible to set up on a contoured surface. Overall patch dimensions are also limited by the maximum practical size of the rigid outer box (in practice, relatively portable vacuum boxes are a maximum of approximately 24 in. (61 cm).

If larger repair patches are required or if no portable vacuum box is available the technician can build box from materials readily available at the hardware store. Figure 11-3-2 shows the instructions to make a debulking box and Figure 11-3-3 shows the set up when the custom box is used.

In-Process Quality Control

Bonded repairs require more in-process quality control than bolted repairs to obtain structurally sound results. Composite materials and adhesives require extensive record keeping ensuring they are within life, such as to storage time in the refrigerator, warm-up time and out time on the shop floor.

Lay-up operations need to be inspected as to the correct fiber orientation. Cure cycles must be monitored to assure they follow specifications.

For large repairs, a small companion panel is cured with the repair (Figure 11-3-4). It is used for coupon testing to provide confidence in the quality of the repair, repair patch and adhesive bond.

Bolted repairs require inspection of holes for damage and size. Assembled repairs also require inspection of fastener installations.

is applied through a heat blanket that is controlled using thermocouples placed directly on the heat blanket, in order to limit the amount of resin advancement during the debulk cycle.

Once the debulking cycle is completed, the laminate is compacted to consolidate the plies by venting the vacuum source attached to the outer rigid box, thus allowing atmospheric pressure to re-enter the box and provide positive pressure against the inner vacuum bag. Upon completion of the compaction cycle, the laminate is removed from the assembly and is prepared for cure.

In the case of prepreg repair patch laminates, the prepreg plies are cut, stacked and placed within the double vacuum debulking assembly shown in Figure 11-3-1. In this process, the thermocouples are placed along the edges of the laminate, to ensure that all areas of the laminate reach the required debulking and compaction temperatures. No bleeder material is used in the prepreg staging process, in contrast to the wet lay-up staging process.

To begin the staging process, the inner vacuum bag and outer box are evacuated. The prepreg laminate is then heated to the debulking temperature. Once the debulking cycle is completed, the laminate is compacted at tempera-

Repair Validation

Successful inspection of a repair is not sufficient to guarantee that the repair will perform as designed and implemented. Repair designs need to be supported by an experimentally verified database and analysis. This helps to ensure the repair's capability to carry the intended loads or to replace the capability of the parent structure. The repair material allowables used in the design should be generated using approved testing and data reduction methods that reflect the amount of testing completed, material and process controls in place and the criticality of the structure.

Both strength and stiffness must be taken into account when designing the repair. Analyses need to be done in each fiber direction with careful attention to limit the effects of hard points. It must be understood that increases in stiffness do not correlate to increases in the repair factor of safety. Environments that the parent material was designed for and details such as edge bands, cutouts and fastener penetrations must also be considered.

Repair designs are based on using a specific material or a family of materials. Design properties are usually obtained by mechanical property testing specimens that mimic the particular repair process. Typically this testing is not as extensive as for the parent material and does not involve sufficient replication to obtain statistically based properties. Batch-to-batch variation of repair materials will occur, which can be somewhat problematic for wet lay-up materials.

Typically two practices are utilized for obtaining repair allowables. Allowables can be based on the parent material properties with knockdown factors that reflect lower cure temperatures and pressures of the repair material relative to the parent material, or allowables and material properties are derived for the repair material to be used in the repair analysis. It is common to use large reductions from the mean value to the allowable design value since the process parameters (fiber volume, pressure and temperature) of repair patches have more variability than the parent material.

In addition to coupon testing, a variety of elements are tested to validate repair designs. These are usually performed to support repair designs included in the SRM and range from simple joint specimens, representing bolted or bonded load transfer, to tests of full-scale repairs.

Simple joint specimens are used for development of repair designs. These are usually two-dimensional. Examples of such elements

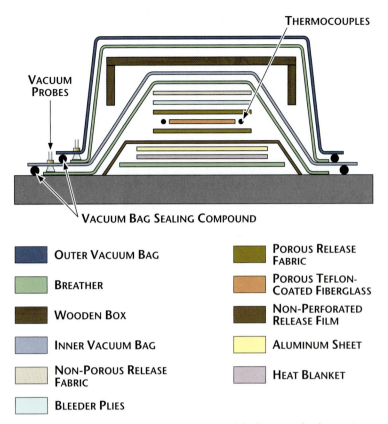

Figure 11-3-3. Wooden box double-vacuum debulking tool schematic

would be single- or double-bolt specimens to obtain bearing, bearing/bypass and net tensile values; and lap-bonded specimens to obtain joint shear strengths. The more complex elements are used to validate the repair design and repair process. These are full-scale representations of the repair.

Final validation of bolted and bonded repairs relies on strict attention to all details, including damage removal and site preparation, repair design, appropriate use of materials, repair analysis, material and fabrication processes,

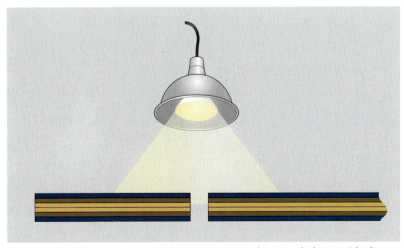

Figure 11-3-4. A small piece of the repair material is cured along with the repair for use in testing the quality of the repair.

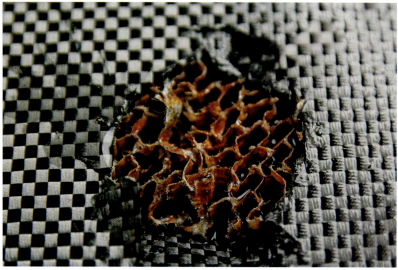

Figure 11-3-5. The water in this honeycomb core must be removed before the carbon fiber material is repaired.

It is extremely important to ensure water and moisture is removed prior to performing any bonding, especially one incorporating a heated curing process. Standing water, like that pictured in Figure 11-3-5, as well as water vapor and absorbed moisture in laminates and honeycomb can produce blistering, delamination and microcrack damage in the composite, and porosity and weak bond line strength in the repair adhesive.

In the field, repair time and equipment may be limited. The parts must be dried as much as possible, and this can be a lengthy process. To mitigate the effects of any moisture not removed during the drying process, cure temperatures of 210°F (99°C) or below should be used if authorized by the system-specific technical data or manufacturer's specification.

Curing at less than the optimum temperature, even when authorized, will prevent adhesives from reaching their ultimate properties; however, loss of adhesive strength is more desirable than inducing damage from water vapor pressure during the cure cycle. The absorption process is reversible and dependent on time, temperature and humidity. The moisture content of a laminate varies through the thickness with the moisture content being highest at the laminate surface. Painted laminates have higher moisture content than unpainted laminates as the paint tends to inhibit the moisture egress from the laminate.

Moisture Removal

Composite skins and sandwich structure inherently absorb water and moisture during use. This water and moisture intrusion may not be obvious by visual inspection of the structure. The structure may look dry, even if it is not. Some composite materials, including resin, fiber and core, have inherent water absorption characteristics. Sandwich or honeycomb panels are particularly prone to water absorption and retention due to the increased air volume in these panels. Cracked coatings, impact damage and loose fasteners all provide paths for moisture intrusion.

inspection and appropriate design values supported by test evidence.

Honeycomb Sandwich Assemblies

Moisture can enter into honeycomb sandwich assemblies through damaged edge closeouts, skin punctures, as shown in Figure 11-3-6, or other defects that expose the core to the environment. This moisture can collect in core cells and become trapped. Moisture in honeycomb sandwich assemblies may not be detectable by X-ray.

When applying heat to cure bonded repairs, the following can occur:

- Moisture in laminate skins desorbs into the adhesive bond line during the cure process and results in bond line voids. This can be alleviated when curing two-part adhesive systems by allowing the adhesive to gel at room temperature prior to beginning the heat cure, or by drying the part.

- Blistering of laminate plies can occur if the vapor pressure of the moisture in the laminate exceeds the strength of the matrix material. The potential for blistering can be reduced by drying the repair area.

Figure 11-3-6. Punctures in composite materials permit moisture to enter into the core of structures and possibly become trapped.

- Skin-to-core disbonds and honeycomb core node bond failures can occur if the pressure in the core due to heating air and trapped moisture in the core cells, exceeds the strength of the skin-to-honeycomb core bond or the strength of the core node bond. The potential for node bond failure and skin-to-core disbonds can be lessened by reducing the repair cure temperature.

For example, FM300-2, which cures 50°F (10°C) lower than FM300, has been qualified as a repair adhesive to replace FM300 and reduces the possibility of skin-to-core disbonds attributable to the presence of moisture. Laminate drying is still required prior to performing the cure cycle to reduce bond line porosity and the potential for laminate blistering. If liquid water is present in the honeycomb sandwich assembly (as detected by X-ray), use one of the water removal procedures described below.

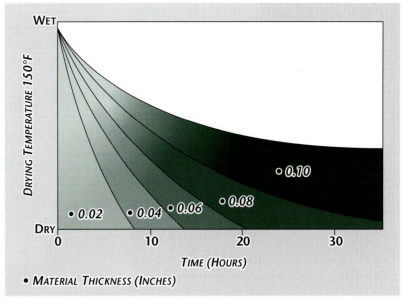

Figure 11-3-7. Drying times for wet laminates

Procedure for Laminate Drying Prior to Bonding

Absorbed moisture in composite laminates can cause problems when heat is applied during the curing process. It is necessary to dry the part prior to curing using drying temperatures that do not allow the moisture vapor pressure to exceed the matrix strength.

Generally, the part is never dried at a temperature higher than the service temperature of the material used to manufacture the part. The time required to completely dry the skin varies with skin thickness, initial moisture content and drying temperature. The graph in Figure 11-3-7 shows drying times for materials of varying thicknesses.

It is not necessary to completely dry the skin to prevent laminate blistering or bond line porosity as completely drying thin skins (4 to 10 plies) may take more than 10 hours. Completely drying thicker skins (12 plies or more) can take more than 30 hours. It is only necessary to reduce the near surface moisture content by using the following laminate drying procedure.

Water Removal from Honeycomb Core

Water in the honeycomb core, either visually apparent or detected by X-ray, must be removed to prevent corrosion of metallic core or moisture-related degradation of nonmetallic core. Areas containing water will appear lighter than adjacent areas in an X-ray film; however, the presence of cured liquid adhesive from a previous disbond or delamination repair can give a similar appearance.

If the water indication is in proximity to a previous repair, obtain assistance from an NDI technician to determine whether water is present. Water must be removed prior to a cure temperature of 200°F (93°C) or higher being used. Generally, water removal is performed at a lower temperature than the laminate drying temperature to prevent damage to the honeycomb sandwich assemblies from steam pressure.

Two water removal procedures are listed below. Which procedure to use depends on the availability of equipment and materials, whether the part can be removed from the aircraft and whether the water is located in a repairable area.

Heat blanket drying. This procedure uses a heat blanket (Figure 11-3-8) to locally heat the water in the assembly causing it to egress out of the part. It is the easiest method to use and is effective only when the moisture in the area

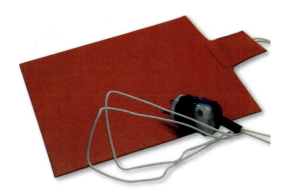

Figure 11-3-8. Heat blanket

Figure 11-3-9. A vacuum connection attached to a vacuum bag

Figure 11-3-10. Moisture indicator

being heated has an open path to the vacuum bag.

1. Perform NDI of the part to determine the location of water in the core.

2. If the part has water in a non-repairable zone, as defined in the part's SRM, proceed to the procedure for oven drying.

3. If the part has water in a repairable zone, as defined in the part's SRM, drill holes through skin in the area containing water. Use a 125-in. (318-cm) diameter carbide drill bit. For each square inch of water accumulation, drill two holes.

4. Lay up heat blanket, thermocouples and vacuum bag over the area containing water.

5. For parts manufactured from 250°F (121°C) service temperature materials, dry at 190°F (88°C). For parts manufactured from 180°F (82°C) service temperature materials, dry at 160°F (71°C).

6. Apply 20 to 30 inches of mercury vacuum to the vacuum bag. Heat affected area to the specified drying temperature at a rise rate of 2 to 6°F (1 to 3°C) per minute. Figure 11-3-9 shows a typical vacuum–vacuum bag connection.

7. Upon reaching the specified temperature, hold for 6 hours while maintaining 20 to 30 inches of mercury vacuum.

8. Test for the presence of water during the last hour of the drying cycle by connecting a moisture indicator in the vacuum line.

9. If the desiccant in the moisture indicator changes from blue to pink, dry the part for an additional 6 hours. Remove the discolored desiccant. Repack the filter with fresh desiccant using Rymplecloth® at each end of the filter. An example of a moisture indicator is shown in Figure 11-3-10.

10. Repeat steps 7 through 9 until there is no color change.

11. Cool to below 150°F (66°C) at a rate not to exceed 5°F (3°C) per minute.

12. Disassemble heat blanket, vacuum bag and thermocouples.

13. Reinspect area using NDI to determine if water has been removed or if it has migrated to another location.

14. If water has been removed from the assembly, proceed to step 17

15. If water is still present in the assembly, repeat the process starting at step 4

16. If water has migrated as a result of the drying process or if the above procedures prove unsuccessful and the water is still in a repairable zone, remove the skin from the area containing water. Remove the skin cautiously to minimize damage to the core underneath. After skin removal repeat the process starting at step 4

17. If holes were drilled in skin, seal holes with liquid adhesive. Bond an external patch over the drilled holes.

18. If the skin was removed or the core was damaged, repair skin and core.

Oven drying. Use this procedure when an oven (Figure 11-3-11) is the heat source for performing bonded repairs. This will ensure any undetectable water vapor in the core assemblies will not cause part damage. It is also used for removal of water from a non-repairable zone.

The oven is used to heat the water in the part and to drive it out the way it came in. An envelope vacuum bag, a vacuum bag that completely surrounds the part, is used to ensure that a path exists for moisture egress. A moisture indicator is used to determine when drying is complete.

This procedure can only be used when the part can be removed from the aircraft and an oven large enough to hold the part is available.

1. Completely surround the part with an envelope vacuum bag. Tape two thermocouples to the part under the vacuum bag. Apply 20 to 30 inches of mercury vacuum.

2. Place the enveloped bagged assembly in an air circulating oven at least 3 ft. (0.9m) above the oven floor. Apply 20 to 30 in. of mercury vacuum.

3. The drying temperature and time should be recorded either using the thermocouples applied to the part and a temperature recording device (preferred) or the oven temperature recorder. In aviation applications, a heat bonder with thermocouple input, as shown in Figure 11-3-12, is typically used to record temperature. If neither of the recorders is available, temperature recordings should be made manually at 15-minute intervals.

4. Dry parts using a two-step drying cycle (Figure 11-3-13). For parts manufactured from 250°F (121°C) service temperature materials, dry at 190°F (88°C) for 32 hours followed by 225°F (107°C) for 16 hours. For parts manufactured from 180°F (82°C) service temperature materials, dry at 160°F (71°C) for 32 hours followed by 180°F (82°C) for 16 hours.

5. Dry the part using the specified drying cycle. Heat oven to the required temperature at a rise rate of 2 to 6°F (1 to 3°C) per minute. Maintain 20 to 30 in. of mercury vacuum during the entire drying cycle.

6. Test for the presence of water during the last hour of the drying cycle by connecting a moisture indicator outside of the oven in the vacuum line.

7. If the desiccant in the moisture indicator changes from blue to pink, dry the part for an additional 6 hours. Remove the discolored desiccant. Repack the filter with

Figure 11-3-11. Industrial oven used for curing and drying of composites.

Figure 11-3-12. A heat bonder with thermocouple input is used to record temperature readings.

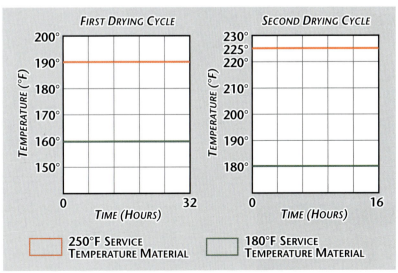

Figure 11-3-13. A two-cycle drying process is used for parts manufactured from 250°F and 180°F service materials.

fresh desiccant using Rymplecloth® at each end of the filter.

8. Repeat steps 5 through 7 until there is no color change.
9. Cool to below 150°F (66°C) at a rate not to exceed 5°F (3°C) per minute.
10. Remove part from oven and debag.
11. Inspect the part to determine the moisture/water entry point. If the entry point can be determined, seal the area with liquid adhesive and cure.

Surface Preparation

Prior to the part being processed for repair, the part surface must be cleaned and dried to remove dirt, grease, aircraft fluids and NDI couplant. This prevents potential contamination of the repair adhesive bond line as well as contamination of equipment and facilities. Hand sanding will remove dry contaminants and improve the bonding surface. Whenever possible, sand parallel to the fiber direction with fine-grit sandpaper. Cleaning solvents may then be used to remove any remaining contaminants.

Wiping Cloths

Approved cloths are low lint and are tested to contain a minimal amount of contaminates. Care should be taken to ensure the solvent of choice does not affect the wipe cloth. Methyl ethyl ketone (MEK) dissolves polyester blend and most other synthetic blend cloths, leaving a residue on the surface that will affect the bond strength (Figure 11-3-14).

Figure 11-3-14. Methyl ethyl ketone is a solvent commonly used in composite repair.

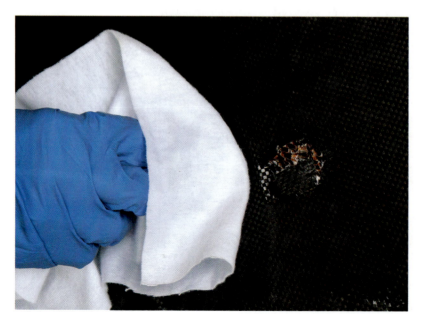

Figure 11-3-15. A lint-free cloth should be used to clean the surface for repair.

Solvent Wiping

Solvents must be used only when wearing approved health and safety equipment. Most solvents are flammable and have low flash points. DO NOT USE flammable solvents near open flames. Inhaling solvent vapors and mists may cause respiratory irritation.

In extreme cases, exposure can cause fluid accumulation in the lungs and central nervous system depression. In case of accidental ingestion, a physician or local poison control center must be contacted immediately. Solvents are used to clean an area of dust, oils, adhesives and other contaminants prior to bonding or painting. Care must be taken to prevent these solvents from being contaminated.

Wiping Process

Use a squeeze bottle or pour the solvent onto the rag and not onto the surface. Do not dip the rag or the part into the solvent container. Do not place contaminated rags against the solvent container opening.

Several applications of the cleaning solvent should be used and applied each time with a clean, dry, lint-free cloth (Figure 11-3-15). Clean an area at least twice the size of the repair. Use one of the following methods:

Method 1. Start from the center of the repair area and wipe towards the outside. After one pass has been made, fold or flip the rag so a clean area of the rag will be used. Dry wipe before solvent evaporates.

Switch to clean cloths frequently. Repeat the entire wiping process until the rags show no signs of contamination. Allow the surface to dry completely (usually 15 minutes after solvent has evaporated) before applying adhesive or repair plies.

Method 2. Start from one side of the repair and wipe straight across to the other side. After one pass has been made, fold or flip the rag so a clean area of the rag will be used. Dry wipe before solvent evaporates.

Switch to clean cloths frequently. Repeat until the entire area is wiped. Repeat the entire wiping process; however, wipe a slightly smaller area, being careful not to pull contaminates from areas that were not wiped. Repeat until the rags show no signs of contamination. Allow the surface to dry completely, usually 15 minutes after solvent has evaporated, before applying adhesive or repair plies.

Metal Surface Preparation

Scuff sanding and solvent wipe is not an acceptable surface preparation treatment for metals. Metal treatment for bonding is also critical and care must be taken to create an active surface for bonding in addition to removing contaminates.

Additional methods must be used to prepare the surface for bonding. Some of the methods include, but are not limited to, phosphoric acid anodizing, grit-blast silane, sol gel application or chemical-conversion coatings.

Paint Removal

The use of chemical paint stripper is prohibited because it will degrade the composite resin system. Mechanical abrasion paint removal methods work well if done with care. The area of paint removal should extend 2 in. (5 cm) beyond the repair area and the surfaces surrounding the area of paint removal should be masked off.

Paint stripping of composite parts has been a source of concern for many years because the techniques used to strip metal are often too harsh to strip composites. Stripping composites is normally accomplished by power sanding to the primer then hand sanding through the primer.

Chemical paint strippers can seriously damage epoxy matrix resins; their use is prohibited on polymer matrix composites.

Abrasive blasting has great potential to harm the matrix and fibers. The type of blast media and pressure can affect the removal rate and also can damage the surface of the composite materials. This method should only be performed on large parts by experienced personnel, and only when authorized by the SRM.

Water jet blasters can severely damage a polymer matrix material and must not be used on composites. Laser stripping methods are being used more every day and have proven to be an effective method in the removal of paint from a composite surface. Table 11-3-1 lists paint removal methods and if they can be used on composite repairs.

Process Overview

Perform a solvent wipe prior to removing paint to prevent driving contaminants and oils into the composite. Paint and any other surface coatings within the repair area boundary must be removed prior to any surface repair activity.

PAINT REMOVAL METHODS	
REMOVAL METHOD	RECOMMENDED USE
Sanding (power and hand)	Effective
Chemical stripping	Prohibited
Abrasive blasting	Only on large parts by experienced personnel with SRM authorization
Water jet blasting	Prohibited
Laser stripping	Effective

Table 11-3-1. Permissible and prohibited paint removal methods

The coatings should be removed from the repair area. During the paint removal process, it is crucial that no additional damage be caused by excessive material removal. Great care must be taken to not sand into composite fibers or remove excess material from metallic structures.

Generally, the only field-authorized method for paint removal from composite substrates is sanding. Pneumatic sanders are preferred for initial paint removal (Figure 11-3-16). Other types of power sanders should not be used because of the high potential for laminate damage.

Using a pneumatic sander, remove the paint until the primer is exposed. Switch to hand sanding to complete the paint removal process. The paint must be removed 2 in. (5 cm) beyond of the repair area.

Figure 11-3-16. Sanding should be used to remove paint in the field, and a pneumatic sander is the preferred tool for initial paint removal.

Figure 11-3-17. Hand sanding is the preferred method of removing paint from small areas of a composite structure.

Figure 11-3-18. Power sanders, such as the dual-action type, provide an efficient and rapid means of paint removal.

Paint must be removed from repair surfaces to ensure adequate adhesion of bonded repairs and adequate friction in bolted joints. The following methods will remove the paint or surface coatings from graphite/epoxy (GR/EP), boron/epoxy (B/EP), aramid/epoxy (A/EP), fiberglass/epoxy and graphite/bismaleaimide (GR/BMI) composites in preparation for a bonded or bolted repair.

Hand Sanding

Hand sanding with 80- to 100-grit sandpaper on a soft sanding block removes paint satisfactorily in many applications (Figure 11-3-17). However, a light touch is needed and the sanding block must be moved in a direction parallel to the surface fibers to prevent damage to the surface ply.

This technique requires minimal preparation and cleanup time and costs little. The removal rate is very slow and the process is labor-intensive. This is the preferred method for sanding small areas.

Power Sanding

Paint removal can be performed by a dual action (DA) or jitterbug sander (Figure 11-3-18). A disk sander can be very aggressive and should not be used for paint removal. As with hand sanding, care should be taken to sand in the direction of surface fibers to avoid damaging them. Power sanding provides a rapid means of paint removal. Care must be used to prevent gouging or damaging more material than the needed repair.

Abrasive Blasting

Composites may be blasted using wheat starch. This technique provides a quick removal rate, moderate preparation and cleanup time and is not labor-intensive. The blast media may be reused and this technique, if properly performed, does not harm the composite surface. Other type of blast media are available but should be tested before used on the aircraft.

Cleaning

Surface cleaning is critical both before and after almost every step of the bonded repair process. Precleaning removes all the oils, greases, dirt, etc., that might otherwise contaminate the repair surface and any tool or material used in subsequent steps. Ground-in contaminants can be very difficult to remove; therefore, it is recommended to preclean all repair areas before performing any machining or sanding.

Solid Laminate Repair

This section describes the processes used to lay up adhesives and precured patches. Surfaces to be bonded and uncured adhesive materials are sensitive to contamination, moisture and heat during this process. Surfaces include both the patch as well as the part.

The utmost care is required to minimize exposure to these elements during the material preparation and lay-up to ensure the repair strength is not degraded. Perform repair material preparation and lay-up in an environmentally controlled area.

If an environmentally controlled area is not available for lay-up, as in the case of an on-aircraft repair, prepare the repair materials in an environmentally controlled area and expedite lay-up of the repair materials, heat blanket and vacuum bag to minimize exposure.

Patch installation. If the required overlap between the patch and the part is not attained, reduced strength of the repair will result. Since the adhesive is first applied to the part surface, it is critical that the adhesive be correctly located on the part surface. Refer to the SRM to obtain the required patch overlap.

In addition, orientation sensitive patches must be properly aligned with the part being repaired during patch installation to ensure the required strength and stiffness is obtained. Generally the patch's 0° fiber direction is aligned with the part's primary load direction.

- Patch alignment may be specified by orienting the patch 0° fiber direction with respect to the part's 0° fiber direction. Patch alignment may also be specified by orienting the patch's 0° fiber direction with respect to a prominent feature on the part surface, such as a defined line of fasteners. Consult the SRM for determination of part 0° fiber direction or other means of aligning patch. Typical tolerance for patch alignment is ±1°.
- Thin metallic bonded patches and pre-cured six-ply quasi-isotropic patches are not orientation sensitive from a strength or stiffness standpoint. Patch alignment during installation is not a requirement for these types of patches.

Film Adhesive Repairs (Externally Bonded Patch)

Figure 11-3-19 shows a typical film adhesive repair. Follow these steps to perform a film adhesive repair.

1. Remove film adhesive from 0°F (-18°C) storage. Inspect label to ensure the material has not exceeded its shelf life.
2. Allow adhesive to thaw at room temperature until moisture no longer condenses on the sealed bag. This will be at least 2 hours for adhesive kits and at least 4 hours for large rolls. Material exposed to temperatures above 0°F (-18°C) for more than 24 hours must be considered suspect and should be tested before using.
3. Using the patch as a guide, cut the film adhesive 0.25 in. (0.64 cm) larger than the

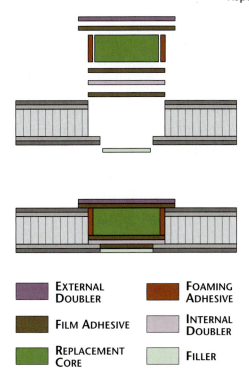

Figure 11-3-19. External repair using doublers

EXTERNAL DOUBLER	FOAMING ADHESIVE
FILM ADHESIVE	INTERNAL DOUBLER
REPLACEMENT CORE	FILLER

patch periphery. Note out-time and return unused material to cold storage.

4. Remove the barrier material from the patch bond area. Use care not to damage the composite surfaces during tape removal.
5. Wipe bond surfaces with clean, dry Rymplecloth®.
6. Remove the separator film from both sides of the film adhesive.
7. Apply the embossed surface, if applicable, of the film adhesive to the part surface. Apply the film adhesive over the repair area to ensure required patch overlap is achieved.
8. Determine the part 0° direction or primary load direction from the SRM. Align the patch 0° direction, if applicable, with the part 0° direction during layup.
9. Center the patch over the film adhesive previously applied to the part surface. Tape patch and adhesive in place. Check to ensure the required patch overlap is achieved.
10. Sometimes multiple stacked patches are required. In that case, stack the largest patch over the film adhesive previously applied to the part surface. Follow by application of increasingly smaller patches. Apply a layer of film adhesive between each patch in the stack.

Figure 11-3-20. A technician calibrates ultrasonic inspection equipment prior to examining an aircraft for damage. Ultrasonic inspection is one type of NDI used to detect flaws and damage in composite materials.

11. Lay-up the heat blanket and vacuum bag materials.

12. To prevent degradation of the adhesive, initiate the cure process as soon as possible but not later than 2 hours after the layup is complete. If repair is performed on-aircraft, initiate cure within 15 minutes of lay-up.

Paste Adhesive Repairs (Externally Bonded Patch)

Follow these steps to perform a paste adhesive repair.

1. To ensure the paste adhesive adequately wets the surfaces to be bonded, it is important to apply paste adhesive to both surfaces. Bond line thickness is important to control when using paste adhesives to preclude reduced strength and unacceptable porosity.

   After applying adhesive to the part and patch surfaces, an adhesive comb is used to remove excess adhesive and provide the correct amount of adhesive on the surfaces to be bonded. Scrim cloth is applied over the adhesive on the part surface prior to installing the patch to prevent excessive adhesive squeeze out during the cure cycle.

2. Remove paste adhesive from refrigerated storage. Allow the material to reach room temperature before opening the containers.

3. Using the patch as a guide, cut a piece of scrim cloth 0.25 in. (0.64 cm) larger than the repair patch periphery. If stacked patches are required for the repair, cut separate layers of scrim cloth 0.25 in. (0.64 cm) larger than each succeeding patch in the stack.

4. Apply solvent to a clean, dry Rymplecloth®. Wipe clean the adhesive comb. Allow to air dry for 30 minutes.

5. Prepare approximately 1.75 oz. (50 g) of paste adhesive for patch bond.

6. Using a spatula, apply a thin layer of paste adhesive on the part surface. The adhesive should extend a minimum of 0.25 in. (0.64 cm) beyond the patch surface. Apply additional adhesive over any exposed honeycomb core.

7. Draw adhesive comb over the part surface to remove excess adhesive. After each stroke, remove the excess adhesive from the comb with a clean, dry Rymplecloth®. Ensure the comb remains perpendicular to the surface during use. Avoid resin starving any areas of the part surface during the combing operation.

8. Apply the scrim cloth that was cut in step 3 to the paste adhesive on the part surface. Press the scrim cloth into the part surface with the spatula and work out wrinkles.

9. Using a spatula, apply a thin layer of paste adhesive to the bond surface of the patch.

10. Draw adhesive comb over the bond surface of the patch to remove excess adhesive. After each stroke, remove the excess adhesive from the comb with a clean, dry Rymplecloth®. Ensure the comb remains perpendicular to the surface during use. Avoid resin starving any areas of the patch surface during the combing operation.

11. Determine the part 0° direction (or primary load direction) from the SRM. Align the patch 0° direction (if applicable) with the part 0° direction during lay-up.

12. Apply the patch containing adhesive to the part surface containing the adhesive and scrim cloth. Ensure the patch is aligned on the part surface to maintain the required patch overlap. Tape patch in place using high temperature tape.

13. If multiple stacked patches are required, stack the largest patch on the part surface followed by increasingly smaller patches. Apply scrim cloth and adhesive between each patch in the stack.

14. Lay-up the heat blanket and vacuum bag materials or lay-up the heat/vacuum blanket.

15. Wipe with clean, dry Rymplecloth® to remove residual adhesive on the adhesive comb. Apply methyl isobutyl ketone

(MIBK) to another clean, dry Rymplecloth®. Wipe the adhesive comb clean. Allow to air dry for 30 minutes. Ensure adhesive comb is free of adhesive residue.

Damage Removal

Damaged material must be removed down to the sound material to perform a structural repair. This means that damage must be removed along with a minimum amount of good material.

First, use NDI to determine the damage extent (Figure 11-3-20). Then, determine the cutout shape for removing damage.

A circle is the most practical cutout shape for small damage; however, large damage can rarely be confined to a circle without removing an excessive amount of good material. Cutouts required to remove large areas of damage may take any form. However, maintain generous radii at the corners to prevent excessive stress concentrations and the resultant overstress of the repair joint.

The cut-out radius should not be less than 0.5 in. (1.25 cm) To avoid causing additional damage during the damage removal process, use the correct cutter type and the correct cutter feed/speed for the composite material being machined.

Outlining the Damage

Outline the damage to be removed (Figure 11-3-21). Use a permanent ink marker on light colored painted surfaces or a yellow pencil on dark surfaces. A correct damage outline encompasses the damaged area and a minimum amount of good material while maintaining the minimum required cut-out radius.

For noncircular damage, use a straight edge to draw straight lines that encompass the damaged area as indicated by NDI. Connect the lines using a circle with a radius not less than 0.5 in. (1.25 cm).

Penetration Damage

Remove the damage using a 90° router motor and a diamond-coated cutting wheel or a $1/4$-in. (0.64-cm) diameter diamond-coated router bit (Figure 11-3-22). A hand-operated cutting wheel is adequate for most thin laminates up to 0.1 in. (0.25 cm) thick. For thicker laminates or when a controlled-depth cut is required, remove the damage using a 0° router motor and a $1/4$-in. (0.64-cm) diameter router bit. This will prevent damage to honeycomb core or substructure elements.

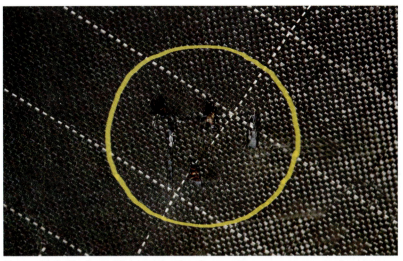

Figure 11-3-21. An outline marks the damaged area on a composite wing.

Template method. A template works well for stabilizing the router bit during the routing operation. Templates can be fabricated from aluminum or fiberglass stock and should be a minimum of $1/8$-in. (0.32 cm) thick.

A 0° router motor, router attachment and router guide are required for this operation. The router setback distance must be considered when making the template to ensure the correct damage outline is attained.

Adjust the position of the router bit in the router assembly to compensate for the template thickness and to achieve the depth of cut desired. Firmly attach the template to the part surface with tape to prevent movement during routing.

Then move the router guide along the template edge to establish the damage cutout shape.

Templates are limited to fairly flat surfaces. A new template must be manufactured for each nonstandard damage shape encountered.

Figure 11-3-22. A router is used to remove the damaged section.

Figure 11-3-23. A technician performs a bond repair on the flap of a transport aircraft.

Hand method. Hand routing operations can be performed without a template, using either a 0° or 90° router motor. Remain $1/8$ in. (0.32 cm) inside the damage outline while routing. Then, finish sand the damage cleanup hole edge to the damage outline.

Use a 90° router motor, a sanding drum with an 80-grit abrasive sleeve or a 1-in. (2.5-cm) diameter diamond-coated router bit for finish sanding of the damage cleanup hole edge.

Partial Thickness Damage

Partial-thickness damage (skin gouges, delamination damage, etc.) must be sanded down to undamaged material.

After determining the damage depth and damage outline, sand down to the damage depth using a 90° router motor and an 80-grit abrasive disk. Sand carefully as the material is removed quickly. Since multilevel delaminations may be present, reinspect the area in question using NDI after the damage is removed.

If delaminations are present in the skin below the original damage area, remove them by sanding and reinspect using NDI. Taper the edge of the partial thickness damage removal area to provide a smooth transition between the damage depth and the outer skin surface. The length of the taper should be 10 times the damage depth.

Bond Line Thickness Control

Controlling the thickness of the adhesive bond line is a critical factor in bond strength. This control can be obtained by matching the quantity of available adhesive to the size of the gap between the mating surfaces under actual bonding conditions (heat and pressure).

A scrim cloth, wires or glass beads are sometimes used to control the bond-line thickness to ensure that a uniform adhesive thickness is maintained. It also helps to contain the adhesive in the bond area. Scrim materials vary in thickness and type, though they are typically 1 to 7 mils (0.025 to 0.18 mm) thick and of mesh cloth material.

Bonded Repair of Metal Structures

Composite materials can be used to structurally repair, restore, or enhance aluminum, steel and titanium components (Figure 11-3-23). Bonded composite doublers have the ability to slow or stop fatigue crack growth, replace lost structural area due to corrosion grind outs, and structurally enhance areas with small and negative margins.

This technology has often been referred to as a combination of metal bonding and conventional on-aircraft composite bonded repair. The U.S. Air Force and the Royal Australian Air Force have been using the technology for more than 25 years on aircraft ranging from Boeing 747s to C-130s and B1Bs.

Commercial aircraft manufacturers and airlines are starting to adapt this technology to their needs. Boron epoxy, GLARE and graphite epoxy materials have been used as composite patches to restore damaged metallic wing skins, fuselage sections, floor beams and bulkheads.

As a crack growth inhibitor, the stiff bonded composite materials constrain the cracked area, reduce the gross stress in the metal and provide an alternate load path around the crack. As a structural enhancement or blendout filler, the high modulus fiber composites offer negligible aerodynamic resistance and tailorable properties.

Secondarily bonded pre-cured doublers and in-situ-cured doublers have been used on a variety of structural geometries ranging from fuselage frames to door cutouts to blade stiffeners. Vacuum bags are used to apply the bonding and curing pressure between the doubler and metallic surface. Autoclaves and a tooling splash from the repair area are used to prepare pre-cured doublers.

Film adhesives with a 250°F (121°C) cure are used routinely to bond doublers to metallic structures. Critical areas of the installation process include a good thermal cure control, having and maintaining water break-free bond surfaces, chemically and physically prepared bond surfaces, technician training and certification and managing a quality bonding site.

Metal Surface Preparation

Metal treatment for bonding is critical and care must be taken to create an active surface for bonding in addition to removing contaminates. Additional methods must be used to prepare the surface for bonding. Some of the methods include, but are not limited to, phosphoric acid anodizing, grit-blast silane, sol gel application or chemical-conversion coatings.

Fastener Hole Repair for Load Bearing Structures

This procedure is used to repair small punctures or incorrectly located fastener holes in a composite laminate (Figure 11-3-24).

1. Clean the repair area.
2. Lightly abrade the surface area around the entrance and, if possible, the exit of the puncture or fastener hole with 150- to 180-grit sandpaper. Abrade 1 in. (2.5 cm) beyond the hole.
3. Dry the component thoroughly.
4. Determine the hole size. For nonround holes, determine the maximum width of the damage.
5. Select a repair fastener. The repair fastener diameter should be slightly larger than the damaged or mislocated hole.
6. Ream the damaged or mislocated hole true and round for the diameter of the repair fastener.
7. Vacuum to remove sanding and reaming residue.
8. Using cotton-tipped applicators and solvent, thoroughly clean the reamed hole and abraded part surfaces with repeated wiping until no residue is left on the applicators. Allow the solvent to evaporate for 30 minutes.
9. Install repair fastener.

Potting Repair for Damaged Fastener Holes

This method is used to repair minor damage to fastener holes. The potting method should not be used if the laminate surrounding the damaged fastener holes is delaminated or damaged in other ways.

1. Clean the repair area.
2. Lightly abrade the surface area around the entrance and exit sides of the fastener hole with 180-grit sandpaper. Abrade 1 in. (2.5 cm) beyond the fastener hole.
3. Dry the component thoroughly.
4. Using cotton-tipped applicators and solvent, clean the fastener hole, countersink area and abraded part surfaces. Thoroughly clean these areas with repeated wiping until no residue is left on the applicators. Allow the solvent to evaporate for 30 minutes.
5. Prepare plies of repair fabric (i.e., fiberglass, graphite or aramid) to overlay the repair. Typically two or more overlay plies are used on each side of a potted repair on load-bearing structures.

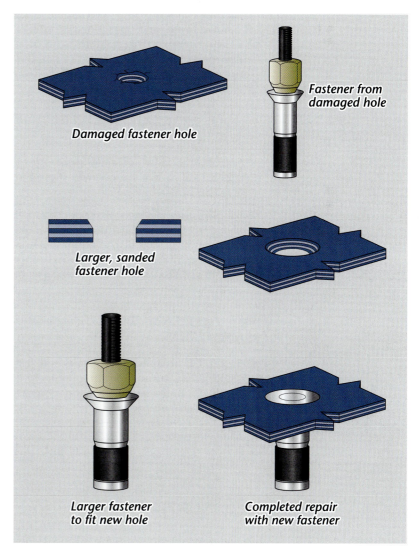

Figure 11-3-24. Repair procedure for a damaged fastener hole

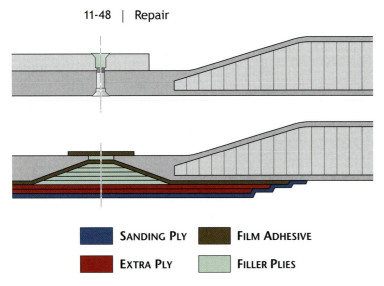

Figure 11-3-25. Fastener hole repair

Legend: SANDING PLY, FILM ADHESIVE, EXTRA PLY, FILLER PLIES

6. Impregnate the repair plies with laminating resin. Apply two of the repair plies to the exit side of the fastener hole. Orient the repair plies in the same direction as the original outer parent ply.

7. Prepare the potting compound. If technical data is not provided, prepare 0.2 oz. (5 g) mixed resin and fiber for each fastener hole (minimum 0.5 oz [15 g]). Ensure fiber, chopped to 0.25-in. (0.64 cm) or smaller, accounts for 5 to 20 percent of the mixture weight.

8. Carefully fill the hole with the potting compound. Apply in layers to avoid air entrapment.

9. Smooth the potting compound with a spatula or square-cut mixing stick and wipe off excess.

10. Apply the remaining repair plies, impregnated in Step 6 to the entrance side of the fastener hole. Orient the repair plies in the same direction as the original outer parent ply. Work out any air bubbles from both the upper and lower plies.

Fabric Layup Repair for Damaged Fastener Holes

This method is used to repair damaged fastener holes when the surrounding laminate is delaminated or damaged in other ways. Figure 11-3-25 shows a typical repair.

1. Clean the repair area.

2. Taper sand the entrance side of the fastener hole, typically 120 to 150° C/L of the fastener hole. Vacuum the area to remove sanding residue.

3. Lightly abrade the surface area around the entrance and exit sides of the fastener hole with 180-grit sandpaper. Abrade 1 in. (2.5 cm) beyond the cleanup area. Vacuum the area to remove sanding residue.

4. Dry the component thoroughly.

5. Using cotton-tipped applicators and solvent, clean the fastener hole, countersink area and abraded part surface. Thoroughly clean these areas with repeated wiping until no residue is left on the applicators. Allow the solvent to evaporate for 30 minutes.

6. Prepare plies of repair fabric (i.e., fiberglass, graphite or aramid) to fill the fastener hole and overlay the repair.

7. Impregnate the repair and overlay plies.

8. Stack the repair plies into the tapered fastener hole cleanout until it is filled.

9. Apply overlay plies to the upper and lower repair surfaces. Orient the repair plies in the same direction as the original outer parent plies.

Fastener Hole Repair Completion

Complete either the potting method or fabric lay-up method by performing the following steps:

1. Apply a porous release film over the repair. Ensure film extends 2 in. (5 cm) beyond the potted fastener hole or the overlay repair plies.

2. Place a bleeder ply over the porous release film.

3. Cover the bleeder with a nonporous film.

4. Place backup plates of 0.063-in. (0.16 cm) or thicker metal on both sides of the repair. These plates should extend 1 to 2 in. (2.5 to 5 cm) beyond the repair area and will ensure even pressure is applied to the repair.

5. Apply pressure with shot bags, pressure blocks, clamps or a vacuum bag.

6. Cure the repair. If an elevated temperature cure is required, use a heat lamp, heat blanket or other heating equipment. Place a thermocouple next to the repair on the same side as the heat source.

7. Smooth the cured repair area after it has cooled to room temperature using 240-grit sandpaper.

8. Locate and redrill or countersink the repaired fastener holes as required.

Figure 11-3-26. A composite fuselage corporate jet is ready for the application of paint.

Fastener Hole Repair for Lightly Loaded Structure, Doors and Panels

The following procedures are used to repair damaged fastener holes in lightly loaded structures.

Fill then drill method. This method uses a two-part resin filled with chopped fibers to restore damaged fastener holes and part surfaces. It is used to repair over-sized countersinks and gouged surfaces that are caused by fastener wear around the head or by fastener removal. This method is intended only for damage that does not extend through the full thickness of the laminate.

Fill then drill plus overlay method. This method uses a wet layup fabric plus a resin filled with chopped fibers to restore damaged fastener holes and part surfaces. It is used to repair incorrectly drilled, oblong, or angled holes in addition to oversized countersinks and gouged surfaces. This method is intended for damage that extends through the full thickness of the laminate.

Vacuum injection fastener hole repair. This method is used when little or no airflow is possible, such as delaminations around fastener holes. The delaminated area is heated to the minimum viscosity temperature of the adhesive, and then adhesive is added to a vacuum chamber that has been placed over the delaminated area. The adhesive is maintained at this minimum viscosity temperature under vacuum to allow outgassing of air and volatiles, then vented to atmosphere to force the resin into the delaminated area.

The vacuum chamber is then removed and a fastener or clamp is installed to provide positive pressure for curing the adhesive. NDI is performed on the delaminated area when the repair is complete to ensure successful injection.

Sealing and Painting

Sealing and painting are important to prevent damage to the composite structure (Figure 11-3-26). Environmental effects such as UV light, moisture or common aircraft fluids such as fuel, hydraulic fluid and deicing fluid that can come in contact with the structure are harmful to the composite. Galvanic corrosion becomes an issue when dissimilar materials are used such as aluminum and carbon fiber.

Corrosion Control

Control of galvanic corrosion in aircraft structures usually involves corrosion prevention or retardation of the corrosion rate. Prevention

Figure 11-3-27. A fay seal separates parts.

Figure 11-3-28. A composite-to-metal joint

The primer or organic coating could also be in the retardation category, since anticorrosion compounds could be added to their chemistry.

Assembly-applied preventatives include sealants and gaskets. A wet-curing sealant called a fay seal is applied between the parts making up the assembly (Figure 11-3-27). A wet-curing sealant called a butt-joint seal is applied between the ends of two parts. A wet-curing sealant can also be applied around the fastener shank or fastener head; this is called a wet installation.

In some cases, an O-ring rubber seal can be placed on the fastener shank to form the seal. Seals around removable doors can use a form-in-place (FIP) seal or a formed gasket installed.

Materials changes. Corrosion prevention via material selection includes using a more cathodic material in place of the aluminum with the CFRC. However, when using CFRC, aluminum, titanium or stainless steel in aircraft structures, thermal expansion within the joint must also be considered along with the galvanic potential difference of the materials.

The combination of CFRC and aluminum would result in the greatest thermal expansion mismatch, which would increase loads on the fasteners, adhesives or sealants as the joint is subjected to in-service temperature variations. A thermal expansion mismatch also results in bonded joints when the bonding or co-curing is accomplished at elevated temperatures. In fact, adhesive bonds between CFRC and aluminum have been known to fail when exposed to subzero temperatures (e.g., -65°F [-54°C]), due to the large thermally induced stress gradient.

The design of a CFRC-metal joint thus involves finding a balance between low cost, lightweight, availability, ease of fabrication, material mechanical property match, galvanic potential match and thermal match. Figure 11-3-28 shows an example of a composite-to-metal joint. A good alternative consideration would be a CFRC-CFRC joint. However, the CFRC-CFRC joint still presents a galvanic corrosion problem with metallic fasteners, since they will be in contact with the carbon fiber ends.

Isolation. Elimination of the moisture or electrolyte is the final method of corrosion prevention. This essentially is the "keep it out and keep it in" philosophy. Fay surface, fillet and butt-joint seals satisfy this requirement.

Retardation of the corrosion rate. Retardation of the corrosion rate includes

methods include barriers, material changes and isolation (elimination of the moisture). Retardation methods include leaching of anticorrosion materials and consumable materials.

Barriers. Barriers are the predominant method for corrosion prevention, applied either during fabrication or assembly. Fabrication-applied preventatives include materials such as fiberglass ply being co-cured onto the carbon fiber-reinforced composite (CFRC) part surface.

Another example of a fabrication barrier is a primer coat of paint or other organic coating applied to the part after machining and before assembly. This prevents the two materials from coming into contact.

leaching of anticorrosion materials or a coating of a consumable/sacrificial material. The leaching compound may be found in the primer on fabricated parts or in the sealant that is applied during the assembly of the parts. Generally, the leachate has been a compound of cadmium or chromium.

Due to environmental concerns, the current requirement is for an anticorrosion compound without cadmium or chromium. The material manufacturers are working to make this formulation. A sacrificial material is generally a very thin layer of a material (e.g., pure aluminum) applied to a part via ion vapor deposition during the fabrication process.

Sealant Joints

Sealant joint design and installation workmanship usually are not the first consideration when structures requiring joints are designed. Therefore, sealants in joints often fail, resulting in a significant replacement costs or, in some cases, a complete joint redesign. Since most joint designs are unique to the rest of the structure design, some general guidelines are useful. Figure 11-3-29 shows an example of a sealant joint.

Shear, tension and compression stresses are typically encountered in the sealant joint. Thermal expansion or contraction, structure movement and environmental forces are the source of these stresses, which can deform the sealant and cause strain. Sealants must be able to accommodate a certain amount of movement; this property of a sealant is called percent elongation.

Good joint design is dependent on the mechanical and chemical resistance properties of the sealant material, the characteristics of the materials forming the joint (substrates) and on the joint configuration. Assuming that the general sealant properties such as chemical resistance and temperature capability are suitable for the joint application, there are certain other sealant and substrate material characteristics that must be considered by the designer. These include sealant adhesion capability to the substrate, cohesive strength of the sealant material, percent elongation and cohesive capability of the substrate.

Adhesion of the sealant to the substrate is an inherent property of the sealant-substrate interface and may be enhanced by the use of a primer, generally called an adhesion promoter. The cohesion, or resistance to tearing, is an internal physical property of the sealant material. This will determine the minimum cross-sectional area of the joint.

Percent elongation and elastic recovery is the capability of the cured sealant material to stretch. Cohesive strength of the substrate is usually associated with composite materials. A substrate that does not have sufficient strength to support the stresses that develop at the sealant-substrate interface will fail internally.

There are several important design considerations for the joint itself:

- Sufficient sealant-substrate interface to provide adequate adhesion
- Sufficient cross-sectional area to avoid cohesive failures
- Maximum surface area-to-volume ratio to reduce strain
- Accessibility for seal installation
- Accommodations for sealant cure requirements

Because sealant may fail either cohesively or adhesively, both properties are important and must be balanced to the joint requirements.

Sealing

Common methods used to seal aircraft structures are: fay surface, fillet, butt-joint and FIP seals. While there are various tools and equipment available, numerous dimensions to be held, different materials to use, and an adhesion promoter and a detackifier to use before and after application, there is one requirement that cannot be stressed enough: the sealing surfaces must be clean.

The water-break-free test is the most common method to verify that a surface is clean.

Figure 11-3-29. A sealant joint with multiple composite layers

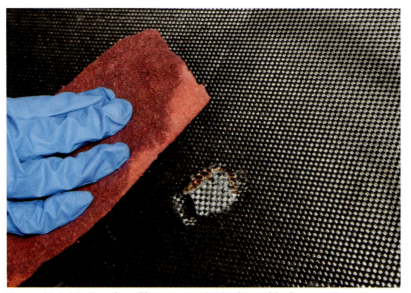

Figure 11-3-30. A carbon fiber composite is cleaned before repair.

However, it should be noted that a water-break-free test cannot be used in many production operations. Many procedures have been developed to obtain a water-break-free surface. The area to be sealed, primed or coated must be free from all grease, oil, dirt and other foreign materials that can hinder the adhesion of the applied material.

Cleaning of the structure (Figure 11-3-30) can take the form of a water and detergent scrub, followed by a solvent material wipe and then the "two-wiper cleaning" process. This last step removes the foreign materials that might be left behind if the cleaner were left to evaporate. In this cleaning process, one wiper is dampened with the solvent and the other is dry. The dampened one is applied to the part first, and, before the solvent can evaporate, the second dry wiper is used to dry the part.

Figure 11-3-31. Fillet seals prevent fuel, water or air from entering areas.

Repeated turning of the wiper presents a new surface to the part. In some instances, the surface is lightly abraded and re-cleaned prior to sealing. In some cases, the water and detergent scrub are skipped as part of the cleaning process.

Sealant materials are categorized into several groups: base material types, temperature ranges, fuel-wetted surfaces and noncorrosion ability. The most common base material is polysulfide. The polysulfides typically use an accelerator material to cure the base rubber. This material is available within a normal temperature range of -65 to 250°F (-55 to 120°C) with short time exposure to 360°F (180°C).

These sealants are available in a wide variety of types, including those specifically formulated for fay surface sealing and wet fastener installation. Other types are specifically formulated for fillet seals, butt-joint seals, fuel tank sealing and low-density, low-adhesion for removable panels. Formulations are also available for other special conditions.

Within each of these categories, there are short and long application times (pot life) fast cure, minimum/low-viscosity applications (spray or brush) and extrusion gun or spatula grades. It should be noted that the polysulfide sealants vary somewhat in their maximum service temperature and their continuous versus peak temperatures.

Material suppliers and company/military/commercial specifications should be consulted for specific selections.

The second-most-used material is the silicone category. These materials typically are used for the next higher temperature regime, in the range of -80 to 500 °F (-60 to 260°C). The silicones use two different cure mechanisms, catalytic or moisture (from humidity).

Fay surface sealing. Fay sealing is a process that seals two surfaces that come into contact with each other in a fastened joint. The fay seal is mandatory for adequate corrosion protection. Wet sealant fastener installation is also mandatory.

The two surfaces are cleaned, and an application of an adhesion promoter may be applied to the two surfaces. Sealant material is next applied in a manner to coat entirely one of the mating surfaces, monitored by material squeeze-out on the edges of the party boundary.

Lower-viscosity materials are used for fay sealing thin sheets. When thick parts are assembled, a higher-viscosity material is used. Longer assembly-time materials are required for large assemblies, such as large skins over spars, ribs, stringers and longerons.

The roller often is used to obtain a uniform pre-assembly sealant thickness. The comb nozzle is used for small or narrow parts that need to be fay sealed. The notched comb also is used to apply a uniform pre-assembly sealant thickness.

Fillet sealing. Fillet sealing is a process that seals the edge of two surfaces that come into contact with each other in a fastened joint (Figure 11-3-31). The fillet seal is used to prevent fuel, water, or air from getting out of where it should be or getting in where it should not be.

The fillet seal constitutes the primary seal in many joint designs. It is backed up by the fay seal.

Fillet seals are usually located inside the aircraft mold line. Wet sealant fastener installation is also mandatory.

The two surfaces are cleaned, and an application of an adhesion promoter may be applied to the two surfaces. Sealant material is next applied to cover the interface of one part to the other. A high-viscosity material is used for fillet seals, so that the fillet shape will be retained with the thixotropic properties of the material.

Short assembly times are desired for the fillet application. A detackifier may be used over the sealant material to allow work to resume over the fillet before the fillet seal is cured enough to be tack free. The detackifier minimizes the potential for drilling chips to stick to the sealant material. Special filleting tools are used to obtain the correct size and shape of the fillet bead.

Brush sealing. Bush sealing is used to overcoat the collar, buck rivet tail, or other nut element of the installed fastener. This process uses a lower-viscosity material and short assembly times. Detackifier may be used over the brushable sealant.

This process is used in pressure areas, such as the cockpit, crew station, or cabin areas (Figure 11-3-32). Spray sealing is beginning to replace brush sealing for large areas. The spray is produced using a 2,000 p.s.i.g. (14 MPa) pump and an airless spray head. The orifice and the spray cap determine the fan size and shape. The spray uses a low-viscosity, brushable-grade, polysulfide material and further thins it with a solvent to obtain a specific Zahn cup time.

Two to four applications are required with a solvent flash-off time between applications. The same cleaning process is used for spray sealing. A nonwater-based adhesion promoter is spray applied prior to the actual spray seal

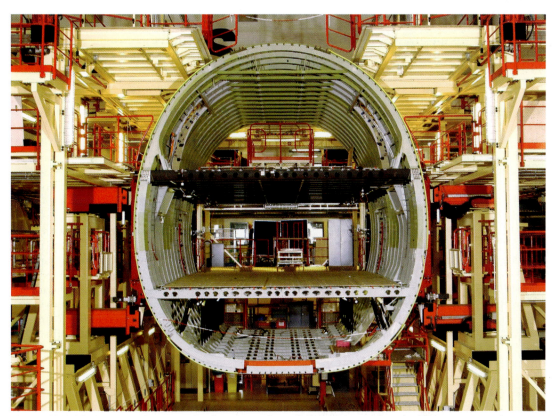

Figure 11-3-32. Fasteners in pressurized areas, such as the cockpit, crew and cabin areas, are often brush sealed with a low-viscosity material.

Courtesy of Airbus

Figure 11-3-33. FIP seals are used to seal access-doors, like the one shown here, and panels in composite structures.

process. The spray is applied approximately halfway up a spar web and 2 to 4 in. (50 to 100 mm) out onto the inner mold line of the skin.

Butt-joint sealing and FIP seals. Butt-joint sealing and FIP seals are the last sealing processes during assembly. The butt-joint seal is applied between the edges of two parts to fill in the gap between them. Nozzles are used to apply the sealant in the gap between the two skins.

The FIP seal is used to seal access bay doors and removable doors and panels. Figure 11-3-33 shows an example of an access door in a composite structure. The door sill is cleaned like in the other sealing processes. Spacers are attached to the sill to provide a specific seal thickness when completed.

The location can be around the fastener using a donut-shaped spacer, or it can be located away from the fastener using the hole of the donut or some other shape. When the second location is used, the volume where the spacer was removed is then filled in with the sealant used for the seal.

The width of the FIP seal is dictated by the general design requirements for the assembly, but is usually approximately 0.5 in. (13 mm). After all of the spacers are located, an adhesion promoter is applied to the sill and is allowed to dry. Any puddling of the adhesion promoter must be soaked up with a wiper. During this time, mold release is applied to the edge of the door and the sealant contact surface and then allowed to dry.

Two or three coats of mold release may be required, depending on the specific mold release used. Masking tape is applied to the door and the skin area around the door to facilitate cleanup. Sealant is applied to the door-sill and the door is installed with a specific sequence of fasteners.

When the sealant is cured, the door is removed with the aid of a plastic wedge. Care is required to prevent damage to the seal. After the door is removed, the excess cured sealant and the mold release is cleaned up, and a powder parting agent is applied to prevent the door from sticking to the sealant.

Many fuel tanks use a noncuring sealant injected into a seal groove. This is considered to be a repairable fuel-boundary seal. It can be a polysulfide or a fluorosilicone material and is called the groove or channel sealant.

The channel sealant can have beads or chopped rubber, as a filler, mixed into the paste sealant. The filler material will migrate in the sealant when a flow of fuel begins to swell the paste. The filler material then moves to where the flow is exiting.

The filler material forms a "log jam" at this point and the sealant flows around it, resealing the groove. This material is injected into a channel that goes around the periphery of the tank. The material is injected in such a manner as to apply pressure to the sealant in the channel groove.

Injection of this material is done at elevated pressures of 2,000 to 4,000 p.s.i.g. (14 to 28 MPa) at the nozzle tip. The tip pressure is dependent on the material thickness of the skin and frame; thicker parts have higher allowed tip pressure. This sealing method is generally used in conjunction with the fay and fillet seal previously described.

A typical wing tank without a bladder would use a fay seal between the skin and the spar caps, then a fillet seal at the edge of the spar cap of the wet side of the wing skin. This would be followed by either a brush overcoat of the fasteners with sealant or spray sealing over the fasteners, up the spar web and out over some of the inner mold line of the skin. After the polysulfide has cured, the channel seal material would be pumped into the channel.

Channel seals. Channel seals require a channel groove machined or formed into the spar cap. The width, depth and location are determined based on the structural loading, volume

Figure 11-3-34. A Beechcraft Premier is parked on the ramp ready for surface preparation prior to priming and painting.

contained in the channel groove and the general design requirements.

If the groove follows the fastener pattern, then the width will be greater than if the groove is on one side or the other of the fastener pattern. Groove depth must be minimized because the groove is counted as a gap in the fastener design.

However, the groove needs to be deep enough to contain a sufficient volume of sealant material to maintain a good seal. Injection of sealant into the groove also must be considered because sealant materials are very viscous and require a significant amount of pressure to move them through the groove, typically 2,000 to 4,000 p.s.i.g. (14 to 28 MPa) nozzle tip pressure.

Injection points need to be designed at approximately every 4 to 6 in. (100 to 150 mm). The injection can take place through the fastener, through a fastener hole with an injection tool, or through a hole in the skin that gets plugged.

Sealant Application Equipment

Sealant application equipment includes pneumatic application guns with different sealant extrusion nozzles and with various size sealant cartridges ranging from 1 to 20 fl. oz. (0.03 to 0.6 L); pneumatic channel sealant injection equipment with a pressure regulator and gauge for reduced tip pressures (used for sealing short lengths of channel groove and for field repairs); and airless spray sealing equipment. Sealant filleting and scraping is done using various hand tools.

Primer and Topcoat Systems

The primer and topcoat function as a system; therefore, the topcoat must be chemically and physically compatible with the primer system. The capability of the system to meet the user performance requirements are determined by how well the surface is prepared prior to coating. Figure 11-3-34 shows a Beechraft Premier ready for surface preparation.

Surface preparation. CFRC surfaces are prepared by scuff sanding or grit blasting to obtain visible dense scratches and loss of gloss. Priming or painting is conducted as soon as possible after surface preparation, and painting must take place within 36 hours. If the part will not be painted within 12 hours, it should be wrapped in clean roll paper until it is painted.

Abrasive cleaning (grit blasting) is the preferred method of preparing unpainted CFRC surfaces (it is required for the mold-line surface) followed by dry wiping. Parts containing close tolerance holes are grit blasted and primed before holes are drilled in the detail skin.

Figure 11-3-35. A technician sands a primed composite surface by hand.

CFCR parts that are not grit blasted—such as parts with complex geometry or locations inaccessible to grit blasting, reworked areas and parts with thin, unsupported cross sections—are processed by removing any peel ply if present on the surface, dry wiping the composite surface, scuff sanding with 150- or 180- grit sandpaper by hand or with a pneumatic sander and removing all sanding dust from the surface by dry wiping. Care must be taken not to sand into a free edge because it may cause edge delamination.

The entire primed or painted exterior composite surface is sanded using 180-grit or finer sandpaper to remove all surface gloss and contamination using an air-driven sander attached to an air-driven high-efficiency particulate air (HEPA) vacuum. Hand sanding is permissible for areas of less than 4 ft. 2 in. (0.4 m2) where mechanical sanding is not feasible (Figure 11-3-35).

Aircraft exterior mold-line surfaces are cleaned with detergent using the following process:

1. Wet down the aircraft, spray detergent on the surfaces and scrub previously sanded areas with nylon abrasive pads. The detergent is allowed to set approximately 2 to 3 minutes on the aircraft, but not allowed to dry.
2. Rinse the aircraft with hot water, 120 to 140°F (50 to 60°C), until the runoff water is free of detergent residue and evidence of the detergent, such as bubbles, on the aircraft is gone.
3. Wipe the exterior mold line using clean wipers; it is not necessary to wipe dry. The wiper is visually examined for contamination, if the aircraft surface still appears dirty. After the second cleaning, areas still dirty are allowed to dry and are locally hand cleaned.

Following detergent cleaning, the aircraft exterior mold-line surfaces are steam cleaned using a minimum steam pressure of 200 p.s.i.g. (1,379 kPa), and the surfaces are raised using ambient-temperature, clean tap water. Proper steam cleaning of intersecting surfaces and door fastener areas is particularly important.

Surfaces should not be touched or contacted in any way after steam cleaning unless personnel are wearing proper protective clothing or covering, such as gloves, overalls, boots and protective caps. The aircraft is allowed to dry for a minimum of 4 hours before painting, and surfaces to be painted are inspected for water, aircraft fluid drips and surface contamination immediately before painting.

Application of primer. For all CFRC parts requiring primer, one smooth, wet, continuous coat of the applicable catalyzed primer is applied to achieve 0.8 to 1.4 mils (0.02 to 0.035 mm) dry film thickness, a wet film thickness of approximately 3.5 to 5 mils (0.09 to 0.13 mm) will achieve the desired dry film thickness. The primer is allowed to dry a minimum of 5 minutes before applying additional primer to meet thickness requirements.

Parts are cured 6 hours prior to further processing. If more than 24 hours elapse between primer applications, the surface must be hand solvent cleaned and scuff sanded prior to applying additional primer coats.

Primer drying time depends on the atmospheric temperature and humidity conditions. Curing of a waterborne primer requires that the water evaporate first, which is achieved in the quickest way by air movement over the part. Elevated-temperature drying cycles may be used instead of air drying. Baking a part before the water evaporates will cause small blisters. Follow the material manufacturer's recommendation for elevated-temperature cure (Cure temperatures must not exceed 250°F, or 121°C, for composite parts.) To ensure that drying is satisfactory:

- Primer film may not show any sign of solvent pop or blistering due to insufficient flash-off time.
- Primer film must resist marring by No. 250 tape and to pass a dry tape test upon cooling to room temperature.

Figure 11-3-36. A team of technicians applies the topcoat of paint to the wing of an Airbus A380 inside one of Airbus' manufacturing facilities.
Courtesy of Airbus

Application of topcoat. Parts should be at room temperature before topcoat applications (Figure 11-3-36). Surface roughness or overspray is removed by sanding with nylon abrasive pads or 320-grit or finer sandpaper after the primer has dried sufficiently to allow sanding. Areas containing excessively heavy roughness, runs, or sags are sanded using 240-grit sandpaper.

Remove sanding dust from seams by blowing with air and from skin surfaces by wiping with wipers dampened with TT-N-95 aliphatic naphtha. If the interval between primer and topcoat application exceeds 24 hours, areas must be sanded using 320 grit or finer sand paper, cleaned, primed and allowed to dry a minimum of 1 hour before applying the topcoat.

The topcoat should be allowed to dry for a minimum of 8 hours at 75°F (24°C) minimum and less than 90 percent relative humidity before the aircraft is removed from the paint booth. Allow 16 hours minimum dry time if the aircraft will be exposed to moisture after moving from the paint booth.

If outdoor temperatures average less than 65°F (18°C), the aircraft is dried for a minimum of 48 hours in a heated indoor area before storing outdoors. Time limits apply from the last paint application on the aircraft, excluding touch-up.

12

Health and Safety

Composite materials are often toxic. The typical health areas at risk are vision, skin and respiration.

Resins, solvents, initiators, dust and particles commonly cause visual risks. Visual problems include symptoms such as watering, redness, swelling, itching and burning of the eyes.

Chemical goggles and glasses with side shields are effective in protecting the eyes from direct contact with toxic materials. However, vapors coming from these materials can still be harmful.

Dermal (skin) risks are commonly caused by fibers, coatings, chemicals (resin, solvents and mold release), foams and dust. Dermal problems include symptoms such as redness, rash, itching, burning and dry or cracking of the skin. Protection from these risks includes covering exposed skin, wearing gloves and using barrier cream.

Respiratory risks are commonly caused by fumes and vapors that are chemical and generated by grinding and dust and particles from grinding as well as glass bubbles. Respiratory problems include symptoms such as headache, nausea, tightness in the chest, trouble breathing, shortness of breath and dizziness.

Avoiding prolonged exposure to certain products and selecting products with the least amount of toxicity can help reduce these risks. Other protective equipment such as dust masks for dust and particle protection only, charcoal respirators for vapor protection over a limited period only, and supplied-air masks can reduce respiratory risks.

Learning Objective

REVIEW
- composite manufacturing health and safety practices
- health and safety considerations in composite repair
- composite material toxicity
- hazards encountered when working with composites
- personal protective equipment used when working with composite materials

DESCRIBE
- Material Safety Data Sheets (MSDS)

Left: Technicians must protect themselves when working on composites with items such as gloves, safety glasses and dust masks.

Section 1
Material Safety Data Sheet

Many of the materials used for composite manufacturing and repair require a Material Safety Data Sheet (MSDS). The MSDS provides important information relating to the product. There is no set format for the MSDS but the Occupational Safety and Health Administration (OSHA) recommends that MSDS follow a 16-section format consisting of the following:

1. Identification
2. Hazard Identification
3. Composition/Information on Ingredients
4. First-Aid Measures
5. Firefighting Measures
6. Accidental Release Measures
7. Handling and Storage
8. Exposure Controls/Personal Protection
9. Physical and Chemical Properties
10. Stability and Reactivity
11. Toxicological Information
12. Ecological Information
13. Disposal Considerations
14. Transport Information
15. Regulatory Information
16. Other Information

Companies that manufacture, sell or ship products are required by law to provide an MSDS. These sheets are included with the product or they can be downloaded from the company's website. All personnel should have a good understanding of the MSDS before they use the product. This includes managers and support personnel who do not directly use the product.

The MSDS must be readily available in the work area where the product is used. A sample MSDS sheet for an epoxy resin system is included in Appendix A. Figure 12-1-1 shows an MSDS for a carbon fiber prepreg material that indicates a possible cancer hazard associated with the product. Personnel working with this type of material should take precautions to minimize their exposure to this product.

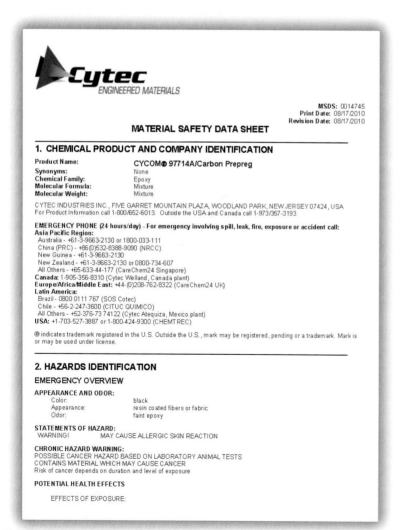

Figure 12-1-1. MSDS indicating possible cancer hazard

Section 2
Toxicity and Hazards of Composite Materials

Toxicity

Toxicity is the inherent harmful effect of a material. Most materials, no matter how "safe" one thinks they may be, are toxic. On the other hand, if materials are handled correctly and carefully, even the most toxic materials may pose little hazard to the worker. No substance is a hazard by itself. The dosage makes a substance a hazard. The term hazard takes into account not only the material's inherent toxicity, but also a person's exposure to the material. For example, if one is exposed to a large amount of a chemical with relatively low toxicity, the resultant hazard may be great. However, without exposure even the most toxic chemical presents no hazard.

Acute Toxicity

The acute toxicity of a material is the harmful effect after a single or short-term exposure. Materials exhibiting acute toxicity are normally classified as irritants, corrosives or sensitizers.

Irritants. An irritant causes a localized reaction resulting from either a single or multiple exposures. It is characterized by the presence of redness and swelling. It may or may not cause cell death. Irritants are classified as mild, moderate or severe depending on the degree of damage they inflict.

Corrosives. Corrosive materials cause tissue destruction without normal healing.

Sensitizers. Repeated exposure to a material that is a sensitizer may result in sensitization. Sensitization results in an allergic reaction either to the skin or in the respiratory system upon re-exposure to the material. Persons sensitized to a certain material can react strongly to trace amounts of that material upon re-exposure. Sensitized persons require zero exposure to that material to prevent a repeat of the allergic reaction.

Chronic Toxicity

Chronic toxicity refers to the adverse health effects caused by exposure to a toxic material over a long period of time. Chronic toxicity testing is performed to determine a specific dose or exposure level that will produce a long-term toxic effect. Some of these effects include blood disease, liver damage, kidney damage, and even cancer.

Figure 12-2-1 shows OSHA hazard communication warning symbols that are displayed on toxic or otherwise dangerous materials to warn the user of a potential hazard. Additional labeling may be present on shipping containers.

Exposure Routes

During handling and processing, toxic materials can enter the body through three main methods: direct contact, inhalation and ingestion.

Direct Contact

Direct contact with a toxic material can result in surface damage to skin or eyes and internal damage to organs if the material is absorbed. The areas of the body most susceptible to exposure are the unprotected parts of the skin, such as the hands, lower arms and face.

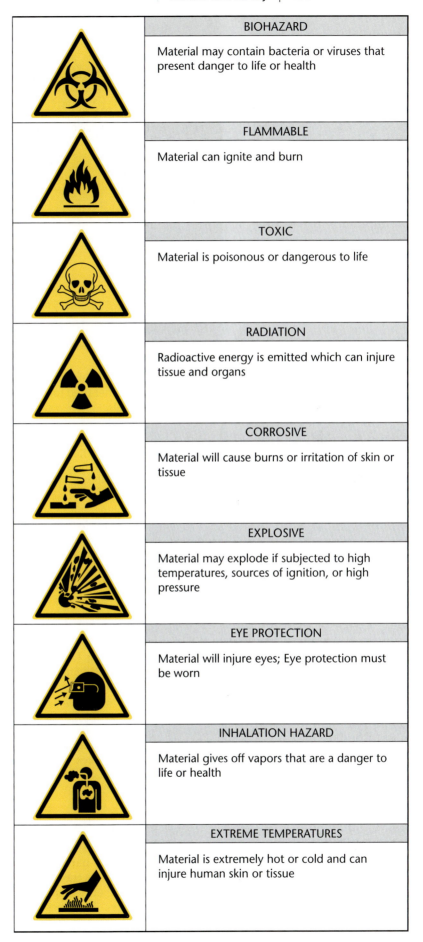

Figure 12-2-1. OSHA Material warning symbols

Figure 12-2-3. A fire-rated cabinet used for the storage of flammable materials.

Skin or eye contact with liquids, gases, vapors and particulate materials (dusts) should be minimized. Special precautions should be taken to prevent contact with chemicals absorbed through the skin. Direct contact can also take the form of secondary exposure caused by handling gloves pencils, mixing cups, etc., that are contaminated with a toxic material after removal of protective equipment.

Inhalation

Inhalation is the process by which material is drawn into the body by breathing. During mixing and lay-up of adhesives and patch materials, the release of solvents and other vapors may occur. Inhalation of these materials should be kept to a minimum by providing adequate ventilation and using local exhaust hoods or respirators. Damage removal, sanding, drilling and machining of cured laminates can generate composite dust. Inhalation of dust can be harmful to respiratory organs.

Total Dust. This refers to all the dust generated by an operation. Only the particles that are able to penetrate to the deep lung (respirable particles) are potentially harmful. The rest of the dust (non-respirable) is trapped and cleared by nasal hairs and other normal respiratory defense mechanisms. Non-respirable particulates are generally treated as "nuisance dusts"; that is, they are not known to cause adverse effects in the lungs and do not produce significant organic disease or toxic reaction.

Respirable Dust. Particles smaller than about 3.5 microns in diameter are able to bypass normal respiratory defenses and reach the deep lung where they can cause respiratory damage. There are respirable exposure limits for some dusts, based only on the fraction that is able to penetrate into the deep lung.

Ingestion

To ingest means literally "to take into the body as food or liquid." While it is doubtful that anyone would purposefully ingest these materials, it is definitely possible to ingest them accidentally. This commonly occurs via secondary contamination. Simple measures such as thorough washing of hands prior to eating or drinking provide significant protection from accidental ingestion.

Hazards

Smoke

Smoke emissions from burning carbon-epoxy and carbon-bismaleimide composites consist primarily of carbon monoxide. Burning carbon-epoxy materials also emit small amounts of carbon dioxide, hydrogen cyanide and hydrogen chloride. The toxic gases emitted from burning epoxy matrix materials are as toxic as the gases emitted from any burning aircraft. Breathing these emitted gases should be avoided.

Fire

Fire and explosion hazards are always present. The grounding or bonding of all conductive parts of the system is an effective means of controlling hazards created by electrostatic energy. Grounding is the process of connecting one or more metallic objects and ground conductors to ground electrodes. Bonding is the process of connecting two or more metallic objects together by means of a conductor. Bonding is done to equalize electrostatic potential between two or more conductive objects.

Most solvents used are flammable. Close all containers with solvents and store in fire proof cabinet when not used. Figure 12-2-3 shows a typical fire rated cabinet. Make sure that solvents are kept away from areas where static electricity can occur.

Static electricity can occur during sanding operations or when bagging material is unrolled. Preferable use air driven tools, if electric tools are used make sure that they are of the enclosed type. Do not mix too much resin. The resin could overheat and start smoking caused by an exothermal process. Always make sure that a fire extinguisher is nearby to fight a fire.

Section 3
Personal Protective Equipment

Personal protective equipment (PPE) (eye protection, gloves, aprons, respirators, etc.) should be worn during handling and repair of advanced composite materials. The PPE required to safely handle a specific material is provided in the supplier's MSDS, which should be consulted to determine what PPE to use.

During composite repair work the skin needs to be protected from hazardous materials. Always wear gloves and clothing that offer protection against toxic materials. Use only approved gloves that protect your skin and do not contaminate the composite material.

Always wash your hands prior to using the toilet or eating. Chemicals could remain on your hands that will burn sensitive skin. Make sure that the gloves do not contaminate your composite materials. Damaged composite components should be handled with care. Single fibers can easily penetrate the skin, break off, and become splinters lodged in the skin.

Guidelines for the Use of Gloves

Gloves are one of the most important defenses used for protection during processing and repair of advanced composite materials. Hands are the primary means of transferring contaminants to other parts of the body. There is no such thing as an all-purpose glove. The selection of the proper glove is dependent upon the operations being performed and the materials being handled.

Puncture and abrasion resistant gloves. Leather and leather palmed gloves provide protection against fiber penetration and abrasion. They also provide some thermal insulation when handling parts subjected to elevated temperatures (less than 300°F). They are not impermeable to chemicals and will allow them to soak through to the skin.

Chemical resistant gloves. Chemical resistant gloves of different materials vary in their ability to prevent certain chemicals from soaking

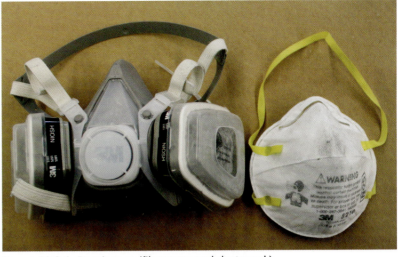

Figure 12-3-1. Respirators (filter type and dust mask)

through to your skin. The gloves must provide a positive liquid-proof barrier to the chemicals used. The gloves must neither degrade upon exposure to these chemicals nor permit permeation of them. Gloves used for repair operations should allow enough dexterity to facilitate hand lay-up operations as well as being free of powder, silicone or other loose surface particles.

Respirators

Respiratory protection is provided against dusts and fibers by wearing a respirator equipped with a HEPA filter (Figure 12-3-1). The respirator will also require chemical cartridges (probably organic vapor) if protection is needed against chemical vapors or gases. A half mask is the minimum recommended. Only National Institute of Occupational Safety and Health/Mine Safety and Health Administration approved respirators shall be worn. Personnel wearing respirators must be medically qualified and trained.

Do not breathe carbon fiber dust and always make sure that there is a good flow of air where the work is performed. Always use equipment to help you breathe when you work in a confined space. Use a vacuum near the source of the dust to remove the dust from the air. When sanding or applying paint, a dust mask or a respirator is needed. A properly fitted dust mask will provide the protection needed. For application of paints, a sealed respirator with the correct filters or a fresh air supply respirator is required.

Eye Protection

Goggles must be worn when performing damage removal, machining and drilling of advanced composite materials unless a full-face respirator is used. Chemical splash goggles or

WORK ACTIVITY	PERSONAL PROTECTIVE EQUIPMENT (PPE)	EQUIPMENT/FACILITIES	PERSONAL HYGIENE
Handling Damaged Composite	• Leather-palmed gloves • Goggles	• None	• Wash hands, face and arms with soap and water before breaks and at end of shift
Handling of Fire-Damaged Composite Parts	• Respirator with 0.3 micron HEPA filter • Leather-palmed gloves • Goggles • Long-sleeved, loose fitting, disposable coveralls, taped closed at the wrist	• Vacuum cleaner with 0.3 micron HEPA filter	• Wash hands, face and arms with soap and water before breaks and at end of shift • Dispose of coveralls after each shift
Handling Prepreg/Uncured Film Adhesives	• Plastic gloves • White cotton gloves (worn over plastic gloves) • Long-sleeved coveralls	• Well-ventilated area	• Wash hands with soap and water after removing plastic gloves
Mixing/Handling Liquid and Paste Adhesives	• Plastic gloves • Face shield or splash goggles • Rubber-coated apron	• Local exhaust hood for mixing • Well-ventilated area for application • Emergency eyewash/deluge shower within 100 feet	• Clean up residual adhesive from work area, tools and PPE • Dispose of gloves after each use • Wash hands, face and arms with soap and water before breaks and at end of shift
Working with Solvents	• Work inside a chemical hood when applicable or use a respirator with a chemical cartridge if PEL is exceeded • Face shield or splash goggles • Rubber-coated apron • Long-sleeved coveralls or laboratory coats • Gloves appropriate for chemicals being used (e.g., polyethylene nitrite, butyl rubber). • Consult the solvent MSDS for proper protection	• Well-ventilated area • Emergency eyewash/deluge shower within 100 feet	• Wash hands, face and arms with soap and water before breaks and at end of shift
Machining, Drilling, Sanding Composite Parts	• Respirator with 0.3 micron HEPA filter • Leather or plastic gloves • Goggles • Long-sleeved, loose-fitting coveralls, taped closed at the wrist	• Vacuum cleaner with 0.3 micron HEPA filter • Emergency eyewash/deluge shower within 100 feet	• Wash hands, face and arms with soap and water before breaks and at end of shift • Wash or dispose of coveralls after each shift • Vacuum dust and debris frequently and at the end of each shift

Table 12-3-1. Personal protective equipment/facilities and personal hygiene for working with advanced composite materials

face shields must be worn when working with liquid adhesives, paste adhesives and solvents. Safety glasses must be worn with face shields.

Clothing

Long-sleeved and long-legged clothing should be worn to minimize skin contact. Openings should be taped closed with masking tape. When dealing with liquid chemicals, a rubber-coated apron should be worn. Figure 12-3-2 shows a technician with protective gear during sanding operations.

See Table 12-3-1 for a summary of PPE requirements for various tasks and products.

Figure 12-3-2. Personal protection equipment for sanding composites

Section 4
Emergency and First Aid Procedures

Damaged composite components should be handled with care. Single fibers can easily penetrate the skin, break off, and become lodged in the skin. Sharp tweezers and a magnification lens are generally required to remove the splinter. If the splinter is hard to remove, seek medical attention immediately.

Accidental chemical spills, runaway exothermic reactions and heat blanket fires are some of the potential emergencies that can be encountered during the manufacturing and repair process. Some general guidelines for dealing with these types of emergencies are listed below. Always refer to the material-specific MSDS for emergency and first aid procedures.

Accidental Spills and Leaks

If accidental contact, inhalation or ingestion occurs, proceed as follows:

Eyes. Immediately flush with large amounts of low-pressure water for a minimum of 15 minutes. Remove any contact lenses to ensure thorough flushing. Seek immediate medical attention.

Skin. Promptly flush with running water. Wash with soap and water. If an allergic reaction is encountered, seek medical attention. Do not clean up resin on skin with solvents, as they will crack the skin and cause a path for resin entry.

Inhalation. Remove the person to fresh air at once. Seek prompt medical attention.

Ingestion. The guidelines for ingestion vary depending upon the materials ingested. Some specify large quantities of liquid be given to dilute the ingested material as well as inducing vomiting. Guidelines for other materials recommend vomiting not be induced. The specific material's MSDS should be consulted for the correct procedures.

Runaway Exothermic Reaction

Do not handle containers with materials undergoing a runaway exothermic reaction. Exothermic emissions can be toxic and extreme temperatures can be generated. Do not approach the container or attempt to control the reaction. Do not breathe toxic gases. Depart the area immediately. Do not return until the reaction is complete and the workspace has been ventilated to remove toxic exothermic reaction products.

Heat Blanket Fires

Turn off electrical power to the hot bonder. Avoid breathing smoke and gases. If fire persists, extinguish with dry chemical or carbon dioxide fire extinguisher while someone calls the fire department. Depart the area as soon as practical. Ventilate the workspace before returning to work.

Appendix A

MSDS: 0010803
Print Date: 10/09/2009
Revision Date: 10/09/2009

MATERIAL SAFETY DATA SHEET

1. CHEMICAL PRODUCT AND COMPANY IDENTIFICATION

Product Name: CYCOM® 823 RTM Resin, Part A
Synonyms: None
Chemical Family: Epoxy
Molecular Formula: Mixture
Molecular Weight: Mixture

CYTEC INDUSTRIES INC., FIVE GARRET MOUNTAIN PLAZA, WOODLAND PARK, NEW JERSEY 07424, USA
For Product Information call 1-800/652-6013. Outside the USA and Canada call 1-973/357-3193.

EMERGENCY PHONE (24 hours/day) - For emergency involving spill, leak, fire, exposure or accident call:
Asia Pacific Region:
  Australia - +61-3-9663-2130 or 1800-033-111
  China (PRC) - +86(0)532-8388-9090 (NRCC)
  New Guinea - +61-3-9663-2130
  New Zealand - +61-3-9663-2130 or 0800-734-607
  All Others - +65-633-44-177 (CareChem24 Singapore)
Canada: 1-905-356-8310 (Cytec Welland, Canada plant)
Europe/Africa/Middle East: +44-(0)208-762-8322 (CareChem24 UK)
Latin America:
  Brazil - 0800 0111 767 (SOS Cotec)
  Chile - +56-2-247-3600 (CITUC QUIMICO)
  All Others - +52-376-73 74122 (Cytec Atequiza, Mexico plant)
USA: +1-703-527-3887 or 1-800-424-9300 (CHEMTREC)

® indicates trademark registered in the U.S. Outside the U.S., mark may be registered, pending or a trademark. Mark is or may be used under license.

2. COMPOSITION/INFORMATION ON INGREDIENTS

OSHA REGULATED COMPONENTS

Component / CAS No.	% (w/w)	OSHA (PEL):	ACGIH (TLV):	Carcinogen
Anhydride -	30-60	Not established	Not established	-
Phenolic epoxy resin -	40-70	Not established	Not established	-

3. HAZARDS IDENTIFICATION

EMERGENCY OVERVIEW

APPEARANCE AND ODOR:

MSDS sheet of two-part epoxy resin

3. HAZARDS IDENTIFICATION

Color: orange
Appearance: liquid
Odor: slight

STATEMENTS OF HAZARD:
WARNING!   MAY CAUSE ALLERGIC SKIN OR RESPIRATORY REACTION
CAUSES EYE IRRITATION

POTENTIAL HEALTH EFFECTS

EFFECTS OF EXPOSURE:
The acute oral (rat) LD50 and dermal (rabbit) LD50 values are estimated to be >3300 mg/kg and >2000 mg/kg, respectively. Inhalation exposure may cause allergic respiratory reaction. Repeated or prolonged dermal contact may cause allergic skin reactions. Direct contact with this material may cause moderate eye and skin irritation. Refer to Section 11 for toxicology information on the regulated components of this product.

4. FIRST AID MEASURES

Ingestion:
If swallowed, call a physician immediately. Only induce vomiting at the instruction of a physician. Never give anything by mouth to an unconscious person.

Skin Contact:
Wash immediately with plenty of water and soap. Remove contaminated clothing and shoes without delay. Obtain medical attention. Do not reuse contaminated clothing without laundering. Destroy or thoroughly clean shoes before reuse.

Eye Contact:
Rinse immediately with plenty of water for at least 15 minutes. Obtain medical advice if there are persistent symptoms.

Inhalation:
Remove to fresh air. If breathing is difficult, give oxygen. Apply artificial respiration if patient is not breathing. Obtain medical attention immediately.

5. FIRE-FIGHTING MEASURES

Suitable Extinguishing Media:
Use water spray or fog, carbon dioxide or dry chemical.

Protective Equipment:
Firefighters, and others exposed, wear self-contained breathing apparatus. Wear full firefighting protective clothing. See MSDS Section 8 (Exposure Controls/Personal Protection).

Special Hazards:
Keep containers cool by spraying with water if exposed to fire.

6. ACCIDENTAL RELEASE MEASURES

Personal precautions:
Where exposure level is known, wear approved respirator suitable for level of exposure. Where exposure level is not known, wear approved, positive pressure, self-contained respirator. In addition to the protective clothing/equipment in Section 8 (Exposure Controls/Personal Protection), wear impermeable boots.

CYCOM® 823 RTM Resin, Part A   MSDS: 0010803   Print Date: 10/09/2009

Methods For Cleaning Up:
Cover spills with some inert absorbent material; sweep up and place in a waste disposal container. Flush spill area with water.

Environmental Precautions:
Use appropriate containment to avoid environmental contamination.

7. HANDLING AND STORAGE

HANDLING

Precautionary Measures: Avoid breathing vapor. Avoid prolonged or repeated contact with skin. Avoid contact with eyes. Keep container closed. Use with adequate ventilation. Wash thoroughly after handling.

Special Handling Statements: None

STORAGE
None

Storage Temperature: Room temperature 20 - 35 °C 68 - 95 °F
Reason: Quality.

8. EXPOSURE CONTROLS/PERSONAL PROTECTION

Engineering Measures:
Where this material is not used in a closed system, good enclosure and local exhaust ventilation should be provided to control exposure when spraying or curing at elevated temperatures.

Respiratory Protection:
In case of insufficient ventilation, wear suitable respiratory equipment. A full facepiece respirator also provides eye and face protection.

Eye Protection:
Wear eye/face protection such as chemical splash proof goggles or face shield. Eyewash equipment and safety shower should be provided in areas of potential exposure.

Skin Protection:
Wear impermeable gloves and suitable protective clothing. Barrier creams may be used in conjunction with the gloves to provide additional skin protection.

Additional Advice:
Food, beverages, and tobacco products should not be carried, stored, or consumed where this material is in use. Before eating, drinking, or smoking, wash face and hands thoroughly with soap and water.

9. PHYSICAL AND CHEMICAL PROPERTIES

Color:	orange
Appearance:	liquid
Odor:	slight
Boiling Point:	Not available
Melting Point:	Not available
Vapor Pressure:	Not available
Specific Gravity/Density:	Not available
Vapor Density:	Not available
Percent Volatile (% by wt.):	Not available
pH:	Not available
Saturation In Air (% By Vol.):	Not available

9. PHYSICAL AND CHEMICAL PROPERTIES

Evaporation Rate:	Negligible
Solubility In Water:	Reacts with water
Volatile Organic Content:	Not available
Flash Point:	>93.3 °C 200 °F Pensky-Martens Closed Cup
Flammable Limits (% By Vol):	Not available
Autoignition Temperature:	Not available
Decomposition Temperature:	Not available
Partition coefficient (n-octanol/water):	Not available
Odor Threshold:	Not available

10. STABILITY AND REACTIVITY

Stability:	Stable
Conditions To Avoid:	None known Will cure at high temperatures with some evolution of heat.
Polymerization:	Will not occur
Conditions To Avoid:	Avoid contact with bases or amines. Do not heat material above 71.1 C (160 F).
Materials To Avoid:	No specific incompatibility
Hazardous Decomposition Products:	Carbon dioxide Carbon monoxide (CO) oxides of nitrogen

11. TOXICOLOGICAL INFORMATION

Toxicological information for the product is found under Section 3. HAZARDS IDENTIFICATION.
Toxicological information on the regulated components of this product is as follows:

Phenolic epoxy resin has acute oral (rat) and dermal (rabbit) LD50 values of >5000 mg/kg and 6000 mg/kg, respectively. Direct contact with this material caused moderate skin and mild eye irritation when tested in rabbits. Prolonged or repeated contact with this material may cause allergic skin reaction.

Anhydride has an acute oral (rat) LD50 and acute dermal (rabbit) LD50 values of >2100 mg/kg and >1400 mg/kg, respectively. Allergic skin reactions or primary skin irritation may be produced by prolonged or repeated contact. Inhalation overexposure may cause an allergic respiratory reaction or respiratory tract irritation. Direct contact with this material may cause moderate eye and skin irritation.

12. ECOLOGICAL INFORMATION

Toxic to aquatic organisms, may cause long-term adverse effects in the aquatic environment.
The ecological assessment for this material is based on an evaluation of its components.

13. DISPOSAL CONSIDERATIONS

The information on RCRA waste classification and disposal methodology provided below applies only to the product, as supplied. If the material has been altered or contaminated, or it has exceeded its recommended shelf life, the guidance may be inapplicable. Hazardous waste classification under federal regulations (40 CFR Part 261 et seq) is dependent upon whether a material is a RCRA `listed hazardous waste` or has any of the four RCRA `hazardous waste characteristics.` Refer to 40 CFR Part 261.33 to determine if a given material to be disposed of is a RCRA `listed hazardous waste`; information contained in Section 15 of this MSDS is not intended to indicate if the product is a `listed hazardous waste.` RCRA Hazardous Waste Characteristics: There are four characteristics defined in 40 CFR Section 261.21-61.24: Ignitability, Corrosivity, Reactivity, and Toxicity. To determine Ignitability, see Section 9 of this MSDS (flash point). For Corrosivity, see Sections 9 and 14 (pH and DOT corrosivity). For Reactivity, see Section 10 (incompatible materials). For Toxicity, see Section 2 (composition). Federal regulations are subject to change. State and local requirements, which may differ from or be more stringent than the federal regulations, may also apply to the classification of the material if it is to be disposed. The Company encourages the recycle, recovery and reuse of materials, where permitted, as an alternate to disposal as a waste. The Company recommends that organic materials classified as RCRA hazardous wastes be disposed of by thermal treatment or incineration at EPA approved facilities. The Company has provided the foregoing for information only; the person generating the waste is responsible for determining the waste classification and disposal method.

14. TRANSPORT INFORMATION

This section provides basic shipping classification information. Refer to appropriate transportation regulations for specific requirements.

US DOT

Dangerous Goods? X
    Proper Shipping Name: Environmentally hazardous substance, liquid, n.o.s.
    Hazard Class: 9
    Packing Group: III
    UN/ID Number: UN3082
    Transport Label Required: Miscellaneous
                                                Marine Pollutant
    Marine Pollutant
    Technical Name (N.O.S.):   phenolic epoxy resin(s)

    Comments: Marine Pollutants - DOT requirements specific to Marine Pollutants do not apply to non-bulk packagings transported by motor vehicles, rail cars or aircraft.

TRANSPORT CANADA

Dangerous Goods? X
    Proper Shipping Name: Environmentally hazardous substance, liquid, n.o.s.
    Hazard Class: 9
    Packing Group: III
    UN Number: UN3082
    Transport Label Required: Miscellaneous
                                               Marine Pollutant
    Marine Pollutant
    Technical Name (N.O.S.):   phenolic epoxy resin(s)

ICAO / IATA

Dangerous Goods? X
    Proper Shipping Name: Environmentally hazardous substance, liquid, n.o.s.
    Hazard Class: 9
    Packing Group: III
    UN Number: UN3082

Transport Label Required: Miscellaneous
Packing Instructions/Maximum Net Quantity Per Package:
   Passenger Aircraft: 914;   450 L
   Cargo Aircraft: 914;   450 L
Technical Name (N.O.S.):   phenolic epoxy resin(s)

IMO

Dangerous Goods? X
   Proper Shipping Name: Environmentally hazardous substance, liquid, n.o.s.
   Hazard Class: 9
   UN Number: UN3082
   Packing Group: III
   Transport Label Required: Miscellaneous
                                Marine Pollutant
   Marine Pollutant
   Technical Name (N.O.S.):   phenolic epoxy resin(s)

15. REGULATORY INFORMATION

Inventory Information

United States (USA): All components of this product are included on the TSCA Chemical Inventory or are not required to be listed on the TSCA Chemical Inventory.

Canada: This product contains components not on the Domestic Substances List. These components are on the Non-Domestic Substances List.

Australia: All components of this product are included in the Australian Inventory of Chemical Substances (AICS) or are not required to be listed on AICS.

China: All components of this product are included on the Chinese inventory or are not required to be listed on the Chinese inventory.

Japan: All components of this product are included on the Japanese (ENCS) inventory or are not required to be listed on the Japanese inventory.

Korea: All components of this product are included on the Korean (ECL) inventory or are not required to be listed on the Korean inventory.

Philippines: All components of this product are NOT included on the Philippine (PICCS) inventory.

OTHER ENVIRONMENTAL INFORMATION
The following components of this product may be subject to reporting requirements pursuant to Section 313 of CERCLA (40 CFR 372), Section 12(b) of TSCA, or may be subject to release reporting requirements (40 CFR 307, 40 CFR 311, etc.) See Section 13 for information on waste classification and waste disposal of this product.

This product does not contain any components regulated under these sections of the EPA

PRODUCT HAZARD CLASSIFICATION UNDER SECTION 311 OF SARA
- Acute

16. OTHER INFORMATION

NFPA Hazard Rating (National Fire Protection Association)
   Health: 2 - Materials that, under emergency conditions, can cause temporary incapacitation or residual injury.

CYCOM® 823 RTM Resin, Part A   MSDS: 0010803   Print Date: 10/09/2009

Fire: 1 - Materials that must be preheated before ignition can occur.

Instability: 0 - Materials that in themselves are normally stable, even under fire exposure conditions.

Reasons For Issue: Revised Section 15

Randy Deskin, Ph.D., DABT +1-973-357-3100

This information is given without any warranty or representation. We do not assume any legal responsibility for same, nor do we give permission, inducement, or recommendation to practice any patented invention without a license. It is offered solely for your consideration, investigation, and verification. Before using any product, read its label.

Index

A

abrasion   10-1
abrasives   6-11
Accu-Lok™ Blind Fastening System   6-20
acute toxicity   12-3
adhesive bonding   6-21
adhesives   2-15
AFP   4-13
Airbus 320/330/340   1-3
Airbus 350   1-1
Airbus A300   1-3
air hose   4-18
alarm condition   7-2
aluminum honeycomb, surface treatment for   6-29
aluminum mesh   10-3
aluminum sheet, surface treatment of   6-29
anisotropic   3-2
Aramid   2-3
aramid countersink   6-6
Aramid (Kevlar®)   2-1, 2-3
A-scan   8-4
assembly operations   6-1
A stage   2-22
ASTM D3039/D3039M   9-5
ASTM D3171   9-14
ASTM D3410   9-6
ASTM D3518/D3518M   9-7
ASTM D4255   9-7
ASTM D5467   9-6
ASTM D5528   9-7
ATL   4-11
autoclave   7-3
autoclave curing   2-27
auto-ignition temperature   7-3
automated tape laying (ATL)   4-11
automated ultrasound system   8-11
automatic fiber placement (AFP)   4-13

B

B-2 bomber   1-3
back counterboring   6-4
balance   3-5
band saw   6-13
basket weave   2-8
bearing failure   11-3
Beech Starship   1-3
benzoxazine resin   2-15
bidirectional fiber   3-3
bismaleimide resins (BMI)   2-15
bleeder cloths   2-31
bleeder ply   4-17
bleeding   2-25
bleed-out technique   4-19
blind fastener   6-20
Boeing 777   1-3
Boeing 787   1-1
bolted repair   11-3, 11-9
bonded composite repair   7-10
bonded repair   11-2, 11-8
bonding   12-4
bond line thickness   2-16
bond testers   8-7
box beam construction   3-9
brad point drill   6-3
braiding   2-2, 2-9
breather material   2-30, 4-18
bridging   4-3
bristle disc   6-12
B stage   2-22

C

CAPRI   4-6
carbide cutter   6-6
carbide reamer   6-5
carbon-epoxy composite, machining of   6-1
carbon fiber   1-1, 2-1, 2-4
carbon rovings   2-23
chemical attack   10-1
Cherry Maxibolt®   6-20
Chromic Acid Anodizing (CAA)   6-30
Chromic/Sulphuric Acid Pickling (CSA)   6-29
Chronic toxicity   12-3
coated abrasive disc   6-12
co-curing   3-9
coin tap   8-2
consolidation   2-25, 4-3
continuous rovings   2-2
Controlled Atmospheric Pressure Resin Infusion (CAPRI)   4-6
core damage   11-21
corrosion   10-3
corrosion problems   6-17
corrosion resistance   1-1
corrosives   12-3
cosmetic repair   10-8
countersink cutter   6-6
countersinking   6-6
coupling medium   8-5
C-scan   8-5
C stage   2-22
cure cycle   7-13
cure processes   2-25
cure time   7-15
curing   4-4
curing lamp   7-1
curing oven   7-6
curing recipe   7-13
cutoff wheels   6-12

D

damage assessment   10-4
damage tolerance   10-7, 10-11, 11-6
damage, type of
   corrosion   10-3
   delamination   10-2
   dent   10-2
   disbond   10-2
   erosion   10-3
   heat/burn   10-3
   laminate splitting   10-2
   moisture   10-4
   negligible   10-4
   non-repairable   10-5
   puncture   10-2
   repairable   10-4
   scratch and gouge   10-2
   surface scratch   10-2
   UV   10-4
debulking   4-3, 4-20
debulking process   11-33
de Havilland Mosquito   1-3
delamination   6-5, 8-3, 10-2
dent   10-2
dermal (skin) risk   12-1
design criteria   3-1
diamond abrasive hole saw   6-7
diamond coated carbine tool   6-2
diamond coated circular saw   6-7
die grinder   6-10
differential scanning calorimetry (DSC)   9-2
DIN 65448 wedge test   9-12
disbond   10-2
double-vacuum bag processing   11-33
downdraft table   6-8
dry fibers   2-1

E

Eddie-Bolt® fastener   6-19
edge closures   3-19
edge distance   11-12
E-glass   2-2
electrical glass   2-2
elevated-temperature requirement   11-7
end-grain balsa wood core   3-16

epoxy   2-14
epoxy matrix materials   10-3
erosion   10-1
erosion damage   10-3
exothermic   2-17
expansion method   3-13
E-Z Buck® rivet   6-19

F

F-22 fighter   1-3
F-35 fighter   1-3
fabric   2-7
failure   11-3
   bearing   11-3
   peel   11-4
   shear-out   11-3
fairings   1-1
fastener
   interference   11-13
fastener fatigue   11-6
fastener selection   11-10
fatigue   1-3, 2-4, 10-7
fatigue test   9-16, 9-17
fiberglass   1-3, 2-1
fibers   3-2
filament   2-7
filament winder   2-5
filament winding   4-7
fill direction   2-8, 3-4
film adhesives   2-16
film transfer   2-22
flash tape   2-31
flexible core   3-14
flight controls   1-1
flush head fastener   6-6
flutter   11-5
flutter, aerodynamic   11-5
foam cores   3-15
foam core sandwich structure   11-30
foaming adhesives   2-18
foams   5-1
fracture
   adhesive   9-10
   cohesive   9-10
freezer storage   2-29
full-scale test   9-16
fuselage   1-1
fuselage frames   1-1

G

glass transition temperature (Tg)   2-12
Global Flyer   1-4

gouging   10-1
graphite   2-4
grounding   12-4

H

hand lay-up method   4-1
hazardous environment   7-3
heat blanket   7-2, 11-17
heat bonder   7-1
heat/burn damage   10-3
heat deflection temperature (HDT)   2-13
heated press   7-9
heat gun   7-8
heating equipment   7-1
heterogeneous   3-2
hexagonal honeycomb core   3-14
Hi-Lok®   6-18
hole drilling   6-3
hole saw   6-7
homogeneous   3-2
honeycomb   1-3
honeycomb core   3-10
honeycomb processing   3-17
honeycomb sandwich   3-9
honeycomb structure   11-22
hot-air unit (HAM)   7-8
hot debulked   4-4
hot melt process   2-22
hygroscopic   2-3

I

impact   10-1
impregnation machine   2-24
infrared heat lamps   7-8
infusible cores   3-16
integrally heated tooling   2-29
interference fastener   11-13
interim repairs   10-7
Invar   5-4
irritant   12-3
isotropic   3-2

J

joint   6-13
joint, adhesive   6-14
joint, bonded   9-9
joint, double-lap   6-24
joint, double strap   6-24
joint, mechanically fastened   6-14
joint, scarf   6-14, 6-25
joint, single-lap   6-24, 9-11

joint, stepped lap   6-25

K

kitting   2-18
Klenk drill   6-4
Korex®   3-18

L

laminate   3-6
laminate orientation code   3-3
laminate properties   3-2
laminate splitting   10-2
laminate structure   11-32
laser projection   4-3
laser projection equipment   4-2
laser vibrometer   8-10
lay-up tape   4-18
leading edges   1-1
lightning protection   2-6
lightning protection materials,
   corrosion of   10-3
lightning strike   2-6
lightning strikes   10-6
lightning strike zones   2-6, 10-7
linear porosity   4-17
liquid adhesives   2-16
liquid and paste adhesives   2-16
liquid ingression   10-2, 10-4
load
   dynamic   9-16
   static   9-16
LockBolt   6-18

M

manufacturing processes   4-1
master model   5-1
Material Safety Data Sheet (MSDS)   12-2
matrix   2-4, 2-11, 3-2
maximum service temperature   2-11
mechanical fastener   6-15
   multi-row design   6-15
   single-row design   6-15
mechanical properties   1-5
microballoon   11-21
microscopy   9-13
microspheres   2-17
microstop countersink gauge   6-6
mini bonder   7-1
minimum bond line thickness   6-26
moisture   11-7
moisture damage   10-4

mold release 4-3
mold release agents 4-17
MSDS 12-2
multiaxial fabric 2-8

N

negligible damage 10-4
net resin prepreg 4-16
Nickel vapor deposition (NVD) tools 5-6
nitrogen 7-4
no-bleed system 4-19
Nomex® 3-18
nondestructive test (NDT) 8-1
non-repairable damage 10-5
Nutplates 6-21

O

operating temperature 11-7
oscillating saw 6-10
out-of-autoclave prepreg 4-4
oven controller 7-6
over expanded honeycomb core 3-14
overheating 10-1
oxygen 7-4

P

PAN-based carbon fiber 2-5
panel buckling 11-5
paste adhesives 2-17
peck drilling 6-3
peel failure 11-4
peel plies 2-30
peel ply 4-17, 6-28
perforated release film 2-30, 4-18
personal protective equipment (PPE) 12-5
phased-array testing 8-7
phenol-formaldehyde resin 2-14
phenolic resin 2-14
Phosphoric Acid Anodizing (PAA) 6-30
photo initiators 7-9
PITCH process 2-5
plain weave 2-8
ply cutting table 4-2
ply orientation 3-3
ply sequence 3-3
polyacrylonitrile (PAN) 2-5
polycrystalline cutting tool 6-2
polyester resin 2-13
polyimide resin 2-15
polymer 2-10
polymer precursor material 2-10

porosity 2-25, 4-17, 11-8
portable vacuum pump 7-3
pot life 2-17
PPE 12-5
preform 4-10
prepreg 2-1, 2-22
prepreg lay-up method 4-1
prepreg material 2-21
prepreg tack 2-24
pressure intensifiers 5-8
primary structure 1-5, 11-3
processing materials 2-29
production tooling 5-3
Proteus 1-4
pulse-echo ultrasonic testing 8-6
pultrusion 4-14
puncture 10-2

Q

quasi-isotropic 3-2
quasi-isotropic layup 11-4

R

ramp checker 8-7
ramp-down rate 7-14
ramp-up rate 7-14
reciprocating saw 6-11
reference direction 3-3
reference plane 3-3
reference standard 8-5
refrigerated storage 2-17
release agent 4-3, 4-17
release fabrics and films 2-30
repair 11-2
  bolted 11-3, 11-9
  bonded 11-2, 11-8
  stepped 11-33
  stringer 11-9
repairable damage 10-4
repair design criteria 11-4
resin 2-10
resin content 9-14
resin film infusion (RFI) 4-11
resin transfer molding 4-5
resin transfer molding (RTM) 4-9
resonance ultrasonics 8-6
respirable dust 12-4
respirator 12-5
respiratory risk 12-1
RFI 4-11
router 6-9
router bit 6-10

roving 2-7
RTM 4-5, 4-9

S

S2-glass 2-2
safety features 7-5
sanding 6-11
sandwich peel test 9-12
satin weave 2-8
Scaled Composites 1-4
scarved repair method 11-33
scratch and gouge 10-2
scratching 10-1
SCRIMP 4-6
sealant tape 2-31
secondary bonding 3-17
secondary structure 11-2
Seeman Composites Resin Infusion Molding Process (SCRIMP) 4-6
sensitizers 12-3
S-glass 2-2
shear loads 3-3
shearography 8-10
Shear-out failure 11-3
shelf life 2-17, 2-29
shrink tape 2-27, 7-6
shrink-wrapping 2-27, 7-6
sickle-shaped drill 6-4
simultaneous stitch manufacture 2-9
Skydrol® 10-4
solid carbide 6-2
solid carbide reamer 6-7
solid release film 2-30, 4-18
solution technique 2-22
Spaceship One 1-4
Spaceship Two 1-4
spade drill 6-3
specific modulus 1-4
specific strength 1-4
splash tooling 5-8
spoilers 1-1
spots, hot or cold 7-3
spring in 5-7
stabilizer
  horizontal 1-5
  vertical 1-5
standardized testing methods 9-5
Standard Laminate Code 3-4
standard test machine 9-2
standard twist drill bit 6-3
static electricity 12-4
stepped repair 11-33
stiffness-to-weight ratios 1-4
storage life 2-29

straight-fluted carbide drill reamer 6-4
strand 2-7
strength-to-weight 1-4
stress concentrations 6-14
stresses
   peel 6-22, 6-26, 9-9
   shear 6-22
stringer repair 11-9
structural properties 1-4
Structural Repair Manual (SRM) 11-1
structure 11-2
   foam core sandwich 11-30
   honeycomb 11-22
   laminate 11-32
   primary 11-3
   secondary 11-2
surface conditioning disc 6-12
surface conditioning pad 6-12
surface preparation 6-15, 6-27
surface pretreatment 6-27
surface scratch 10-2
symmetric laminates 3-5

T

table saw 6-13
tape product 2-7
technical data sheet 2-13
temperature 11-7
   operating 11-7
thermal expansion, coefficient of 5-4
thermal survey 7-2, 7-10
thermal variations 7-11
thermocouple 7-1, 7-9, 11-17
   J-type 7-10
   K-type 7-10
thermocouple placement 7-2
thermocouple wire 7-10
thermography 8-9
thermoplastic 2-11, 6-31
thermoplastic polymers, surface treatment of 6-29
thermoset 2-11, 7-4
titanium 1-1
titanium alloys, surface treatment of 6-30
titanium alloy (Ti-6Al-4V) 6-17
Tooling 5-1
tooling board 5-3
toughening 2-16
tows 2-7
toxicity 12-2
   acute 12-3
   chronic 12-3
transfer medium 4-7
Tube-Core 3-14

twist drill 6-3

U

UAB™ blind bolt system 6-20
ultimate design load level 11-5
ultrasonic inspection 8-3
unidirectional fiber 3-3
unidirectional tape 2-7
UV curing 7-8
UV damage 10-4

V

V-22 tilt rotor 1-3
vacuum-assisted processing (VAP) 4-7
vacuum-assisted resin transfer molding (VARTM) 4-5
vacuum bag material 4-18
vacuum bag molding 2-27, 4-16
vacuum bag pressure 7-2
vacuum bag process 4-3
vacuum bag sealing tape 4-18
vacuum compaction table 4-19
vacuum line 4-18
vacuum pressure 7-3
vacuum pump 4-18
VAP 4-7
VARTM 4-5
vinyl ester resin 2-13
visual inspection 8-1
void content 9-13, 9-14

W

warp 3-3
warp clock 3-3
warp direction 2-8
water-break test 6-28
waterjet 6-9
weave and stitch method 2-9
weaving machine 2-5
weight and balance 11-7
wet lay-up method 4-1
White Knight 1-4
wicking 2-9
wing ribs 1-1
wing structures 1-1
working time 2-17
Woven structural fabric 2-7

Y

yarn 2-2, 2-7

Z

zero (0°) direction 3-3
zoning 11-4